History of the World Economy in the Twentieth Century
General Editor: Wolfram Fischer

From Versailles to Wall Street

1919–1929

Derek H. Aldcroft

University of California Press
Berkeley and Los Angeles

In memory of L.H.A.

University of California Press
Berkeley and Los Angeles

ISBN: 0–520–03336–1
Library of Congress Catalog Card Number: 76–40824

Printed in Great Britain

Contents

List of Tables

Preface

When invited by Professor Fischer to write a volume on the world economy in the 1920s I never envisaged that it would present such a challenge. Having devoted some considerable time to writing and teaching on the inter-war period I initially felt that it would be comparatively easy to organize my thoughts and material on paper. I soon found how ignorant I was about many topics and countries and how vast was the literature I had not read. I realized therefore that I would not be able to put pen to paper for some time and began an intensive campaign of reading as much literature on the period as I could lay my hands on. Some time later, by which time I had consumed vast quantities of literature and collected a great store of notes and statistics, I came to the conclusion that if I did not start to write I should never be able to digest all the material I had. In any case the time allotted for the volume was fast running out.

The results are contained in the chapters which follow. I am fully conscious of the deficiencies which remain but I trust that my ignorance on certain topics and countries will not appear too glaring to all the inquisitive specialists. The coverage of some topics is far from complete, while some are not covered at all, but that remains inevitable in a volume so wide in scope. Each chapter in fact contains the seeds of a separate volume and a lengthy

period of research. Moreover, though the literature in aggregate
is vast, much of it is of mediocre quality and some subjects still
await proper analysis. A wealth of statistical data requires
processing and as time goes on more statistical series are appearing
for individual countries. Ideally I should have liked to collect and
process much of this data, and to present it in an analytical format,
but it is still too patchy to provide good comparative analysis and
requires much more work than time and resources allow. However,
some of the main data have been used for the final chapter on
long-term trends.

A word should be said about the arrangement of the volume. A
strictly geographical treatment of the subject has been rejected for
a number of reasons. First, working on some kind of regional
basis would result in a series of potted histories of countries
and/or regions which would be of no great value and would prove
very tedious to read. Secondly, it would still involve some analytical and thematic treatment which would make the volume very
lengthy indeed. And thirdly, it is unrealistic to assume that any
one author, and especially this one, has an intimate knowledge of
every country in the world.

A thematic treatment is in any case preferable since it gets away
from the purely descriptive and narrative style of text, that is it
tends to explain rather than simply to detail facts, and it enables
the author to convey to the reader some of the broader problems
and issues which were of importance at the time. In a sense I
have attempted a partially chronological approach but at the
same time focused attention on what I felt were the key issues of
the period. At times this leads to some back-tracking and cross-
referencing but I feel that it is preferable to any other approach.
Of course the volume is by no means an exhaustive study of the
world economy in the 1920s, but I doubt whether any single
volume ever could be.

Though geographical coverage is subordinate, in that it is not
allowed to dominate the text, it is by no means neglected, since
reference is frequently made to countries and regions, with
occasional lengthy digressions. Most areas of the world, if not all
countries, do, I hope, feature somewhere in the text though their
appearance on stage may sometimes be too brief. In the final
chapter I have attempted a broader perspective by examining
some long-term trends for the world economy; otherwise readers

may feel that they obtain a somewhat blinkered and short-sighted view of the 1920s.

The word 'billion' is used throughout with the meaning one thousand million.

Much of this work was written in the peaceful and congenial surroundings of St Andrew's College in the University of Sydney.

Special thanks are due to Miss Vina Smith for her expertise in typing successive drafts of the work and to Miss Charmaine Symonds for checking the text and tracking down bibliographical references.

Derek H. Aldcroft
St Andrew's College,
University of Sydney,
August 1974

1

Introduction

It is difficult to say exactly what would have happened to economic and social life had the First World War never occurred, though no doubt one day this counterfactual proposition will be put to the econometric test. There are reasons for assuming that the international economy would have continued developing in much the same way as it had in the half century or so before the outbreak of hostilities, though certainly there would have been ever-increasing symptoms of strain. But the type of development, the growth structure and spread of incomes etc. would not have departed radically from the secular trends which had been going on for some time.

If this assumption is correct we are justified in treating the war as a large exogenous shock which so upset the pattern of development and its underlying equilibrium that it eventually resulted in the breakdown of the type of integrated international framework which characterized the nineteenth century, especially the latter half. Alternatively, if this assumption is incorrect, the war may be seen as an initial shock which for a time disturbed both the cyclical and secular processes of economic development, but that after a short adjustment stage economies reverted to their previous trends without marked effects. In this case the impact of the war had little bearing on the 1929 downturn in economic activity and the subsequent disintegration of the international economy.

Objections can be raised to both these extreme lines of reasoning. To take the second hypothesis first: it is possible to argue that the war produced a fairly severe initial impact, upsetting both cyclical and secular forces, but that the readjustment was soon made and by the middle of the 1920s pre-war patterns of development were re-emerging as the economic process adapted itself. Recovery was strong in the latter half of the decade, and all that happened was a delay to the growth process, an occurrence not without precedent as an examination of past history will show. Moreover, if we ignore the small oscillations in economic activity during the 1920s the pattern of fluctuations was not all that different from that before the war, apart from the somewhat steeper amplitude. On the other hand, if one probes a little more deeply there appear all sorts of distortions and maladjustments in the international economy at large and within individual countries; and there is the dramatic and prolonged downturn of 1929, longer and more severe than most of the cyclical upsets of the nineteenth century. The question which then arises is whether these things would have occurred had there been no war. It seems that the repercussions of war were so profound and long-lasting that it is not possible to write the war off as a once-and-for-all short-term disturbance.

Unfortunately the first line of reasoning is also open to debate. The war did shock in the traumatic sense, it did release new forces, forces which exerted almost 'evil' influences on the international economic mechanism, and it did leave behind a legacy of partly insoluble problems. Yet to associate the economic downturn of 1929, or the 1931 financial crisis which more or less completed the dissolution of the old economic order, directly with the war would perhaps stretch things too far. Though the war did create new forces and new problems it also aggravated or accentuated tendencies which were already present before 1914. And again, the smooth operation of the international economic mechanism before 1914 was perhaps more apparent than real. It *worked* in a sense partly because of a fortuitous set of favourable circumstances, a convergence process, and partly because the costs, especially the social ones, of its operation were either ignored or not accepted as important at the time. In a different situation, when the convergence of favourable factors ceased to operate and when the consequences of human actions counted for more, the system worked miserably. Whether the change in circumstances can be ascribed solely to the war is another matter. On this line of argument we are probably forced to rule out endogenous cyclical forces as causes of the slump of 1929–32.

Thus neither explanation squares with the facts neatly and we are left, as so often in economic matters, floundering in the dirty grey area where 'this, that and the other' all have some bearing on the situation, but unable to attach quantitative measurements to the factors involved. Yet we cannot say that the 1929–32 depression was caused by the war and nothing but the war, nor can we dismiss the war as having no impact on the crisis of capitalism of the inter-war period.

As a way of escape for the moment from this 'awkward corner' (the phrase is Joan Robinson's) let us see what contemporaries thought about the matter. They had few doubts. They felt that the pre-war machinery had worked well and that there was every reason to expect it to do so in the future. The pre-war direction had been all right, and little guidance or management had been required to steer development along the desired route. Hence it was simply a question of getting things quickly back to normal, and to all intents and purposes normal meant the way things were before 1914. Nor was there any doubt that it would be possible to skip merrily back into a bygone age. Such attitudes were reflected in the almost indecent haste with which war-time controls were abandoned and governments reduced their economic commitments, in the desire of America to withdraw from western Europe and not participate in the League of Nations, and in the almost fanatical belief that monetary and exchange stability must be restored at all costs. The latter desire was embodied in the frantic attempt to restore the gold standard; so great was the faith in the virtue of the former 'golden age' that statesmen and administrators were prepared to devote much of their energy during the 1920s towards the resurrection of the system. How different the position was to be after the Second World War. Then there was no question of looking back to old ideals; it was a matter of 'facing the future' with a new set of ideas and tools to guide development in a different direction.

This belief or faith in the old order may well have been genuine, though with hindsight it often appears more like a blind act of faith in the virtues of the known as opposed to the unknown. The businessmen, politicians and others who regarded the normal as the world of 1913 'failed to appreciate that modern war is a revolution, and that the economic world of 1913 had already passed into history as much as had the Habsburg and Romanoff Empires'.[1] This judgement may be harsh. It is possible that the system could have been made to work again had some of the major economic powers been prepared to make greater sacrifices. Failure was not due to any defects inherent in the system itself; it was partly because national powers failed to recognize that circumstances had so changed as to make the system less easy to work, and partly because the powers no longer accepted the costs of operating it. And from this it follows that they were no longer ready to pursue policies which would have assisted its survival. Furthermore, this failure to appreciate that conditions had changed and a keen desire to restore the well-tried monetary system meant that little attention was paid to adapting the system to changed circumstances.

Such motives and attitudes were reflected in national economic policies throughout the 1920s. The restoration of currency stability and with it the gold standard came to be regarded as a prestige symbol or as a sign of national economic virility. But no coordinated plan of restoration was ever attempted: countries fixed their exchange rates on an *ad hoc* basis almost without reference to one another and regardless of whether the rates accorded properly with relevant costs and prices. Currency stabilization was a long drawn out affair which occupied virtually the whole of the decade; in the event many countries emerged with the wrong parities, the most notable cases being those of France and the United Kingdom. Having restored the pre-war system with great effort, or what amounted to an image of it, most countries were not prepared to behave in the way which had ensured its success before. The pre-1914 international monetary mechanism was essentially an exchange system in that its primary purpose was to safeguard external stability even if this meant, which it often did, sacrificing domestic stability. After the war counting the domestic cost of policy actions became much more common so that national policies were often geared more towards domestic needs. This was particularly true of debtor countries anxious to foster their own industrial development but it was also

1. D. Thomson, *Europe Since Napoleon* (1966), p. 601.

true of some creditor nations, for example France, the U.S.A. and even the U.K. at times. Economic policy became more self-centred or nationalistic: in effect it was more concerned than previously with safeguarding domestic interests and less concerned with ensuring that the international economic mechanism worked smoothly. In other words, the domestic situation was no longer sacrificed completely to external needs and hence external equilibrium had to be secured by more restrictive policies. This was manifest in increasing restrictions on trade, capital and labour flows, the freedom of movement of which had been the sheet-anchor of the pre-war system. Such measures however only served to weaken the system and assist its collapse.

It is easy, however, to get the events of the 1920s out of perspective since one's views are readily influenced by the experience of the 1930s. The shift in policy emphasis was only partial in the 1920s: such restrictions and policies as were imposed to protect external equilibrium were nothing compared to the extremes of the following decade. In any case, it would be difficult to argue, given the variety of factors which complicated the situation, that policy shifts were of crucial importance in reducing the viability of the international economic system. The war left behind a legacy of problems which upset the process of readjustment and made the restoration of 'normal' conditions almost impossible. For example, war debts and reparations were on a scale so vast that the problem of their solution and means of payment occupied the entire decade; this caused much international friction and intensified the difficulties of operating the international monetary system. The war also aggravated the problems of debtor countries, especially those in eastern Europe which suffered from military activity and later from currency depreciation. Supply and structural problems also featured prominently. Some of the more mature industrial economies faced excess capacity and structural problems as a result of lopsided war-time expansion, while certain primary producing countries were confronted with an over-supply situation, a factor which led to falling incomes and a decline in their imports of industrial products in the later 1920s. A consequence was increasing resort to restrictive action to maintain prices which, together with increasing tariffs and other restrictions, only made adjustment more difficult.

Yet apart from war debts and reparations, the war alone did not create all these difficulties. The origins of many can be traced back to the late nineteenth and early twentieth centuries. Increasing industrialization and competition in Europe, in Japan and even in some of the primary producing territories on the periphery of the international system gave rise to adjustments in tariff barriers and started off the drive towards economic nationalism, which became such a powerful force in the inter-war years. Problems of over-supply in primary products were not endemic in this period but the rate at which new territories were being made productive, Canada and the Argentine for example, together with the speed of technological advance, brought forward an enormous surge in the supply of certain basic products, notably coffee, wheat, and rubber, which spelled difficulties for the future. Control of prices and production of both primary commodities and manufactured goods was still in its infancy but becoming more common. And similarly, though excess capacity in industrial economies was still fairly rare, visible signs of it, especially in Britain, were certainly present. Even the international financial mechanism was not working so smoothly in 1914 as it appeared to have done some ten to fifteen years earlier.[2]

Though many post-war problems can be traced back to the period before 1914 there can be no denying that the war greatly aggravated or accentuated them. It intensified the drive towards industrialization in the as yet underdeveloped or semi-industrial areas, India, south-east Asia, Japan, Australia and parts of Latin America, and at the same time fostered the nationalistic sentiments which were burgeoning prior to the war. The war distorted the normal demand and supply relationships so that some sectors were greatly expanded in relation to normal peacetime needs. Perhaps the most striking examples were the vast expansion in shipbuilding capacity and the increase in cereals production in the regions of recent settlement. On top of these long-run problems the war also gave birth to new difficulties; it caused much physical

2. Hints to this effect are given in W. A. Brown, Jnr, *The International Gold Standard Reinterpreted, 1914–1934* (1940, 2 vols.). It should be noted, however, that recent research has shown that the international monetary system never worked as smoothly or as automatically as many contemporaries imagined. See A. I. Bloomfield, *Monetary Policy under the International Gold Standard, 1880–1914* (1959), and 'Rules of the Game of International Adjustment', in C. R. Whittlesey and J. S. G. Wilson (eds), *Essays in Money and Banking in Honour of R. S. Sayers* (1968).

destruction and loss of human life; it created a number of new nation states and left a legacy of political debts and currency problems.

It is clear therefore that the 1920s faced difficult economic problems of a type and severity never before experienced. Many remained partly unsolved at the end of the decade. It is equally clear that but for the war the magnitude of many would have been very much less. At this point we turn back to the question raised earlier: would the 1929–32 crisis have occurred without the war? Did the war produce so many fundamental maladjustments that the international economy could never regain its former equilibrium and the only way out was in the Great Crash?[3] Or can the crash simply be attributed to factors which are not connected with the war in any specific way? Here I am thinking of an explanation of the downturn purely in terms of internally-generated causes in which policy factors dominate. The crucial role accorded to U.S. monetary policy by some writers fits the bill in this case.[4] This certainly proves very much simpler since it relieves one of the task of assigning weight to a series of war-induced causes, though it does not solve the problem completely.

We should also consider at this stage whether the 1929 downturn needs explaining in any special way. Was it not simply part of the business cycle process? It could be argued, on the basis of past business cycle history, that the 1929–32 depression was not

3. Briggs has suggested that it can be shown generally, using Frisch's pendulum analogy, that the dislocation caused by war produced such a shock to the economic system that great swings followed, the greatest in 1929–32, and continued throughout the entire inter-war period. But Frisch believed that the economic system was disposed to produce damped fluctuations which were only prevented from dying away by periodic shocks of one sort or another. On this basis therefore the war shock would produce its most violent reaction in 1919–21, and in the absence of a further shock the 1929–32 downswing should have been damped. The fact that it was not and that there was no additional shock of comparable magnitude suggests that we must look to other causes. See A. Briggs, 'The World Economy: Interdependence and Planning', Chapter 37, C. L. Mowat (ed.), *The Shifting Balance of World Forces, 1898–1945* (1968, vol. XII of the *New Cambridge Modern History*), p. 54.

4. See M. Friedman and A. J. Schwartz, *A Monetary History of the United States, 1867–1960* (1963), and J. Pedersen, 'Some Notes on the Economic Policy of the United States during the Period 1919–1932', in H. Hegeland (ed.), *Money, Growth and Methodology: Essays in Honour of Johan Åkerman* (1961).

unexpected and that it was no more spectacular than some previous crises except possibly in terms of duration and world-wide pervasiveness.[5] The war did not break the pre-war pattern of business cycles.[6] In 1914 most industrial countries were about to move into a depression phase but the outbreak of war postponed this and produced a distorted continuation of the major upswing which eventually peaked in 1919–20. The reaction came in the sharp slump of 1920–21 which was then followed, with minor interruptions, by another major upswing to a peak in 1928–9. Thus the Juglar pattern was preserved and a depression was due in about 1929. Moreover, the 1929–32 depression was no greater in amplitude in some cases than the immediate post-war slump, while its duration had been matched in crises of the nineteenth century though not simultaneously with the same intensity. Even the world-wide scope of the depression was not entirely without precedent; the post-war slump fell not far short in this respect,[7] while international recessions were not unknown in the nineteenth century. The question is therefore whether we should simply regard it as another contraction of the business cycle sequence, or whether it was unique in itself and needs to be explained by special circumstances, in particular by the maladjustments in the economic system associated with the wartime shock.[8] Obviously we shall have cause to consider this question.

Turning to a different matter we may ask whether the 1920s are an unusual decade, a special or transitional decade. Most authors cannot resist the temptation to describe their particular period as special or different from the periods immediately preceding or following. It is difficult not to succumb when so many unusual features and dramatic events dominate the period. As against the

5. Though even this requires some modification.

6. D. H. Aldcroft and P. Fearon (eds), *British Economic Fluctuations, 1790–1939* (1972), p. 13. For what seems to be a similar view see R. A. Gordon, 'Cyclical Experience in the Interwar Period: The Investment Boom of the "Twenties"', in *National Bureau of Economic Research, Conference on Business Cycles* (1951). p. 164.

7. Given the severity of the post-war downturn it is surprising how much less attention has been paid to it compared with the one of 1929–32.

8. The 1929–32 crisis may be regarded as unique in that it can be said to represent the grand climax to trade cycle history (ignoring the minor dip of 1937–38) after which the growth cycle took its place. See M. Bronfenbrenner (ed.), *Is the Business Cycle Obsolete?* (1968).

decade or so before the war it certainly seems spectacular, and even compared with the 1930s, a period fraught with the problems of recovery and the social consequences of massive unemployment, the 1920s appear eventful and lively. Beyen has described the 1920s as 'years of hope and vigour' which 'ended in despair', whereas the 1930s were simply 'years of frustration'.[9] The decade is bounded by the aftermath of the Great War and all it entailed in reconstruction and adjustment, and by the beginnings of a severe economic crisis. Economic problems not only dominated the period but were of international scope: they involved continents as well as nations. And some issues were of such magnitude that they exercised the minds of statesmen for the entire period.

Since other volumes in this series cover the war period and the 1930s[10] the present study will stick fairly closely to the confines of the 1920s. This does not mean that reference will not be made to other periods, but for the most part the study begins with the aftermath of war and ends on the point of depression in 1929. No attempt will be made to discuss the depression in detail[11] but an appraisal of its causes forms the basis of one later chapter. Because of its attempted world-wide coverage it is impossible to deal with all aspects of economic development in detail. Attention is therefore focused on some of the main issues and problems which appear to be important in this period. The chapter sequence may be outlined briefly as follows.

Chapter 2 discusses the main consequences of war and the problems of adjustment while Chapter 3 examines in some detail the relief of Europe and then goes on to look at the boom and slump of 1919–21. The chronological sequence is then broken in order to deal with war debts and reparations which form the basis of Chapter 4. Chapter 5 takes up the story of recovery and reconstruction down to the middle of the 1920s. Two chapters are then devoted to monetary matters: Chapter 6 covers the stabilization problem and Chapter 7 looks more closely at the operation of the international monetary mechanism and its weaknesses. The boom of the later 1920s forms the subject of Chapter 8, which is then followed by Chapters 9 and 10 dealing with the problems of

9. J. W. Beyen, *Money in Maelstrom* (1951), p. 3.

10. Gerd Hardach, *The First World War, 1914–1918* (1977), and C. P. Kindleberger, *The World in Depression, 1929–1939* (1973).

11. For which see C. P. Kindleberger, *The World in Depression, 1929–1939.*

primary producers, debtor countries and the whole question of international lending. Chapter 11 reviews some explanations of the turning-point of 1929 and suggests a possible sequence of events based on the analysis of the previous chapters. The final Chapter 12 then shifts ground and analyses the overall performance of the 1920s against the longer-term perspective.

2

The Aftermath of War

A war on a scale larger than any before conceived possible could not fail to leave its mark on the economic and social life of the world economy. Though military activity was centred on European soil nearly every country, however remote from the actual theatre of war, was affected in one way or another by the hostilities. It involved an enormous mobilization of economic resources – in total some 65 million men were drafted between 1914 and 1918 though not all were engaged in fighting at any one time – and, in the belligerent countries at least, an extensive control of economic activity that represented a sharp departure from the liberal doctrines of nineteenth-century political economy.

The details of wartime activity and resource utilization are covered in a companion volume in this series.[1] Our main interest in this chapter is in those important economic consequences of war which have a bearing on subsequent events. Few would deny that the economic repercussions were widespread and far reaching: 'The economic losses resulting from the shattering of the international economic organization . . . extended literally to the ends of the earth.'[2] No complete tally has ever been made of the total

1. Gerd Hardach, *The First World War, 1914–1918* (1977). See generally H. G. Mendershausen, *The Economics of War* (1941).

2. H. G. Moulton and L. Pasvolsky, *War Debts and World Prosperity* (1932), p. 374.

monetary cost of all the direct and indirect effects, some of which are not readily amenable to monetary interpretation. The monetary cost of the actual war and the short-term physical impact in destruction of property, population loss etc., may be fairly easily quantified, but the long-term and more indirect consequences, e.g. the shifts in trade flows, the reorganization of territorial boundaries and the like, are much more difficult to translate into meaningful economic terms.

Even apart from the obvious difficulties involved in making a reliable assessment the fact that war affected nearly every aspect of economic and social life makes it almost impossible to provide a comprehensive account in the space of one chapter. Apart from the immediate direct impact – the loss of income growth, the destruction of physical assets, and the loss and injury of human beings – a whole host of other economic and social repercussions needs to be taken into consideration. The peace treaty settlements, apart from denuding Germany of many valuable resources and assets, imposed heavy reparation settlements, and provided for extensive territorial reorganization in central and eastern Europe which involved, *inter alia*, the dissolution of the Austro-Hungarian Empire (out of which were created several autonomous states) and the partial dismemberment of the former Turkish Empire. Most belligerent countries, and a few others besides, were weakened financially as a result of the war; large budgetary deficits and monetary inflation were the inevitable outcome, and indeed inflationary forces were prevalent the world over throughout the period 1914–20. These countries also suffered a check to output and real income growth while the pattern of production was distorted by the needs of the war machine. On the other hand, many countries outside the European axis received a stimulus from the insatiable demand for primary commodities, both food and raw materials, and the curtailment of supplies of manufactures from the belligerent countries. Thus Canada, some Latin American countries, Japan, the United States and parts of Asia and Australia benefited through increased primary production or a shift to industrial production or both. In the long term these changes shifted the balance of economic power away from Europe towards the North American continent and, to a lesser extent, the Pacific.

Population losses and physical destruction

The war undoubtedly occasioned a serious loss of population and physical assets. The demographic incidence of war is difficult to estimate precisely partly because the data are unreliable but also because there are difficulties in determining the indirect repercussions on the civilian population including the effects on the birth rate. The total loss from war was much greater than the military casualties.

As far as the latter are concerned the records are fairly accurate. Of more than 60 million men mobilized in Europe during the period of hostilities over 8 million (including tentative guesses for Russia), or about 15 per cent of the total, lost their lives in active service. This loss amounted to less than 2 per cent of the total European population and about 8 per cent of all male workers.[3] In addition, 7 million men were permanently disabled and a further 15 million were more or less seriously wounded.[4]

The incidence of loss varied from country to country; those countries heavily engaged in hostilities tended to fare worst, at least in absolute terms. Thus 2 million Germans were killed or died from disease, and probably 1·5–2 million Russians.[5] Of the other major belligerents France lost 1·4 million, Austro-Hungary 1·1 million, the U.K. 744,000 and Italy a similar number. Some of the minor countries also suffered considerable losses with Serbia and Montenegro (325,000) and Romania (250,000) heading the list. Bulgaria and Belgium, on the other hand, had relatively small losses. In most countries, however, the losses represented only a small proportion of the total population. Of the major powers France bore the brunt of the whole proceedings, losing some 3·3 per cent of her population through military casualties, as against 0·5 per cent in Belgium, 1·6 per cent in the U.K., 2 per cent in Italy and Austro-Hungary, and 3 per cent in Germany. The greatest proportionate losses occurred in some of the lesser

3. F. W. Notestein *et alia*, *The Future Population of Europe and the Soviet Union* (1944), pp. 74–5.

4. These latter estimates are more tentative and probably include some civilian members of the population. See S. B. Clough, *The Economic Development of Western Civilization* (1968, revised edition), p. 431; P. N. Stearns, *European Society in Upheaval* (1967), p. 313; E. L. Bogart, *Direct and Indirect Costs of the Great War* (1919), pp. 272–7.

5. But see below, pages 15–17.

belligerents with Serbia and Montenegro losing no less than 10 per cent of their pre-war population.

The overall impact was greater than these figures indicate since most of the dead were in the prime of life and constituted the most productive part of the labour force. In Germany, for instance, 40 per cent of the fatalities were aged between 20 and 24 and 63 per cent were between 20 and 30, while only 4·5 per cent were aged 40 or over. France and Germany each lost about 10 per cent of their male gainful workers, Italy 6 per cent and the U.K. 5 per cent. Some idea of the magnitude of the loss may be gained from the estimated time it would take to replace the war casualties in the male population between the ages of 20 and 44; it would require 10 years for the U.K., 12 years for Germany, 38 years for Italy and 66 years for France.[6] Moreover, these figures take no account of the civilian losses nor of the men wholly or partially incapacitated for work as a result of war injuries of one sort or another.

Civilian casualties are more difficult to estimate, and can only really be inferred by comparing actual mortality with what might have been expected in the absence of war. The figures for civilian losses include deaths resulting from disease, famine, and privation consequent on the war as well as those wrought by military conflict. Altogether Europe (excluding Russia) probably lost over 5 million civilians through war-induced causes, with Austro-Hungary the greatest sufferer (nearly 1 million). Italy too fared badly, partly because of poor health conditions, recording a loss of 800,000, while in absolute terms the German loss was almost as great. In relative terms Serbia and Montenegro suffered by far the worst, whereas the losses in France and the U.K. were comparatively moderate.

The combined death toll for Europe (excluding Russia), that is, military and civilian casualties as a result of war, amounted to more than 11 million of which just over 6·5 million were due to military causes. In other words, $3\frac{1}{2}$ per cent of the European population was removed by war. The greatest quantitative losses occurred in Germany and Austro-Hungary. In relative terms mortality ranged from about 1 per cent of the pre-war population in Scandinavia to as much as 20 per cent in Serbia. France, Italy, Germany and Austro-Hungary lost about 4 per cent of their populations, while

6. Bogart, *Direct and Indirect Costs of the Great War*, p. 283.

for the U.K. and Belgium the proportionate losses were under
2·5 per cent. But none could compare with Russia in numerical
terms. Total mortality there probably amounted to 16 million
(largely as a result of the civil war), or over 11 per cent of the pre-
war population.

To complete the picture, estimates of the number unborn as
a result of military mobilization need to be considered. Some
belligerents experienced very high birth deficits from this factor,
Austro-Hungary one of no less than 3·6 million while in Germany
it was over 3 million. France and Italy had deficits of around 1½
million, the U.K. over 700,000 and Romania just over 500,000.
All told the loss in births (Europe excluding Russia) probably
slightly exceeded the combined figure for total casualties.

TABLE 1
ESTIMATED POPULATION DEFICITS AS A RESULT OF
THE FIRST WORLD WAR

Country (pre-war boundaries)	Total deficit of population ('000)	Deficit as a percentage of pre-war population
United Kingdom	1,788	3·9
France	3,074	7·7
Belgium	416	5·4
Italy	2,735	7·6
Serbia and Montenegro	1,064	31·3
Romania	1,088	14·0
Greece	295	6·2
Portugal	264	4·3
Germany	5,436	8·0
Austro-Hungary	5,063	9·5
Bulgaria	444	9·2
Norway	26	1·0
Sweden	81	1·4
Denmark	19	0·7
Netherlands	93	1·5
Switzerland	77	2·0
Spain	434	2·1
Europe (excluding Russia)	22,397	7·0
Russia	26,000	18·5

NOTE: The figures for total deficits include military losses, excess civilian (or
war-induced) deaths and wartime birth deficits.

SOURCE: F. W. Notestein et alia, The Future Population of Europe and the
Soviet Union (1944), p. 75.

The estimated losses under the three headings considered above give a combined population deficit as a result of the war of around 22 million for Europe without Russia. In other words, Europe lost 7 per cent of her pre-war population, or the equivalent of all her natural increase between 1914 and 1919. As a result the population of Europe in 1920 was about the same as it had been at the beginning of the war. The largest absolute losses were in Germany and Austro-Hungary with over 5 million apiece, but in relative terms Serbia and Montenegro easily headed the list (see Table 1). The neutral powers easily came off the best with losses of 2 per cent or less. Of the Allied powers France and Italy suffered the worst. France's total population deficit amounted to just over 3 million or 7·7 per cent of her pre-war population. This includes a shortfall of some 1·4 million in births as a result of a dramatic decline in the birth rate. The net result was that France's population by the middle of 1919, at 38·7 million, was some 1·1 million down on 1914 even with the inclusion of Alsace–Lorraine which she recovered by the Treaty of Versailles.[7] Nor was this the end of the matter. A further million or more were injured or wounded in one way or another, while over 100,000 were wholly incapacitated.[8]

The data for Russia are much less reliable. The following figures therefore can only indicate rough orders of magnitude. Mendershausen suggests over 5 million military deaths in the former Russian Empire and nearly as many civilian losses.[9] Though these figures are high they take no account of the enormous death toll of the civil war and the subsequent famine. Notestein gives a combined loss in the region of 26 million, mostly in the civil war period, and this figure excludes the losses in the territories ceded by Russia.[10] But whatever the final tally it is clear that the total

7. A. Sauvy, *Histoire économique de la France entre les deux guerres, 1918–1931* (1965), pp. 21–2.

8. T. Kemp, *The French Economy 1919–1939: The History of a Decline* (1972). Mantoux gives figures of 3 million wounded and nearly 750,000 crippled but these figures seem far too high. E. Mantoux, *The Carthaginian Peace or the Economic Consequences of Mr Keynes* (1946).

9. Mendershausen, *The Economics of War*, p. 307. His figures for war population losses differ somewhat from those of Notestein for individual countries because of the different method of assessment.

10. Notestein *et alia, The Future Population of Europe and the Soviet Union*, p. 83.

Russian losses of population throughout this war period exceeded the combined figure for the rest of Europe.

The war caused a serious depletion and deterioration in the quality of Europe's population. Moreover, the calculations given above are not strictly complete since they do not include losses following the influenza epidemic in 1918–19, which was indirectly caused by the war, or the deaths occurring through famine, disease and continued military activity in some countries in the armistice period. Undoubtedly the most serious of these was the world-wide epidemic of influenza which carried off millions of people in Asia, particularly India, and caused considerable loss of life in Europe and America. Altogether the attack probably claimed some 15 million victims, or nearly twice the number lost on the European battle-fields.[11] In addition, substantial losses of population also occurred in eastern Europe and the Balkans as a result of post-war famine, while massacres of various nationalities in the post-war border conflicts, notably the Armenians, Syrians, Jews, Poles and Greeks, brought further casualties, though the totals were fairly small.

Thus the final casualty list for what might be termed the entire war period, 1914–21, runs into many millions; it probably exceeds 60 million even making allowances for some double counting. Russia alone accounted for nearly half this total. Direct military losses were responsible for only a relatively small proportion of the loss in world population of this period.

Great though the loss of life and injury sustained in the war and shortly afterwards it is to be doubted whether it had any severe or lasting economic impact on the countries concerned. The war drained the belligerents of some of their best manpower, many of whom were highly skilled, but as the post-war period was marked by high unemployment in many of the countries which lost men at the front it could be argued that wartime casualties and the check to population growth were something of a mixed blessing. So too in the central and eastern European countries the period between the wars was one of excess or underemployed labour especially in agrarian activities.

11. Mendershausen, *The Economics of War*, p. 260; H. W. V. Temperley (ed.), *A History of the Peace Conference of Paris*, vol. I (1920), p. 138; R. Butler, 'The Peace Treaty Settlement of Versailles', chapter 8 of C. L. Mowat (ed.), *The Shifting Balance of World Forces, 1898–1945* (1968, vol. XII of the *New Cambridge Modern History*), p. 212.

To some extent the physical devastation wrought by the war seemed much worse, partly because it was visible for all to see, and partly because it was more difficult to put right; it required money and real resources which were both scarce after the war, though the speed with which restitution was made must be regarded as impressive. Various global estimates have been made of the total capital losses incurred. One suggests that at pre-war prices the value of property destroyed in the world was roughly £2,000 million, though this does not include armaments, munitions and other military supplies. Stamp calculated that the war destroyed some three to four years' normal growth of income-yielding property in Europe (excluding Russia), or one part in thirty of its original value. To this needs to be added the deterioration of the physical capital through neglect or lack of maintenance. On the other hand, some areas of activity, those servicing the war machine, probably increased their total assets; while countries not engaged in the conflict or on the periphery almost certainly ended the war in better physical shape. This led Bowley to conclude that in 1919 the world found itself with its physical capital in bad shape and in quantity no greater than in 1911.[12] This is but a rough estimate yet it is the best we have.

Europe was the main sufferer. About one-thirtieth of her assets was destroyed and physical damage was greatest in France, Belgium, Serbia and eastern Europe, whereas the U.K., Austria and Germany, though major participants, came off fairly lightly. Bulgaria too was much better placed than her neighbours on the Balkan peninsula; there was virtually no destruction or despoliation of property since the country never became a theatre of war and so the productive apparatus of the economy at the end of hostilities was in a reasonable state.[13] The occupied territories suffered the worst ravages since they shared the privations of the Central Empires and at the same time were exploited to the utmost for the good of their temporary masters. It was rough justice that two of the victors, Belgium and France, should

12. A. L. Bowley, *Some Economic Consequences of the Great War* (1930), pp. 89–90. Various estimates of the cost of the war in monetary terms are given in Bogart, *Direct and Indirect Costs of the Great War*, p. 299.

13. Bulgaria was probably more adversely affected by the social and political turmoil immediately following the war which partly paralysed the economy. G. T. Danaillow, *Les Effets de la guerre en Bulgarie* (1932), pp. 547–52, 602–4.

experience the worst ordeal. Practically the whole area of Belgium was invaded, crops were ruined and land became unfit for cultivation, factories, mines and houses were destroyed, and general destruction and pillage were widespread, though the enemy eventually appreciated the need to keep the economy running in order to serve its own needs. The extent of the damage can readily be listed. Some 100,000 houses, equivalent to 6 per cent of the 1914 stock, were destroyed or damaged beyond repair; three-quarters of the railway rolling stock and one-quarter of the fixed stock were destroyed, and by the Armistice only eighty locomotives were in reasonable working order; about half the steel mills were smashed completely and most of the remainder badly damaged. The position was little better on the land. Over 240,000 acres (97,000 hectares) of land were rendered unfit for cultivation by shelling, while the animal population was decimated. One-half of the horned beasts, two-thirds of the swine, one-half of the horses, 1,500 million fowl and 35,000 goats perished or were seized during the course of hostilities.[14] France's destruction makes equally dismal reading. The main devastated area was in the north where ten departments were invaded and liberated. In all some 6,000 square miles (15,500 square kilometres), or 2 per cent of France, with a total population of 2 million, were laid waste, and losses of livestock in this area exceeded 50 per cent of the immediate prewar levels. These regions accounted for a high proportion of French agricultural and industrial activity – 20 per cent of her crops, 70 per cent of her coal output, 90 per cent of iron ore output and 65 per cent of steel output. Much machinery, equipment and factories were also destroyed, while destruction of property covered an even wider area than the invaded departments. Altogether about 500,000 buildings were damaged, and at least 250,000 completely destroyed. In addition, there were many other damages including 1·2 million acres (0·485 million hectares) of forest which were laid waste.[15]

14. F. Baudhuin, *Histoire économique de la Belgique, 1914–1939*, vol. I, 2nd edition (1946), pp. 63–76; H. L. Shepherd, *The Monetary Experience of Belgium, 1914–1936* (1936), pp. 14–16; D. Thomson, *Europe since Napoleon* (1966), p. 603.

15. See C. B. Clough, T. Moodie and C. Moodie (eds), *Economic History of Europe: Twentieth Century* (1969), pp. 58–61; S. Pollard and C. Holmes, *Documents of European Economic History: Vol. 3 The End of the Old Europe*

France and Belgium accounted for the bulk of the property losses, $17,000 million out of a total of $29,960 million estimated by Bogart. In comparison the destruction suffered by other countries was quite modest, although in some cases it involved a large proportion of the total net worth of the countries in question. Thus Poland, Serbia, Romania and Italy came off quite badly on this reckoning. Paradoxically, Germany fared the best with a total property loss of only $1,750 million, most of it due to air raids late in the war.[16] However, monetary values do not always register an accurate assessment of the havoc wrought by war. In value Poland's loss of property was placed only a little way below that of Germany but the impact was very much greater. The occupying powers literally devastated Polish territory, taking cash, securities, cattle and farm implements, and stripping factories. Half the bridges, station buildings and railway work-shops were destroyed and 1·8 million buildings were lost by fire. Nearly 11 million acres (4·45 million hectares) of agricultural land were put out of use, 6 million acres (2·43 million hectares) of forest were totally destroyed, and 7,600 million cubic feet (215 million cubic metres) of timber were removed by alien armies. Many factories were denuded of equipment, the metallurgical industry was completely immobilized, much of the railway rolling stock was taken, large tracks of good agricultural land were laid waste and 60 per cent of the cattle stock disappeared. To make matters worse the administrative and financial apparatus was completely disorganized, partly as a result of the new territorial groupings contained in the peace treaties, while Poland as an enemy country had no right to reparations and had to pay debts not only to the Allies but also indemnities for German and Austrian State properties in occupation.[17]

Serbia, which was subsequently incorporated into the new state of Yugoslavia, also suffered extreme devastation. After the Austro-Hungarian retreat nearly all the factories and industrial establish-ments were in a useless condition. The saw-mills, cement works, and brick kilns had been wrecked, and the farms stripped of most

1914–1939 (1973), pp. 50–53; C. Gide and W. Oualid, *Le Bilan de la guerre pour la France* (1931), pp. 170–84.

16. Bogart, *Direct and Indirect Costs of the Great War*, pp. 285–7.

17. F. Zweig, *Poland between Two Wars* (1944), pp. 29–33; J. Taylor, *The Economic Development of Poland, 1919–1950* (1952), pp. 140–42.

of their livestock and implements. The railways had been rendered unworkable and even the houses in some districts had been stripped of furniture and fittings. The same story was true of Austrian Galicia. Many dwellings and farm buildings had been destroyed completely and peasants were living in hovels or temporary accommodation, without proper food or clothing, and in some cases without seed to sow in their fields.[18]

Destruction was so great and complete in some of the occupied or invaded areas that the advisability of attempting to rebuild many towns and villages which had once been prosperous was considered an open question. In the west as well as the east, especially Belgium, northern France and northern Italy, ruined industries had to be restored almost from the foundations. Virtually all stocks of raw materials had gone, the machinery either removed or rendered unworkable, and almost nothing remained but the bare walls of the factories, an army of hungry unemployed men and the manufacturers 'whose capital consisted of their own brains and some amount of depreciated currency'.[19] For these countries the price of war was indeed a heavy one.

Exactions under the peace treaties

If some of the enemy powers got off rather lightly in terms of physical destruction and territorial devastation retribution was not long in forthcoming. The peace treaties[20] not only imposed heavy penalties on the vanquished, including large reparation indemnities, but also made extensive territorial changes in central and eastern Europe which were to have significant repercussions in the short and medium term. The post-war settlements constituted

18. H. W. V. Temperley (ed.), *A History of the Peace Conference of Paris*, vol. I (1920), p. 147. For other countries in eastern Europe see G. T. Danaillow, *Les Effets de la guerre en Bulgarie* (1932); D. Mitrany, *The Effect of the War in South-Eastern Europe* (1936); I. T. Berend and G. Ranki, *Economic Development of East-Central Europe in the 19th and 20th Centuries* (1974).

19. Temperley, *A History of the Peace Conference of Paris*, vol. II, p. 148.

20. Separate peace treaties were made with each of the enemy powers. They were as follows: Treaty of Versailles with Germany (28 June 1919), Treaty of St Germain-en-Laye with Austria (10 September 1919), Treaty of Neuilly with Bulgaria (27 November 1919), Treaty of Trianon with Hungary (4 June 1920), and the Treaty of Sèvres with Turkey (20 August 1920). The latter Treaty was rejected and it was not until July 1923, by the Treaty of Lausanne, that eventual agreement was reached with Turkey.

the biggest exercise in the reshaping of the political geography of Europe ever undertaken.[21] The process involved the greater part of the continent and the only countries not affected (that is if we exclude minor independences) were Holland, Luxemburg, Switzerland, Spain and Portugal. Altogether the number of separate customs units in Europe was increased from twenty to twenty-seven, while political frontiers were lengthened by 12,500 miles (20,000 kilometres).[22] The newly created independent states comprised Poland, Finland, Estonia, Latvia, Lithuania, Czechoslovakia and Yugoslavia.[23]

Both Germany and the former Austro-Hungarian Empire suffered heavy territorial losses by the peace treaties. Under the Treaty of Versailles Germany lost all her colonies, Alsace–Lorraine, the Saar basin, most of Posen and part of west Prussia, the industrial region of Upper Silesia, Schleswig, Danzig, the Baltic port of Memel, the frontier districts of Eupen and Malmédy and a small area near Troppau.[24] In total she was deprived of about

21. D. Thomson, *Europe Since Napoleon* (1966), p. 626.

22. Margaret S. Gordon, *Barriers to World Trade: A Study of Recent Commercial Policy* (1941), p. 19.

23. The number is enlarged if one includes Southern Ireland, Danzig, Iceland (which subsequently became independent of Denmark), and even more if one separates Georgia, Armenia etc. from Russia.

24. The distribution of the territories ceded was as follows: The German colonies were distributed under mandate to the powers which already occupied them; Alsace–Lorraine went to France, the coal mines of the Saar were given to France and the area put under League trusteeship with provision for a plebiscite after fifteen years; in 1935 the Saar voted overwhelmingly to go back to Germany and the latter then repurchased the coal mines from France. Posen and west Prussia went to Poland and a corridor to the Baltic was provided through the German port of Danzig, which became a free city under the League but incorporated into the Polish customs system. Plebiscites were to determine the attribution of Upper Silesia and the east Prussian districts of Allenstein and Marienwerder; the latter two voted to return to Germany in July 1920 while the Silesian plebiscite of March 1921 decided 60 per cent in favour of Germany and 40 per cent for Poland with the result that the League decided to split the territory with the smaller and economically richer part being awarded to Poland. The Schleswig borderland was also subject to a plebiscite in both zones; the northern half went to Denmark and the southern to Germany. The port of Memel eventually went to Lithuania as her access to the sea, Eupen and Malmédy were ceded to Belgium, and Troppau became part of Czechoslovakia. For full details see D. Thomson, *Europe Since Napoleon* (1966), pp. 623–66 and R. Butler, 'The Peace Treaty Settlement of Versailles, 1918–1933', chapter 8 of C. L. Mowat (ed.), *The Shifting Balance of*

$13\frac{1}{2}$ per cent of her pre-war territory and 10 per cent of the population of 1910. But these figures somewhat underestimate the extent of the damage since the areas ceded contained some of the richest agricultural and industrial resources. Consequently Germany in effect lost 15 per cent of her arable land and 12 per cent of the livestock, 48 per cent of her iron ore, 15·7 per cent of her coal, 63 per cent of zinc ore, 24 per cent of lead mines and smelting plants, 19 per cent of iron and steel capacity, including 40 per cent of the blast furnace equipment. Altogether about 15 per cent of her pre-war capacity was forfeited. These percentages moreover refer to the proportion of pre-war output produced by the ceded territories and the losses in terms of potential output were even greater, ranging from 36 per cent in the case of coal to 72 per cent for iron ore.[25]

In addition to these penalties the Allies confiscated nearly 90 per cent of the German mercantile fleet, almost all her foreign investments, while payments in kind were demanded in the transitional period before the heavy reparations bill was presented.[26] Finally, the Treaty also provided for the disarmament of Germany; she was forbidden to have an air force, the army and navy were reduced to minor proportions and conscription was abolished, while provision was also made for an Allied occupation force in the Rhineland.

The loss of resources was severe but not incapacitating. Far worse was the dislocation caused by the partition of industrial regions which formed single integrated units, such as Upper Silesia, and the breaking of the link between Ruhr coal and the iron of Lorraine. But partitioning was not confined to Germany since the peacemakers, in their infinite wisdom but absence of economic sense, repeated the exercise again and again during their course in treaty formulation for the European continent.

World Forces, 1898–1945 (1968, vol. XII of the *New Cambridge Modern History*), pp. 219–20.

25. C. R. S. Harris, *Germany's Foreign Indebtedness* (1935), p. 1; Mantoux, *The Carthaginian Peace or the Economic Consequences of Mr Keynes*, pp. 69–70; H. Moulton and C. E. McGuire, *Germany's Capacity to Pay* (1923), pp. 107–09; L. Grebler and W. Winkler, *The Cost of the War to Germany and Austria–Hungary* (1940).

26. The reparations bill was not fixed by the Treaty but left to be determined by a Reparations Commission. This aspect is dealt with fully in Chapter 4.

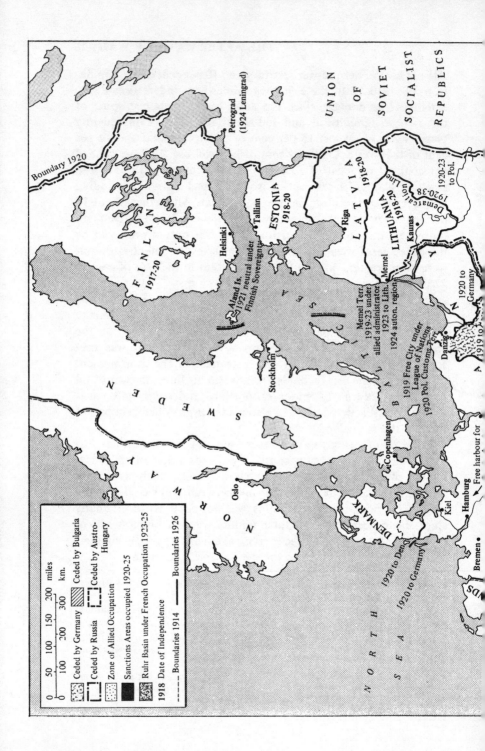

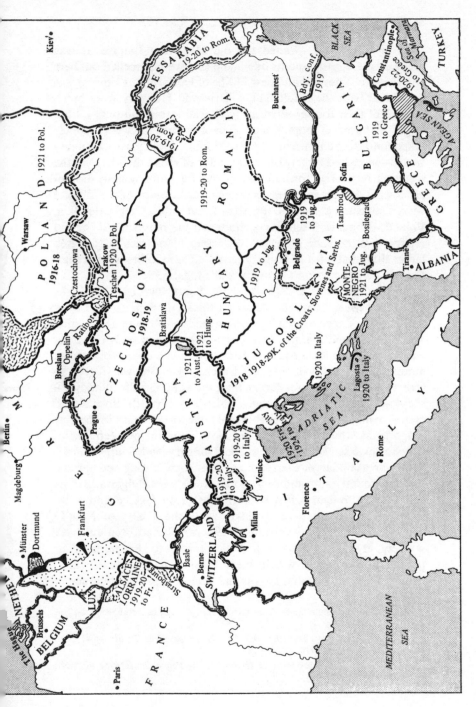

Treaty settlements in Europe, 1919-26

A far worse fate awaited the old Hapsburg Empire. It was sliced up mercilessly and its bits and pieces were parcelled out here and there to states old and new.[27] The old amorphous Empire was decimated with the result that Austria and Hungary were but a quarter of their former selves in territorial terms and only a little larger in terms of population. Economic criteria were scarcely taken into account when the partitioning took place. Hungary was dismembered largely on the grounds of racial diversity yet the resulting territorial formations proved no more racially homogeneous and made even less economic sense. Slabs of the Empire were distributed among no less than seven states, Czechoslovakia, Poland, Romania, Yugoslavia, Italy and the remnants of the old regime, Austria and Hungary. Romania alone secured an area larger than that left to Hungary herself. These losses were greater than those inflicted on Germany and Bulgaria.[28]

Austria lost Trieste, Istria and the South Tyrol to Italy; she ceded Bohemia, Moravia, Austrian Silesia and parts of Lower Austria to Czechoslovakia; Bukovina to Romania; Bosnia, Herzegovina and Dalmatia to Yugoslavia. Union with Germany was forbidden and her armed forces were cut down to a token amount. Hungary probably fared even worse. She was forced to cede to Romania an area larger than she kept herself; in addition she lost Croatia and Slovania which, along with Bosnia and Herzegovina, went to join Serbia and later Montenegro in the new Yugoslavia, while she also yielded Slovakia to the new republic of Czechoslovakia. Both Austria and Hungary ended up as landlocked areas no larger than some of their surrounding neighbours.

Other countries to suffer territorial losses were Bulgaria, Russia and Turkey. Bulgaria lost western Thrace to Greece and some small frontier areas to Yugoslavia while the Treaty of Neuilly confirmed the frontiers existing in 1914 which had been cut back severely in 1913.[29] Russia lost Bessarabia to Romania, four peripheral territories which were created independent states, namely Finland, Estonia, Latvia and Lithuania, and subsequently

27. In actual fact the Hapsburg monarchy had already ceased to exist before the treaty settlements.

28. C. A. Macartney, *Hungary and Her Successors: The Treaty of Trianon and its Consequences, 1919-1937* (1937), pp. 1-2.

29. H. W. V. Temperley (ed.), *A History of the Peace Conference of Paris*, vol. IV (1921), p. 459.

a large slice of her western frontier after the Polish defeat of the drive on Warsaw in 1920. Negotiating a settlement with Turkey was more complicated and dragged on since the Turks rejected the Treaty of Sèvres of 1920. Eventually however, by the Treaty of Lausanne of 1923, Turkey renounced claims to territories with Arab majorities but retained a foothold in Europe by securing eastern Thrace from Greece. [30]

The main beneficiaries from the peace settlements were Poland, Yugoslavia, Czechoslovakia and Romania. Poland, back on the map after more than a century, secured substantial chunks of territory from Germany, Austria and Russia, the original partitioning powers. The new independent states of Czechoslovakia and Yugoslavia also did well from the break-up of the Hapsburg Empire, while Romania more than doubled its former size in gains from neighbouring countries. The territorial gains of most other countries were quite minor by comparison.

One can scarcely conclude that the territorial realignments of the peace treaties were satisfactory and it is probable, as Thomson suggests, that they created more problems than they removed.[31] The reorganization of boundaries created several new states, greatly increased the length of European political frontiers and increased the number of separate tariff units; it left many national minorities under alien rule and created enormous problems of economic integration. Possibly these difficulties were the inevitable outcome of an attempt to satisfy several objectives at one and the same time, namely ethnic delineation, national self-determination, the reconstruction of historic frontiers and economic requirements, since to satisfy one required the modification of another. Thus to give Poland access to the Baltic it was necessary to award her territory that included a German-speaking element, while the predominantly German Sudetenland was incorporated in Czechoslovakia in order to give Czechoslovakia a defensible frontier

30. R. A. C. Parker, *Europe 1919–45* (1969), p. 39. The complex territorial rearrangements of this period are perhaps best followed in the excellent maps in H. C. Darby and H. Fullard (eds), *New Cambridge Modern History*, vol. XIV, *Atlas* (1970). For statistical detail on territorial and population changes in central and eastern Europe see I. T. Berend and G. Ranki, *Economic Development of East-Central Europe in the 19th and 20th Centuries*, Chapter 8 and N. Spulber, *The State and Economic Development in Eastern Europe* (1966), pp. 54–5.

31. Thomson, *Europe Since Napoleon*, p. 633.

for Bohemia and Moravia. But given the complex mixture of nationalities within eastern Europe ethnic problems were bound to arise even had national self-determination been followed to the letter of Wilson's doctrine.

Though economic factors were not completely ignored in the peace-making process it would certainly appear from the results that they were given short shrift when defining the boundaries of newly created and reconstituted states. Each country received whatever resources and equipment happened to be located in the territory assigned to it.[32] This often meant the complete break-up of former trading patterns and lines of communication and the separation of mutually dependent branches of industry. Such problems were particularly acute in central and eastern Europe. Yugoslavia, for example, inherited five railway systems with four different gauges; each system seived different centres so that they were practically unconnected with each other, and unifying these disparate parts took the best part of a decade. The textile industry of Austria was split apart; the spindles were located in Bohemia and Moravia, which became part of Czechoslovakia, while the weaving looms were mainly in and around Vienna.[33] Hungary, a country which prior to 1914 had been making reasonable industrial progress, was shorn of some important raw materials needed to service her developing industries. She was left with about half her industrial undertakings, including the important manufacturing centre of Budapest, but lost many raw material sources, including 84 per cent of the forests, a similar proportion of iron ore, all her salt, copper and most other non-ferrous metals, 90 per cent of her water power and 30 per cent of her lignite. Losses in the industrial sector were very uneven, ranging from 89 per cent in the case of saw-mills to 18 per cent of the machine industries. The net result was that Hungary retained proportionately more industrial activities than raw material resources with the paradoxical result that she emerged from the war more industrialized than when she began it.[34] Such changes did more to hinder than promote economic recovery after the war and in the long term they created

32. L. Pasvolsky, *Economic Nationalism of the Danubian States* (1928), p. 548.

33. ibid., pp. 527, 548.

34. Macartney, *Hungary and Her Successors*, pp. 461–2; I. T. Berend and G. Ranki, *Hungary: A Century of Economic Development* (1974), pp. 92–3.

resentment and frustration which was partly reflected in the growing tide of nationalism throughout the inter-war period.

Apart from the task of physical reconstruction, which relatively speaking was greater in central and eastern Europe than anywhere else, the new states generally had to build new economic organizations out of the multiple segments of the territories acquired. This usually involved the creation of new administrative units, new currencies, new lines of communication[35] and the forging of fresh economic and trading links to replace those which had been destroyed. Inevitably it increased the role of the state in the economic sphere and in turn this was expressed in a drive towards greater self-sufficiency. The gainers as well as the losers faced equally difficult tasks. Romania and Yugoslavia, with their domains greatly enlarged through ceded territories, had to integrate the diverse parts, with their ethnic contrasts, into unified states.[36] Czechoslovakia landed up with a host of racial minorities to consolidate. Welding together the three separate segments which constituted the revived state of Poland was even more difficult, especially as she began her existence with no natural frontiers, without a port,[37] and little in the way of highly developed industry except in the part of Upper Silesia awarded to her by the plebiscite of 1921. 'On the day of their political unification the three parts of Poland did not constitute a single economic unit. They had different systems of civil, commercial, and fiscal legislation. They belonged to differing customs units, to differing money and credit systems. Nor did they constitute a unity in the sense that they had been developed after an organized pattern by constant and mutual testing. On the contrary some parts were over- and some under-developed.'[38]

35. Apart from the severe physical destruction suffered by transport systems and deterioration in rolling stock and equipment resulting from maintenance neglect, frontier changes meant that former lines of communication became disorganized and useless in some cases. Repair work was also held up by shortages of materials, labour, fuel and strikes. See League of Nations, *Transport Problems which arose from the War of 1914–1918 and the Work of Restoration Undertaken in this Field by the League of Nations* (1945), pp. 10–12.

36. N. Spulber, *The State and Economic Development in Eastern Europe* (1966), pp. 26–7.

37. This problem was solved by making the German city of Danzig an independent city state within the Polish customs area and hence represented by Poland abroad.

38. Zweig, *Poland between Two Wars*, p. 13.

Austria and Hungary, on the other hand, had the reverse problem of creating viable economic units out of the remnants of the old monarchy; not that this had been a very coherent and efficient economic organization anyway but the resulting dislocation was even worse. The best portions of the former Empire were sliced off and Austria and Hungary were left with the rump. Austria ended up with a head much larger than its body compared to pre-war in that Vienna, the once glittering capital city of Europe, which harboured an overgrown bureaucracy, tended to dwarf the rest of the country. With a population of under 6½ million, nearly one-third of whom were in Vienna, Austria had become a top-heavy and economically precarious state.[39] Hungary secured a rather larger population but since she lost many of her most valuable resources to her neighbours her economic system was considerably weakened and disrupted.[40]

The financial legacy of war

Apart from the loss of life and property, the direct costs of the war need to be considered since the method of finance created serious problems in the immediate post-war period. The direct cost of the war to all the belligerents amounted to some $260 billion, of which the Allied share accounted for $176 billion. The largest expenditures were incurred by the U.K., the United States, Germany, France, Austro-Hungary and Italy in that order. Some idea of the magnitude of the total outlay can be gained from the fact that it represented 6½ times the sum of all the national debt accumulated in the world from the end of the eighteenth century up to the outbreak of the First World War.[41]

The crux of the problem was not so much the magnitude of the outlay involved as the way in which it was financed. The rigid financial orthodoxy which had prevailed throughout the nineteenth century disintegrated almost overnight as governments throughout the world abandoned the gold standard and resorted

39. Butler, 'The Peace Treaty Settlement of Versailles, 1918–1933', p. 222.
40. R. Donald, *The Tragedy of Trianon* (1928), Chapter 18.
41. W. S. and E. S. Woytinsky, *World Commerce and Governments* (1955), p. 743. Total war expenditure converted to a gold basis amounted to $200 billion, which represented five times normal expenditure and was equivalent to five times the national debt at the beginning of the war.

to deficit financing.[42] Only a very small proportion of the war expenditures was financed by taxation and the bulk was met out of credit operations of one sort or another. Thus France and Germany relied almost entirely on borrowing to finance the war, and less than 2 per cent of the cost was derived from revenue sources. Italy did somewhat better, since 16·2 per cent of its war expenditures came from war revenues while for the United Kingdom the proportion was 20·3 per cent.[43] Even in the United States only just over 23 per cent of war expenditures was covered from revenue sources.[44] Taking all the belligerent powers together some 80 per cent or more of the excess of actual wartime expenditure over those of the last three years of peace was financed by borrowing.[45] This method of financing need not have been inflationary had the loans been derived from genuine savings but in fact much of the finance was raised through bank credit. Banks either granted loans to governments by creating new money or else received 'promises to pay' from the governments and then increased the supply of money with these promises as reserves. The details of the mechanism varied from one country to another but the end result was the same. Public debts rose rapidly and the proportion of short-term debt increased,[46] the money supply was vastly expanded and the banks' metallic reserves in relation to their notes and deposits fell sharply. Thus in Germany by the end of 1918 the money supply had risen nine times, the budgetary

42. See J. Stamp, *Taxation during the War* (1932) and *The Financial Aftermath of War* (1932).

43. Though if certain non-tax revenues are excluded the British proportion falls to 18·3 per cent. C. Gilbert, *American Financing of World War I* (1970), pp. 222–3.

44. Gilbert, *American Financing of World War I*, p. 223. See also S. Mac-Clintock, 'French Finances and Economic Resources', *Journal of Political Economy*, vol. xxx (1922), p. 232; H. Truchy, *Les Finances de Guerre de la France* (1926); D. T. Jack, *The Restoration of European Currencies* (1927), p. 6; R. Knauerhase, *An Introduction to National Socialism 1920 to 1939* (1972), p. 25; F. A. Knox, 'Canadian War Finance and Balance of Payments, 1914–1918', *Canadian Journal of Economics and Political Science*, vol. vi (1940); P. N. Apostol *et alia*, *Russian Public Finance During the War* (1928).

45. Mendershausen, *The Economics of War*, p. 306.

46. In Italy, for example, by the end of the fiscal year 1918–19 short-term debt constituted 43 per cent of total domestic indebtedness, while taxation furnished less than one-eighth of aggregate expenditure. C. E. McGuire, *Italy's International Economic Position* (1927), pp. 90, 97.

deficit by six times while the metallic reserves as a proportion of bank notes and deposits had fallen to 10 per cent from 57 per cent in 1914. The position in Austria–Hungary was even worse, while France and Belgium also suffered severely. In general the expansion of currency, increase in debt and fall in metallic reserves went farthest in the central European countries; the European entente powers suffered moderately, while the European neutrals, Japan and the United States fared somewhat better.[47]

These conditions inevitably gave rise to rapid price inflation and currency depreciation since virtually all countries abandoned fixed parities with gold during the course of the war. In most countries prices at the end of the war were two to three times the level of 1913–14. Countries which fared the worst in this respect were those which had experienced the greatest degree of monetary inflation. Thus in Germany wholesale prices at the end of 1918 were five times the level of pre-war, despite internal controls, while the mark had slumped to 50 per cent of its former par value; Austria and Hungary experienced even greater inflation and their currency was worth between 30 and 40 per cent of its former value. Other countries whose currencies had begun to depreciate significantly were Finland, France, Italy and Portugal. On the other hand, many neutral countries, in particular the Netherlands, Norway, Sweden and Switzerland, managed to retain and even improve the value of their currencies despite significant inflation.[48]

But with one or two exceptions, notably Germany and Austria–Hungary, inflation had not really become unmanageable by the end of the war. It became much worse soon after the end of hostilities as continued lax monetary and fiscal policies, coupled with

47. J. S. Davis, 'World Currency Expansion During the War and in 1919', *Review of Economic Statistics*, vol. II (1920), pp. 10–13; B. M. Anderson, *Effect of the War on Money, Credit and Banking in France and the United States* (1919).

48. P. Alpert, 'The Impact of World War I on the European Economy', in W. C. Scoville and J. C. La Force (eds), *The Economic Development of Western Europe from 1914 to the Present* (1970), pp. 17–27; L. B. Yeager, *International Monetary Relations: Theory, History and Policy* (1966), p. 268; League of Nations, *Europe's Overseas Needs 1919–1920 and How They were Met* (1943), p. 42. For Latin America see J. H. Williams, 'Latin American Foreign Exchange and International Balances during the War', *Quarterly Journal of Economics*, vol. XXXIII (1918–19).

other forces, for a time served to stoke the fires of inflation. The choice then was between pressing on with inflation, which had advantages as well as drawbacks, or calling a halt to the process. Some European countries, notably Germany, Hungary and Austria, as well as a number of others, chose the former course with ultimately disastrous consequences. Others, the U.K. and the U.S. in particular, clamped down very quickly with consequences in some ways equally severe though of a different nature.

Apart from internal debt and its inflationary implications the war left a legacy of inter-governmental debts contracted among the Allied powers; and eventually, after the Reparations Commission had deliberated, an enormous reparations bill was imposed on Germany and other enemy nations.[49] Negotiations over the payment of these debts were to occupy statesmen for the rest of the decade and they were never paid in full. More important, the debts themselves caused great friction and resentment among the major powers; and reparations in particular gave rise in part to some unfortunate consequences.[50]

Europe and the world economy

War losses, destruction and devastation were one thing but perhaps more serious from the long-term point of view was the decline in economic importance Europe suffered vis-à-vis the rest of the world as a result of her exertions between 1914 and 1918. Her economic machine became impoverished and run-down during the course of hostilities, while she became increasingly dependent on external sources of supply and finance. The United States became the great provider, and as Europe lost overseas investments and contacts so America increased her influence and emerged from the war as a strong net creditor. But the United States was not the only country to gain from the ordeal. Many countries on the periphery of the international economy received a stimulus from wartime demand for raw materials and foodstuffs, while the shortfall of supply in manufactures from Europe also accelerated industrial development in some countries.

By the end of the war the world as a whole was almost certainly

49. Actually reparations for the other enemies were fixed by the respective peace treaties.
50. These matters are dealt with more fully later.

worse off than in 1913–14. Even by 1920 world manufacturing production was still about 7 per cent less than in 1913 while the volume of world exports was not much more than one-half that of pre-war.[51] In terms of production and income almost the whole cost of the war fell on Europe. Svennilson has calculated that if there had been no war and the 1881–1913 European rate of industrial output growth of $3\frac{1}{4}$ per cent per annum had been maintained then the 1929 level of production would have been achieved in 1921. Thus, on a crude basis, one may say that the war caused an eight-year setback to the growth of output. But since expansion did take place in some countries during the war the check to industrial production on a world basis amounted to about four and a half years.[52]

In many countries output and exports suffered a reversal during the course of the war, and with the run-down of plant and machinery and dislocation following the war, levels of activity in 1919 and 1920 were some way below those of 1913. By far the worst performance was recorded in Russia where industrial output in 1920 was down to about 13 per cent of the 1913 figure. But here special circumstances accounted for the disastrous record, in particular the continuing border conflicts, the repercussions of the civil war through 1920 and the general chaos and mismanagement of the new Soviet regime. Indeed, the economy was in a state of complete collapse in 1920 which Nove calls 'nightmare conditions'.[53] At the other extreme South Africa experienced an increase in industrial activity of the order of 200 per cent, while the number of establishments and employees nearly tripled between 1911 and the early 1920s. This was very much a case of import substitution as overseas supplies of manufactures were cut off, since exports changed very little. Nearly all sectors benefited with the sole exception of the once-flourishing ostrich feather industry which almost completely collapsed as a result of fashion

51. See League of Nations, *Industrialization and Foreign Trade* (1945), p. 134 and Woytinsky and Woytinsky, *World Commerce and Governments*, p. 39.

52. I. Svennilson, *Growth and Stagnation in the European Economy* (1954), p. 19.

53. A. Nove, *An Economic History of the U.S.S.R.* (1969), pp. 55–63; also N. Jasney, *Soviet Economists of the Twenties: Names to be Remembered* (1972), p. 9; see also M. Dobb, *Soviet Economic Development Since 1917* (revised edition, 1968), and S. Kohn and A. F. Meyendorff, *The Cost of the War to Russia* (1932).

changes! For the Union it represented a marked shift towards the manufacturing sector, a process that continued throughout the inter-war period when South Africa achieved one of the highest rates of growth on record.[54]

Aside from these extremes there was a group of countries, mainly enemy nations or those heavily engaged in military conflict, whose output was severely checked in the latter half of the war and thence recovered only slowly. By 1920 manufacturing output in Germany, France, Belgium,[55] Bulgaria, Poland, Czechoslovakia, Austria, Hungary, Romania and Latvia was at least 30 per cent or more down on 1913.[56] Yet even this was an improvement from the position prevailing immediately after the war. Tentative figures put out by the League of Nations suggest that industrial production in central and eastern Europe was more than one-half below normal, while in Belgium, Germany and Austria it was about 60 per cent below par.[57] Agriculture held up slightly better though even here there was a serious shortfall. Production was about one-third below normal in Continental Europe; in some of the devastated areas of France wheat production in 1919 was only 34 per cent of 1913, oats 38 per cent, sugarbeet 17 per cent and potatoes 60 per cent.[58] Declines of this magnitude however were by no means uncommon in central and eastern Europe where much good land had been sacrificed.

54. C. G. W. Schumann, *Structural Changes and Business Cycles in South Africa, 1806–1936* (1938), pp. 154–7, 168, 174–5, 214–23; J. C. Du Plessis, *Economic Fluctuations in South Africa, 1910–1949* (1950), pp. 21, 36.

55. Belgium is a doubtful case since there are a number of conflicting estimates. The common range is between 20 and 35 per cent below pre-war but Shepherd reckons that in 1920 industrial output had reached 88 per cent of the pre-war level, compared with 45 per cent in 1919. Shepherd, *The Monetary Experience of Belgium 1914–1936*, p. 16.

56. Most of the data on manufacturing production is drawn from League of Nations, *Industrialization and Foreign Trade* (1945), pp. 134–36. Cf. OEEC, *Industrial Statistics 1900–1959* (1960), p. 9 which gives figures for industrial production but for a lesser range of countries. See also Svennilson, *Growth and Stagnation in the European Economy*, pp. 304–5.

57. League of Nations, *Europe's Overseas Needs 1919–20 and How They Were Met* (1943), p. 9; League of Nations, *Agricultural Production in Continental Europe during the 1914–18 War and the Reconstruction Period* (1943), p. 12.

58. Sauvy, *Histoire économique de la France entre les deux guerres, 1918–1931*, p. 26.

Some neutrals and one or two other countries fared reasonably well and by 1920 achieved production levels close to those of 1913 and occasionally beyond. The U.K. just about managed to scrape home on this count, and Italy, surprisingly, was not that far off, though in both cases the recovery was not that very soundly based. The Scandinavian and European neutrals did better. Sweden in particular benefited considerably from wartime demands, which caused a rapid expansion of heavy manufacturing, and which gave rise to a great number of innovations, new production and distribution methods and new forms of industrial organization. For example, the kerosene shortage accelerated electrification, and the metal shortage gave a boost to new methods of ore prospecting, while the rapid breakthrough in lightweight metals can be attributed to the same cause. No doubt these developments would have occurred in time but they would have taken much longer but for the pressure exerted by wartime demands. Finally, as in many other countries, Swedish scientific research received a considerable stimulus during the period of hostilities.[59]

However, one can easily exaggerate the benefits derived by the neutrals. Their recovery was rapid and some sectors gained enormously from the war, but there were losses as well as gains and both were unevenly distributed. Moreover, in the short term the neutrals experienced considerable difficulties as a result of hostilities. As Temperley remarked: 'A survey of their condition in 1918 will convince any unprejudiced reader that, however greatly particular classes and interests in Holland, Switzerland, and Scandinavia may have enriched themselves by the war, these countries were, as a whole, suffering severely by the long continuance of hostilities.'[60] Apparent prosperity was purchased at the expense of a sharp rise in the cost of living, a shortage of essential commodities and the stagnation or decline of certain trades and classes of exports.

It was outside the European axis that the real gains were made.

59. E. Dahmén, *Entrepreneurial Activity and the Development of Swedish Industry, 1919–1939* (1970, translated by Å. Leijonhufvud), pp. 387–8.

60. H. W. V. Temperley (ed.), *A History of the Peace Conference of Paris*, vol. I (1920), p. 144; see also E. Heckscher *et alia*, *Sweden, Norway, Denmark and Iceland in the World War* (1930), and R. Lank, *Der Wirtschaftskrieg und die Neutralen, 1914–1918* (1940).

Two of the most prominent beneficiaries were the United States and Japan. The former supplied much of the Allied requirements in wartime both in physical resources and financial aid. Production was boosted by the strong demand for American products by countries, mainly European, unable to supply their own needs so that America ended up with a large excess balance in commodity trade; in turn the U.S. became much less dependent on imports from Europe.[61] Moreover, largely as a result of loans floated on behalf of the Allies and the liquidation of foreign holdings of U.S. securities, the international investment position of the United States underwent a dramatic change. A net debtor status of some $3,700 million dollars pre-war was transformed into a net creditor status of a similar amount by 1919, exclusive of inter-governmental debts.[62] During the war the U.S. became a creditor nation second only to the U.K. and in the 1920s America's international influence was to increase further as many European and Latin American nations became dependent on American capital.

Japan also emerged from the war in a much stronger position. Her participation in the war was only marginal and so she was able to benefit from the opportunities opened up by the indisposition of the major belligerents. She became far more industrialized and technically mature, a creditor instead of a debtor with a short-term balance abroad of over 1,300 million yen (£151·5 million), and a large increase in output to her credit. The volume of manufacturing output increased by 78 per cent and the industrial base was widened considerably with important developments in engineering, chemicals and iron and steel. New capacity in the iron and steel industry equivalent to that of the Imperial Steel Works which had formerly supplied 70–80 per cent of domestic production was brought into existence during this period.[63] But probably the greatest gains were made in shipping and foreign trade. The mercantile marine increased by 80 per cent and now carried the bulk of Japan's foreign trade. The shortage of manufactured goods in Europe and restricted shipping space gave Japan a great

61. A. G. V. Peel, *The Economic Impact of America* (1928), pp. 135–6.

62. H. B. Lary, *The United States in the World Economy* (1943), p. 122; Cleona Lewis, *America's Stake in International Investments* (1938), pp. 447, 450, 455.

63. See K. Yamasaki and G. Ogawa, *The Effects of the World War upon the Commerce and Industry of Japan* (1929).

opportunity for expanding her commerce by penetrating markets in the Western Pacific and even further afield. Between 1913 and 1918 Japan's exports trebled in value, though in volume terms the expansion was somewhat less, and markets in which she established a footing or strengthened her previous hold upon included India, China, the Netherlands East Indies, Oceania, parts of South America and Africa, and to a lesser extent European countries. In short, Japan became a much strengthened competitor of western nations as she steadily replaced former suppliers in underdeveloped countries. Thus her share of the Chinese market rose from 20 to 36 per cent between 1913 and 1919 while that of the U.K. fell from 16·5 to 9·5 per cent.[64] Clearly this boded ill for the industrial nations of western Europe.

But there were losses as well as gains even in Japan. Some of the plants and firms set up in wartime failed to survive the post-war deflation, while others could only be kept going in peace-time with government assistance. Japan also experienced serious inflation which left a legacy of over-inflated capital values and high operating costs in industry together with severe financial disorders, the repercussions of which were felt throughout the first post-war decade.[65]

Japanese competition was not the only source of worry for the European industrial countries. In many less developed countries wartime shortages and the suspension of competition had provided the opportunity for expanding the industrial sector. Wherever one looks the story is the same: in the Far East, in Asia, in Latin America, in the White Dominions and even in parts of Africa the acceleration of industrial activity is not difficult to find. Chinese industrialization went forward rapidly with a growth rate of well over 10 per cent in the modern industrial sector, with textiles accounting for a substantial part of the increase. And after the post-war recession the high rate of expansion continued throughout the 1920s.[66] In India the same process occurred, probably on

64. G. E. Hubbard, *Eastern Industrialization and its Effects on the West* (1938), pp. 40–42; A. Feuerwerker, *The Chinese Economy, 1912–1949* (1968), p. 74.

65. W. W. Lockwood, *The Economic Development of Japan* (1968), pp. 40, 57.

66. Kate L. Mitchell, *Industrialisation of the Western Pacific* (1942), p. 99; J. K. Chang, *Industrial Development in Pre-Communist China* (1969), pp. 60, 71-2.

a wider basis. Demand for Indian manufactured goods rose sharply partly because certain former imports were eliminated and partly as a result of the military requirements of Indian troops, Mesopotamia and other eastern war centres and of the Allied powers. By 1919 India had supplied equipment and stores to various theatres of war to the value of £80 million. India lacked the plant and equipment to take full advantage of the situation, a limitation which allowed Japan to penetrate the Indian market.[67] But in the long term, particularly for Lancashire's interests, the most significant development was the expansion of the indigenous cotton textile industry and the intrusion of the Japanese into the Indian textile market. It was the wartime developments more than anything else that prepared the way for the competition in cotton between Lancashire, Japan and India which became such a notable feature of the post-war period.

The Latin American record is more mixed. The war administered a temporary shock to the region; it curtailed the influx of foreign capital, equipment and immigrants and for a time checked exports, especially to Europe. Exports however soon recovered with the urgent demand for food and raw materials, while the reduced flow of manufactured imports gave some encouragement to industrial development, especially in textiles and the canning and preserving of food. This trend towards greater industrial self-sufficiency continued after the war with varying degrees of success. But the impact of war was far from universally beneficial in Latin America. Argentina, for example, came off quite badly. Machinery imports in 1917 were down to one-third those of 1913, construction activity declined and the output of manufacturing and mining fell by nearly 17 per cent between 1914 and 1917, despite a certain amount of import substitution, though she did make large grain sales to the Allies in the latter half of the war.[68] 'The common opinion that the war boosted industrialization

67. A. K. Bagchi, *Private Investment in India 1900–1939* (1972), p. 78; V. Anstey, *The Economic Development of India* (4th edition, 1952), pp. 215–20; S. G. Panandikar, *Some Aspects of the Economic Consequences of the War for India* (1921).

68. The beef industry of Argentina, and also of Uruguay, was adversely affected by the increasing demand for tinned and frozen beef which encouraged the breeding and sale of inferior animals. See J. H. Parry, 'Latin America', Chapter xix in C. L. Mowat (ed.), *The Shifting Balance of World Forces, 1898–1945* (1968, vol. xii of the *New Cambridge Modern History*), p. 597.

appears to be at best a very partial view.'[69] Brazil seems to have laboured under somewhat similar difficulties. If anything, Leff argues, the war retarded rather than promoted industrial development.[70] This is possibly an extreme view since certain industries, especially food processing and textiles, took advantage of the interruption of overseas supplies and expanded rapidly.[71] On the other hand, the domestic response was often restrained by a lack of raw materials and capital goods. Energy consumption in particular was seriously curtailed because of the difficulty of getting hold of imported fuels. Brazil in fact received little more than one-quarter of her normal imports of coal in 1918, while the Argentine railways were forced to experiment with grain as a fuel. Moreover, Brazil's wartime industrial expansion by no means transformed the structure of the economy – many of the new firms were little more than the workshop variety – and it received a considerable setback once overseas competition re-emerged.[72] By contrast the response in Chile was better. The curtailment of imports gave a vigorous boost to industrial output and the economy was able to achieve its first massive effort towards import substitution. Industrial production rose by 9 per cent per annum during the war years, and the rate of progress in the inter-war years though slower was by no means negligible.[73] This was perhaps fortunate in view of Chile's loss of her nitrate monopoly to low-cost synthetic nitrates during the war.[74] A

69. C. F. Diaz Alejandro, *Essays on the Economic History of the Argentine Republic* (1970), pp. 52–3, 217–18.

70. N. H. Leff, 'Long-term Brazilian Economic Development', *Journal of Economic History*, vol. xxix (1969), p. 475; see also W. Dean, *The Industrialization of São Paulo, 1800–1945* (1969), p. 104.

71. W. Baer, *Industrialisation and Economic Development in Brazil* (1965), pp. 16–17; S. J. Stein, *The Brazilian Cotton Manufacture: Textile Enterprise in an Underdeveloped Area, 1850–1950* (1957), p. 107.

72. Baer, *Industrialisation and Economic Development in Brazil*, pp. 18–19.

73. O. E. Munoz, 'An Essay on the Process of Industrialisation in Chile since 1914', *Yale Economic Essays*, vol. viii (1968), pp. 146–9.

74. Chile's nitrate exports dropped sharply between 1918 and 1919 due to the cessation of wartime demand but by this time her former monopoly was already being undermined by the vast increase in synthetic production. By 1922 Chile accounted for only about 24 per cent of the world production of nitrogen as against over one-half in 1913. M. Mamalakis and C. W. Reynolds, *Essays on the Chilean Economy* (1965), p. 215; F. W. Fetter, *Monetary Inflation in Chile* (1931), pp. 146–7; B. B. Wallace and L. R. Edminster, *International Control of Raw Materials* (1930), pp. 28–9.

similar process, though less spectacular, took place in Uruguay. With 1,000 new enterprises created between 1915 and 1919 the total number virtually doubled. Many however were small-scale and inefficient and after the war required protection to keep them going.[75] Elsewhere in Latin America the war certainly fostered import substitution though the general conclusion seems to be that it essentially accelerated a process already in progress before 1914 rather than unleashed new economic forces.[76]

Outside Japan and the United States probably the major beneficiaries were the White Dominions, Canada, Australia and New Zealand. Not only did they receive a boost to industrial development but their agrarian sectors also benefited from the impoverishment of agricultural output in Europe during the course of the war. For example, the expansion in Canadian wheat acreage in 1913–20 equalled that of the period 1900–13, while meat and dairy products also received a stimulus. But the most significant long-term feature was the strong incentive given to industrial and mining activity as a result of the demand for munitions, the protection afforded by high ocean freight rates and the steep fall in imports from Europe. Hence there was a sharp rise in mineral production and non-ferrous metal refining; the quantity of iron and steel produced rose from 1 to 2½ million ingot tons; pulp production more than doubled; the number of motor vehicles in use rose from 51,000 to 276,000, while 350,000 dead-weight tons of shipping were being produced by the end of the war, and the Canadian aircraft industry was turning out some 3,000 military training planes. In addition, a wide range of secondary industries was also stimulated. Indeed, the war accelerated the shift from a relatively simple staple economy[77] to a complex industrial economy and set the stage for the vigorous expansion of the 1920s. By the end of the war Canadian manufacturing output had surpassed that of agriculture, accounting for 44 per cent of the total product.[78] 'The nasty truth remains . . .

75. P. C. M. Teichert, *Economic Policy, Revolution and Industrialization in Latin America* (1959), pp. 79–80.

76. W. Glade, *The Latin American Economies* (1969), p. 395.

77. See G. W. Bertram, 'Economic Growth in Canadian Industry, 1870–1915: The Staple Model and the Take-Off Hypothesis', *Canadian Journal of Economic and Political Science*, vol. XXIX (1963).

78. A. E. Safarian, *The Canadian Economy in the Great Depression* (1959), pp. 18–19; W. T. Easterbrook and H. G. J. Aitken, *Canadian Economic*

that World War I advanced Canada's industrial facilities and skills in ways which would have taken much longer under normal peace-time stimuli.'[79]

Australia did not fare so well, and certainly less well than her neighbour, New Zealand. The Australian record is very patchy. Real income per head fell quite sharply, by some 20 per cent during the course of the war (though the estimates for this period are far from reliable).[80] This no doubt is explained by the decline in activity in construction, mining, certain domestic manufactures and exports, despite the Allied demand for agrarian products. Nevertheless, gains were made in some sectors, notably capital-intensive, import-competing industries, and it has been argued that the war set off a chain of events which changed Australia into a mature industrial economy.[81] The inability of overseas suppliers to meet demand provided scope for several heavy industries to expand, particularly iron and steel, engineering, metal processing and chemicals. Altogether over 400 products were manufactured for the first time, and some new export trades were created. The Allied demand for jams, jellies and fruit preserves gave rise to £2 million worth of exports in 1918–19 as against negligible quantities in 1913.[82] Many gains were permanent and made more so in that practically all commodities which began manufacture

History (1956), pp. 518–21; H. A. Innis, Essays in Canadian Economic History (1956), pp. 291–301.

79. R. E. Caves and R. H. Holten, The Canadian Economy: Prospect and Retrospect (1959), p. 71.

80. Calculated from data given in N. G. Butlin, Australian Domestic Product, Investment and Foreign Borrowing, 1861–1938/39 (1962), pp. 7, 34, and Commonwealth Bureau of Census and Statistics, Demography Bulletin, no. 47 (1949), p. 155. The odd thing is that real income per head remained below the pre-war level throughout the 1920s despite considerable industrial expansion. Lydall drew attention to the stagnation in income revealed in Butlin's figures for the first third of the twentieth century, and one feels that there is need for either revision or explanation. But Australian economic historians have not so far responded. H. F. Lydall, 'N. G. Butlin's Anatomy of Australian Economic Growth', Business Archives and History, vol. III (1963), p. 209.

81. C. Forster, 'Australian Manufacturing and the War of 1914–18', Economic Record, vol. XXIX (1953), p. 230. Overall manufacturing declined absolutely and relatively. See Butlin, Australian Domestic Product, Investment and Foreign Borrowing, 1861–1938/39, pp. 13, 461.

82. Forster, 'Australian Manufacturing and the War of 1914–18', pp. 217, 228.

on any reasonable scale during the war received tariff protection afterwards. For some industries, especially those in the heavy sector, this was essential since the small Australian market limited their competitive ability.[83]

In general then the war did give some stimulus to industrial activity in those countries which previously had relied heavily on the primary sector. Some was hot-house growth which withered or became stunted once trading conditions returned to normal and foreign supply was resumed. Developments in Spain and Egypt might be placed in this category.[84] More often than not the infant industries developed during the war needed protection to keep them going and this they often got during the 1920s. Few of the non-industrialized countries received a sufficiently large 'push' to propel them on to the path of modern economic growth. Despite an impressive rate of growth, industrialization in China did not get very far and there were signs of it beginning to fade away by the end of the 1920s as the wartime stimulus lost its effectiveness. 'The short-lived "industrialization boom" during and immediately following World War I did not, and indeed could not, take root and flourish in China against the then-existing economic and socio-political backgrounds.'[85] By the early 1930s modern manufacturing and mining accounted for less than 10 per cent of the national product and agriculture still contributed over 60 per cent. In the majority of cases new industrial developments remained little enclaves to serve the domestic market, with protection to hide their inefficiency. For some, moreover, the war merely stimulated existing extraction of resources with little lasting or worthwhile broadening of the industrial base. The high demand for rubber and tin left the 1918 pattern of the Malayan trading

83. Pat Brown and Helen Hughes, 'The Market Structure of Australian Manufacturing Industry, 1914 to 1963–4', Chapter 4 in C. Forster (ed.), *Australian Economic Development in the Twentieth Century* (1970), p. 182.

84. H. G. Moulton, 'Economic Conditions in Europe', *American Economic Review*, vol. XIII (1923), p. 58; P. O'Brien, *The Revolution in Egypt's Economic System* (1966), pp. 12–13; C. Issawi, *Egypt in Revolution: An Economic Analysis* (1963), pp. 30–32.

85. Y. Cheng, *Foreign Trade and Industrial Development of China* (1956), pp. 37–42. Population pressure, lack of capital, educational backwardness, feudalistic social structure, weak central government and foreign interference 'formed a vicious circle handicapping her industrial development. Each link reinforced and perpetuated the other, thus strangling Chinese economy in an ever-tightening ring' (p. 42).

economy little different from what it had been in 1914.[86] The same would probably apply to Bolivia. All the war did was to give such countries the added headache of an over-supply problem once the war demand terminated. Inevitably it was the already high-income countries who stood to gain most since they had a sound base from which to expand and diversify.

Indeed it could be argued that the war was far from an unmixed blessing for the countries not engaged in hostilities whether in Europe or elsewhere. It is true that those countries fortunate enough to possess foodstuffs and raw materials which were urgently demanded by the Allies did very well. Thus the sugar planters of Java and Cuba reaped a golden harvest as a result of the exclusion of German and Austrian sugarbeet from the world markets. Similarly many other primary producers benefited from the demand for particular commodities such as Chilean nitrates or Argentine grain. But gains in one country were often offset by losses elsewhere while the subsequent collapse of wartime demand brought hardship to many countries. In some cases products accumulated in the country of origin either because Germany or other enemy powers had previously provided the main market or because the Allied powers refused shipping facilities in order to economize on scarce tonnage. Brazil, for example, had to finance her unexportable coffee, while the warehouses of the Dutch East Indies were overflowing with copra and other oleaginous commodities. The export trade of some countries with products not deemed essential for the prosecution of the war was almost strangled by the dearth of shipping and the closure of markets. Many Latin American countries suffered severe difficulties in this respect because of the loss of the German market and the difficulty of obtaining capital and manufactured products from the Allied powers and where possible this gave an incentive to industrialization. But probably the worst-hit country was Persia. The closing of the Dardanelles in 1914 and the subsequent collapse of Russia deprived the country of many trade channels. Her exports of raw cotton and agricultural products were sharply reduced while high prices and the difficulty of access to markets forced Persia to curtail drastically her imports of all but the most essential commodities. European products when available could only be

86. P. P. Courtenay, *A Geography of Trade and Development in Malaya* (1972), p. 117.

supplied through Mesopotamia and India and the conditions of war made this both a difficult and costly exercise.[87]

That said, it remains true that the balance of economic power swung away from Europe towards the Americas and to a lesser extent the Pacific. Much of the gain accrued to North America, but the war fostered sufficient interest in industrial activity in the lesser developed areas to ensure that import substitution and subsequently export competition would increase rather than diminish after 1918, and that this would act to the detriment of Europe. The extent of the shift in balance can be appreciated from the figures for the distribution of world trade; by 1920 the Americas accounted for 32·1 per cent of world trade as against 22·4 per cent in 1913, while Asia's share rose from 12·1 to 13·4 per cent. The main loss was suffered by Europe and the U.S.S.R. whose combined share fell from 58·4 to 49·2 per cent during these years.[88]

Structural problems

According to Svennilson the inter-war period can be regarded as a prolonged transformation crisis for the European economy; growth was slowed down by the formidable structural problems faced after the First World War and the slowness with which adjustments took place.[89] The thesis is not without its attractions, and it is significant that countries which adapted their economies rapidly, such as Sweden, achieved a fairly impressive performance during the period. The purpose here is not to challenge the thesis but rather to outline some of the chief maladjustments arising out of the war in the European context and to show that the problem was not simply a European one *per se*.

By the late 1920s it became clear that the dislocation caused by the war was far more serious than the actual physical destruction. The war created a series of maladjustments and impediments to

87. H. W. V. Temperley (ed.), *A History of the Peace Conference of Paris*, vol. I (1920), p. 144.

88. Woytinsky and Woytinsky, *World Population and Production*, p. 45. A good survey of Europe's decline in relation to the wider world is given by P. Renouvin, *Les Crises du XXᵉ siècle. I. de 1914 à 1929* (*Histoire des relations internationales*, vol. VII, 1957), especially Chapters 5 and 14.

89. Svennilson, *Growth and Stagnation in the European Economy*, p. 44.

economic relationships and destroyed the elaborate and complex, often delicate, trading connections in several ways. Some of the features need only be mentioned briefly here as they will be taken up and discussed more fully in later chapters. The whole system of banking, credit and organization of money markets was suspended, controlled or modified during the war and had to be reestablished or adjusted to new conditions. The delicate mechanism of the gold standard had been abandoned, most currencies had lost much of their former value and stability and the problem of currency restoration became one of the crucial issues during the post-war years. 'Everywhere currency and exchange disorder is hampering trade and retarding reconstruction. In some countries it is a prime factor amongst those which are causing a breakdown of the economic and social system.'[90] New problems – large internal debts, war debts among the Allied powers and massive reparations imposed on the vanquished – made currency stabilization even more difficult. Severe capital shortages in central and eastern Europe hampered reconstruction which in turn accentuated the problem of currency stabilization. Added to which the redrawing of many boundaries in Europe entailed the recasting of trading connections and lines of transport, the adoption of new currencies and, in some cases, the entire replanning of economic systems.

During the war the productive effort of belligerent and neutral countries alike was directed to new purposes, new trading links were often hastily improvised and relations with former customers severed. Few commodities or trading connections escaped unscathed; Newfoundland cod and Lancashire cotton may make strange bed-fellows but equally their trade channels were disrupted between 1914 and 1918.[91] Many trading links were lost for ever, others had to be painfully rekindled during the 1920s at a time when import substitution and increasing protection made the going more difficult. Thus Russia, the main source of some materials and an important supplier of timber and wheat, was cut

90. League of Nations, *Currencies after the War: A Survey of Conditions in Various Countries* (1920), p. IX.
91. The big expansion in the production of Icelandic cod pushed Newfoundland fish out of European and South American markets. See Innis, *Essays in Canadian Economic History*, pp. 299–300 and W. C. Chamberlain, *Economic Development of Iceland through World War II* (1947), pp. 62–7.

off for years after the war and then emerged again as an exporter at the very time when her products were least required. The trading operations of the Baltic ports, Riga, Reval and Narva, as suppliers of industrial products to the Russian empire and as entrepôt centres in the trade between Russia and Western Europe, were shattered beyond repair by 1918.[92] The economic attachments of Latin America shifted more towards the U.S.A. who superseded Britain as a chief source of capital. In some cases technical developments served to destroy certain channels of trade; the introduction of synthetic nitrates, for example, ruined the Chilean monopoly of the nitrate trade. Quite often whole new selling and trading arrangements had to be developed after the war to regain former trading connections or else to exploit new channels of trade. Not much is usually said about such matters, a somewhat surprising neglect given the fact that the intricate and complex international trading mechanisms developed during the nineteenth century were considerably undermined during the course of the war.[93]

One of the serious and intractable problems of the inter-war period was excess capacity. There were signs even before 1914 that this was becoming a problem as some industrial economies were beginning a structural transformation associated with new technologies. The war accelerated this process and at the same time brought several new and more important forces into play. For one thing as economies were geared to servicing the war machine certain sectors became seriously over-expanded in relation to peace-time requirements; unfortunately they sometimes tended to be sectors where the long-term growth potential was limited. Thus shipbuilding, iron and steel, engineering and coal (the latter to a lesser extent) were considerably expanded in war-time and inevitably excess capacity developed in the 1920s. World shipbuilding capacity almost doubled during the war and by the time the post-war boom was complete there was enough shipping in existence to last a whole decade without further building. Iron and steel capacity of continental Europe and the U.K. was some 50 per cent higher by the mid 1920s than before war yet for much of the inter-war period output remained below

92. Royal Institute of International Affairs, *The Baltic States* (1938), p. 104.
93. One of the few books that contains some interesting comments on these aspects is J. B. Condliffe, *The Reconstruction of World Trade* (1941).

the 1913 level.[94] Coal was another field in which serious excess capacity prevailed though here the main causes were a sharp deceleration in the growth of demand and the opening up of new seams on the continent.[95] However, over-capacity was by no means a problem confined to the European industrial powers. Many countries had in fact over-expanded some sectors during the course of the war, be it raw materials, agricultural or industrial products. The vast expansion of wheat production in Canada, America and Australia presented problems once European production recuperated.[96] The same applied to many other primary products. Sugar might be taken as a good illustration. European production contracted by two-thirds between 1914 and 1918 and the resulting high prices stimulated an enormous expansion in Cuban cane production. Further cane plantings in Cuba and elsewhere shortly after the war together with a sharp rise in productivity following the introduction of new varieties of cane were met with a fairly rapid revival of European beet production, assisted by tariffs and bounties. By the mid 1920s Cuba was suffering severely from falling sugar prices which depressed incomes and led to a curtailment of imports.[97] Several other agricultural products were affected in like manner, and raw materials were not exempt. Malaya and Bolivia faced difficulties once the boom in demand for rubber and tin had passed its peak.

Secondly, import substitution was greatly stimulated in many countries for reasons already outlined earlier. The process continued after the war, helped along by the growth of economic nationalism. One notable sufferer from this development was the Lancashire cotton industry, but it was only one of many. Indeed, the major industrial nations faced the same process over a wide range of manufactured commodities, and they themselves were also participants in the game. The production of dyestuffs provides a vivid illustration. Before the war Germany produced four-fifths of the world output of dyes. When this source of supply was cut

94. Svennilson, *Growth and Stagnation in the European Economy*, pp. 120, 124.

95. League of Nations, *The Problem of the Coal Industry: Interim Report on its International Aspects* (1929), p. 9.

96. See M. Tracy, *Agriculture in Western Europe: Crisis and Adaptation Since 1880* (1964), pp. 117–18.

97. Lary, *The United States in the World Economy*, p.155; League of Nations, *Economic Stability in the Post-war World* (1945), Part II, p. 35.

off during the war several countries, including the U.K., U.S.A., France, Italy and Japan, were forced to increase their self-sufficiency in this field. Important dye industries were established and subsequently protected with the result that Germany's share of the world total declined to 46 per cent by 1924.[98]

Finally, new technical developments or the accelerated application of existing ones again added to the structural problem and made capacity redundant in competing industries. The boost given to the use of electricity and oil, the internal combustion engine and rayon are the most obvious examples, all of which had implications for the future prosperity of existing industries. And in the very long term one might mention aviation, the feasibility of which was clearly demonstrated by wartime activities, but which did not present a real threat to surface or ocean transport until after the Second World War. But examples on a smaller scale could be multiplied indefinitely. Dahmén in his study of Swedish industry has shown how the war gave rise to a great number of innovations or speeded up existing ones; and, as he points out, their combined magnitude coupled with their simultaneous emergence created serious tensions between new and old sectors so that the old activities had to be liquidated quickly and painfully. Fortunately Sweden accomplished this transformation process fairly rapidly and thereby avoided some of the more severe structural problems which were such a feature of the older capitalist countries during the inter-war period.[99]

Political and social tensions

Political and social life could scarcely remain immune after a war of such magnitude. Historians have argued for some time now about the extent to which new social forces were unleashed though few would be prepared to submit that it had no impact at all in this respect.[100] Indeed, the great admixture of the social classes within the military ranks, the influx of women into industrial occupations, the strengthening of trade unionism and workers'

98. V. Trivanovitch, *Rationalization of German Industry* (1931), p. 14.

99. Dahmén, *Entrepreneurial Activity and the Development of Swedish Industry, 1919–1939*, pp. 389–90.

100. There is a useful summary of the debate in A. S. Milward, *The Economic Effects of the World Wars on Britain* (1970).

participation in industry and the levelling effect of high taxation, could scarcely fail to have some impact on society as a whole. It found expression in demands for more democratic government and greater equality, and though the response fell short of the ideal there can be little doubt that the heightened social consciousness paved the way for improved conditions for the less fortunate classes of society.[101] Progress may have seemed slow and imperceptible at times but the lower orders stood to benefit in the long term from the increasing participation of the State in economic and social affairs. And the latter in turn can be attributed directly to the war. First, it gave governments considerable experience in managing economic affairs, and though most of the war-time control apparatus and machinery were scrapped in the enthusiasm to get back to what was considered the normal pre-war conditions, there could not fail to be some legacies left over for the future.[102] Indeed, there are many examples, notably the massive railway legislations in Britain and America which were designed to profit from the experience of running the railways on a more unified basis during wartime. Secondly, and more important with regard to the State's spending capacity, the war raised the tolerable or acceptable levels of taxation. Peacock and Wiseman have shown in the case of the U.K. how the displacement effect worked in favour of permanently higher peacetime levels of taxation since the reduction from the very high levels during the war proved a sufficient consolation to the tax-paying sector of the community.[103] This therefore gave the government much greater leverage in economic matters, since even if it had had the will before 1914 it had lacked the means necessary for extensive participation. There is good reason to suppose that a similar process took place in other countries.[104]

101. See A. Marwick, *The Deluge* (1965) and *Britain in the Century of Total War* (1968) for the social repercussions of war. Unfortunately, there are no really comparable studies for other countries.

102. See A. Marwick, 'The Impact of the First World War on British Society', *Journal of Contemporary History*, vol. III (1968), pp. 53–4.

103. A. T. Peacock and J. Wiseman, *The Growth of Public Expenditure in the United Kingdom* (1961).

104. On the question of increasing state activity generally see A. Briggs, 'The World Economy: Interdependence and Planning', Chapter III in C. L. Mowat (ed.), *The Shifting Balance of World Forces, 1898–1945* (1968, vol. XII of the *New Cambridge Modern History*).

In a wider context the war undoubtedly weakened the stability of existing social structures – the net result being to accord greater power to the lower orders. Since they considered themselves the oppressed sector of society their discontent was expressed visibly once they felt they had enough strength. This paved the way for much greater upheaval and turmoil in society, politically and socially though the two are closely linked, as the lower orders clashed with the entrenched establishment in society. Russia provides the shining example (hardly the most apt description in view of subsequent events but politically it was a complete success) of what could be achieved in the political field. The seeds of change had been sown long before 1914 but whether they would have borne fruit so early, if at all, but for the war, is a moot point. The existing regimes in Germany, Bulgaria and Turkey were disposed of, but the replacements constituted nothing very revolutionary. Nevertheless, the political and social turmoil which ensued had a harmful effect on the countries in question. Bulgaria, for example, was seriously affected by the political upheavals following the war and these were to result in policies – notably victimization of owners of wealth and capital – which penalized economic initiative and paralysed the forces of economic recovery.[105] Elsewhere leaders of the lower orders in several countries attempted to seize power, though success was both limited and short-lived. Hungary spawned a communist dictatorship under Bela Kun in 1919. In Italy there was a wave of strikes – the number of days lost through strikes in industry rose from under 1 million in 1918 to nearly 19 million in the following year – and workers occupied factories and large farm estates, though ultimately gaining precious little from the exercise.[106] But strikes were commonplace within the western world and beyond. The growth in the size and importance of labour organizations during the war (e.g. trade union numbers doubled in the U.K. and more than trebled in France) strengthened the power of the workers and gave rise to severe industrial unrest in many countries. France, Britain and the United States in particular were hit by massive strikes following the war, some of them inspired by

105. Danaillow, *Les effets de la guerre en Bulgarie*, pp. 550–52, 602–604.

106. S. B. Clough, *The Economic History of Modern Italy* (1964), p. 208.

political motives, but for the most part the concrete achievements were either very limited or lost in the subsequent depression. Latin America too suffered from political upheavals as a reaction to the war or to the collapse following the post-war boom of 1919–20. A period of political stability was rudely shattered by violent outbreaks of disorder followed in some cases by a resort to unconstitutional methods of control. Peru enjoyed a *coup d'état* in 1919; Argentina suffered from severe industrial unrest followed by a bloodbath as the military sought to restore the peace. Serious disorders of one type or another occurred in Brazil, Chile, Ecuador, Paraguay and Bolivia during the early 1920s and eventually most of the republics were once again contaminated by a disease all too common in this part of the world.[107]

Finally new regimes emerged in central and eastern Europe together with widespread demands for land reform which envisaged the break-up of large estates and the redistribution of the land to small impoverished farmers (contrast the position in Russia where the ultimate aim was to liquidate the independent farmer). Altogether twelve European countries carried out agrarian reforms and some 60 million acres (24·28 million hectares) or 11 per cent of the total territory was redistributed. More than one-half the acreage was allotted to former tenants, landless labourers and owners of small plots, one quarter was acquired by the State and the landlords were allowed to retain the rest. The area redistributed was highest in Latvia and Romania, approximately 42 and 30 per cent respectively, and lowest in Finland and Bulgaria, about 2 per cent. More often than not expropriation began with the alien landlords – e.g. in Romania it was taken from Hungarian, Russian, Bulgarian and Turkish owners, and in Hungary and Czechoslovakia from German and Russian landlords.[108] But while the peasant acquired a greater stake in the land the changes, as with so many other reforms, did not bring immediate economic benefits. Indeed, the marketable surpluses of agricultural products often

107. Royal Institute of International Affairs, *The Republics of South America* (1937), p. 147.

108. Details from W. S. and E. S. Woytinsky, *World Population and Production: Trends and Outlook* (1953), p. 497. For a case study see D. Mitrany, *The Land and the Peasant in Rumania: The War and Agrarian Reform (1917–1921)* (1930).

fell after the completion of reform, because of the increased fragmentation of holdings.

Some final comments

The above commentary makes no pretence at a comprehensive coverage of all the ramifications of the First World War. The aim rather has been to show that the war did have world-wide repercussions in that the impact was felt almost as much outside Europe as within, and to draw attention to some important implications which were to have a direct bearing on later events. Some of these, notably reparations, are touched upon only briefly at this point since they come up again for discussion later. No attempt has been made to differentiate specifically between long-term and short-term consequences since these are not always readily distinguishable, and in any case some of the immediate post-war events are covered in later chapters.

The war had an unfavourable impact on economic systems generally. This is not to say that there were no beneficial results though the comments so far mostly point in the opposite direction. There were gains even if these were far outweighed by the losses. The pressure of war needs did much for technical innovation and production processes. A series of new technical developments came on stream, while many which had been in the embryonic stage prior to the war were activated more rapidly than would otherwise have been the case. The movement towards new productive methods in shell production spread to other manufacturing activities, the car industry being a substantial beneficiary of this development after the war. Notable advances were made in the application of work study methods and in the development of industrial research. The heightened awareness of the social problems of society, which occurred as a result of the mixing of the classes on the battlefield and in the workshop, can again be counted as a significant gain. Yet when all is said and done war is a high price to pay for these benefits given the magnitude of the losses incurred.

At the time of the Armistice few statesmen appreciated the enormity of the economic problems which the war left as a legacy. The popular impression was that the problems would soon disappear once things got back to normal, and getting back to normal meant recreating the world that had been lost, and for good. Thus in contrast to the position after 1945, when economic conditions were much worse,[109] governments vainly sought to move back into the past without realizing that there could be no return. Only by the time it was too late, when a new set of problems emerged in the form of a world slump, was it realized that the past held no special attractions. Maybe this is too harsh a judgement. It could well be that statesmen were overtaken by the series of events which demanded solution as a result of which they had little time or energy to spare for the more fundamental problems. Certainly in the early years of the 1920s there was much to occupy the policy makers, though some of their decisions suggest that the previous comments are not far wide of the mark. The years immediately following the war were not to be marked by wise decisions.

109. 'The economic situation of the world at the end of 1918 appeared at this time difficult and depressing, but by comparison with 1945 it now seems a relatively simple and manageable sort of problem.' J. W. F. Rowe, *Primary Commodities in International Trade* (1965), p. 78.

3

Years of Chaos 1919-21: Famine and Relief - Boom and Slump

It is surprising to us now, after the experience of another world war, how many people after the Armistice of 1918 considered that the clocks could be turned back quite rapidly and the course of events take up where it left off in 1913. Once the peace treaties had been signed and Europe had been sorted out, the vanquished had been penalized, the war-time economic restrictions abandoned and the great god of gold had been restored, life could carry on as before. This might do a little injustice to the position but it does not seem very wide of the mark.[1] However, it should, one might say, have been clear from the start that conditions in 1918–19 were very different from what they had been prior to the outbreak of war. Even if the long-term and more indirect implications of the war could not have been properly foreseen at least it should have been obvious that there were immediate problems which required careful attention: in particular the relief and reconstruction of Europe and the task of adjusting economies to peacetime conditions. The manner in which these problems were tackled

1. The idea of a return to normalcy was certainly current in a number of countries other than the U.S.A. and the U.K. See Pearl S. Buck, *How it Happens: Talk about the German People, 1914–1933, with Erna von Pustau* (1947), pp. 104–5.

scarcely suggests that their significance was fully appreciated, and the policies adopted, by the Allied powers in particular, simply created more problems than they solved.

The relief of Europe

At the end of the war the greater part of Europe was impoverished in nearly every conceivable respect. Output was low, famine was imminent, capital and raw materials in desperately short supply, transport systems were completely disorganized and financial and currency mechanisms were running out of control:

> All countries in Europe were suffering from a lack of working capital and from a loss through wear and tear or physical destruction of fixed capital . . . stocks (of food, raw materials and manufactured goods) had been exhausted during the war. . . . Durable consumers' goods were likewise largely worn out, destroyed or in need of repair. Housebuilding and repair in particular had been practically at a standstill during the war, and in the war zones whole towns and villages had been devastated . . . much of the machinery had not been replaced and in certain areas machinery had been deliberately destroyed by retreating armies. . . . The mechanism of transportation was particularly affected. Railway rolling stock was in a deplorable condition all over Central and Eastern Europe. . . . The state of roadbeds was often inadequate for rapid traffic, and many bridges were in a dangerous state.[2]

Central and eastern Europe were the most severely affected; indeed the position in some countries was described as chaotic with economic and social systems bordering on collapse.[3] Russian society had already disintegrated and economic activity in 1919–20 was virtually at a standstill.[4] Prospects of recovery without external assistance were slim indeed since inexperienced governments battled against almost insuperable odds. The failure to organize comprehensive reconstruction eventually resulted in the collapse of some economic systems.

On one front concerted action was forced on the Allies, namely

2. League of Nations, *Europe's Overseas Needs 1919–20 and How They Were Met* (1943).

3. K. W. Rothschild, *Austria's Economic Development Between the Two Wars* (1947), p. 16 et seq.

4. N. Jasny, *Soviet Economists of the Twenties: Names to be Remembered* (1972), p. 9.

the relief of poverty and hunger. By the end of 1918 the spectre of famine prevailed over a wide area of central and eastern Europe. Food was in very short supply since output of agricultural products was one-third or more below pre-war levels, while the countries in this region had little means to pay for imports of food even had these been readily available. Some areas were close to starvation and a graphic illustration of the suffering this meant is given by Mrs Snowden's observations on Vienna, a city which had lost all its former glitter. Her account is worth quoting in full:

What sad sights were there for the observant in the streets and cafés of the once gay city of Vienna. The postman who delivered the letters at the hotel was dressed in rags. The porters at the railway stations were in worn cotton uniforms, and were glad of tips in the form of hard-boiled eggs and cigarettes. Uniformed officers sold roses in the cafés. Delicate women in faded finery begged with their children at street corners. Grass was growing in the principal streets. The shops were empty of customers. There was no roar and rush of traffic. The one-time beautiful horses of the Ringstrasse looked thin and limp. Frequently they dropped dead in the streets, of hunger. . . . At the Labour Exchanges many thousands of men and women stood in long lines to receive their out-of-work pay. . . . In every one of the hundred one-roomed dwellings I visited were pitiful babes, small, misshapen or idiotic through the lack of proper food. Consumptive mothers dragged themselves about the rooms tearful about the lack of milk, which their plentiful paper money would not buy because there was none to sell. Gallant doctors struggled in clinic and hospital with puny children covered with running sores, with practically no medicines, no soap, no disinfectants. . . . As it is tens of thousands of child lives and old lives have been ended by famine and the diseases of famine; whilst over a long period the number of suicides from hunger and despair amounted to scores in every week.[5]

Conditions were equally bad in other central and east European countries. Poland presented a pathetic picture in the early post-war period. She had been occupied by the Germans and overrun by several armies, while border hostilities continued on a number of

5. Mrs P. Snowden, *A Political Pilgrim in Europe* (1921), pp. 113–14, quoted in S. Pollard and C. Holmes, *Documents of European Economic History*, vol. III. *The End of the Old Europe 1914–1939* (1973), p. 64. For further observations on conditions in central Europe see the reports of the British Director of Relief in *Economic Conditions in Central Europe I and II*, Cd 521 and 641 (1920).

fronts after the end of the war. As a result much damage had been done to the country; currency and finance were in a chaotic state; nearly everything, and especially food, was in short supply, unemployment was high and malnutrition and disease widespread. The British Director of Relief described the position in the devastated regions as follows:

> The country . . . had undergone four or five occupations by different armies, each of which had combed the land for supplies. Most of the villages had been burnt down by the Russians in their retreat (of 1915); land had been uncultivated for four years and had been cleared of cattle, grain, horses and agricultural machinery by both Germans and Bolsheviks. The population here was living upon roots, grass, acorns and heather. The only bread obtainable was composed of those ingredients, with perhaps about 5 per cent of rye flour. Their clothes were in the last stages of dilapidation; the majority were without boots and shoes and had reached the lowest depths of misery and degradation. The distribution of food in the towns was very unequal. It was possible to buy almost anything in the restaurants at a price, and cafés and cake shops were well supplied, but in other parts of the same towns it was impossible to obtain any food.[6]

The returning soldiers swelled the level of unemployment, added to the food problem and spread disease. Half the population of Warsaw was in receipt of unemployment relief and nearly all that of Lodz. In some areas children were dying for lack of milk and in parts of the east famine conditions prevailed. Disease was widespread, especially typhus brought in by returning soldiers, and up to 60 per cent of the population was affected in some way. Malnutrition and disease forced up the mortality rate which rose to more than 40 per thousand while birth rates in Warsaw fell to just under 12 per thousand.

Clearly the most urgent task of the Allied governments was to organize the feeding of starving Europe. The bulk of the relief was provided by or through American organizations, principally the American Relief Administration created early in 1919 as the executive agency of the Allied Supreme Council responsible for relief.[7] Under its arrangements a steady stream of food deliveries

6. Quoted in S. B. Clough, T. Moodie and C. Moodie (eds), *Economic History of Europe: Twentieth Century* (1965), p. 100.

7. Soon after the Supreme Council was wound up in June 1919 the American Relief Administration became an unofficial body responsible for relief.

began and by August 1919 food to the value of $1,250 million had been delivered to Europe. Most of this was provided on a cash or credit basis, and less than 10 per cent consisted of outright gifts. The Allied and liberated countries generally got their provisions on credit (most of which was never repaid) while enemy countries had to pay in cash.[8]

After the signing of the Peace Treaty in June 1919 official relief programmes were sharply curtailed, and subsequently relief activities were mainly confined to private and semi-official organizations. These managed to distribute about $500-million-worth of foodstuffs over a period of two to three years, mostly in the form of gifts. This small, though welcome, contribution mostly went to assist children. However, the basic task of feeding the people of Europe was left once again to the respective governments.[9]

Useful though the relief programme was it fell far short of real needs; it was too little and too short. Except for deliveries to Belgium and northern France, supplies on any scale never really got under way until the beginning of February 1919, and then they came to almost an abrupt halt in the summer of that year, long before the problem of hunger and poverty had been solved. On average every child of central and eastern Europe was fed for one month only by the U.S. relief organizations. Child poverty alone therefore remained critical in many of these countries; a medical inquiry in March 1921 in Czechoslovakia showed that 60 per cent of the children remained undernourished or lacking in vitality.[10] The real extent of the problem was never adequately surveyed; the whole relief exercise was hastily improvised and there were innumerable difficulties in coordinating the relief efforts of the United States and the Allies. It should be borne in mind that the U.S.A. had huge food stocks at the end of the war and this was obviously an important consideration in drawing up the relief programmes. Furthermore, the fact that the enemy states were expected to pay their way only made their economic reconstruction more difficult.

8. League of Nations, *Europe's Overseas Needs 1919–1920 and How They Were Met* (1943), p. 34.

9. ibid., p. 34.

10. League of Nations, *Relief Deliveries and Relief Loans 1919–1923* (1943), pp. 21–3.

Relief of famine was only the first step in the process of reconstruction. Europe was short of raw materials, capital and consumer goods, and supplies of the first two were equally important for purposes of recovery. But no overall plan of reconstruction relief was ever conceived and international efforts apart from meeting food requirements were very limited indeed. Little effective action was taken over raw materials; indeed, one of the major tragedies of the post-Armistice period was the failure to supply and finance the import of raw materials necessary to restart industrial activity in the impoverished and devastated regions of Europe.[11] Some attempt to preserve and extend the wartime Allied cooperation for raw materials seemed likely with the establishment of the Supreme Economic Council in February 1919. Its main functions were to examine measures which might ensure an adequate supply of raw materials and other commodities for the devastated areas including ex-enemy countries, and the Council duly established special sections to deal with various aspects of the problem. But its activities and powers were very limited; it had no specific authority to deal with the distribution of raw materials while its mandate ran out at the end of the Armistice period. Moreover, its effectiveness was further reduced by the abrupt withdrawal of economic controls, especially in the U.K. and U.S.A., in 1919, and America's desire to disengage herself as quickly as possible from inter-Allied organizations.[12] Consequently the prospects of worthwhile action appeared extremely bleak and efforts to form new organizations came to very little. A European Coal Commission was formed in August 1919 to coordinate coal production and distribution throughout Europe but, lacking the necessary authority to put its recommendations into effect, it devoted most of its energies to the pressing problem of supplying Austria with coal until this task was assumed by an organ of the Reparations Commission.[13]

Nor did the peace treaties have much to say on this matter.

11. M. Hill, *The Economic and Financial Organization of the League of Nations* (1946), pp. 16–17.

12. Even before the Armistice Herbert Hoover had made it quite clear that the United States would not be willing to be a party to any international programme of resource control in peacetime. A. Zimmern, *The League of Nations and the Rule of Law, 1918–1935* (1936), p. 157.

13. League of Nations, *Raw Material Problems and Policies* (1946), pp. 17–18; B. B. Wallace and L. R. Edminster, *International Control of Raw Materials* (1930), pp. 320–21.

They dealt with raw material problems only incidentally in connection with commercial policy, and contained no provisions for ensuring the supply of raw materials to newly created states or defeated powers.[14] Little more was heard about raw materials until October 1920, when the International Financial Conference at Brussels (the first of the League's economic conferences) recommended the ter Meulen Plan, designed to provide international credits for the import of raw materials and primary necessities. But the scheme, limited and piecemeal though it was, never came into operation although it was favourably received by creditor countries including the United States. In any case, by 1920 it was already too late, since the rot had gone too far for the successful application of any kind of general scheme.[15] The scramble for raw materials in the boom of 1919–20 had left many central and eastern European countries with a minimal supply.[16] Consequently rehabilitation was seriously retarded, their economies were further weakened and exchange depreciation and inflation were already reaching serious proportions. Under such conditions the problem required a country-by-country approach with credits linked to a definite and comprehensive plan of reconstruction under supervision. This approach was eventually adopted by the League for Austria and Hungary. But had a bold attempt been made at an early date to deal with problems of reconstruction the economic chaos which befell some countries in central and eastern Europe might have been avoided.

The overall position with regard to the supply of continental

14. The treaties dealt with raw material exactions for reparations purposes. Germany, for instance, was required to deliver specified quantities of coal to France, Belgium and Italy for ten years, and an option accorded to the Reparations Commission to require Germany to deliver other materials was subsequently taken up. The defeated powers were also under an obligation to restore or replace, so far as the Commission saw fit to demand, animals, machinery, equipment, stocks of materials etc., destroyed or seized by them in war. There was, in addition, provision for reciprocal supplies of raw materials between successor states. However, these provisions did not provide an adequate substitute for international action to control the distribution of raw materials.

15. Hill, *The Economic and Financial Organization of the League of Nations*, p. 26.

16. The League put it in stronger terms: 'the major part of continental Europe continued to be starved of primary products'. League of Nations, *Raw Material Problems and Policies* (1946), p. 71.

Europe may now be summarized. In 1919 and 1920 the area imported $17·5 billion worth of goods from overseas as against exports of only $5 billion. Foodstuffs and finished goods formed a high proportion of total imports, while imports of raw materials were fairly small in relation to requirements. Moreover, the areas most in need, central and eastern Europe, received proportionately

TABLE 2

INDICES OF OVERSEAS IMPORTS INTO CONTINENTAL COUNTRIES (1913 = 100)

	Total	Foodstuffs	Raw materials and semi-manufactures	Finished goods
1919	83	110	53	137
1920	65	76	52	88
1927	87	92	86	82

SOURCE: League of Nations, *Europe's Overseas Needs 1919–1920 and How They Were Met* (1943), p. 14.

less than northern and western Europe. The indices in Table 2 give a breakdown into the main categories of imports. The most serious shortfall was in raw materials, imports of which were only just over 50 per cent of pre-war in both 1919 and 1920. Food imports were relatively high in 1919, probably reflecting relief deliveries, though given the deficiency in agricultural output they were still far from adequate. The cessation of relief deliveries in the autumn of 1919 brought a sharp drop in food imports during 1920. Rather surprisingly, however, imports of manufactures in 1919 were some 37 per cent above the pre-war level, though they fell off sharply in 1920 when the capacity of many countries to pay became exhausted. The high volume of these imports in 1919 can be explained by pent-up demand and the slow revival of local industries, though one wonders whether more could not have been done to check this class of imports so as to conserve resources for food and raw material purchases. Moreover, much of the demand for manufactures was accounted for by the western Allies and neutral countries and the sharp fall in this category in 1920 can be attributed largely to the revival of domestic production. Overall imports into these countries were well up on 1913, whereas for other countries they were less than one-third and raw material imports only a fraction of the pre-war level.[17]

17. League of Nations, *Europe's Overseas Needs 1919–1920 and How They Were Met* (1943), pp. 13–21.

In monetary terms the total European import surplus on trade account was $12·5 billion; less than half this total was covered by invisible receipts and the export of gold, leaving $6·7 billion to be financed by the import of capital. Much of this was derived from governmental loans (mainly from the U.S.A.) of one sort or another, since private capital was not easily attracted into countries unstable both financially and politically. Thus relief loans or credits accounted for nearly $1 billion, inter-governmental loans and other long-term borrowings for about $3 billion, leaving about $2½ billion to be found as best it could from short-term borrowings or the sale of domestic currencies to speculators.[18]

International efforts to promote reconstruction in Europe were woefully inadequate after the First World War, a lesson which was appreciated by the planners responsible for the same task after 1945. A coordinated plan for the reconstruction of Europe was never conceived at any stage and what relief was given was very inadequate. Moreover, relief tended to be regarded as a form of charity which should be extended to some countries but not to others. Political considerations rather than capacity to pay determined whether cash payment was demanded, and the probable effect of cash payments or of the issue of relief loans on a country's capacity to acquire raw materials had little influence on policy.

The consequences of this inadequate action have a direct bearing on later events. Since many countries were unable to obtain sufficient raw materials recovery was delayed, factories remained idle and unemployment high. Unemployment benefits, relief programmes, and continued military spending kept government spending high and this, coupled with the low taxable capacity of the population, ruled balanced budgets out of the question.[19] Furthermore, inadequate foreign credits to finance imports meant pressure on the demand for foreign exchange and a consequent depreciation of currency values. It is true that each depreciation of the exchange helped to promote exports and create employment. But the final consequences were disastrous. The price paid for temporary export stimuli was increasing inflation,

18. League of Nations, *The Transition from War to Peace Economy: Report of the Delegation on Economic Depressions*, Part 1 (1943), p. 68.

19. In 1921 over one-half the total expenditures of the Austrian government went on food subsidies. L. Pasvolsky, *Economic Nationalism of the Danubian States* (1928), p. 97.

declining real income of the bulk of the population, loss of confidence and eventually the flight of capital from productive activity. Ultimately it led to the disintegration of the whole economic and social fabric of several countries. As the League of Nations noted in a report, for several years the whole economic and social organization of many countries was allowed to rot away and 'when it was finally faced, it had ceased to be a general problem of transition and reconstruction and had become a problem of cutting the gangrene out of the most affected areas one by one'.[20]

Thus the breakdown of many European countries in the early 1920s can be attributed partly to the absence of speedy and effective international action. Their disease required adequate provision for the stricken areas to permit more rapid recovery and hence obviate the need for exchange depreciation, and the immediate support of currencies weakened by inflation rather than waiting until the collapse was well under way. Finally, if the price boom of 1919–20 had been curbed the costs of imported goods to Europe would have been considerably less burdensome. It is to this aspect that we now turn.

Boom and slump 1919–21

While much of Europe was struggling with famine, poverty and reconstruction, the western Allies, and not a few other countries besides, were enjoying one of the most spectacular booms in history. They were soon to enjoy an equally spectacular slump. The factors behind this boom are of considerable interest, but even more so are those related to its collapse since misguided government policy again played no small role. Important too are the consequences.

It was initially anticipated that a slump would follow the period of hostilities as wartime orders were cancelled, soldiers were demobilized and economies began the difficult conversion to peacetime production. In the first few months after the Armistice there was a mild recession but this soon gave way in the spring of 1919 to 'a boom of astonishing dimensions',[21] probably one of

20. League of Nations, *The Transition from War to Peace Economy: Report of the Delegation on Economic Depressions*, Part 1 (1943), p. 70.
21. W. A. Lewis, *Economic Survey, 1919–1939* (1949), p. 18.

the shortest and sharpest booms ever recorded. In the United States it lasted for about nine months, from April 1919 to January 1920, in the U.K. and France a little longer, from April 1919 through to the spring or summer of 1920. A notable feature was the very sharp rise in prices as pent-up demand for commodities was unleashed at a time when production was still recovering from the effects of war. Factories were swamped with orders and the consequent demand for labour assisted demobilization. Within just over a year from the Armistice Britain had demobilized some 4 million men and abandoned most of the wartime controls. The process of conversion was even more rapid in the United States.

The boom was most marked in the United States, the U.K., Japan and some of the smaller neutral countries since these economies were in better shape to meet the sudden upsurge in demand. Much of continental Europe and Russia were in no fit state to participate properly though inflationary conditions continued unchecked. For this reason it is difficult to describe it as a world-wide boom, though outside Europe there was certainly much activity. Many primary producers benefited from the sharp rise in commodity prices, though quite often, as in Malaya and Canada, the boom was very much speculative, based on temporary shortages with no great rise in output.[22] India too, despite the severe influenza epidemic of 1918-19, participated in the bonanza. Many companies there had done quite well in the war and were in a highly liquid state though in many cases profits were frittered away in very large dividends. Nevertheless, there was a sharp rise in company formation; the number of companies floated rose by 75 per cent and the paid-up capital doubled, while the figures for imported machinery suggest a considerable rise in industrial investment.[23]

One of the main factors in the boom of 1919-20 was undoubtedly the repercussions of the war. A fairly large pent-up demand for goods was backed by financial assets accumulated during the

22. J. W. F. Rowe, *Markets and Men: A Study of Artificial Control Schemes in Some Primary Industries* (1936), p. 158; E. Marcus, *Canada and the International Business Cycle 1927-1939* (1954), p. 99.

23. D. R. Gadgil, *The Industrial Evolution of India in Recent Times*, 4th edition (1942), p. 226; A. K. Bagchi, *Private Investment in India 1900-1939* (1972), pp. 79-81.

period of hostilities. 'All over the world larders, wardrobes and shops were empty; all over the world, too, purchasing power had accumulated.'[24] Demand was released at a time when stocks were low and productive activity still recovering so that initially it was simply translated into soaring prices. The price rise was aggravated by several factors. Shortages of shipping space and dislocation of internal transport systems in the immediate post-war period created artificial shortages when considerable accumulations of primary commodities were waiting overseas to be moved.[25] There was also considerable speculative stockholding in anticipation of rapid upward price movements. The possible gains (or losses) to be made from cornering the market far outweighed any changes in the cost of keeping stocks. It has been estimated that in the U.K. an interest rate of 45 per cent per annum (less the percentage costs of handling and storage) would have been required to remove all the profit from stockholding an average commodity on borrowed money, yet at no time did the relevant short-money rates exceed 7 per cent.[26] It is impossible to estimate the precise role of speculative activities in the price boom but by all accounts it certainly made an important contribution to inflating prices.

Government policies also share the blame. For one thing government controls over economic activity were abandoned very rapidly at the end of the war. Businessmen demanded the end of controls and governments, especially in the U.S.A. and U.K., acquiesced fairly readily. Thus, despite the short supply of commodities, many wartime controls were dismantled before the summer of 1919. Relaxation of control in nearly every instance was followed by a sharp and simultaneous price increase and it seems evident that retention of price control for somewhat longer might have avoided much of the severe spiral in prices.[27]

The upswing was also materially supported by fiscal and monetary policies which pumped funds into the economy and expanded credit. United States government spending was still at a high level and the net deficit in the Federal budget for the fiscal year to the

24. Lewis, *Economic Survey, 1919–1939*, p. 19.

25. On this aspect see D. H. Aldcroft, 'Port Congestion and the Shipping Boom of 1919–20', *Business History*, vol. III (1961).

26. League of Nations, *Economic Fluctuations in the United States and the United Kingdom, 1918–1922* (1942), pp. 54–5.

27. R. H. Tawney, 'The Abolition of Economic Controls, 1918–1921', *Economic History Review*, vol. XIII (1943).

end of June 1919 was nearly 50 per cent higher than in the previous year. Easy credit conditions encouraged business activity and an expansion in building and construction work.[28] Similar policies were followed in the U.K. Public spending remained high and credit conditions were fairly easy. In fact the Bank rate was quite ineffective for a good part of 1919; the market was more or less controlled by the tap Treasury bill rate of $3\frac{1}{2}$ per cent and a special-deposit rate of 3 per cent and the position remained unchanged until well into the summer of 1919.[29] One reason why governments were anxious to keep interest rates low was because of the large amount of short-term debt overhanging the market which they wished to fund on favourable terms.

The U.S.A. and U.K. were not alone in such policies. All over the world governments tended to adopt fiscal and monetary measures which accentuated the cyclical upswing. The inflationary process of course went furthest in central and east Europe where financial and currency conditions were already approaching a chaotic state by the end of the war. The needs of reconstruction, limited tax potential and lax administrations meant a continuation of the inflationary financial and monetary policies pursued during the war. Here little attempt was made to check the process; indeed in most cases policy measures aggravated the inflationary spiral which got worse and eventually ended with disastrous consequences, as we shall presently see.

Elsewhere the boom ended almost as dramatically as it had begun. The first signs of a break came in the United States when early in the New Year (1920) business activity began to slacken. Soon afterwards Canada and Japan experienced a fall in exports to the United States. On 15 March the Tokyo stock market collapsed and Japanese share prices fell by 70–80 per cent in six months. The following month the banks began closing their doors and the crisis deepened. The price of rice and of silk fell by 55 and 75 per cent respectively in little more than a week, a clear indication that the commodity price boom was over.[30] During the

28. R. A. Gordon, 'Cyclical Experience in the Inter-War Period: The Investment Boom of the 'Twenties', in National Bureau of Economic Research, *Conference on Business Cycles* (1951), p. 169; M. W. Lee, *Macroeconomics, Fluctuations, Growth and Stability*, 5th edition (1971), p. 132.

29. A. E. Feavearyear, *The Pound Sterling*, revised edition (1963), p. 354.

30. K. Yamamura, 'Then Came the Great Depression: Japan's Interwar Years', in H. van der Wee (ed.), *The Great Depression Revisited* (1972), p. 184.

spring and summer of 1920 most countries, both primary producers and industrial economies, recorded turning-points in economic activity and prices, and there was no longer any doubt that the bubble had burst. During the remainder of the year production, exports and prices fell far and fast, while unemployment rose rapidly. As a result 1921 proved the worst year on record.

Few countries escaped the severe check to activity between 1920–21 (and for some it ran on until 1922) except those in central and eastern Europe whose currencies had so depreciated that they were enjoying a temporary boost from exports.[31] Germany, Austria, Czechoslovakia, Poland and a number of others in this area actually recorded increases in industrial production in 1921. Elsewhere the picture was grim and for some the downturn proved to be more severe, though of shorter duration, than that of 1929–32. In Sweden, for example, production and income in percentage terms fell twice as far in 1920–21 as they were to do in the 1929 downturn.[32] Though much more moderate by comparison, real national income in South Africa declined more than twice as much as in 1929–32.[33] The U.K. too experienced a much sharper decline in this period,[34] while calculated on a monthly basis the depression in the United States was far more severe than that at the end of the decade (see Table 3). The main blessing was that the post-war depression was very much shorter; by 1922 most countries began to show signs of revival.

The explanation of this sudden and sharp contraction is not so straightforward as it might seem. One simple and commonly

31. Recent estimates for New Zealand suggest that activity continued to rise during 1921 with a slight relapse occurring in 1922. G. R. Hawke, 'The Government and the Depression of the 1930s in New Zealand: An Essay Towards a Revision', *Australian Economic History Review*, vol. XIII, March 1973.

32. E. Lundberg, 'Business Cycle Experiences in Sweden, with Special Reference to Economic Policy Issues', in E. Lundberg (ed.), *The Business Cycle in the Post-War World* (1955), p. 56. The declines were hefty in 1920–21: 27 per cent for income, 25 per cent for industrial production and 24 per cent for export volumes. Only exports recorded a greater percentage fall in 1929–32.

33. 8·6 as against 3·8 per cent per annum. C. W. G. Schumann, 'Aspects of Economic Development in South Africa', Chapter 1 of M. Kooy (ed.), *Studies in Economics and Economic History: Essays in Honour of Professor H. M. Robertson* (1972), pp. 7–9.

34. For the U.K. see the data in D. H. Aldcroft, *The Interwar Economy: Britain 1919–1939* (1970), p. 34.

TABLE 3
PERCENTAGE DECLINES IN SELECTED INDICATORS IN THE UNITED
STATES (ON MONTHLY BASIS), 1920–21 AND 1929–32

	1920–21	1929–32
Wholesale prices (all commodities)	3·4	0·88
Total industrial production	2·4	1·53
Durables	5·0	1·76
Non-durables	3·3	0·91

SOURCE: R. A. Gordon, 'Cyclical Experience in the Inter-War Period: The Investment Boom of the 'Twenties', in National Bureau of Economic Research, *Conference on Business Cycles* (1951), p. 172.

quoted reason is that it was the inevitable reaction to the previous boom; as output began to catch up with demand and commodities arrived from overseas the basis of the boom disintegrated. However, this line of reasoning is not consistent with the facts. For one thing if the pent-up demand for goods was so large after the war, and inventories so low, as is usually stated to be the case, how was the productive mechanism, which was still recovering from the war, able to satisfy this demand so quickly? True the Japanese and American economies were in fairly good shape after the war and able to supply part of the needs of other countries. But in many countries the boom was one of prices rather than production so that it is unlikely that they could meet all the unsatisfied demand. Moreover, the time period is short, a year or less, so that even if all countries had had their productive mechanisms in good fettle it is still difficult to conceive of their coping with the problem in so short a space of time.

Raw materials and foodstuffs were clearly in short supply at the end of the war though part of the problem was distribution and the means of payment. Shipping space was still scarce and it is said that some countries held stocks of materials accumulated during the war. The boom also encouraged further production. Thus when supplies became more readily available prices declined. But again one must ask whether the supply side was crucial in breaking the upward spiral in prices of commodities, and if so why did this cause industrial recession elsewhere. Cheaper and improved supplies of raw materials should have allowed the industrial boom to continue, so doubts must be cast on the supply-oriented hypothesis. Unfortunately we know little about the existing stock position but in any case there is reason to believe that boom was broken in the industrial countries and then spread to primary producing countries.[35]

One possibility is that the price inflation produced its own cure in that rapidly rising prices and lagging wages checked the growth of real incomes and led to consumer resistance. Moreover, the rapid rise in industrial costs produced uncertainty, while in some countries, notably the U.S.A., supply inelasticities became operative in the winter of 1919–20. Rapid industrial expansion coupled with strikes in basic industries and transportation caused output to reach a ceiling late in 1919 and the first quarter of 1920.[36] This accelerated the pace of inflation and increased consumer resistance. Pilgrim argues that supply constraints were not the primary cause of the turning-point since they were removed after the first quarter of 1920, yet a contraction began. In fact the turning point occurred in the January[37] so that the timing would seem to fit quite well.

Many writers place considerable emphasis on the role of government policy in checking the boom. Néré regards the 1920–21 setback as the first and most grave of the stabilization crises. Restrictive fiscal and monetary policies, especially in the U.S.A. and U.K., checked expansion and also reduced the flow of credits abroad. This in turn checked the demand for exports, and the export lag at the upper turning-point is consistent with an internally generated explanation.[38] The timing of government measures certainly fits this sequence. In the United States government expenditures declined after the middle of 1919 while tax revenues rose, so that by the end of the year government finance was exerting a strong deflationary impulse.[39] Pilgrim feels however

---

35. Alpert suggests that the boom originated overseas in the primary producing countries which were the first to be hit by the curtailment of European purchases. But a few lines later he says it started first in Japan and then spread rapidly to Europe. P. Alpert, *Twentieth Century Economic History of Europe* (1951), p. 50.

36. Bottlenecks were experienced in other countries, especially the U.K., at around the same time partly as a result of strikes and transportation difficulties.

37. J. D. Pilgrim, 'The Upper Turning Point of 1920', Ph.D. thesis, Vanderbilt University (1969), p. 149, and 'The Upper Turning Point of 1920: A Reappraisal', *Explorations in Economic History*, vol. xi (Spring 1974).

38. J. Néré, *La Crise de 1929* (1968), p. 21.

39. Gordon, *loc. cit.*, p. 170.

that the impact was too early to have much to do with the upper turning-point though it certainly made the economy more vulnerable. He argues that monetary policy was the crucial factor. Increases in the cost of credit together with a reduction in credit availability towards the end of 1919 caused a check in total construction and hence fixed investment declined after the last quarter of 1919. This was sufficient to cause a contraction in income early in 1920.[40] This accords very closely with the views of Pedersen, who regards the Federal Reserve's policy as a serious blunder.[41]

There seems fairly wide agreement that policy played a crucial part in the U.S. upper turning-point, though whether a different policy could have prevented some degree of recession in 1920–21 is another matter. The strategic role of the United States in the world economy and the fact that its economy peaked before most others make it reasonable to conclude that the international depression of 1921 had its origins there.[42] The check to income affected the demand for imports while credit restrictions reduced the outflow of financial assistance, especially to Europe.

Inflation and continued currency depreciation prompted several other countries to resort to policy tightening during the course of 1919–20 which thereby aggravated the downswing. Japan and Sweden, for example, adopted severe retrenchment policies. It is often difficult to determine, however, whether policy action was critical to the breaking of the boom. In Britain both monetary and fiscal policy became increasingly restrictive in late 1919 and early 1920; but policy action was probably less crucial to the turning-point than in the U.S.A., since there were already indications that the economy was peaking before the measures really began to bite. Consumer demand began to tail off in the

40. Pilgrim, 'The Upper Turning Point of 1920', p. 150.

41. J. Pedersen, 'Some Notes on the Economic Policy of the United States during the Period 1919–1932', in H. Hegeland (ed.), *Money, Growth and Methodology: Essays in Honour of Johan Åkerman* (1961), p. 477; cf. E. R. Wicker, *Federal Reserve Monetary Policy, 1917–1933* (1966), p. 47. For an earlier view which downgrades the role of money see B. M. Anderson, *Economics and the Public Welfare* (1949), pp. 57–8.

42. More so possibly than the one in 1929. For a similar view see M. Friedman and Anna J. Schwartz, *A Monetary History of the United States, 1867–1960* (1963), p. 360. These authors attribute the origins to the U.S.A. in both cases.

first months of 1920 so that it is unlikely that the final shift to dear money in April 1920, when the Bank rate was raised to 7 per cent, caused the boom to break. But, as Miss Howson rightly points out, 'The 7 per cent Bank rate came just at the right time to ensure that the (over-)optimistic expectations of businessmen (who had apparently believed the prosperity generated by the restocking boom would last for ever) which were fading fast, and had been for some three to four months, were replaced in the shortest possible time by deep pessimism, which was later reflected in a drastic downturn in investment.'[43] Moreover, there can be little doubt that the sharp monetary contraction which followed together with severe fiscal retrenchment greatly exacerbated the downswing once it was under way.[44] The government's action certainly got rid of inflation but must be condemned for being too severe and too late.

Why did governments act so harshly at this time? Even if one believes that they did not start the downswing one can hardly fail to agree that the ensuing depression was made very much worse by their actions. Pedersen expresses some surprise and doubt about the apparent absence of motivation in U.S. policy. There was no clear policy statement, he says, and the objective could hardly have been to stabilize economic activity or prices since the measures had the opposite effect. 'Rather the authorities seem to have been guided by a somewhat vague idea that conditions were unsound, that prices were too high, that the budget should be balanced, that things could not correct themselves, and that some action "cleaning up" the aftermath of the unsound wartime policy was necessary.'[45] Certainly U.S. policy seems less clear cut than the British, since the Bank of England at least had the specific

43. And as the author notes, this pessimism was all the stronger and well-founded since the authorities, by their acceptance of the Cunliffe Committee *Reports* in the previous December, had made it clear that dear money once imposed would be consistently maintained. S. Howson, 'The Origins of Dear Money, 1919–20', *Economic History Review*, vol. xxvii (1974), p. 106, and *Domestic Monetary Management in Britain, 1919–38* (1975), pp. 23–9.

44. Other, non-policy, factors which contributed to the slump included the widespread cancellation of orders in 1920, the collapse of exports and the coal strike of 1921. See Howson, 'The Origins of Dear Money', p. 106, and D. H. Aldcroft, 'British Monetary Policy and Economic Activity in the 1920s', *Revue Internationale d'Histoire de la Banque*, vol. v (1972), pp. 283–5.

45. Pedersen, 'Some Notes on the Economic Policy of the United States during the Period 1919–1932', p. 477.

objective of regaining its control of the market which it had lost in wartime.[46] But in the circumstances the corrective action of governments was understandable. The boom did appear to be getting out of hand during 1919 and the rapid rise in prices was almost bound to give grounds for alarm since lax financial administrations were a powerful force in the inflationary spiral in Europe. If the boom had not broken of its own accord continuing inflation was a real danger, given no change in government policy. In any case, there was almost bound to be a reaction against wartime financial practices towards the prevailing belief in the virtue of sound finance. This and other adjustments in policy were regarded as vital prerequisites for a return to normalcy in economic affairs. As Condliffe has observed, 'Abandonment of government controls over production and prices, reduction of government expenditure and taxes, balanced budgets, removal of trade barriers, and a speedy return to gold as the basis for national currencies were almost unchallenged objectives.'[47] It is not so much that the policies were wrong, but rather that they were pursued too vigorously and for too long. It could even be argued that action to curb the boom should have been taken somewhat earlier. However, worse still, the lessons of this episode went unheeded in 1929.

The consequences of the post-war boom-and-bust mentality are worth considering. They were not as disastrous as those which followed the great inflations in central and eastern Europe, though this no doubt was of limited consolation to those who suffered in the slump. Moreover, had the authorities acted somewhat earlier to control the boom the consequences could well have been even more serious. Einzig, for example, feels that postponement of the slump until 1920-21 probably saved several countries from grave internal political disorders,[48] no doubt on the grounds that a depression following on immediately from the war would have proved intolerable, especially given the enormous demobilization programmes to be carried through.

46. I have not included the decision to get back to the gold standard as an objective since policy was not specifically geared to this until later.

47. J. B. Condliffe, *The Commerce of Nations* (1951), p. 440.

48. P. Einzig, *World Finance since 1914* (1935), p. 51; see also J. A. Dowie, '1919-20 is in Need of Attention', *Economic History Review*, vol. xxviii (1975), pp. 447-8.

These speculations apart, the repercussions of the episode cannot be dismissed lightly. The prospects of a smooth and speedy transition to peacetime conditions were shattered. In 1921 many factories were idle, millions of men and women were without work and industrial unrest was widespread as wages were forced down sharply under sliding-scale agreements. Reconstruction was brought to a halt almost overnight and as a consequence was prolonged well into the 1920s. For debtor countries the problem was worse. The relapse of commodity prices in 1920 destroyed the prospect of a solution to the international debt problem. Henceforward the commodity value of international indebtedness continued to rise almost incessantly until March 1933 when depreciation of the U.S. dollar provided some relief. But by that time the real burden of the debts was practically twice what it was when they were contracted.

Pedersen lays much of the blame for the difficulties of other countries in the 1920s on U.S. policy. It hindered reconstruction and added to their burden. He argues that if the U.S. monetary authorities had stimulated demand in the spring of 1920 instead of contracting it they would have prevented the permanent depression of countries struggling to return to the gold standard, mitigated inflation in a number of countries and made monetary reconstruction in these countries that much easier.[49] There is undoubtedly some truth in these allegations. The break in the business cycle in 1920 reduced U.S. imports and her favourable trade balances so that the volume of dollars supplied to foreigners had to be cut – by no less than 50 per cent between 1919 and 1921. By late 1920 the dollar shortage had become so acute in Europe as to require an increasingly large outflow of gold. In addition, U.S. imports from other areas declined, largely because of the collapse in primary product prices. Thus a sizeable surplus was recorded with primary producers in 1921, reversing the previous gold outflow to them, and the net inflow of gold to the U.S.A. in 1921 amounted to $686 million, the largest in any year prior to the devaluation of the dollar in 1933.[50] Unfortunately the drain of gold from European countries did not lead to a reform of financial affairs via credit restriction and currency stabilization since the

49. Pedersen, 'Some Notes on the Economic Policy of the United States during the Period 1919–1932', p. 477.
50. H. B. Lary, *The United States in the World Economy* (1943), pp. 140–45.

Europeans allowed their exchanges to slide further, thus aggravating the inflationary spiral.

Debtor countries were particularly hard hit by the sharp fluctuations in prices. They wasted reserves and credits in bidding for commodities on a high and rising market. Then when the bottom fell out of the market they were in difficulties. The drop of more than 40 per cent in the general level of dollar prices imposed a heavy burden on all debtors who had contracted debt at inflated prices. The transfer problem was aggravated since it was difficult to service the debt at lower prices; primary producers strove to increase output in an attempt to maximize income. The price decline also accentuated the deflationary difficulties of countries attempting to restore their currencies to pre-war parity. This is particularly true in the case of the U.K. since prices in sterling had risen more than dollar prices during the war.

In effect the United States failed to take full account of its changed status during the war – to a large creditor nation with a strategic role in the world economy. Adjustment to a positive trade balance required it to enlarge its imports and lend abroad. The cut-back in both respects in 1920–21 was a vital blow to the debtor countries. Subsequently the United States resumed lending on a large scale (though it shrank from its obligations on the import front) but only to pull down the chopper again at the most inopportune time.

But to attribute all the blame to the U.S. authorities (and the monetary authorities at that, which Pedersen does) is perhaps unfair. They were by no means the only culprits. The violent fluctuations in commodity prices cannot be ascribed solely to U.S. policy; it is quite probable that commodity prices would have declined regardless of the retrenchment measures. Furthermore, it is doubtful if continued boom in America would have done much to check inflation and currency collapse in continental Europe. And in any case, it would scarcely have been wise to allow a speculative boom to go unchecked, while if policy measures had further fuelled the boom the ultimate reaction might have been even more catastrophic.

The boom was certainly not an unmixed blessing for the industrial countries and others who participated, not because of the subsequent reaction, but because of some unsavoury features in the boom itself. In many respects it was an artificial boom created by paper shortages and supply bottlenecks arising partly out of the dislocation caused by war. Though production expanded it could not in the short term keep pace with rising demand and hence inflationary conditions dominated the upswing of the cycle, which developed into a speculative ramp. The boom's outstanding feature was speculative buying in commodities, securities and real estate and the very large number of industrial transactions at inflated prices. 'Houses, ships and especially the equities of firms were sold at fancy prices, with a flurry of mergers, combines and public flotations of private companies, with heavy burdens for the future in debt service to bond holders, especially banks, and in customary dividends.'[51] The financial orgy was made possible by the extremely liquid state of firms as a result of high wartime profits, relatively easy money conditions and large-scale creation of bank credit. A good deal of the speculative activity was based on borrowed money. Between January 1919 and April 1920 nearly £400 million of bank credit was made available in the U.K. for industrial and other purposes, while total bank clearings nearly doubled in the years 1918 to 1920. Activity in the new issue market reached phenomenal proportions. New capital issues on the London money market rose from £65·3 million in 1918 to £237·5 million in 1919 and to a peak of £384·2 million in 1920, and most of the increase in new issues represented flotations for domestic purposes.[52]

The worst excesses occurred in some of the older industries, coal, cotton, shipbuilding and steel, where prospects remained bright but for a very short time. The flotation of new companies, the sale of old ones and the issue of new shares became almost a daily event in 1919. Prospects of high profits attracted speculators and a large number of companies were bought up and refloated at inflated capital values, often with the assistance of the banks. In the U.K. cotton industry, for example, 109 mills with an original share capital of £4·5 million were sold for £31·7 million.[53] Judging by the rapid rise in the price of old and new ships even greater speculation occurred in the maritime industries. For these industries such transactions had disastrous consequences. Their wartime profits were dissipated in a frivolous manner and once

51. C. P. Kindleberger, *The World in Depression, 1929–1939* (1973), p. 33.
52. Aldcroft, *The Inter-War Economy: Britain, 1919–1939*, p. 35.
53. F. Utley, *Lancashire and the Far East* (1931), p. 45.

the bottom fell out of the market they were often left with virtually worthless assets together with a heavy burden of debt as a result of increased interest liabilities, the issue of bonus shares and the watering of capital stock. The cost of over-capitalization in the boom was to remain a heavy burden on some industries throughout the inter-war period. Worse still, it was in those industries whose future growth prospects were weakest that the worst excesses took place.

Finally the boom tended to stimulate far too much capacity, often in the very sectors whose future growth potential was limited. Shipping and shipbuilding capacity increased enormously in the period: in fact sufficient capacity came into existence to last a decade or more. Many countries, particularly India and Japan, over-extended their textile capacity to the detriment of Lancashire. American agriculture over-stretched and over-capitalized itself so that its productive capacity acted as a drag on the market. Primary producers the world over expanded on too lavish a scale, and continued to do so for a time after prices had fallen in a desperate effort to maintain their returns.

All told therefore, the boom and slump of the immediate post-war period did not provide a very auspicious opening to the decade. The upswing itself was marked by undesirable features while the subsequent reaction cut short reconstruction and recovery from the war.[54] Government policies both aggravated the boom and contributed to the slump and for this reason must share some of the blame for the consequences and repercussions of this episode. Yet while one part of the world was following a policy of orthodox retrenchment, another part, continental Europe, was continuing to enjoy the delights of inflation. It was soon to learn that these were short-lived.

54. Many reconstruction plans disappeared as a result. See P. B. Johnson, *Land Fit for Heroes: The Planning of British Reconstruction 1916–1919* (1968).

4

War Debts and Reparations

War debts and reparations were one of the most controversial issues of the 1920s. The negotiations and wrangles over who was to pay for which of the costs and debts arising from the war dragged on endlessly, partly because the main participants could not readily agree a solution. Ironically, after much time and energy had been expended most of the debts were never paid, and in the 1930s they were rendered moribund largely as a consequence of the slump. The economic consequences of the debt collection may not have directly caused the slump but they certainly provided one additional impediment to the smooth functioning of the international economic mechanism in the 1920s. Moreover, in Germany they were directly relevant to the economic crisis of 1923.

Extent of the problem

Altogether some twenty-eight countries (excluding three self-governing dominions of the British Commonwealth) were involved in one way or another with war debts and reparations. In effect every European belligerent apart from Turkey was involved, all the new states carved out of the enemy territories, every European neutral except Spain, and finally the United States and Japan. Five of these countries were debtors only and ten creditors only, while the remaining thirteen were both debtors and creditors: the final tally produced ten net debtors and eighteen net creditors. Russia is excluded here since the new Soviet regime repudiated all the debts of the former Tsarist Empire. With many countries however the amounts involved were relatively small and by far the most important participants were Germany, the United States, the U.K., France, Italy and Belgium. Germany was of course easily the largest debtor with eleven creditors to her name while the U.S. had sixteen debtors. The U.K. had no less than seventeen debtors and France ten, while even some of the smaller debtors, such as Czechoslovakia, Hungary and Bulgaria, were under an obligation to nine or ten creditors apiece.[1]

The sums involved are almost incomprehensible to the ordinary person. Inter-Allied war debts amounted to some $26·5 billion, mostly owed to the United States and the U.K., while France was the principal debtor. The burden imposed on Germany, as fixed by the Reparations Commission in 1921, was even larger at $33 billion, the greater part to be paid to France and the U.K. These amounts were varied downwards during the 1920s as a result of endless negotiations though the sums, together with accrued interest, still remained large: too large to be met in full, they were ultimately declared moribund.

Whether sums on this scale should have been imposed is debatable. There has been much criticism of the whole question of war debts,[2] especially of such a size, and it has often been asked whether they could not have been modified, scaled down or even abolished altogether. Apart from the problems involved in negotiating the settlements, the debts created a great deal of bad feeling, involved complex difficulties regarding their transfer and imposed severe burdens on the debtor countries. Certainly the process could have been simplified but politically it would have been impossible to avoid war debts altogether. The United States certainly wanted payment for services rendered to the Allies, while the French insisted on their pound of flesh from the

---

1. H. G. Moulton and L. Pasvolsky, *War Debts and World Prosperity* (1932), p. 5.

2. The first and most famous being J. M. Keynes, *The Economic Consequences of the Peace* (1919) to which Mantoux replied more than a generation later. E. Mantoux, *The Carthaginian Peace or the Economic Consequences of Mr Keynes* (1952).

enemy: the intransigence of these two powers ruled out any prospects of a deal, regardless of what other countries felt. In the case of the Allied powers some scaling down or pooling of costs incurred in a common cause would seem to have been eminently sensible. This could have made the issue so very much more simple. On the other hand, a good case could be made for exacting retribution from the enemy. A warmonger, just as a naughty child or a criminal, must expect to receive punishment for misdeeds committed, otherwise society would ever be at the mercy of the lawless. But whether the punishment is fair and just in any particular instance nearly always remains open to debate. In fact, as we shall see later, after the scaling down of reparations the German burden was not so large as many commentators have tried to make out.

Why were reparations and inter-Allied war debts kept separate when they could have been easily linked? The U.K. and France were the largest debtors of the United States and at the same time the main recipients of reparations from Germany. Their debts and credits could have been offset and Germany could then have settled with the U.S.A. Most of the European powers would gladly have negotiated along these lines had it not been for America's obstinate refusal to accept reparations from Germany. America had rendered aid to the Allied powers and insisted that they alone should be responsible for repayment. She opposed the mixing of claims partly no doubt because there was a much greater likelihood of Germany defaulting on her obligations than the Allies, in which case America would be left with a much larger balance of bad debts than if one of the Allies ceased payment. For purposes of the following discussion it will be convenient to treat them separately.

German reparations[3]

Most of the reparations bill fell to Germany. The exactions from the other enemies were small by comparison though burdensome in individual cases.[4] Unlike those of Germany the latter were

3. There is a vast literature on the subject, a selection of which has been included in the bibliography. Much of it is very repetitive however.

4. For example, the amount fixed for Bulgaria represented 22·5 per cent of the national wealth of the country, and this percentage rose appreciably after inclusion of other payments demanded by the Treaty of Neuilly. The

fixed by the individual peace treaties[5] and since similar principles and issues are involved there is no merit in discussing each in detail. The Versailles Treaty had been unable to agree an amount for German reparations since the Allies had rather different ideas as to what should be included. The Europeans, and especially the French who took a very hard line throughout the negotiations, wanted Germany to pay all Allied war damages and all the Allied costs of the war but the United States felt that war damages were all that Germany could be expected to pay. The final settlement was to be worked out by a special Reparations Commission which was instructed to draw up a statement of account by May 1921. In the interim the Treaty made provision for transitional payments in the form of foreign exchange, gold and in kind, all of which were to be credited to the reparations account at arbitrary valuations. Germany was required to surrender the greater part of her merchant marine, her entire navy and all her armament material; to deliver specified amounts of livestock, industrial equipment (mainly railway rolling stock), coal and other goods to the Allies, to build 200,000 tons of shipping a year for the Allies, and lose all public property in the ceded territories and colonies as well as most foreign investments. In addition, she had to pay all the costs of Allied occupation of troops on German territory, none of which was to be credited to the reparations account.[6]

In April 1921 the Reparations Commission came up with a final bill of 132 billion gold marks or about $33 billion, an amount far in excess of the sum considered feasible by Keynes and the U.S. experts at Paris. Against this were to be credited payments of some 8 billion marks already made, though the Germans, using a different basis of valuation and inserting additional items, claimed a very much higher figure for the transitional payments, most of which were in kind.[7] The total sum bore a 6 per cent interest

---

annual payments for extinguishing the debt over a specified thirty-seven years would absorb 55 per cent of the equivalent pre-war budget. Needless to say the liabilities were subsequently scaled down. L. Pasvolsky, *Bulgaria's Economic Position* (1930), pp. 65-7.

5. Namely the Treaty of Neuilly (Bulgaria); Treaty of Trianon (Hungary).

6. G. Stolper *et alia*, *The German Economy: 1870 to the Present* (1967), p. 75.

7. See Mantoux, *The Carthaginian Peace or the Economic Consequences of Mr Keynes*, pp. 152-3. Mantoux added the following cynical remark: 'It is only to be wondered that the whole of Germany's war costs were not included as reparation payments.'

charge and a schedule of payments drawn up by the Commission provided for the transfer of fixed instalments of gold marks. The first reparation annuities were set at 2 billion gold marks per annum, to be paid quarterly commencing in January 1922, while an immediate down payment of 1 billion gold marks was demanded. In addition, a variable annuity, amounting to 26 per cent of Germany's export proceeds, was to be paid quarterly from November 1921. Deliveries in kind were to continue and the Reparations Commission could demand payment in kind for any part of the reparations bill.

The plan was accepted reluctantly by the German government and put into operation rapidly. Initially Germany was able to comply with the obligations, but towards the end of 1921 the government informed the Commission that it would be unable to meet the instalments due early in 1922 and requested a reduction. After protracted negotiations that year's bill for payments both in cash and kind was reduced. This relief soon proved inadequate however.

During 1922 Germany's financial system, and along with it her capacity to pay, rapidly deteriorated. Payments so far had consisted largely of cessions of property abroad, the surrender of various types of equipment and certain deliveries of commodities, whereas cash payments had formed only a minor part. Since German citizens had to be compensated by the State for these losses government spending rose rapidly. The cost of the treaty obligations, including reparation payments, absorbed over 80 per cent of the total unborrowed revenues of the government and in 1922–23 they exceeded these revenues. This burden was imposed at a time when domestic expenditure was rising rapidly for reconstruction purposes. The tax system, not the most efficient anyway, could not cope with the pressure and the result was large budgetary deficits and a resort to the large-scale issue of paper money to meet the government's expenditure.

At the same time the transfer problem was becoming acute. This had previously been obscured by the utilization of foreign assets and deliveries in kind, but the former were exhausted by May 1921 and Germany was finding increasing difficulty in paying in kind. The obligation to make cash payments forced the government into further weakening her financial system. New measures included the sale of large quantities of paper marks to foreigners, the release of most of her already depleted gold and foreign exchange reserves, which provided a base for the monetary system, and the utilization of the proceeds from the sale of German securities and real estate to foreigners.[8]

The result of these activities was accelerating inflation and depreciation of the currency. By November 1921 the mark was down to 1·5 per cent of its par value, and though there was some respite early in 1922 the mark very soon began to plunge again under the pressure of further cash payments and speculation. In desperation, therefore, the German government in July 1922 pleaded for a postponement of cash payments for that year and a moratorium for a further two years, with a warning that financial collapse would ensue if these were not granted. The Allied powers met in August but were unable to agree over the request for a lengthy moratorium; all that they could offer was temporary relief for the rest of 1922 by accepting short-term Treasury Bills in lieu of cash. Deliveries in kind were still to continue and Germany would be liable for the full payments in the following year. The mark therefore continued on its downward course and towards the end of the year internal flight from the currency had set in. One last attempt was made by Germany, in November, to secure a complete moratorium on payments to allow her to stabilize the mark, but the French firmly resisted the request at Allied meetings in London and Paris.[9] By this time the German government had all but lost control of the situation; its capacity to meet its external obligations had more or less been exhausted and the prospect of further payments being made looked bleak. Fearing the worst the French and Belgian governments marched their troops into the Ruhr on 11 January 1923.[10]

The invasion completed the collapse of Germany's financial system. The objective was to enforce payment by direct control of

8. Moulton and Pasvolsky, *War Debts and World Prosperity*, pp. 271–272.

9. W. M. Jordan, *Great Britain, France and the German Problem, 1918–1939* (1943), pp. 108–9.

10. The French government took this action to enforce collection on the grounds that reparation payments were in arrears. By all accounts deliveries to France had been dwindling during the course of 1922 but by how much is not exactly clear. Certainly it was more than the 100,000 telegraph poles which Colin Cross cites as the pretext for invasion. C. Cross, *Adolf Hitler* (1973), p. 78.

the Ruhr industrial system, but passive resistance by the Germans thwarted the French while financing the process sent the mark up to 'stellar magnitudes'.[11] Neither side gained but the struggle continued until the mark was worthless. Whether the German government deliberately provoked the inflationary crisis to prove that it could not pay reparations is a moot point, but the effect was certainly spectacular. By September 1923 the currency was in such a state that Germany called off the passive resistance and proposed the introduction of a new currency, the Rentenmark. Two months later the currency was stabilized at the rate of 1,000 billion paper marks for one gold mark.[12]

The upshot of this disaster was a rethinking of the reparations issue. In November the Reparations Commission nominated two committees of non-political experts to examine various aspects of the problem and to propose solutions. The more important of the two, under the chairmanship of General Charles C. Dawes, a future Vice-President of the United States, was to consider means of stabilizing German financial affairs and the possibilities of a new and more feasible schedule of reparations.[13] The Dawes Committee came up with a solution in April 1924 which was accepted by the Reparations Commission and subsequently by all governments concerned at a specially convened conference in London in August. The Dawes Plan, as it became known, was put into force in September 1924.

The Dawes Plan certainly represented an improvement, though some would argue that it only prolonged the agony.[14] It did not reduce the total amount owed but it recognized Germany was not in a position to pay annuities on the former scale. The annual payments were therefore reduced to more manageable proportions, the payments period was extended, and ways of raising revenue to make the payments were suggested. The new schedule of payments was to start at 1,000 million gold marks annually, rising to 2,500 million in 1929. A Reparations Agency was set up in Berlin to keep an eye on the situation; in the event of transfer difficulties it

11. J. W. Angell, *The Recovery of Germany* (1929), p. 23.

12. The mechanics of the inflation and stabilization are dealt with more fully in Chapter 6.

13. The other committee was to investigate the amount of capital expatriated from Germany.

14. S. B. Clough, *The Economic Development of Western Civilization* (1968), p. 440.

could recommend a postponement of payments. Since capital was desperately short in Germany at this time and her credit was too weak to borrow abroad a large loan of 800 million gold marks was underwritten and floated under the Dawes banner. It proved an immediate success which seemed to guarantee the future economic stability of Germany. Henceforth large amounts of capital poured into Germany which enabled the reparation payments to run smoothly.

On the surface the Dawes Plan worked to perfection; the annuities were paid regularly without much apparent difficulty to the creditors. Altogether some 7·6 billion marks were paid under the scheme.[15] But the underlying weaknesses in the payments mechanism were masked by an entirely new factor, massive foreign borrowing. Because of budgetary and balance of payments difficulties Germany borrowed around 28 billion marks abroad in the period 1924–30 inclusive, out of which she paid reparations amounting to 10·3 billion. In other words, her reparation payments were covered at least two-and-one-half times by the import of capital. So long and only so long as foreign capital poured into the country the settlement of reparations ran smoothly. The crunch came in the first half of 1929 when American lending was sharply curtailed, which set off a chain reaction among foreign banks demanding the withdrawal of short-term loans from Germany.[16] The position was extremely tricky since not only had Germany piled up large foreign liabilities, but many of these were short-term debts liable to immediate recall.

Recognition of Germany's precarious financial position together with pressure from the German government led to one last attempt to solve the reparations issue. A new committee of experts was set up early in 1929 under Owen D. Young, with the task of preparing a final statement of account. After much wrangling a solution was finally thrashed out which was acceptable to all parties. Only the briefest details need be given since the Plan scarcely got off the ground before the Hoover moratorium put an end to reparations. It provided for a substantial reduction in the capital sum and a scaling down of the annuities, starting at

15. Mantoux, *The Carthaginian Peace or the Economic Consequences of Mr Keynes*, p. 152.
16. S. Flink, *The German Reichsbank and Economic Recovery* (1929), p. 251.

1,650 million gold marks in the first year and eventually rising to 2,300 million. The Reparations Agency was to be withdrawn and the Plan was inaugurated by a $300 million loan. It took effect in April 1930. By this time the depression was making it increasingly difficult to comply even with the scaled-down obligations. Within a year Germany was engulfed in financial crisis and President Hoover proposed a moratorium on reparations in June 1931. The following year the signatories to the Lausanne Agreement put an end to reparations for good.

After all these changes what did Germany eventually pay on reparations account? It is not easy to say precisely how much since a considerable part was transferred in goods the exact valuation of which is very difficult. Moreover, Allied and German estimates vary considerably, as one might expect. The commonly quoted figure is for a total payment of around 21,000 million gold marks equivalent approximately to $5 billion, though the Germans put it at least three times as high.[17] Other non-German estimates suggest a sum of about $8·5 billion.[18] Either way the amount was only a fraction of the $33 billion originally proposed by the Reparations Commission in 1921.

Germany's capacity to pay

A great amount has been written about the reparations issue and much has been critical of the whole deal. The attempt to collect such large debts eventually proved futile and kept Europe in a state of political and economic turmoil for more than a decade. The large inter-governmental debts unrelated to current production and trade also tended to hamper a return to economic and financial tranquillity in Europe. The debt burdens also had unfortunate economic consequences for Germany, especially in 1923 and again in 1931. But let us leave aside these repercussions for the moment to examine the vexed question of Germany's ability to pay. Many writers have been very critical of reparations

17. Mantoux, *The Carthaginian Peace or the Economic Consequences of Mr Keynes*, p. 152; Moulton and Pasvolsky, *War Debts and World Prosperity*, p. 269. Mantoux suggests that 35–38 billion marks were received by Germany from abroad between 1920 and 1931.

18. L. B. Yeager, *International Monetary Relations: Theory, History and Policy* (1966), p. 273.

on the grounds that it was quite impossible for Germany to meet the obligations imposed. A closer inspection of the facts suggests that this conclusion requires some modification.

The following analysis relates to the period mainly from the Dawes Plan (1924) onwards. Prior to this Germany was clearly in no position to pay since during late 1922 and 1923 she was in the throes of hyperinflation. And before then much of the payment consisted of goods and property etc. and so the capacity to pay did not arise in quite the same form as later.[19]

For the payment of reparations to operate smoothly two conditions had to be met. First, large sums had to be extracted from the Germans through taxation and, secondly, these sums had to be transferred into foreign currencies (ultimately mostly dollars) to effect the payments. Now the first of these centred on the taxable capacity of the nation and was the less difficult of the two. The maximum amount of public funds available for reparation purposes in any one year was the difference between the maximum taxable capacity of the nation and the minimum amount required by the State for domestic purposes. At the end of the 1920s German taxes were about 25 per cent of national income, while reparations accounted for some 10 per cent of total taxation or 2·5 per cent of the national income.[20] This was a heavy but certainly not an impossible burden. Indeed U.K. taxes were probably higher than this in the 1920s,[21] and tax rates were by no means excessive by post-1945 standards.

However, there is reason to believe that this by no means exhausted the German ability to raise the cash internally. Given the rising incomes of the later 1920s a case could be argued for increasing the rate of taxation to provide more for reparations. In fact the government not only failed to make a bigger effort in this direction but deliberately ran budgetary deficits throughout the entire period of the Dawes Loan. In the seven-year period 1925–31 (ending 31 March) the federal budgetary deficit amounted

19. A budgetary problem yes but no transfer problem.
20. P. T. Ellsworth, *The International Economy*, 3rd edition (1964), p. 403; Mantoux, *The Carthaginian Peace or the Economic Consequences of Mr Keynes*, p. 147.
21. International comparisons are difficult but figures given by Bowley suggest that on a per capita basis the U.K. was considerably more heavily taxed. A. L. Bowley, *Some Economic Consequences of the Great War* (1930), pp. 116–17, 120.

to some 4 billion marks, while the budgetary outlays for reparations totalled just over 5 billion marks. The nominal federal debt rose by 6·6 billion marks in this period about half of which was financed through foreign borrowing and about half internally. At the same time the states and municipalities were running into even greater debt, though a large part of their deficits were financed by internal borrowing. Local bodies borrowed 11·6 billion marks, 1·6 billion of which came from abroad. By March 1931 the total German public debt (federal plus local) amounted to 24·2 billion marks, about 18 billion of which had been contracted in the period 1925–31. Moreover, less than one-third of this sum was derived from foreign borrowing, the remainder being raised internally.[22]

Since the greater part of these deficits was financed internally there seems no sound reason why the money could not have been drawn from taxation rather than borrowing. This for a start would have provided a healthy budgetary position. Secondly, part of this revenue, from whatever source it was raised, could almost certainly have gone towards the reparations bill. Both federal and state governments were spending large sums on projects or activities which raised the standard of living of the people but had no direct bearing on reparations. For example, the social expenditure of the Reich more than doubled during this period, while more than a few parks, sports stadia and similar luxuries were built by the municipal authorities. Had the borrowing been devoted mainly to export-revenue raising projects[23] to earn foreign exchange to effect the transfer of reparations one could be less critical of the budgetary deficits. As it was the government ran steadily deeper into debt both with foreigners and its own citizens and used the proceeds to improve the welfare of the nation. Even if only part of the large deficit had been shifted over to taxation the proceeds would have been enough to meet the existing reparations bill and more besides.

On the first condition alone, therefore, there are grounds for believing that Germany's internal capacity to pay was by no means exhausted. The transfer issue was far more complicated and proved the main stumbling block. After the money had been raised

22. Moulton and Pasvolsky, *War Debts and World Prosperity*, pp. 280–82.
23. Part of it was of course.

internally it had to be transferred through the exchanges to the recipients. For such large sums involved transfer could only take place in the form of goods and services, which ultimately meant that Germany had to earn sufficient surplus on her trading account to cover the annual bill. This was no easy task since many of the options were partially closed. There were several possible ways of boosting exports but each presented certain difficulties. Keynes suggested that the easiest way was to let the exchange value of the mark fall to make German exports more attractive to foreigners. But after the recent disastrous experience of the mark in 1923 the Germans were in no way eager to adopt this solution, and in any case the Dawes device of 'transfer protection' precluded it.[24] A second alternative was to adopt a deflationary policy which would reduce prices and costs (thereby making exports more competitive) and restrict domestic consumption, and this in turn would release resources for export industries and reduce the demand for imports. But the compression required to achieve a substantial increase in the value of exports would have been intolerable. Assuming a 10 per cent fall in export prices gave rise to a 20 per cent increase in the volume of exports this would raise the value of exports by 8 per cent only ($1 \cdot 20 \times 90 = 108$). Moreover, since German industry was heavily dependent on imported raw materials the gross rise in exports would have to be greater still to cover the cost of the raw materials. Keynes estimated that finished exports would have to rise by some 40 per cent which would entail a very substantial reduction in costs unless foreign demand was very elastic.[25] In fact it has recently been shown in the case of the U.S.A. that the price elasticities of demand for imports were relatively low so that the scope for shifting more German goods into this market was relatively limited.[26] In addition to this most of Germany's customers were not in a particularly receptive mood towards imports partly because of excess capacity in their own industries. One final possibility was the reduction of imports, a point taken up below.

24. J. M. Keynes, 'The German Transfer Problem', *Economic Journal*, vol. xxix (1929), p. 168.

25. ibid., pp. 165–6.

26. M. E. Falkus, 'United States Economic Policy and the "Dollar Gap" of the 1920s', *Economic History Review*, vol. xxiv (November 1971), p. 601.

Not surprisingly, therefore, Germany had substantial deficits on her external account throughout the 1920s. In the period 1925–31 her international income fell short of payments by 18 billion marks, more than half of which was absorbed by reparations. The only way to cover these deficits was by borrowing abroad. Estimates of the total amount of capital flowing into the country vary but it was probably in the region of 28 billion marks in the period up to the middle of 1930, over 50 per cent of which was in the form of short-term debt (under three years). Only 10·3 billion was used for reparations purposes, while the rest went to financing a large import surplus (6·3 billion marks), accumulating assets abroad (9·7 billion),[27] paying interest on commercial debt and adding to her gold and foreign exchange reserves.[28] On the basis of these figures Harris argued that the larger part of Germany's foreign borrowings was devoted to objects that had no direct connection with reparations, namely the building-up of capital assets depleted by war and inflation, and the financing of a substantial rise in the standard of living by the large import surplus. In the latter context loans were used for re-equipping industry, building social overhead capital and the like with the result that real wages rose by about 20 per cent during the period 1925–30.[29] However, the allegation of misuse is not entirely proven, since exports benefited indirectly from the improved industrial productivity arising from re-equipment, while part of the import surplus consisted of raw materials used in the production of export goods. Nevertheless, even if we assume that all foreign borrowing except for the payment of reparations could have been dispensed with, Germany would still have had a large debt problem though a manageable one in the short term. Borrowing on that scale could not have continued for ever so that long-term viability would depend on how quickly Germany could have improved her external earnings position. The task here was far from easy but not hopeless, though events as they turned out shattered the prospects of the point ever being put to the test. The

27. Thereby giving a net capital inflow of 18 billion marks.

28. The figures quoted are approximate orders of magnitude since estimates vary slightly. C. T. Schmidt, *German Business Cycles 1924–1933* (1934), p. 110; Moulton and Pasvolsky, *War Debts and World Prosperity*, p. 285; C. R. S. Harris, *Germany's Foreign Indebtedness* (1935), pp. 6–10.

29. Harris, *Germany's Foreign Indebtedness*, pp. 10–11. See Chapter 10.

upshot of the argument is that reparations on the scale envisaged were not outside the bounds of reality but a reduction in them would certainly have made things a lot easier.[30]

Foreign borrowing on the scale of the later 1920s did have some perverse effects for Germany. Large capital imports aggravated the transfer problem in so far as they raised Germany's propensity to import, and reduced the buying power of lending countries and hence their import of German goods. In addition, the rise in German purchasing power occasioned by capital inflows meant a diversion of resources towards production for the home market rather than for export. In a wider context the massive foreign borrowing simply stored up trouble for the future. Had Germany been left to fend for herself a crisis might have occurred much earlier and then the real nature of the transfer problem would have been appreciated. As it was Germany was able to meet her payments without any great hardship and with the minimum disturbance to creditor nations in the form of unwanted German goods. But as Moulton and Pasvolsky have pointed out, German and European borrowing on such a scale could not go on indefinitely nor fail to accentuate the existing maladjustments. 'Even if the world depression had not begun at the end of 1929 and international lending had not suddenly decreased almost to vanishing point, it was inconceivable that new loans could have continued to exceed the rising reparation and Allied debt instalments, plus interest charges on the vast volume of private indebtedness that had already been created. The loan policy which constituted the second phase of post-war reparation and inter-Allied debt policy thus did not solve the war debt problem nor lay the foundation for enduring world prosperity.'[31] It would be difficult to argue that reparations and war debts were the immediate cause of the turning-point of 1929, but the serious maladjustments they created and the large borrowing they entailed simply concealed the disequilibrium and did little to improve the situation.[32] Furthermore, once foreign lending dried up as a result of the decline in in-

30. This conclusion runs counter to the views of most authorities on the subject though Ohlin expressed a similar feeling in 1929. B. Ohlin, 'The Reparation Problem: A Discussion', *Economic Journal*, vol. xxxix (June 1929), p. 172.

31. Moulton and Pasvolsky, *War Debts and World Prosperity*, pp. 384–5.

32. H. W. Arndt, *The Economic Lessons of the Nineteen-Thirties* (1944), p. 13.

comes in creditor countries the basic unsoundness of the situation was exposed. The second stage of the crisis, the financial breakdown in central Europe in 1931, can be directly attributed to the debt problem. Once credits were no longer freely available Germany in particular, with a large volume of insecure short-term debt, was unable to stand the strain and financial collapse was therefore inevitable.

In the light of the known consequences[33] it is difficult to put a strong case for reparations of the magnitude imposed in the 1920s. Even though Germany's ability to pay may have been greater than is often assumed the fact is that she did not manage to meet her obligations without external assistance, which simply made things more difficult for the future. The first mistake of the Allies was not simply that they fixed total reparations unrealistically high – largely as a result of the intransigent French attitude – but that the annuities were set at too high a level to begin with. These could easily have been made more reasonable in the early years when Germany was recovering from the shock of 1923, and then adjusted as the German economic position improved. By fixing them as they did the Allies left Germany with what seemed an impossible task and hence little effort was made to meet either the budgetary or transfer objectives. The second mistake was for the Allies to bale Germany out by loans once these objectives fell by the wayside. By doing this Germany was simply incurring one debt to pay another (in fact building up an even larger debt in the process) so that the problem of real redemption was never faced squarely. Capital imports no doubt assisted Germany's recovery and improved her ability to export but since the end result was an increasing burden of debt the net return was negative. This process could only go on for so long; once foreign lending dried up the collapse was inevitable.

Inter-Allied war debts

The settlement of debts among the Allies presented less of a

33. These were not of course confined to Germany. France, for example, financed a large programme of reconstruction in the early 1920s on the assumption that the cost would be met by German reparations. When these did not materialize on the scale envisaged France ran into severe budgetary difficulties with serious consequences in terms of inflation and the currency.

problem than reparations though similar difficulties were experienced. About 15 per cent of the total costs of the war were met through inter-Allied debts contracted during the period of hostilities, the bulk of which were loaned by the U.S.A., the U.K. and France in that order. Further debts were run up during the immediate post-war period in relief and reconstruction aid to stricken Europe. All told the final tally amounted to around $26·5 billion or $23·0 if irrecoverable Russian debts are excluded. By far the largest creditor was the U.S.A., accounting for about one half the total, most of which had been lent to the U.K., France and Italy.[34] Britain was the next largest creditor; she owed $4·7 billion to the U.S. but had claims on other countries amounting to $11·1 billion leaving her a net creditor of $6·4 billion, or $3·9 if we discount the Russian debt. The third main creditor, France, was owed $3·5 billion, but since she was in debt to the U.S. and U.K. for a total of $7·0 billion she ended up a net debtor of $3·5 billion (or $4·4 billion excluding the Russian debts).[35] France was easily the largest single net debtor but there were a number of other important net debtors among the Allies, notably Italy and Belgium.

Several attemps to find a solution to the problem of war debts all ran foul of the United States who insisted on being paid in full. The European Allies felt that the large balance in favour of the U.S.A. was unjustified in the conditions under which the debts were contracted. The money had been spent in dealing with a common enemy and therefore a fairer distribution of the burden was in order. On the other hand, the loans had been contracted in good faith and the United States had never at any time intimated that they would be cancelled, scaled down or adjusted in any way. The U.S.A. therefore had a perfect legal right to insist on collecting its claims, if not a moral one.

One of the first proposals, originally put forward by Keynes, was that all the debts should be cancelled. This possibility was raised with the United States by Lloyd George but received very short shrift. Similarly an attempt to distinguish between war costs

34. C. Gilbert, *American Financing of World War I* (1970).

35. See Bowley, *Some Economic Consequences of the Great War*, p. 100 and A. Sauvy, *Histoire économique de la France entre les deux guerres, 1918–1931* (1965), p. 169; H. E. Fisk, *The Inter-Ally Debts: An Analysis of War and Post-War Public Finance, 1914–1923* (1924).

and post-Armistice obligations came to nothing since the U.S.A. insisted on collecting the lot, including the accrued interest. Nor would the U.S.A. entertain any suggestion that war debts and reparations should be linked. This could have immensely simplified the process of transaction since most of the Allied debts to the U.S.A. could have been cleared by German reparations being paid directly to America. Finally, one proposal for a more equitable distribution of the debt burden was put forward by Sir Josiah Stamp. This suggested a pooling of all wartime obligations as a common responsibility of the Allies and a redistribution of the sum among them in proportion to each one's ability to pay. Then the claims of each country would be compared with its share in the common responsibility. If its claims exceeded its responsibility it would be credited with the difference, otherwise the difference would be charged against it. On this basis of assessment the U.K. would have been left with a net debt of about $2 billion, France with $4·7 billion; Italy and Belgium would have been entitled to repayments, while the American claim on Europe would have been reduced to $2·1 billion or a fraction of the $12 billion outstanding.[36] However, neither the U.S.A. nor France was attracted to this scheme, France because she ended up with a larger net debt than the one actually contracted, and the U.S.A. since her claims were drastically reduced – though ironically enough she eventually received very little more from the Allies than the sum proposed under the Stamp plan.

Given America's inflexible attitude the Allies had no alternative but to insist on collecting their own debts including reparations, though both the U.K. and France did make certain concessions to their debtors, adhering to the principle that they would collect no more than they in turn owed to the United States. However, the United States was eventually forced to relax its demand for full repayment as it became clear that the European countries could not meet their obligations. In 1922 Congress appointed a special committee to negotiate revised and final settlements; each country was to be dealt with separately according to the ability to pay. Settlements were eventually arrived at with most of the countries in debt to the U.S.A., though these were not finally completed until 1926. Arrangements varied from country to

36. W. S. and E. S. Woytinsky, *World Commerce and Governments* (1955), p. 745.

country and were more liberal than previously – the repayment period was stretched to sixty-two years and the interest rate was fixed at 3–3½ per cent, with specially low rates being granted to France, Italy, Belgium and Yugoslavia. Most important, the capital sums were scaled down considerably, the effect of which was to halve the original U.S. claims.

Even these concessions did not solve the problem. A large part of the inter-Allied war debts proved as irrecoverable as German reparations. As with the latter, paying the debts raised budgetary and transfer problems for the countries concerned. Easily transferable values were in short supply and creditors were reluctant to accept payment in competing goods. Clearing claims with the United States proved the most difficult since increasing protection in that country and her demand for payment in gold and dollars made it almost impossible for the debtors to raise the requisite funds, especially since nearly all of them had unfavourable payments balances with the U.S.A. Payments were made, but the solution was farcical and indirectly it involved a link with reparations which the Americans were never prepared to sanction in practice. The U.S.A., and to a lesser extent other creditors, made capital loans to Germany who then paid her creditors; the creditors in turn passed back currency to the U.S.A. in settlement of their own debts. This process went on until the flow of funds from America dried up, and when the Allies were forced to release their claims on Germany war debts very soon died a natural death.

The final tally runs as follows. From 1918 to 1931 the U.S.A. received $2·6 billion from the Allies, a small amount compared with the original $12 billion and less than half that specified by the revised settlements of the 1920s. Four countries, U.K., France, Italy and Belgium, were responsible for nearly all the payments collected by America, while these same countries received 93 per cent of the payments made by Germany to all her creditors under the Dawes and Young reparation plans. Reparations received between 1924 and 1931 more than covered the combined Allied debt payments of those four countries though each country fared differently. Italy and Belgium gained on balance by a small amount, while France received some three-and-one-half times as much in reparations as she paid in war debts to the U.S.A. and U.K. The U.K., the only country to continue debt payments on a large scale, was responsible for most of the payments to the U.S. and ended up with a negative balance overall.[37]

Thus after a decade of political wrangling little was paid either in reparations or war debts against the original claims presented. The negotiations involved much valuable time and energy and directed attention from more serious issues, while the continued existence of the problem was a source of international friction throughout the 1920s. The manner in which payments were ultimately effected concealed the real issues involved and gave rise to a basic disequilibrium in the international payments mechanism which was bound to be exposed sooner or later.

37. Moulton and Pasvolsky, *War Debts and World Prosperity*, pp. 291-2; Clough, *The Economic Development of Western Civilization*, p. 442.

5

Reconstruction and Recovery 1921-25

The year 1925 is generally taken to mark the end of the period of reconstruction and recovery from the war and immediate post-war slump. Lewis regards it as 'a cheerful year' both in economics and politics. 'The dark days of post-war dislocation seemed to have been left behind, and the prospects seemed good.'[1] Certainly much had been accomplished within a short space of time. A large part of the wartime physical destruction had been made good and the level of economic activity in many European countries had reached or surpassed that of pre-war. In many areas outside Europe production had advanced rapidly and reached new records, while the volume of world trade was already above that of 1913.[2] Some of the worst currency inflations were over and the progress towards currency stabilization in general was given a boost by Britain's return to gold in April 1925. The fall in commodity prices had been checked and even reversed and primary producers were beginning to feel the benefits of increased industrial activity. Politics too appeared less unsettled. The problems relating to war

1. W. A. Lewis, *Economic Survey 1919–1939* (1949), p. 34; cf. C. P. Kindleberger, *The World in Depression, 1929–1939* (1973), p. 31.

2. See A. Maddison, 'Growth and Fluctuation in the World Economy, 1870–1960', *Banca Nazionale del Lavoro Quarterly Review*, vol. xv (1962), Table 25, p. 186.

debts and reparations had been settled, at least for the time being, which together with the signing of the Locarno pact in 1925 reduced some of the tension and friction in international affairs. In short, the spirit of anxiety, pessimism and even despair of the early 1920s had given way to restrained confidence and determination.[3]

World recovery

It is difficult to give a very accurate account of the pace of economic activity during the early 1920s, since the available data are patchy and not very reliable. There are no global income estimates for the period and the only figures on a reasonably uniform basis for the world as a whole are derived from those collected by the League of Nations for manufacturing and the production of foodstuffs and raw materials. While these are reliable enough to provide broad orders of magnitude, in many cases the individual country series are in the process of revision which in some cases has produced noticeable differences from the earlier series. Unfortunately, until revision is complete we are forced to rely on the League's estimates for world-wide comparisons.

TABLE 4
WORLD INDICES OF MANUFACTURING PRODUCTION, 1913–25
(1913 = 100)

	World	Europe *	U.S.S.R.	U.S.A.	Rest of world
1920	93·6	77·3	12·8	122·2	109·5
1921	81·4	70·0	23·3	97·9	103·7
1925	121·6	103·5	70·1	148·0	138·1

* Covers 18 countries: U.K., Germany, France, Italy, Belgium, Netherlands, Switzerland, Sweden, Denmark, Norway, Finland, Austria, Czechoslovakia, Hungary, Poland, Romania, Greece, Spain.

SOURCE: I. Svennilson, *Growth and Stagnation in the European Economy* (1954), pp. 204–5.

After the sharp check to activity in 1921 manufacturing output in the world as a whole recovered quite quickly and probably surpassed the 1913 level in 1922–3, while by 1925 it was nearly 22

3. J. S. Davis, 'Economic and Financial Progress in Europe, 1924–25', *Review of Economic Statistics*, vol. XII (1925), p. 61.

per cent above the pre-war level (see Table 4).[4] However the contrast between Europe and the rest of the world is striking. Manufacturing output in Europe only just surpassed the pre-war level by the middle of the decade[5] and in Russia it was still 30 per cent down. Apart from one or two exceptions such as the Netherlands, Italy and Czechoslovakia, most of the countries which recorded gains above the world average between 1913 and 1925 lay outside Europe. They included the U.S.A. (48 per cent), Japan (122 per cent), Australia (41 per cent), India (32 per cent), New Zealand (36 per cent), and South Africa (304 per cent). At the other extreme most central and east European countries (particularly Germany, Poland, Russia, Austria, Hungary and Romania) failed to recover their pre-war levels of activity. Midway between these two extremes several countries recorded quite respectable increases in output (e.g. France, Canada, Norway,

TABLE 5

PRODUCTION INDICES FOR RAW MATERIALS AND FOODSTUFFS
IN 1925 (1913 = 100)

	All products	Raw materials and colonial products	Foodstuffs
Eastern and central Europe (excluding U.S.S.R.)	97	99	97
Eastern and central Europe (including U.S.S.R.)	100	93	102
Rest of Europe	109	109	109
Europe (excluding U.S.S.R.)	103	105	102
Europe (including U.S.S.R.)	103	102	104
North America	127	137	117
South America	130	132	129
Africa	143	170	124
Oceania	118	114	121
Asia (excluding Asiatic Russia)	127	171	109
World	118	130	111

SOURCE: A. Loveday, *Britain and World Trade* (1931), p. 7.

4. The Woytinskys suggest that world industrial output recovered to 1913 by 1922 and that in 1925 it was 23·6 per cent above the pre-war level. See W. S. and E. S. Woytinsky, *World Population and Production* (1953), p. 1002.

5. This accords fairly closely with figures for industrial production produced by OEEC for a similar range of countries. See OEEC, *Industrial Statistics 1900–1959* (1960), p. 9.

Sweden and Spain), though Belgium and the U.K. had a struggle to match their pre-war performance.

Relatively few countries had a large share of their resources devoted to manufacturing activity so that this indicator is not a very reliable guide for the many countries which specialized in primary products. The League of Nations collected extensive data on over sixty commodities (mainly raw materials and foodstuffs) and produced output indices for the main regions of the world. These are given for 1925 in Table 5. World output of foods and raw materials rose by 18 per cent over the period 1913–25, though raw materials had a substantially faster rate of increase. Again similar regional variations in rates of progress to those in manufacturing are apparent. European output did not manage to regain the pre-war level until 1925 and then only marginally surpassed it. By contrast every other continent was producing more both absolutely and per head of population than it had done in 1913, and by a large margin. Oceania increased her production of raw materials and foodstuffs by nearly one-fifth, Asia and North America by over one-quarter, South America by 30 per cent and Africa by over 40 per cent. In each case raw material production rose more rapidly than that of foodstuffs. Quite often development was based on the demand for one or two products and represented growth from a small base. Thus much of the expansion in Asia and Central America reflected the rapid increase in demand for petroleum and rubber for the motor industry, while Africa benefited from a sharp increase in demand for vegetable fats.[6]

There seems little doubt therefore, even in the absence of complete data, that the world as a whole was richer in 1925 than it had been in 1913. Production indices for manufacturing and commodities had risen by around 20 per cent, world trade by about 16 per cent[7] whereas world population had increased by a mere 6 per cent. The rapid development of many new products such as cars, radios, artificial silk, also points to a higher standard of living. But the gains were very unevenly divided. It was the

6. A. Loveday, *Britain and World Trade* (1931), pp. 7–8.

7. Maddison, 'Growth and Fluctuation in the World Economy, 1870–1960', p. 186. This figure is probably an outside limit since other estimates suggest a rather lower increase between 1913 and 1925. Trade figures are notoriously inaccurate for this period.

areas outside Europe where the largest gains were made, especially North America and Japan. Income per head in Europe by 1925 was no doubt still below pre-war, and in eastern Europe even more so. The war and post-war reconstruction phase had shifted the balance of economic power well away from Europe's grasp. This shift is also reflected in the trade statistics. The centre of gravity moved from Europe and the Atlantic to North America, Asia, Oceania and the Pacific Ocean. World trade as a whole grew less rapidly than output between 1913 and 1925 but the gains were distributed even more unevenly. In North America and Asia it increased by well over a third, and in Central America by one-quarter to a third, whereas in Europe as a whole it was more than 10 per cent down on 1913 and in eastern Europe it was probably less than three-quarters of the pre-war level.[8]

The European recovery problem

It took seven years before Europe as a whole regained her former levels of activity and even then recovery was not really complete. Many countries continued to suffer from excess capacity and heavy unemployment; at the end of 1925 there were over 2·5 million unemployed workers in the U.K., Germany, Britain, Italy and Poland alone, not to mention the large number of underemployed workers, especially in agriculture. Secondly, Europe's trade still fell short of its pre-war volume. Thirdly, the fact that production had barely surpassed the 1913 level at a time when population was rising suggests that income per head was still below the previous peak. Taken as a whole therefore the performance cannot be regarded as particularly spectacular.

The rate of recovery was very uneven not only between regions but also between countries within the same area. Figures prepared for one of the League's reports show that the area which lagged seriously behind was central and eastern Europe which had suffered the most from the war and its aftermath. Some countries in this region escaped the post-war slump because of inflation, but this was little consolation since, once out of control, inflation checked economic activity more sharply than in countries which had adopted deflationary policies. By 1925 industrial production

8. Maddison, 'Growth and Fluctuation in the World Economy, 1870-1960', p. 186; Loveday, *Britain and World Trade*, pp. 25-9.

TABLE 6
INDUSTRIAL PRODUCTION AND MINING IN EUROPE, 1913–25
(1913 = 100)

	1920	1921	1922	1923	1924	1925
Western Allies *	70·3	66·2	85·1	94·6	112·2	114·9
Neutrals †	98·7 §	87·3	92·4	98·7	105·1	111·4
Central and eastern Europe ‡	57·6	69·5	76·0	58·6	77·2	87·0
Total continental Europe	66·7	70·2	81·0	75·0	91·7	98·8

* Includes Portugal.
† Denmark, Netherlands, Norway, Spain, Sweden and Switzerland.
‡ Germany, Czechoslovakia, Austria, Bulgaria, Estonia, Finland, Greece, Hungary, Latvia, Poland, Romania and Yugoslavia.
§ Excludes Netherlands and Norway.
SOURCE: League of Nations, *Europe's Overseas Needs 1919–1920 and How They Were Met* (1943), p. 9.

in this area was still 13 per cent below that of 1913 whereas the western Allies and neutral countries were recording gains of a similar magnitude (see Table 6). Within these groupings some countries did very much better than others. Italy, for instance, far surpassed the performance of any of her Allies; Denmark and the Netherlands did better than the other neutrals while Finland outpaced the Scandinavian countries; France and Belgium, though subject to similar destruction, registered somewhat different rates of recovery, while France did better on balance than the U.K.[9] In eastern and central Europe it is more a case of selecting the best out of a bad lot, though Czechoslovakia stands out with an increase in manufacturing output of more than one-third above the pre-war level.

Most countries had special problems in the reconstruction period, some of which will be discussed later when we consider the experience of individual countries, but several general factors can be adduced to explain the relatively slow rate of European recovery.

For one thing the task of reconstruction itself was enormous. Moreover, it was not simply a problem of restoring physical damage though this in itself was a considerable item. The amount

9. These comparisons are borne out by data for the total volume of domestic output which are available for certain countries. See A. Maddison, *Economic Growth in the West* (1964), p. 201.

of physical destruction of land and property may not seem that large but for the countries concerned it often constituted a real burden at a time when resources were short. For many countries, especially in central and eastern Europe, there was the additional problem of literally re-creating viable economic systems out of territories which had been sliced up and reformulated by the provisions of the peace treaties. Economically these countries had not been strong even before 1914 but after the war they were in a very much worse condition.

Economic and political conditions were scarcely conducive to rapid recovery in the first few years after the war. Hardly a year went by without some event or series of events hampering progress. In 1919–22, for example, strikes, political upheavals and border hostilities abounded throughout Europe both in the east and west. The sharp contraction in economic activity in 1920–21 in most west European countries abruptly cut short the recovery, and for some it spelt the beginning of an intermittent policy of deflation in preparation for the return to the gold standard. Throughout these years, too, inflationary pressures were building up in much of Europe and 1922–3 saw the unleashing of these forces in Austria, Poland and Germany, together with the abortive occupation of the German Ruhr by France and Belgium. After 1923 things quietened down somewhat and by the middle of 1924 the outlook was generally more favourable to genuine sustained progress than at any time since the Armistice.[10] Nevertheless some events still gave cause for alarm; Germany and Poland, for example, experienced partial stabilization crises in 1924, and the following year the French and Belgian currencies weakened seriously at a time when other countries, the U.K., Switzerland and Norway in particular, were experiencing deflationary pressures connected with the return to gold. Finally, the U.K. suffered the worst strike in history in 1926.

Some of these events affected particular countries more than others, but there can be little doubt that in total they did much to impede recovery throughout Europe as a whole. But by no means all the problems were of a local nature. Currency difficulties were widespread throughout this period and as Loveday commented, 'the European exchanges for seven years danced and jumped with

10. J. S. Davis, 'Economic and Financial Progress in Europe, 1923–24', *Review of Economic Statistics*, vol. VI (1924), p. 242.

spasmodic and tireless energy'.[11] Currency instability was probably one of the biggest single factors impeding general recovery, even though some countries did gain, especially initially, from depreciated currencies and inflationary financing of reconstruction. But against this have to be set adverse effects. Several countries eventually failed to bring inflation under control and their economies collapsed under the strain. This, as we have argued elsewhere,[12] did more harm than good to their economies and left them in a much weaker state than at any time since the end of the war. Secondly, the uncertainty created by extremely volatile exchanges hindered the revival of foreign trade and made it difficult to plan for the future. Much energy was spent in speculative currency deals rather than in real trade transactions, and the very slow recovery in European trade must in part be attributed to uncertainty caused by currency instability. Thirdly, while certain countries, notably France, did benefit from inflation and a depreciated exchange, many in central and eastern Europe did not. For these countries a depreciated currency often brought little real gain since supply inelasticities precluded them from taking advantage of their more competitive position, while the imports of equipment on which their future development depended were made much more expensive. The long-term consequences of currency depreciation were not beneficial either since the artificial protection which it provided led to the establishment of inefficient enterprises or industries which subsequently had to be given state assistance to keep them in business.

Probably the most important single barrier to recovery and development was shortage of resources. This was certainly the major problem in central and eastern Europe in the immediate post-war years and even beyond. It was not simply a question of a physical shortage of equipment and raw materials though this was certainly an acute problem in the early days after the Armistice. The problem ran much deeper, since it was essentially an acute shortage of capital, both long and short term. These countries were incapable of raising sufficient capital internally, nor were they able to earn sufficient foreign exchange to pay for imports of materials and equipment essential for economic development. The only solution to this problem was recourse to

11. Loveday, *Britain and World Trade*, p. 31.
12. See Chapter 6, pages 138–45.

foreign borrowing but this failed to materialize on anywhere near the scale required. Much of the post-Armistice assistance consisted of governmental lending to alleviate famine and assist with general relief of war-stricken areas, and in any case a good part of this went to the western Allies. When this dried up the import of capital into continental Europe by loans raised abroad (other than inter-governmental loans) was very limited and most of it went to western and northern Europe. Thus between 1919 and 1923 bond issues by continental and east European countries amounted to $210 million compared with $575 million for western and northern Europe.[13] Unsettled political and economic conditions made investors extremely reluctant to grant long-term loans to these areas. In the absence of adequate long-term lending these countries had to struggle on, relying on short-term credits granted by the creditor countries. Even the flow of these was erratic and in any case they provided little solution to the long-term shortage of capital.[14]

Given the conditions of the time it is hardly surprising that international lending on private account was limited. What was required was international cooperative action among creditor nations to provide impoverished countries with access to supplies of capital. Instead the United States and the U.K. provided loans but only to those countries which were reliable borrowers, and able to look after themselves. The League of Nations could have provided a channel but it assisted little apart from once-and-for-all reconstruction loans to countries after the worst had already happened, for example, Austria in 1922, Hungary in 1924, and Bulgaria and Estonia in 1926. In short, the League's work was far too limited and its assistance was too little and too late.

International lending on an adequate scale in the early 1920s would have done much to alleviate the desperate plight of the central and east European countries and might have helped to avoid some later problems. Loans would have facilitated sound

13. League of Nations, *Europe's Overseas Needs 1919-20 and How They Were Met* (1943), p. 29.

14. It meant too that the cost of capital, when available, was extremely high. Charges on credits to first-class borrowers in Austria in 1925 were between 16·15 and 18·65 per cent and these were by no means the highest. F. Hertz, *The Economic Problem of the Danubian States: A Study in Economic Nationalism* (1947), pp. 163-5.

recovery and by so doing have avoided some of the worst financial and currency excesses. In turn, external assistance would facilitate the recovery of international trade and obviate the need for increased protection and other restrictive measures. Not until after 1924, when economic conditions had become more stable, did the flow of lending increase markedly, but by this time the damage had been done.

Western Allies and the neutrals

Of the western powers the two most severely affected by wartime devastation were France and Belgium. France emerged from the war almost bankrupt with large debts and most of her foreign investments either lost or liquidated. Some 10 per cent of the territory was devastated, including some of the most valuable resources, while industrial and agricultural output were about 30–40 per cent below 1913, and exports but a fraction of the pre-war level. In fact France's industry and agriculture were probably more severely crippled than those of her adjacent neighbours with the possible exception of Belgium.[15] By 1919 the franc had lost 50 per cent of its former purchasing power and worse was still to follow. The main consolation was that France was probably marginally better off than the defeated powers, and at least she recovered the important industrial area of Alsace–Lorraine.

Despite the setback France made a relatively rapid recovery. By 1923 the volume of exports had recovered to the pre-war level and two years later they were almost one-quarter larger than in 1913.[16] Industrial output just about doubled between 1921 and 1924 by which time the previous peak had been surpassed, though estimates vary as to by how much.[17] Income estimates are also open to debate. Markovitch suggests that it was not until 1925

15. W. F. Ogburn and W. Jaffé, *The Economic Development of Postwar France* (1929), pp. 20–23.

16. Maddison, 'Growth and Fluctuation in the World Economy, 1870–1960', p. 186.

17. Sauvy suggests an increase of 8–9 per cent above 1913 for 1924 and 1925 as against 17–18 per cent given by Markovitch. A. Sauvy, *Histoire économique de la France entre les deux guerres 1918–1931* (1965), p. 465; T. J. Markovitch, 'L'industrie française de 1789 à 1964 – conclusions générales', in *Histoire quantitative de l'économie française* (1966), p. 170. See also footnote 29, page 109.

that real national income in France just about regained the 1913 level. Sauvy's figures on the other hand, indicate a 12 to 13 per cent increase for 1924 and 1925, which seems to accord more closely with the domestic output figures given by Maddison.[18] Agriculture did not share in the recovery to the same extent and declined in relative importance; it remained dominated by small-scale inefficient farms.

The exact dimensions of growth may still be fuzzy but there seems little doubt that by the middle of the 1920s France, despite financial and currency difficulties, had made a fairly good recovery. In this she was assisted by several factors. Physical reconstruction proceeded quite rapidly, helped along by generous governmental assistance on the assumption that Germany would foot the bill. At the end of 1921, 80 per cent of the injured industrial establishments of any size had recommenced operations, and a start had been made in building new capacity in the devastated areas of the north.[19] By 1925 a large part of the reconstruction had been completed. Much importance is attached to the considerable transformation and modernization of France's industrial structure in the period, especially in metallurgy, chemicals and new high-growth sectors. By all accounts the heavy investment in new equipment and modern technology made French industry more efficient than it had ever been before 1914.[20] Mechanization was no doubt encouraged by a shortage of labour which was partly met by immigration. The extent of the transformation has probably been exaggerated but certainly French industry was very active in this period. The government contributed substantially to the modernization programme while the war had helped to shake up French industrialists and reduce their resistance to change.[21] In addition, the sharp decline in the value of the franc 'made borrowing so profitable that even those entrepreneurs imbued

18. Sauvy, *Histoire économique de la France entre les deux guerres 1918–1931*, p. 282; Markovitch, 'L'industrie française de 1789 à 1964 – conclusions générales', p. 170; Maddison, *Economic Growth in the West*, p. 201.

19. J. S. Davis, 'Recent Economic and Financial Progress in France', *Review of Economic Statistics*, vol. III (1921), p. 224.

20. Ogburn and Jaffé, *The Economic Development of Postwar France*, p. 120; T. Kemp, *The French Economy 1919–39: The History of a Decline* (1972), pp. 67–71, 97; G. Martin, 'The Industrial Reconstruction of France since the War', *Harvard Business Review*, vol. v (1927).

21. Kemp, *The French Economy 1919–1939*, p. 66.

with the traditional abhorrence of credit learned to sacrifice commercial morality to pecuniary advantage'.[22]

Currency depreciation also assisted the country in other ways. It helped to counteract the impact of the 1921 depression and encourage domestic spending. It gave a boost to the tourist trade and to French exports. Exports increased rapidly after 1922; between 1922 and 1926 they rose by 56 per cent at which point they were over one-third greater than in 1913. Kemp implies that it was not until the later 1920s that an export-led boom took over from one based on reconstruction and the home market.[23] In fact the main growth in French exports occurred in the first half of the decade and by 1927-8 exports had flattened out. Elsewhere he argues that France benefited from being a late starter in industrialization in that her major export industries were concentrated not on the less developed countries but rather on the high-income countries of western Europe and North America. Thus she stood to gain from the increased purchasing power of these countries and had little to lose from Japanese and Indian competition in textiles, as in the case of Britain.[24]

The French economy still suffered from weak spots and France nearly paid the price of inflationary financing in a collapse of the currency. Fortunately Poincaré saved the day and France was one of the few countries to benefit significantly on balance from inflation and currency depreciation. Belgium showed a somewhat similar experience though her recovery effort was not so impressive. The country suffered severe war damage and losses and by 1919 industrial production and exports were less than 50 per cent of the pre-war level.[25] But the occupation had by no means paralysed the country since it was in the German interest to keep production going. Nevertheless reconstruction was a substantial task and the government freely assumed almost the entire cost in the belief that compensation would be forthcoming. As in France this resulted in a considerable amount of new plant based

22. D. S. Landes, *The Unbound Prometheus: Technological Change and Industrial Development in Western Europe from 1750 to the Present* (1969), p. 464.

23. T. Kemp, *The French Economy 1919-1939*, p. 97.

24. T. Kemp, 'The French Economy under the Franc Poincaré', *Economic History Review*, vol. xxiv (February 1971), p. 85.

25. F. Baudhuin, *Histoire économique de la Belgique 1914-1939*, vol. i, 2nd edition (1946), pp. 91-104.

on up-to-date techniques. The iron and steel industry, which was almost obliterated by the war, was a major beneficiary. Large-scale government assistance coupled with inflation that eroded much of the fixed debt enabled the Belgian ironmasters to re-equip themselves with modern plant on relatively easy terms. Output of pig iron surpassed the 1913 level in 1924 and by 1927 Belgium had 50 per cent more blast furnace capacity than when she started the war and some of it was the most technically advanced in Europe.[26]

The reconstruction process was more or less complete by 1925. Most of the farms had been restocked and nearly every square yard of devastated area was again under the plough. Belgian agricultural production showed a better record than the average for western Europe in the early 1920s and by 1924 it had attained the pre-war level. All the devastated houses and most of the public buildings had been completely rebuilt and restored.[27] However the limited statistics available suggest that it was not until the mid 1920s that industrial production fully regained pre-war dimensions.[28] It is not obviously apparent why Belgium failed to match France's performance.[29] Belgium suffered more severely in the slump of 1921 though recovery from this setback was quite rapid. Possibly the most important factor was that Belgium failed to recover her lost export markets; currency depreciation, though on par with France's, does not seem to have given much of a fillip to exports which languished badly in the early 1920s.

Of the belligerent powers Italy's post-war performance was by far the best. Italy was less severely affected by the war and post-war slump than either France or Belgium, though by some accounts Italy's economic machinery was badly disorganized

26. Landes, *The Unbound Prometheus*, p. 462.

27. W. H. Pringle (ed.), *Economic Problems in Europe Today* (1927), p. 137.

28. H. L. Shepherd, *The Monetary Experience of Belgium, 1914–1936* (1936), p. 16; OEEC, *Industrial Statistics 1900–1959* (1960), p. 9.

29. When allowance is made for the conflicting and shaky nature of the statistics for this period the difference may be quite marginal. On the basis of the OEEC industrial production data France did very much better than Belgium between 1920 and 1925; on the other hand, Belgium recovered more rapidly between the Armistice and 1920. In 1925 industrial production in Belgium was 6·5 per cent above 1913 and 13·0 per cent above in 1926; the respective increases for France were 9·0 and 20·0 per cent. Both countries surpassed their pre-war peaks in 1924 by a similar margin.

almost to the point of breakdown in the post-Armistice period.[30] If so Italy certainly staged a remarkable revival since by 1922 industrial production had regained the pre-war level and domestic output was some 13 per cent above 1913.[31] Certainly from 1922 onwards Mussolini's industrialization and efficiency drive did much to hasten expansion. Aided by government assistance and a liberal credit policy Italy enjoyed continuous industrial expansion up to 1926. Iron and steel production doubled; rayon output multiplied several times, placing Italy in the forefront of the European producers; the mercantile marine doubled and considerable progress was made in chemicals and the electrical industry. By 1926 industrial output had climbed to 42 per cent above the pre-war figure, with domestic output over a fifth greater.[32] Exports too received a considerable stimulus from currency depreciation and the occupation of the Ruhr, which allowed Italy to re-enter eastern markets, so that by 1925 they were over a third higher than in 1913.[33] Good harvests in 1923 and 1925 and a flow of surplus agrarian labour to France, Belgium and Luxemburg assisted development.[34] But expansion ground almost to a halt as the favourable factors disappeared one by one. Credit facilities, which had been somewhat over-extended, so causing speculation and the creation of many dubious companies – the number of joint stock companies almost doubled between 1922 and 1926 – were sharply curtailed.[35] Emigration declined as Belgium and France completed their reconstruction, and the U.S.A. imposed severe quantitative controls. German recovery spelled the end of Italy's honeymoon in her eastern markets, while bad harvests in

30. Pringle, *Economic Problems in Europe Today*, p. 32; W. G. Welk, *Fascist Economic Policy* (1938), p. 159; S. B. Clough, *The Economic History of Modern Italy* (1964), pp. 198–202, 208.

31. Maddison, *Economic Growth in the West*, p. 201. But Maddison suggests that Italy's total output was already 6·6 per cent above 1913 by 1920 and that it rose slightly in 1921. This hardly seems to square with more indirect evidence on the state of Italy's economy at the time or with the fact that her exports were still 20–25 per cent below the pre-war level in 1921–2.

32. OEEC, *Industrial Statistics 1900–1959*, p. 9; Maddison, *Economic Growth in the West*, p. 201.

33. Maddison, 'Growth and Fluctuation in the World Economy, 1870–1960', p. 186.

34. Pringle, *Economic Problems in Europe Today*, pp. 32–4. In 1925 there were 1·2 million Italians in these three countries.

35. Welk, *Fascist Economic Policy*, p. 162.

1926-7 and the settlement of war debts with the U.S.A. and U.K. (1925-6) added to the burdens. Above all, Mussolini's promise to defend the lira resulted in an overvalued currency after stabilization. Thus unlike most other countries Italy failed to participate in the boom of the later 1920s.

The country least affected by wartime dislocation, Great Britain, had a rather chequered performance in the first half of the 1920s, though more recent statistical inquiries suggest that it was not as bad as was once imagined. The record is too well known to bear repetition in detail. Having recovered her former production and income levels at an early date (1920) Britain suffered a sharp contraction in 1921; industrial production fell by over 18 per cent and unemployment rose to 2·4 million or 22 per cent of those insured. This was one of the worst depressions in British history and apart from investment, which was bolstered up by a large-scale programme of subsidized housebuilding, all indices of economic activity fell substantially. The position was aggravated by strikes in coal, cotton and other industries.

Though the unemployment position began to improve in the latter half of 1921 it was not until early 1922 that economic activity showed real signs of revival. During 1922 production rose strongly despite a decline in investment and real wages, though output in one or two major industries, notably building and shipbuilding, declined quite substantially. However, there was a strong revival in exports, an increase of no less than 38 per cent on 1921, and domestic consumption rose by 3·5 per cent. It seems likely that the initial upswing was generated by the export revival and by developments in the consumer goods industries. This was supplemented by growth in the new industries and later by an upturn in building activity. The recovery continued until 1925 though the pattern of growth was very uneven from year to year. Real income rose more rapidly in the latter part of the recovery when production and exports were tailing off, while the upsurge in investment did not take place until 1924-5.

The strength of the recovery between 1921 and 1925 was quite marked as the following figures indicate: domestic output rose by 20 per cent, industrial production by 41·4 per cent, real income by 9·6 per cent, exports by over 50 per cent and investment by just over one-quarter. These calculations are based on the low levels of the 1921 slump; even so, by 1925 income and production had cleared the levels of 1920 or 1913 by a reasonable margin.[36] But the recovery was by no means complete. Exports were still 25 per cent down on 1913 while unemployment, even at its lowest in June 1924, was still around 1 million, or 9·2 per cent of the insured population. Intermittent deflation in connection with the return to gold helped to depress activity though the main problem was a structural one. A large proportion of resources was tied up in the old basic industries, for example textiles, shipbuilding and coal, the demand for whose products, both at home and abroad, was declining rapidly.[37]

The main neutral countries (Norway, Sweden, Denmark and the Netherlands) had several things in common with the U.K. None had suffered severely as a result of the war though their economic systems had been distorted; a big setback was the loss of export markets, especially in Europe, so that in most cases export volumes were by 1920 some 30–50 per cent down on 1913. Secondly, the neutral countries returned to the gold standard at pre-war parity which meant that they all, with the possible exception of the Netherlands, experienced a bout of deflation during the course of the 1920s. Thirdly, they experienced a sharp contraction in activity after the post-war boom, though again the Netherlands seems to have fared better. On the other hand, most of the neutrals recorded a better performance than Britain in the first half of the 1920s.[38]

Initial recovery from the war was rapid so that by 1920 levels of economic activity were already above the pre-war base, and in Denmark and the Netherlands substantially so. The collapse of the boom coupled with a deflationary policy brought a violent contraction in 1921. Activity declined sharply in all countries except the Netherlands and in some, notably Norway and Sweden, fell well below the pre-war level. The deflationary policy was particularly severe in Sweden since the government was intent on forcing costs and prices down in anticipation of an early return to parity. Wholesale prices fell by about 50 per cent and output declined by over one-quarter, while unemployment rose to

36. The General Strike of 1926 occasioned a sharp check to activity.
37. The above paragraphs are based on D. H. Aldcroft, *The Inter-War Economy: Britain 1919–1939* (1970), pp. 32–3, 37.
38. Though probably not Switzerland, while Sweden's progress was about on par with Britain's.

a peak of 33 per cent at the end of 1922.[39] The appreciation of the krona caused a sharp contraction in exports, and Sweden became the target of exchange dumping by continental countries with very depreciated currencies.[40] Thus Sweden's progress in the early 1920s was severely curtailed and it was not until 1924, when the krona was again fixed to gold, that economic activity approached pre-war dimensions once again.

Norway and Denmark recovered much more rapidly from the 1921 depression since deflationary policies were not forced to such extremes. Both achieved rapid rates of expansion up to 1925 when levels of activity were far higher than in 1913.[41] But their stabilization phase was still to come; after 1925 their prosperity was cut short by extreme deflationary policies in preparation for the return to gold so that growth was limited for most of the remainder of the decade. Only the Netherlands seems to have avoided deflationary crises in the 1920s and as a result she was one of the few countries which enjoyed continuous and rapid growth over the whole decade. A strong and sustained upswing in exports contributed to her successful performance.

Central and eastern Europe

The task of reconstruction and recovery in the territories of central and eastern Europe was on a scale quite different from that of the west. Virtually all the countries in this region were faced with a whole series of almost insuperable problems and with resources very much inferior to those of the west European powers. The list of difficulties seems endless and makes depressing reading: physical devastation; territorial problems and consequent economic disorganization; financial chaos, including unbalanced budgets, inflation and currency instability; balance of payments problems, unemployment, rapidly rising population and agrarian reform; political instability and weak administrative

39. D. T. Jack, *The Restoration of European Currencies* (1927), p. 69; E. Lundberg, *Business Cycles and Economic Policy* (1957), pp. 8–10, 15, 95; H. Clark, *Swedish Unemployment Policy, 1914 to 1940* (1941), p. 60.

40. B. Thomas, *Monetary Policy and Crises: A Study of Swedish Experience* (1936), p. 31.

41. Industrial production was 69 per cent higher in Denmark and 23 per cent in Norway; domestic output 17 and 32 per cent greater. See Maddison, *Economic Growth in the West*, p. 201 and OEEC, *Industrial Statistics 1900–1959*, p. 9.

organizations; lack of a balanced economic structure and shortages of almost everything. Even this does not exhaust the possibilities. Not every country suffered from all these problems at once though it is difficult to find any which did not face at least a large proportion of them. Thus for most of these countries it was a case not of getting back to normal as quickly as possible but of trying to avoid economic disintegration. Though reliable statistical data are limited it seems very unlikely that many of these countries regained their pre-war levels of activity even by the middle of the decade.

For the purposes of this section the main countries of central and eastern Europe include Austria, Czechoslovakia, Bulgaria, Greece, Hungary, Poland, Romania, Yugoslavia and Russia.[32] We shall mainly confine our discussion to general observations on the problems of reconstruction rather than discuss each country in detail.

Most countries in central and eastern Europe were in a weak economic position prior to the war. Industrial development, even in the Czech lands and Russia, was relatively limited and the population was still heavily dependent on agriculture. In the Balkan states of Bulgaria, Romania and Yugoslavia, up to 80 per cent of the population earned a livelihood from the land. The density of farm population was high and techniques of cultivation primitive, hence yields were low. Income per capita was low which meant limited savings for investment outside the primary sector. Apart from Russia most industrial development consisted of light industries, notably textiles and processing facilities for primary products. The most industrialized state was Czechoslovakia which inherited much of the industry of the former Austro-Hungarian Empire, but its agriculture still bore the stamp of feudalism.[43] Bulgaria, on the other hand, had virtually no industry. In most cases trade was confined to primary products with a high dependence on the export of one or two commodities. Yet though economically very backward this region had a degree of economic cohesion and stability prior to the outbreak of hostilities.

The war and its aftermath shattered any semblance of unity and

42. Germany does not feature here partly because her position is somewhat different from that of the group of countries listed and in any case this country is dealt with in detail elsewhere. See Chapter 6, pages 138–45.

43. J. Gruber, *Czechoslovakia: A Survey of Economic and Social Conditions* (1924), p. 43.

stability. The economic, political and social life of virtually all the east European countries was in complete chaos. Famine was rife, destruction and pillage by invading armies had damaged much of the productive facilities, trade was almost non-existent, while financial and currency systems were in ruins. In Austria, for example, economic life was practically at a standstill; unemployment and famine were widespread and serious starvation would have occurred but for relief from abroad.[44] For some, moreover, the Armistice did not spell the end of hostilities. The period of war economy lasted until March 1921 in Poland since she was engaged in fighting for her frontiers in the east. Greece was locked in combat with Turkey until 1922 when she suffered a disastrous defeat and had to provide for over 1 million refugees from Asia Minor. Hungary had civil war to contend with.

The peace treaty settlements did little to improve matters – indeed rather the reverse. Though freedom from foreign domination was secured the new territorial arrangements merely impeded economic progress and recovery. Primary emphasis in geographical restructuring was placed on ethnic delineation and the re-establishment of historic frontiers, and economic considerations were almost completely ignored in defining the territories of the newly created and reconstituted states. The new alignments made little economic sense whatsoever. Former patterns of communication and trading links were severed while the division of territory often sliced up viable economic enterprises or regions as, for example, in Austria and Hungary.[45] 'The Treaties of Peace cut large parts of the economic fabric of the continent into morsels. Industrial centres were divided from their sources of raw materials and their markets, and former trade routes were hastily barricaded by tariffs and prohibitions.'[46] Hence the new states inherited various fragments of territory which required welding into viable and cohesive political and economic units. Not only had they to deal with the ordinary problems of reconstruction but they literally had to create new administrations and national economies out of the motley collection of territories which they inherited. Moreover, they were left to accomplish these tasks almost unaided at a time when resources were desperately short, with financial and

44. L. Pasvolsky, *Economic Nationalism of the Danubian States* (1928), p. 97.
45. These problems are discussed in Chapter 2, pages 27–30.
46. Loveday, *Britain and World Trade*, p. 30.

administration systems far from commensurate with the needs in hand, and when social and political stability left much to be desired. These difficulties were compounded by further problems. Population was rising very much faster than in the west during the 1920s. In Hungary, Yugoslavia, Bulgaria, Romania, Greece and Albania the natural rate of increase was three times or more greater than that of the U.K. At the same time the traditional safety-valve of emigration almost disappeared; between 1920 and 1924 the average annual gross emigration to extra-European countries from south-east Europe amounted to a mere 53,000 persons as against 178,000 per year in the period 1906–10.[47] This meant even further pressure on the already densely populated farm lands while the extensive land reforms led to a fragmentation of land-holdings and a significant increase in small-scale subsistence farming.[48] The effect of the land reforms is difficult to assess precisely since the extent of reform and its impact varied considerably from country to country. Initially it probably had a perverse effect on production and yields by reducing the scope for mechanization and improved efficiency, though the large estates out of which the new holdings were carved had not been noted for their enterprise. As Doreen Warriner observed, the real mistake of reform was not that it destroyed highly efficient farming enterprises but that it perpetuated all the defects of individualistic farming.[49] In Romania, where large estates were confiscated and some 30 per cent of the land was redistributed, the reforms had a harmful impact and delayed recovery. The cultivated area and the output of cereals fell sharply.[50] Yugoslavia also experienced a

47. Royal Institute of International Affairs, *South-Eastern Europe: A Brief Survey* (1940), pp. 76–9. Overseas migration from Europe as a whole was very much reduced after the war partly due to American restrictions on immigration. The average annual overseas emigration from Europe was 629,500 in 1921–5 and 555,600 in 1926–30, compared with over 1·4 million between 1906 and 1910. Most of the reduction was borne by eastern Europe, the Balkans and Italy. See D. Kirk, *Europe's Population in the Inter-war Years* (1946), pp. 83–8, 279.

48. N. Spulber, *The State and Economic Development in Eastern Europe* (1966), p. 69.

49. D. Warriner, *Economics of Peasant Farming* (1939), p. 154.

50. W. S. and E. S. Woytinsky, *World Population and Production: Trends and Outlook* (1953), p. 498; League of Nations, *Agricultural Production in Continental Europe during the 1914–18 War and the Reconstruction Period* (1943), p. 49.

sharp contraction in cereal output during the early 1920s, though in this case land reform covered only a small proportion of agricultural land. By contrast, in Czechoslovakia and the Baltic states (Latvia, Estonia, Lithuania), the results of fairly extensive land reform appear to have been quite favourable. Elsewhere, in Hungary, Poland and Bulgaria, where the reforms were relatively modest, the effect was quite small.

Factors other than land reform were responsible for the slow recovery of agricultural production in eastern Europe, though the relative force of each varied from country to country. The main initial cause was the marked deterioration of the whole productive apparatus as a consequence of wartime devastation, together with the losses suffered by the peace treaties. Hungary, for example, lost much of her livestock and the territories annexed were the best for cattle-breeding.[51] Farmers were desperately short of capital and credit for reconstruction, and the break in primary product prices in the early 1920s squeezed profits. Moreover, new tax burdens were imposed on the agrarian sector in order to finance industrialization. On the other hand, inflationary conditions in some countries eased the problem of financing though the general disorganization arising from inflation ultimately did more harm than good. The result was that in some countries agricultural output still remained below the pre-war level by the middle of the decade.[52]

However, the recovery of agricultural production could provide little real solution to the main problem, namely increasing pressure on the resources of the land. The obvious long-term solution was industrial development but in the conditions then prevailing this was easier said than done. Shortages of plant, raw materials and capital were widespread, while currency depreciation and the financial instability of the new states left little prospect of much assistance from abroad. Moreover, several countries had lost large parts of their industrial interests, either through destruction or pillage or via the terms of the peace treaty settlements. Hungary and Austria, for example, were deprived of a good part of their manufacturing activities, while Poland lost her

51. O. S. Morgan (ed.), *Agricultural Systems of Middle Europe* (1933), pp. 212–15.

52. Though overall production of foodstuffs was not far off the pre-war level. See Loveday, *Britain and World Trade*, p. 7.

eastern market in Russia as a result of the new regime.[53] The disorganization of the infrastructure, particularly communications, the generally chaotic economic conditions after the war and the poverty of the mass of the people, were hardly conducive to rapid industrialization. Export outlets were also limited by the loss of many markets and the inefficient nature of production. Moreover, the State could provide little direct assistance, at least initially, given the inefficient tax systems and the large burden of public debt, both internal and external. Most countries were burdened either with reparations or with some of the debts of the Ottoman and Austro-Hungarian empires, or both.

Given these limitations the only solutions to reconstruction and industrialization were short-term expedients. Thus inflation, currency depreciation and tariff protection became the means by which these countries sought to adjust their economies and foster industrial development. Inflation and exchange depreciation are normally regarded as detrimental to economic systems and so they may be once they get out of control. On the other hand, as we have already seen, they both stimulate investment and exports initially, and for these countries, labouring under so many difficulties, such courses of action were virtually the only ones available. Nearly all the countries concerned temporarily solved their low-capacity problem by inflationary investment. Thus in Austria there was a big expansion in industrial capacity between 1919 and 1923 with the result that industrial equipment was some 20 per cent greater than pre-war. The same was true of Hungary. Between 1913 and 1925 the number of enterprises rose by 50 per cent and virtually every industry except clothing recorded additions to industrial capacity.[54] Similarly physical reconstruction proceeded rapidly in Poland; it began on a large scale in 1921 and was almost complete by 1924–5.[55] Inflation helped Polish industry to establish itself in the home market and the accompanying currency depreciation allowed it to exploit the markets of countries with more stable currencies.[56] At the same time currency deprecia-

53. F. Zweig, *Poland between Two Wars* (1944), p. 89.
54. Pasvolsky, *Economic Nationalism of the Danubian States*, pp. 159–60, 350–52.
55. Zweig, *Poland between Two Wars*, p. 33.
56. By contrast the attempts to stabilize the currency in the mid 1920s were accompanied by an acute industrial crisis and a sharp dip in industrial production. R. Górecki, *Poland and Her Economic Development* (1935), p. 81.

tion and liberal tariff protection helped to protect the domestic market from competing imports. Most of the countries in the region had higher tariffs than before the war, a reflection of what was to become a more sustained drive towards economic autarchy in later years. When completed in 1925–6 the Czech tariff structure was almost double the old Austro-Hungarian, and represented 36·4 per cent of the total value of imports. The new Hungarian tariff averaged 31·1 per cent of imports as against 18·9 per cent under the former tariff. These tariff levels were much higher than those prevailing in most other countries. Both Austria and Hungary used tariffs to protect new undertakings which replaced those lost under the territorial changes of the peace treaty.[57]

It is doubtful whether the expedients employed to effect recovery can be regarded as all that successful. Certainly inflation and currency depreciation gave an initial boost to the economies of these countries, but once it got out of hand, as in the case of Austria, Hungary and Poland, it probably did more harm than good. The German example is instructive in this respect.[58] Moreover, once stabilization and financial control were effected a reaction in economic activity set in. Forced industrialization gave rise to inefficient undertakings and much excess capacity. In fact development was reflected in the expansion of capacity rather than output. Both Austria and Hungary expanded their industrial capacity considerably in the early 1920s, partly to make up for losses suffered by the treaty provisions, but by the mid 1920s industrial output was running at about 75–80 per cent of pre-war, that is about two-thirds the capacity then available.[59] Probably capacity over the region as a whole was expanded far in excess of needs, once the artificial conditions of inflation and currency depreciation had ceased to exist.[60]

Thus the measures resorted to in the early 1920s gave an artificial boost to these economies but produced few real and lasting benefits. Industrial activity in the region as a whole was still well below that of 1913 in 1925, in some cases significantly so.

57. W. T. Layton and C. Rist, *The Economic Situation of Austria* (1925), p. 27.
58. See Chapter 6, pages 138–45.
59. Pasvolsky, *Economic Nationalism of the Danubian States*, pp. 159–60, 350–52. Even by 1929 industrial production in Austria was still only about 80 per cent of capacity. Hertz, *The Economic Problem of the Danubian States*, p. 143.
60. See Layton and Rist, *The Economic Situation of Austria*, p. 27.

The League's manufacturing indices suggest that Poland fell short by 37 per cent, Hungary, which had experienced more rapid growth before 1914, by 23 per cent, Romania by 8 per cent and Austria 5 per cent. Trade too remained well below pre-war though the output of raw materials and foodstuffs made a better recovery.[61] It is significant that Czechoslovakia, which had inherited important industrial interests from Austria–Hungary and had reformed her financial and currency systems at an early date, was the only country to experience rapid growth, with an increase in manufacturing output of 36 per cent compared with 1913.[62] It was not until the late 1920s that manufacturing activity in most countries exceeded the pre-war level, though in at least one case, Poland, even this was not achieved. Moreover, by 1929 income per capita for the whole of south-eastern Europe was only marginally above that of pre-war, while in at least two countries, Poland and Bulgaria, it was well below.[63] Spulber's observations on the 1930s are equally applicable to the 1920s: 'A gigantic backlog of backwardness, increasing demographic pressures, consistently erroneous economic policies, insuperable nationalistic barriers to fruitful cooperation in the area, all but arrested the process of economic growth.'[64] Inflation and currency depreciation could provide only a temporary alleviation of the fundamental problems of this region, and they in turn became problems which ultimately necessitated remedial action. Once some financial stability was restored capital imports provided a source of relief, but again these proved transient since at the crucial moment, in the late 1920s, they were hastily curtailed.[65]

Russia presents a different case and merits a few separate comments. Under the new regime the country was virtually cut off from the west, but in any case the economy ground to a halt in the years 1919–21 under the impact of civil war and external border hostilities, inflation and communization. Recovery from this chaos was long and arduous but the groundwork was laid in the years 1922–4, with the partial return to private enterprise

61. See Table 5, page 99; also Loveday, *Britain and World Trade*, p. 30.
62. League of Nations, *Industrialisation and Foreign Trade* (1945), pp. 134–7.
63. L. J. Zimmerman, 'The Distribution of World Income, 1860–1960', in E. de Vries (ed.), *Essays on Unbalanced Growth* (1962), p. 50; L. Pasvolsky, *Bulgaria's Economic Position* (1930), p. 267.
64. Spulber, *The State and Economic Development in Eastern Europe*, p. 75.
65. See Chapter 10, pages 261–7.

(under the New Economic Policy – NEP), the stabilization of the currency and the restoration of budgetary equilibrium, and the end of civil violence and external conflict. In the first year which might be regarded as near normal (1922–3), output of large-scale industry rose by 50 per cent but this still left it some 60 per cent down on the 1913 level. Not until 1926 did industrial and agricultural output exceed the pre-war base and then only by a small margin. A multiplicity of factors impeded recovery including the famous price 'scissors' crisis, the destruction and neglect of basic capital equipment, shortages of skilled labour, fuel and materials and spare parts, a disorganized transport system and the lack of competent managerial personnel.[66]

Beyond Europe

While most of Europe was struggling to recover from the war and its aftermath in the first half of the 1920s a good part of the rest of the world was enjoying fairly vigorous growth. It is true that most countries, both industrial countries and primary producers, were hit quite badly by the post-war slump, but though its effects were severe its duration was relatively short and by 1922 the upswing had begun. Thus for many countries it was a question not of recovering from the war but of consolidating the gains already made during Europe's indisposition.

The most vigorous and sustained industrial growth occurred in the United States and the White Dominions. The U.S.A. experienced a very sharp burst of expansion from the trough of July 1921, when industrial production rose by over 64 per cent to a peak in June 1923. The boom was led by building and durable goods production, the latter increasing by no less than 140 per cent. Activity fell off in the following year, though durable goods production still remained well above the 1921 trough, but by the middle of 1924 the upswing was resumed.[67] Despite difficulties in

66. On Russia see W. A. Lewis, *Economic Survey 1919–1939* (1949), pp. 29–31; N. Jasny, *Soviet Economists of the Twenties: Names to be Remembered* (1972), pp. 17–26; A. Nove, *An Economic History of the USSR* (1969), pp. 55–68, 86–93; M. Dobb, *Soviet Economic Development since 1917*, revised edition (1968).

67. M. W. Lee, *Macroeconomics Fluctuations, Growth and Stability*, 5th edition (1971), pp. 151–7.

agriculture Canada also experienced a sharp upturn in the latter half of 1921. This was led by a spectacular upsurge in exports which by 1925 were almost double those of 1913, and heavy fixed investment in new sectors, especially non-ferrous metals, car production, electric power and newsprint. These developments set the stage for an even more massive domestic upswing in the later 1920s when the growth of the export sector tailed off.[68] Australia and New Zealand also shared in the boom of the first half of the 1920s. Australian manufacturing output rose faster than in the later 1920s – 6·3 per cent per annum from 1919–20 to 1924–5 as against 4·2 per cent per annum from 1925–6 to 1928–9. As in Canada the shift towards a more industrialized economy, which had begun during the war, continued and was stimulated by rising population and tariff protection (the 1920–21 Greene tariff). The upswing in wool and wheat prices after the post-war collapse in 1921 benefited both Australia and New Zealand.[69] The most spectacular structural shift occurred in South Africa where manufacturing expanded very rapidly both during the war and afterwards. In fact over the whole inter-war period the South African economy was one of the most buoyant in the world, largely due to the massive drive towards industrialization. The decline in the importance of mining, a policy of protection, and the gradual erosion of prejudice against goods made in South Africa contributed to the success of the policy of diversification.[70]

Elsewhere the record was more patchy. India stagnated after the post-war boom, unable to push forward from the promising start made during the war. A severe dose of internal deflation coupled with intense competition from abroad made the prospects of profitable investment in any but the most naturally protected industries appear extremely gloomy in the early 1920s.[71] Not until 1924 was the high level of manufacturing activity achieved

68. R. E. Caves and R. H. Holton, *The Canadian Economy: Prospect and Retrospect* (1959), pp. 99–100; A. E. Safarian, *The Canadian Economy in the Great Depression* (1959), pp. 21, 23–4.

69. C. B. Schedvin, *Australia and the Great Depression* (1970), p. 52; Muriel F. Lloyd Prichard, *An Economic History of New Zealand to 1939* (1970), p. 294; C. Forster, *Industrial Development in Australia in 1920–1930* (1964), pp. 16–17.

70. C. G. W. Schumann, *Structural Changes and Business Cycles in South Africa 1806–1936* (1938), pp. 168, 174.

71. A. K. Bagchi, *Private Investment in India 1900–1939* (1972), p. 65.

in the post-war boom exceeded.[72] Japan's growth slowed down, after the spectacular wartime expansion, under the impact of the government's deflationary policy and the violent earthquake of 1923. Even so it was far from unimpressive.[73]

It is difficult to generalize about Latin America because of the diverse economies of the different republics. The interruption of imports during the war had provided an incentive for industrial expansion and in some cases this was continued after the war. Thus Mexico, Chile and the Argentine all recorded quite significant advances in industrial production in the first half of the 1920s.[74] In Chile a shift towards industrialization was imperative since the increasing use of synthetic nitrates virtually shattered the original basis of that country's development. On the other hand, many countries found difficulty in industrial development once European and American competition reappeared, given the high price and inferior quality of their products. The war-expanded industries of Brazil, for example, suffered a setback, though for a time cotton textiles managed to achieve a considerable advance. But with foreign competition and no assistance from the government, which was more intent on propping up the coffee economy, progress on the industrial front did not proceed very far.[75] By 1924 there were signs that even this limited industrial expansion was coming to an end.

For the most part the Latin American countries remained basically primary producers, often heavily dependent on one or two commodities. The instability to which this gave rise is well known and was particularly marked in the post-war boom and slump which left 'a trail of devastation' throughout the area.[76]

72. Though by the mid 1920s India's manufacturing output was probably one-third higher than pre-war.

73. H. T. Patrick, 'The Economic Muddle of the 1920s', in J. W. Morley (ed.), *Dilemmas of Growth in Prewar Japan* (1971), pp. 213–15.

74. See C. F. Diaz Alejandro, *Essays on the Economic History of the Argentine Republic* (1970), pp. 52–3; Nacional Financiera S.A., *Statistics on the American Economy* (1966, Mexico), p. 89; O. E. Munoz, 'An Essay on the Process of Industrialisation in Chile Since 1914', *Yale Economic Essays*, vol. VIII (1968), pp. 146–7.

75. W. Baer, *Industrialization and Economic Development in Brazil* (1965), pp. 19–20; S. J. Stein, *The Brazilian Cotton Manufacture: Textile Enterprise in an Underdeveloped Area, 1850–1950* (1957), p. 108.

76. D. Joslin, *A Century of Banking in Latin America* (1963), p. 217.

For a time during the 1920s, under the stimulus of U.S. investment and the rising demand from industrial countries for many of their products, Latin American countries enjoyed boom conditions. Raw material producers in particular did very well. Several countries, notably Venezuela, Mexico, Ecuador, Peru and Bolivia, benefited considerably from the motor-car boom which boosted the demand for petroleum and tin. However, once the favourable demand conditions evaporated their economies were subject to severe strain.[77]

Conclusion

There is little doubt that the balance of economic power shifted away from Europe during the period 1913 to 1925. During the protracted phase of European recovery from the aftermath of war, the U.S.A., Japan, the Dominions and a host of smaller countries outside Europe consolidated the gains already made during the war. While Europe struggled to regain her pre-war momentum, output and capacity expanded much faster in these regions and by the mid 1920s they were substantially greater than before the war. For example, in Japan, China, India and Australia alone annual steel production was ten times the amount before the war, while the number of cotton spindles in Japan, China, India and Brazil nearly doubled (10 million to over 18 million) between 1913 and 1925-6. In trade too Europe had lost ground. In the years 1910-14 about one-half of U.S. imports came from Europe, but by 1923 this had been reduced to less than one-third, and Canada and Asia had edged out Europe.[78] During the later 1920s Europe managed a better performance, and probably even gained a little lost ground, but she was never able fully to recover the displacement of economic power suffered in the years 1913 to 1925.

77. See Chapters 9 and 10.
78. A. G. V. Peel, *The Economic Impact of America* (1923), pp. 135-6, 238.

6

The Restoration of Monetary Stability

The problem

Few countries emerged from the war with their monetary and currency systems unscathed. Nearly all currencies, except the dollar, lost their stability and depreciated in value once the tie with gold was broken or the artificial pegging practised in wartime was released. By the end of 1920 most European currencies were below their pre-war par value and the depreciation of some had been rapid indeed. In Russia and parts of central and eastern Europe currencies were worth 50 per cent or less of their original values.[1] The loss in value was not surprising since the war had seriously weakened the productive mechanisms of many economies, it had created balance of payments problems, and, above all, inflationary methods of financing had been widespread.

The restoration of monetary stability was regarded as a matter of some urgency after the war though initially little effort was made in this direction. Large fluctuations in exchange rates had rarely occurred under the pre-war gold standard; their effects on economic activity and trade were viewed with alarm – hence the

---

1. League of Nations, *Currencies after the War: A Survey of Conditions in Various Countries* (1920), p. ix; League of Nations, *Europe's Overseas Needs 1919–1920 and How They Were Met* (1943), p. 42 for a table of values.

desire to return to the orderly monetary system which had prevailed before 1914. Two main ideas dominated the process of monetary reconstruction. First, it was considered highly desirable that each nation should quickly return to a fixed gold parity. This belief resulted in a country-by-country approach to stabilization with little regard to the crucial issue of the viability of the exchange rates selected. Establishing the value of the gold parity was regarded as an act of national sovereignty and the chief concern of central bankers and governments was whether stabilization could be maintained at the chosen rate. Secondly, it was never for a moment questioned that the monetary system should be based on gold. That many nations adopted a variant of the pre-war system, the gold exchange standard, was neither here nor there since most countries regarded it as a first step, or half-way house, to a return to a gold specie standard, or at least a gold bullion standard.[2] Faith in the power of the gold standard was unquestioned. It was the hallmark of a return to 'normalcy'; international imbalances would be readily corrected by the system's 'automatic' adjustment processes, though it was recognized that there might be temporary strains and difficulties in the transitional period.

This chapter is concerned primarily with currency stabilization and the problems associated with it rather than with the operation of the gold standard itself. The working of the revised standard and its inherent weaknesses are the subject of the next chapter.

The progress of stabilization

The stabilization of currencies proved a long-drawn-out affair which lasted most of the decade. No systematic plan was drawn up though the United States, which had little difficulty in readopting the full gold standard in 1919, served as a rough benchmark for the realignment of all other currencies. Each country stabilized and returned to the gold standard as soon as conditions were deemed suitable. Much depended on how quickly countries got their financial affairs under control. Latvia, without foreign aid, put a definite stop to inflation in the summer of 1921, and thereby gained the distinction of being one of the first countries to

2. R. H. Meyer, *Bankers' Diplomacy: Monetary Stabilization in the Twenties* (1970), pp. 6–7.

stabilize her currency. She was soon followed by Albania and Lithuania, where new national currencies were introduced to replace foreign ones, while Austria was the first of the hyper-inflationary countries to bring in a new monetary unit. In 1923 and 1924 several countries effected stabilization including Switzerland, Sweden and the Netherlands, all of which returned to pre-war parity, while in contrast Germany and Hungary were forced to introduce new currency units after bouts of hyper-inflation. Britain's return to gold in April 1925 provided the signal for the British dominions and several other countries to stabilize. By early 1926 stable exchanges existed in thirty-nine countries, seventeen in Europe, two in North America, twelve in Central and South America, two each in Africa and Asia and four in Oceania. During the next two years or so the process was more or less completed. Countries such as Estonia, Bulgaria and Denmark which had already stabilized on a *de facto* basis moved to a *de jure* standard. Several countries still had to carry out *de facto* stabilizations before returning to the gold standard. These included Italy, Poland, Belgium, France, Greece, Brazil, Argentina, Ecuador, Paraguay, Norway and Peru, all of which virtually accomplished both stages by the end of 1928. The new international gold standard was by then more or less complete. In Europe only Spain, Portugal and Romania and in Asia, Japan, had still to complete the task, while the final steps towards *de jure* stabilization still remained in the case of Czechoslovakia, Brazil, Uruguay and Peru.[3] Apart from the gold standard countries several others with stable exchange rates continued to adhere to a silver standard. These included China, Persia, Abyssinia and several other eastern countries.

The manner in which stabilization was carried out and the characteristics of the new standard varied considerably from country to country. At one extreme a select band of countries managed to regain their pre-war parities: these were the U.K. and the Dominions, Switzerland, the Netherlands, Denmark, Sweden, Norway and Japan, the last of which finally returned to gold in the midst of depression. At the other extreme five countries,

3. W. A. Brown, Jnr, *The International Gold Standard Reinterpreted, 1914–1934*, vol. I (1940), pp. 395–402. Spain never managed to stabilize her currency while Portugal completed the process only in June 1931 when the gold standard regime was on the point of disintegration.

Austria, Hungary, Poland, Germany and Russia, were forced to introduce new monetary units[4] since violent bouts of inflation had wrecked their currencies completely. The majority of countries fell between these two extremes in that they stabilized after devaluation. The levels at which stabilization was effected varied considerably, but in general devaluations were greatest in the central and east European countries. The following list provides a representative sample of countries with the figures in brackets showing the percentage dollar value of these currencies as fixed at the date of stabilization: Estonia (1·1), Romania (3·7), Bulgaria (3·7), Portugal (4·6), Greece (6·7), Yugoslavia (9·1), Finland (12·5), Belgium (14·3), Czechoslovakia (14·3), France (20·0), and Italy (25·0).[5]

External financial assistance played some part in assisting stabilization though only in a few cases was it of crucial importance. Only in five European countries (Austria, Belgium, Danzig, Hungary and Poland) was *de facto* stabilization effected with the aid of specific loans, credits obtained in anticipation of such loans, or reconstruction schemes (through the League's auspices) holding forth the promise of foreign loans or credits, though it is doubtful if these were really needed in the case of Belgium and Poland. Seven other countries (Denmark, Italy, Norway, Greece, Portugal, Switzerland and the U.K.) arranged temporary forms of credit though these were not always utilized for this purpose. On the other hand, twelve countries (Bulgaria, Czechoslovakia, Estonia, Finland, Germany, Latvia, Romania, Yugoslavia, Lithuania, France, Sweden and the Netherlands) managed their preliminary stabilizations without any loans or specific credit arrangements. However, for the final stabilization most of them either arranged for temporary credits as a stand-by or effected their currency reforms with the aid of foreign loans.

The League of Nations' role in assisting financial reconstruction and currency reform was very limited and haphazard. The International Financial Conference at Brussels in 1920 stressed the need for a return to financial orthodoxy but offered little assistance to countries already in serious financial difficulties as a

4. Albania, Lithuania and Danzig also introduced new national currencies to replace foreign currencies.
5. League of Nations, *The Course and Control of Inflation: A Review of Monetary Experience in Europe after World War I* (1946), pp. 92–3.

result of inflation. Apart from food relief, Europe was left to fend very much for itself after the Armistice. Only when economies were on the point of disintegration and the damage had been done did the League step in with a reconstruction scheme, and even then its assistance was not usually crucial to effecting the initial stabilization. This was true of Austria (1922), Hungary (1924), Germany (1924), Poland (1927), and Estonia (1927), all of which were aided by the League. The League's efforts usually involved some measure of control over the financial affairs of the countries in question, which they were obviously unwilling to accept until things really became desperate.[6] For this reason countries were reluctant to turn to the League for help and most of the credits and loans for stabilizing purposes were provided by the major central banks.

Despite its fairly extensive nature financial aid was probably not of crucial importance in ensuring the technical success of exchange stabilization taken as a whole. Foreign loans could act as an important confidence-booster where faith in the economy was rapidly dwindling, they could check the motives for capital flight and hence further speculation, and they could also meet the real capital needs of the countries in question. On the other hand, some of the loans or credits were too small or too late to serve a really useful purpose, while many were never utilized. None of the eleven loans generally known as stabilization loans was raised for that purpose alone and hence it is difficult to determine exactly what proportion of the funds was used specifically for currency stabilization. In any case, loans and credits from abroad were often not sufficient in themselves to stabilize a country's exchanges. The German case provides a good example. Stability of the exchange ultimately depended upon domestic reform and so long as the inflation was allowed to continue no amount of foreign assistance would have saved the mark from its headlong depreciation. But when inflation had been checked and preliminary stabilization effected then it was possible for a foreign loan to assist the final reform. Even when the basic conditions for exchange stability had been met external assistance was rarely

6. See League of Nations, *Principles and Methods of Financial Reconstruction Work Undertaken under the Auspices of the League of Nations* (1930), and League of Nations, *Reconstruction Schemes in the Interwar Period* (1945).

indispensable though in some cases, for example Austria and Hungary, it may have had a favourable psychological impact. The fact remains however that many countries never really needed foreign loans and those that had recourse to them in one form or another 'seem to have done so largely for the reason that they had become almost a fashion in the 'twenties'.[7] A fashion which had unfortunate consequences, since, according to Meyer, credit and loan negotiations among central banks gave rise to friction and divisions of opinion which served in part to destroy international monetary and financial cooperation.[8]

The format of the gold standard varied considerably. In few countries was the pre-war monetary organization fully restored in its original form. The full gold standard, or specie standard, in which gold coins circulate internally and all other money is readily convertible into gold, was abandoned almost everywhere with the odd exceptions of the United States, Sweden, the Netherlands and a few Latin American countries. Most countries adopted a watered-down version of the full standard with restrictions on the convertibility of non-commodity money into gold and on the export of gold. In the few countries which went onto the gold bullion standard (e.g. Britain, Denmark, Norway) notes could not readily be converted into gold on demand except for export purposes and then only at a fixed price and in large minimum amounts. The majority of countries opted for the gold exchange standard whereby a country's monetary authority tied its currency to gold indirectly by dealing on the foreign exchange market to maintain a fixed exchange rate with a foreign currency on either a gold coin or gold bullion standard. In other words, the central bank had the obligation to maintain the value of the national currency at par with other gold currency countries by buying and selling foreign exchange at the gold parity. By the end of the 1920s thirty or so countries had adopted the gold exchange standard in one form or another; in each case legal provision was made for central banks to hold foreign exchange reserves in some form and amount against notes or notes and deposits. Only a select band of countries (including the U.S.A., U.K., Canada, Australia, New Zealand, South Africa, the Netherlands, Sweden, Norway and Switzerland) had no legal provisions permitting the inclusion of

7. League of Nations, *The Course and Control of Inflation*, p. 131.
8. Meyer, *Bankers' Diplomacy*, p. 3.

anything except gold in the reserves of central banks, though most of these were in fact substantial holders of foreign exchange.[9]

Despite the great diversity of stabilization techniques and standards it is possible to group countries into certain categories with similar characteristics. There were first of all the great hyperinflationary countries where new currency units were introduced because the previous monetary units became worthless. Secondly, a broad band of countries suffered 'minor' inflations and stabilized at a rate considerably below the pre-war parity. And thirdly, several countries returned to parity after severe deflations. Some of the salient features of each of these may be considered in turn.

The inflationary potential in Europe

Five countries suffered violent inflations in the 1920s and eventually stabilized with new currency units. But most of Europe experienced some inflation at this time which suggests there were common forces at work. Each inflation had its own particular set of characteristics but there were causal factors common to most of them. These may be considered under several headings – the fiscal needs of governments, monetary policies, balance of payment problems, and political and administrative factors – though they were all closely interrelated.

The methods of financing the war had started the inflationary process and the fiscal demands of governments after 1918 ensured that it would continue. The burden of reconstruction was heavy in many parts of Europe and this was undoubtedly the main factor making for large budgetary deficits. But government expenditures were also boosted by other factors. In many countries military outlays continued at a high level after 1918 since sporadic hostilities continued over a wide area of Europe. Poland and Russia did not conclude a peace treaty until March 1921 while Greece and Turkey remained at war until 1923. Even after hostilities had ceased military spending remained high in all the former belligerent countries, apart from Germany and Austria.

9. Brown, *The International Gold Standard Reinterpreted, 1914–1934*, vol. II, p. 732; D. T. Jack, *The Restoration of European Currencies* (1927), pp. 43–4; M. Palyi, *The Twilight of Gold, 1914–1936: Myths and Realities* (1972), pp. 116–17.

France's military expenditure in 1920 was not much less than that on reconstruction; in Poland and Hungary military spending in the early 1920s accounted for one-third of government spending and an even larger proportion of the budgetary deficits. Reparations took the place of military spending in Germany and accounted for one-half the government's deficit in the early 1920s, and when payments tailed off in 1922–3 the budget was strained by financing passive resistance in the Ruhr. Public expenditures in Austria and Hungary were swollen out of all proportion to the resources of the new republics by the maintenance of the large administrative personnel left over from the Austro-Hungarian Empire. Other factors included the settlement of refugees in Greece and Bulgaria and agrarian reforms in eastern Europe, while most countries experienced increased outlays on social welfare including unemployment relief.

These pressures came at a time when savings were low, taxation inadequate and government finances were already in a bad state. Most countries had large public debts and massive budgetary deficits, while in many the tax system was quite inefficient and inadequate for the task in hand. The case of Romania was by no means untypical. Here the League of Nations found that their technical advisers 'were powerless to repress the inefficient accountancy, the over-estimation of revenue, the slowness with which arrears of taxes were collected, and even the wholesale corruption. . . .'[10]

In the absence of large-scale foreign assistance the fiscal requirements for reconstruction and other things could only be carried out by restricting consumption, but this proved difficult for two reasons: first because consumption levels were already low in many cases and to impose further direct sacrifices after the war-time austerity would have caused serious social discontent, and secondly because government policies and administrative systems were not geared to the task. The easiest way out was inflationary spending which imposed sacrifices in a roundabout way. As a form of enforced taxation it was relatively easy to administer and held attractions for governments which were weak, inexperienced and disorganized. Admittedly it was an unsuitable

10. Royal Institute of International Affairs, *The Balkan States. I. Economic: A Review of the Economic and Financial Development of Albania, Bulgaria, Greece, Roumania and Yugoslavia since 1919* (1936), p. 51.

and haphazard method of reconstruction but it achieved a measure of success initially due to the peculiar circumstances. It depended on the fact that the adjustment of wage rates lagged behind commodity prices, and as long as the rise in prices was not accompanied by a comparable increase in many incomes and consumers' expenditure, the consequent restriction of consumption released productive resources for reconstruction equipment; that people were willing to save part of their incomes; and that the majority of those operating in the foreign exchange markets believed exchange depreciation to be temporary and up to a point were willing to hold depreciated currencies. The whole process was ultimately dependent on one factor, namely ignorance about inflation and what it implied, since Europe had not experienced inflation for more than a century. Over Europe as a whole this first phase of relatively moderate inflation lasted surprisingly long and did make an effective contribution to the resources needed for reconstruction.

But in several cases it moved into runaway hyperinflation. The process by which hyperinflation develops is complex and depends partly on the psychological reaction of the people. Once people realize what is happening they take steps to protect themselves and by so doing complicate the fiscal process and throw the monetary mechanism into disorder. First, the lag between money incomes and prices is eliminated by indexing wages and salaries; eventually wages tend to anticipate price changes so that real wages may rise in the final stages of hyperinflation. Secondly, the saving propensity drops rapidly as money loses value and ultimately dis-saving takes place which forces up the velocity of circulation of money. Finally, the initial capital inflow gives way to capital flight as the market loses confidence and anticipates further currency depreciation, and this in turn speeds up the exchange depreciation and the rise in prices. At the same time the fiscal needs of the government are in jeopardy, and the reaction to this makes things worse. The inflation levy tends to plug up certain obvious sources of reconstruction finance (savings and taxation) and becomes less effective in itself, as people speed up the rate at which they spend their incomes and the velocity of money increases. At this stage inflation loses its capital-forming power and the whole process becomes cumulative. A falling propensity to save necessitates greater resort to inflationary financing, while tax yields in real terms fall because of the inevitable lag in collection. In turn the fall in the real value of tax receipts increases budgetary deficits and aggravates the inflationary conditions. This process played an important part in all cases of hyperinflation in the early 1920s. In Germany in 1923 the depreciation of tax revenues reached a point at which taxes cost more to collect than they brought in, so that the budgetary deficit and rate of inflation would have been less had the ordinary machinery of taxation been discarded and the government relied on inflation alone.

It can be argued that hyperinflation could never have occurred but for the continued increase in money supply and the increased velocity of circulation once the upward price movement became persistent. In Germany the velocity of circulation was about ten times greater than normal. But here as elsewhere domestic monetary policy was probably the crucial factor in the final stages, and the process could have been checked at any time had the authorities tapered off the issue of new money, which they finally did. The money supply was pumped up so vigorously because printing money provided the government with real resources in a convenient way and secondly, the effectiveness of the method declined over time as ever larger issues were required. The issue of money provided the government with a means of revenue by a special kind of tax on cash balances held by people, and the rate of tax was the depreciation of the real value of money which was equal to the rise in prices. Not until the tax rates exploded (that is prices) and caused disruption did the authorities substitute a traditional tax programme for a policy of printing money.[11]

There is still some debate however as to the causes of inflation between the monetary school and those that argue for a balance-of-payments theory. The debate has been mostly centred on the German experience though it is relevant to the experience of other countries.[12] The monetarists place the main emphasis on changes in the money supply and see the rise in wages and depreciation of the exchanges as a reflection of the internally-generated inflation. For those who adhere to a balance-of-payments theory of inflation

11. See the very informative analysis of hyperinflations by P. Cagan, 'The Monetary Dynamics of Hyperinflation', in M. Friedman (ed.), *Studies in the Quantity Theory of Money* (1956), pp. 77–8.

12. W. Fischer, *Deutsche Wirtschaftspolitik 1918–1945* (1968), pp. 23–4.

the key is the external deficit which depresses the exchange rate, raises import and domestic prices which in turn increases the budget deficits and calls forth an increase in the note issue.[13] However, such a fine distinction is misleading since both monetary and exchange factors had a part to play. While it is probably true that runaway inflation was ultimately a product of the money supply policy it would be wrong to ignore the influences stemming from the external account. At the end of the war most European countries were short of goods and the intense need for imports automatically put pressure on the exchanges. As the exchange rate depreciated import prices rose and so added to the internal inflation. But at the same time capital imports flowed in from abroad in response to the depreciation, while the fall in the exchange made exports more attractive. In theory these forces should have adjusted the balance of payments and checked inflation. In fact the normal equilibrating forces through exchange rate adjustment were scarcely operative at this time because of the inelastic demand for imports and the inelastic supply in the export sectors, more especially in eastern Europe. Capital imports therefore only provided a temporary stage of equilibrium, and the exchange depreciation had to be repeated to attract further foreign capital to pay for urgent imports. This was especially the case in primary producing countries (e.g. Bulgaria, Poland, Brazil, Chile, Argentina) where the sharp fall in export prices after 1920 led to extreme difficulties. As the depreciation continued the stimulus to capital imports weakened since the expectation of a return to pre-war parities became ever more remote.[14] Once exchange depreciation accelerated and there was no prospect of a return to 'normal',

13. K. Laursen and J. Pedersen, *The German Inflation 1918–1923* (1964), pp. 36–41, argue the case for Germany but adhere to the quantity theory for France. F. D. Graham, *Exchange, Prices, and Production in Hyperinflation Germany, 1920–1923* (1930), p. 76, is somewhat equivocal on this issue and notes that in the last stages of inflation there was little pressure on the exchange rates since all reparation payments had been suspended.

14. The fact that such expectations were held seems difficult to believe now. As the League of Nations noted in one of its reports: 'In the light of subsequent experience, it may seem fantastic that such expectations should have been so widely entertained. They were a product of pre-war psychology, a product of the long period of comparative exchange stability prior to 1914.' League of Nations, *The Course and Control of Inflation: A Review of Monetary Experience in Europe after World War I* (1946), p. 47.

foreign capital was rapidly withdrawn and domestic funds sought refuge in more stable currencies. This of course simply accelerated the process. Frequently the fall in the exchange rate became an important factor in the mechanism of inflation, driving up the cost of living, putting pressure on wages which in turn raised the demand for currency and credit on the part of government and business. Moreover, the exchange depreciation resulting from capital flights aggravated the inflationary problem both through its effects on the balance of payments and more directly since in the later stages of inflation wage rates and other domestic costs tended to be fixed in direct relationship with foreign exchange quotations.

In the final analysis it can be argued that differences in inflation records in various countries were the consequence of political and administrative factors. Political motives for inflation may have been important in some cases. For example, the Russian inflation was officially welcomed for a time as a means of destroying the capitalist economy, while the German inflation may have been partly motivated to prove that the country could not pay reparations.[15] It is also significant that the governments and administrations of all the countries which experienced hyperinflation were weak and incapable of dealing with the enormous problems confronting them. The Austrian currency was adversely affected from the start by doubts as to the viability of the new state, while the German and Polish administrations left much to be desired. Political instability and administrative incompetence were hardly conducive to sound financial policies. In Poland the administration was ill-prepared to cope with reconstruction. Soon after the end of the war, experienced alien officials left the

15. This is a debatable point but not one entirely without foundation. How, for example, does one explain the Reichsbank's reluctance to use its substantial gold reserves to support the exchange? In January 1923 these were sufficient to redeem the total paper circulation at existing exchange rates more than five times, and had the government made a determined effort at an early stage to restrain the rise in prices by withdrawing money from circulation through the sale of gold in support of the exchange rate the problem might have been solved. Actually the Reichsbank did make some effort to maintain the exchange in the first quarter of 1923 but by this time it was too late. The policy of financing passive resistance in the Ruhr opened the floodgates to domestic currency circulation and the use of all the central bank's gold could not have prevented collapse.

country and the new state was left without any proper civil administration. Apart from creating a competent staff there was the problem of unifying the three different tax systems in the three sectors formerly under foreign control, added to which the Polish population regarded tax collectors with some distaste. Similarly, political factors in Germany made resistance to inflation difficult. A new and inexperienced socialist government fought a losing battle to establish its authority against strong opposition from conservative and business classes. The State was therefore thwarted in its attempt to pass tax reforms which would have provided an adequate basis of taxation. As a result the government came increasingly under the influence of business interests who initially were the chief beneficiaries of inflation. And the head of the government which carried on the inflationary financing of Ruhr industrialists in 1923 was a man of big business![16]

The experience of countries with equally great problems but which managed to tackle inflation at an early stage are illustrative. Latvia, without a currency of her own and faced with a larger relative reconstruction than any other country, put a stop to inflation in the summer of 1921 and became one of the first to stabilize her currency. What is more she did this without external assistance. A rigorous fiscal policy was enforced from the beginning of the new republic and this enabled her to check incipient hyperinflation in the first months of 1921. In May 1921 legal provision was made for the collection of all taxes in terms of a new unit of currency, the *lat*, equivalent to one gold franc.[17] Equally rigorous fiscal measures were imposed in Czechoslovakia, and after a brief inflationary flurry in the winter of 1919–20 the State's finances were brought under control. Yet Austria, which suffered little destruction and had no reparations to pay, experienced one of the most violent bouts of inflation. The experience of Latvia and Czechoslovakia and that of other countries suggests that there was nothing inherently impossible in taking decisive

16. It is sometimes argued that the weakness of the defence against inflation can be attributed to the little importance attached to the quantity theory of money by German economists. They refused to believe in the link between money and prices and attributed the main cause to the balance of payments. This argument is not very convincing, and in any case the government never made any real attempt to control inflation in any direction.

17. This was the first case of 'tax valorization' in the history of post-war inflation.

fiscal and monetary measures as a prerequisite to currency stabilization. The moral of this is that strong and competent administrations with the will to succeed had no reason to let inflation go unchecked. Unfortunately, it was these features which were notably absent in many countries in the early 1920s.

Hyperinflation and its consequences

It would serve no useful purpose to recount in detail the history of hyperinflation in the five countries which experienced it.[18] The pattern of events was broadly the same even if the details differ in various respects. The end product was the same: the currencies became worthless and had to be replaced. At the end of the day prices had risen 14,000 times in Austria, 23,000 times in Hungary, 2·5 million in Poland, 4,000 million in Russia and 1 million million in Germany, against the pre-war base.

Apart from the Russian where some rather special factors were operative, the forces behind each inflation were very similar. The war had left all countries in a weak state, with large debts, balance of payments problems and inadequate taxation levels. Large fiscal requirements for reconstruction and other purposes were imposed on governments too weak to raise the finance through the normal channels and the only option left was inflation through the printing press. In the final stage inflation became solely a response to domestic monetary forces and even the printers of bank notes could not cope with the demand for money required to buy goods at vastly inflated prices. In Germany 'Two thousand printing presses turned out bank notes day and night and the economy drowned in a flood of paper money.'[19]

18. The German saga has been recounted many times. Apart from the sources already cited see C. Bresciani-Turroni, *The Economics of Inflation* (1937); F. K. Ringer (ed.), *The German Inflation of 1923* (1969); J. Pedersen, 'A Chapter of the History of Monetary Theory and Policy', in G. Bombach (ed.), *Stabile Preise in wachsender Wirtschaft: Das Inflationsproblem* (1960, Tübingen). There is a useful summary of hyperinflation experiences in W. A. Lewis, *Economic Survey 1919–1939* (1949), pp. 22–31. For Austria see J. van Walré de Bordes, *The Austrian Crown* (1924); for Hungary see I. T. Berend and G. Ranki, *Hungary: A Century of Economic Development* (1974) and *Economic Development in East-Central Europe in the 19th and 20th Centuries* (1974).

19. R. Knauerhase, *An Introduction to National Socialism, 1920 to 1939* (1972), p. 26.

The manner in which these countries eventually stabilized their currencies provides interesting contrasts in methodology. Resolutions of the Brussels Conference in September 1920 had suggested that the way to currency stabilization was through budgetary equilibrium, but at that time things were much less chaotic than they later became. Once hyperinflation had set in no such order of events was possible since it was difficult to balance fiscal accounts when the currency was falling rapidly in value and becoming unserviceable as a unit of account for the assessment and collection of taxes. In fact however two possible options remained open: either the currency could be stabilized by means other than fiscal policy so as to achieve a monetary unit as the basis of an effective fiscal policy; or, following the Latvian example, the national currency could be abandoned for fiscal accounting purposes and taxation collected in terms of gold or some foreign currency.

The first of these courses was adopted by Austria and Hungary, both of which secured the assistance of the League of Nations. Though attempts were made to increase taxes there was no systematic effort to adjust them to the depreciation of the currency through tax 'valorization' schemes. Failing this, currency stabilization became a prerequisite to fiscal reform: 'stabilization of the currency, while simultaneous with a plan for budget reform, preceded its accomplishment'.[20] The initial stabilization of the currencies was achieved by a return of confidence as a result of the League of Nations' financial reconstruction schemes. The League arranged international loans for Austria in 1922 and Hungary in 1924[21] and the League's staff supervised their finances until 1926. Once confidence in the new currencies was secured fiscal policy rapidly became effective and budgetary equilibrium was achieved within a very short space of time.[22]

The alternative solution was adopted by Germany and Poland. In Germany two important measures preceded the stabilization of the mark in November 1923. First the 'passive resistance'

20. League of Nations, *The Course and Control of Inflation: A Review of Monetary Experience in Europe after World War I* (1946), p. 23.

21. The loans were more important in evoking confidence than for purposes of stabilization itself since the Austrian loan was not issued until 1923.

22. See League of Nations, *The Financial Reconstruction of Hungary* (1926) and *The Financial Reconstruction of Austria* (1926).

expenditure in the Ruhr was stopped in September and taxes were assessed in terms of gold and collected in national currency at the rate of the day. Almost simultaneously with these preparations for restoring budgetary equilibrium it was announced that a new currency, the *Rentenmark*, would be introduced to replace the now valueless currency in existence. The new mark, valued at 1 million million old marks, was introduced on 15 November; its success was partly ensured by two factors. First it was backed by the security of an internal loan on the basis of real assets (land and buildings) and secondly, its issue was to be strictly limited to 2,400 million marks. In the final analysis much depended on public confidence. Once there appeared to be a reasonable prospect that the *Rentenmark* would retain its value the public's demand for cash recovered quickly.[23] But there were anxious moments: the new currency had no gold backing and for many months its existence was precarious. Had the government not set about completing its fiscal reforms immediately after stabilization it is doubtful if the new currency would have lasted long. Moreover, it was not until 1924, when Germany secured an international loan (the Dawes loan), that the currency was converted to a more solid base (a gold monetary standard). Angell suggests that without this Germany might well have experienced another bout of inflation.[24]

Poland's efforts at stabilization were more protracted. Up to 1921 little was done to halt inflation since the executive machinery was too weak to impose effective fiscal control, political administrations were short-lived and the country was still engaged in border hostilities.[25] Then several abortive attempts were made to stabilize by fiscal reform. The first two were made between 1921 and 1923, both of which failed after temporary success, largely because the fiscal effort was relaxed too soon. Another

23. The more so in that the public had economized in the use of depreciated mark currency to such an extent as to cause serious inconvenience in everyday transactions. The promise of stability for the new currency was sufficient to create a demand for it which ensured its value.

24. J. W. Angell, *The Recovery of Germany* (1929), p. 26. In August 1924 the new currency was named the Reichsmark.

25. F. Zweig, *Poland between World Wars* (1944), p. 35. The Polish and Austrian monetary problems are well covered in M. A. Heilperin, *La Problème monétaire d' après-guerre et sa solution en Pologne, en Autriche et en Tchécoslovaquie* (1931).

attempt was not made until 1924 by which time Poland was in the throes of hyperinflation. In that year stringent fiscal measures were introduced, including valorization of taxes on a gold basis, which brought hyperinflation under control and stabilized the exchange value of the currency.[26] The success was short-lived, however, partly because the fiscal measures were again relaxed too early and partly because the parliamentary regime was too weak to carry through the drastic measures proper financial reform required.[27] After another bout of inflation the final attempt was made in 1926–7 when a new unit of currency was introduced. This time firm financial measures to bring about budgetary equilibrium and monetary order, together with an international loan arranged by the League, ensured its success.

The consequences of hyperinflation were widespread and varied and it is therefore not easy to provide a short and concise statement. It is an area which would benefit considerably from a rigorous counterfactual analysis. One's immediate reaction is to say that it was a bad thing for all concerned and to conclude that countries made a net loss on the deal. Yet several writers have argued the opposite, at least for the case of Germany, and concluded that there was in fact a net gain.[28] Their arguments are worth considering in a little more detail.

Their case rests substantially on a comparison with countries which carried out restrictive credit and fiscal policies. Had Germany adopted that course after 1920 there would have been serious unemployment which, given the poverty of the German

26. There is some doubt as to what external financial assistance Poland received in 1924. The League suggests that she received practically no financial help from abroad, but Bandera reckons a stabilization loan under League auspices was floated in that year. See League of Nations, *The Course and Control of Inflation: A Review of Monetary Experience in Europe after World War I* (1946), pp. 24–7 and V. N. Bandera, *Foreign Capital as an Instrument of National Economic Policy: A Study Based on the Experience of East European Countries between the World Wars* (1964), pp. 24–5.

27. Zweig, *Poland between World Wars*, pp. 40–46. There were other factors responsible as well including a deterioration of the trade balance, withdrawal of foreign credits and a tariff war with Germany.

28. Graham, *Exchange, Prices, and Production in Hyperinflation Germany, 1920–1923*, pp. 320–24, and Laursen and Pedersen, *The German Inflation 1918–1923*, especially pp. 123–6. For a recent review see P. Czada, 'Ursachen und Folgen der grossen Inflation', in H. Winkel (ed.), *Finanz- und wirtschaftspolitische Fragen der Zwischenkriegszeit* (1973 Berlin).

population and its revolutionary mood, would probably have led to political and social upheavels. As it was the results in terms of welfare were favourable in comparison with those countries which followed an anti-inflation line. A high level of employment was maintained, industrial production and real income were higher than under any alternative system proposed at the time (and its distribution was probably more egalitarian), capital accumulation was encouraged, probably more so than under a full employment non-inflationary state, and less was paid on reparations. Laursen and Pedersen do point out, however, that conditions could have been better without inflation if economic management had been able to find policies which would ensure full employment without inflation. In the absence of these it was better to have inflation rather than sacrifice employment opportunities.

Their case appears to rest on very tenuous grounds. Even leaving aside the obvious adverse effects for the moment it is difficult to be convinced by the points they claim in their favour. Though Germany gained initially from inflation, in so far as she did not suffer a contraction crisis after 1920, she made up for this in 1923 when income and production were checked sharply. By the end of 1923 the real income of Germany was barely one-half that of 1913; the same was true of industrial production which was even below the level of 1920. In fact throughout the years 1920–23 income and production levels remained well below pre-war, while exports were barely one-half their pre-war volume.[29] This dismal record cannot be matched by any of the countries which carried out a deflationary policy! One can scarcely argue that the distribution of income improved or was even optimal. The working classes tended to suffer from the lag in the adjustment of wage rates; real wages fell continuously from 1919 to 1923 by which time they were barely two-thirds those of 1913, which for many meant poverty and even starvation.[30] On the other hand, many businessmen made high profits since costs lagged behind selling prices, and debtors and speculators gained at the expense of

29. OEEC, *Industrial Statistics, 1900–1959* (1960), p. 9; Angell, *The Recovery of Germany*, pp. 33–45; H. Mendershausen, *Two Postwar Recoveries of the German Economy* (1955), Chapter 1.

30. See G. Bry, *Wages in Germany 1871–1945* (1960), p. 230. Data for skilled workers. At times real wages during the inflationary period fell to 50 per cent of the pre-war level.

creditors. Debt was wiped out by inflation since currency depreciation not only allowed debtors to meet their interest payments but
left them with a large net profit. Most middle-class savings were
destroyed since they were invested in fixed interest securities.

The feverish industrial activity of this period which has been so
much acclaimed was more apparent than real. Output rose but
from a very low base; it still remained much below pre-war,
while productivity declined. Exchange depreciation protected
Germany from foreign competition and the lag in wages reduced
the incentive to mechanize so that part of the gain in employment
was at the expense of efficiency. True there was much investment
since, with high profits and abundant credit at trifling costs, many
industrialists rapidly expanded their plant and equipment. Between
20 and 25 per cent of the capital equipment of German industry
was brought into existence during the inflation period. This more
than made good the war losses in absolute terms but qualitatively
it is another matter. While some of this expansion in capacity
was beneficial much of it was badly designed and hastily installed.
It resulted in mushroom concerns and enormous unwieldy trusts,
some of which later collapsed. The most spectacular was the famous
(infamous?) Stinnes combine which was built up on the basis of
huge debts and disintegrated once the mark was stabilized.[31]
Investment resources were hardly optimally allocated in this
period. Indeed the whole direction of investment was deformed
and distorted; most of it was unrelated to needs and made a limited
contribution to the subsequent recovery of the German economy.
Much of the plant laid down in this period was scrapped later.[32]

It is difficult to believe that the balance sheet of hyperinflation,
either in Germany or elsewhere, was anything but adverse, or that
it could have been much worse under deflation. The sacrifices
made for a temporary boost to employment were far too high.[33]

31. C. R. S. Harris, *Germany's Foreign Indebtedness* (1935), pp. 2–3.

32. Austria too experienced a large expansion of capacity in 1919–23 but
most of it proved excessive since in 1924–6 output was only about two-thirds
capacity. L. Pasvolsky, *Economic Nationalism and the Danubian States* (1928),
pp. 159–60; W. Layton and C. Rist, *The Economic Situation of Austria* (1925),
p. 15.

33. 'The inflation was something that no German, no matter how non-
political, could escape and even those who did well out of it . . . were not
disposed to advocate it publicly as a desirable system.' C. Cross, *Adolf Hitler*
(1973), pp. 79–80.

It is true that unemployment was low in 1921 and 1922 and production rising (but from a very low base) at a time when the
deflating countries were suffering contraction. But Germany got
her share in 1923 and 1924. Unemployment among trade union
members in 1923 as a whole averaged 9·6 per cent, and it was
over 20 per cent in the last three months, while in 1924, in the
aftermath of stabilization, unemployment was very high indeed.[34]
Industrial production collapsed in 1923 and took until 1927 to get
back to the pre-war level, while real wages and per capita consumption of various basic commodities were much lower throughout the years of inflation than before the war.[35] 'All in all,' states
Bry, 'it can be said that both the index numbers of industrial
production and the scattered data on per capita consumption
tend to corroborate the broad findings on real wages during
inflation. These levels were substantially below, and during the
last phases of the crisis pitifully below, the real wages that prevailed
before the outbreak of World War I.'[36]

The long-term repercussions of the inflationary episode should
also be borne in mind. Five years of turmoil, poverty, starvation
and tension – since this is what it meant for the ordinary German –
were hardly likely to add to the health and strength of the population. In fact for a generation or more the Germans lived under the
spectre of inflation and their reactions to the depression of 1929–32
were conditioned by this disastrous episode.[37] It took the economy
two years or more to recover from the shock of 1923[38] but the
after-effects were felt for much longer. Though fixed debts had
been cleared many firms found themselves short of working
capital since most liquid capital and savings had been destroyed

34. Bry, *Wages in Germany 1871–1945*, p. 230; K. Wiggs, *Unemployment in
Germany since the War* (1933), p. 210. German's average level of unemploy-
ment for the whole decade was no better than that of other countries. See
E. Lundberg, *Instability and Economic Growth* (1968), p. 32.

35. Real wages did not regain the pre-war level until 1928.

36. Bry, *Wages in Germany 1871–1945*, p. 233.

37. Indeed Laursen and Pedersen, *The German Inflation 1918–1923*, p. 11,
note that the German inflation served as an obstacle to expansionary policies
all over the world in the 1929–32 downturn. For some of the wider social consequences see the selection of essays in Ringer, *The German Inflation of 1923*.

38. Schmidt reckons that the German economy recovered very quickly after
stabilization and that in 1924 real national income was almost as great as in
1913. Other sources and indicators suggest otherwise however. C. T. Schmidt,
German Business Cycles 1924–1933 (1934), p. 73.

in the inflation. As a result the propensity to save was low after 1923, capital was short and interest rates high so that Germany was forced to borrow heavily abroad in the later 1920s.[39] The instability arising from this borrowing is well known and is the subject for comment elsewhere.[40] Finally, depreciation of currencies in Germany and elsewhere provided a very effective customs barrier behind which many inefficient plants were created, and after stabilisation they were kept in being by protection.[41]

Some minor inflations

The term 'minor inflation' is perhaps a misnomer since even by today's standards they were anything but that. But against the countries just discussed which performed in grand style, most other countries experienced relatively moderate inflation. Nevertheless, even in the west European countries the pace of inflation was sufficient to involve quite a considerable devaluation in currencies upon stabilization.

The French currency provides an interesting case study. For much of the 1920s the struggle to save the franc from hyperinflation occupied the attention of the authorities. Apart from a short deflationary period in 1921–2 the franc was continually under pressure until it was stabilized late in 1926.

The French depreciation cannot be attributed to any one particular cause. During the war and immediately thereafter the unsatisfactory system of public finance led to a highly inflationary situation since the government was forced to borrow heavily from the banks and public, and this in turn was accompanied by a large increase in paper currency. Kemp has described France's method of war financing as 'a model of ineptitude',[42] though it was by no

39. Harris suggests, with some justification, that it was inflation rather than reparations which was the chief cause of Germany's subsequent growth in foreign indebtedness. Harris, *Germany's Foreign Indebtedness*, p. 3.

40. See Chapter 10.

41. P. Einzig, *World Finance since 1914* (1935), p. 77. Einzig feels that economic nationalism was to a large extent the outgrowth of the post-war currency chaos.

42. T. Kemp, 'The French Economy under the Franc Poincaré', *Economic History Review*, vol. xxiv (February 1971), p. 83. See G. Jèze, 'The Economic and Financial Position of France in 1920', *Quarterly Journal of Economics*, vol. xxxv (February 1921), which is biased and nationalistic in emphasis.

means the only country which practised unsound finance in this period. After the war public spending continued at a very high level since the government paid liberal compensation to war victims and contributed generously towards the task of reconstruction, assuming that most of the cost would be recovered from Germany. Reparations ultimately covered only a little over one-third of the costs of reconstruction and the rest had to be financed by other means. The government was therefore forced into large-scale borrowing from French citizens. In the period 1919–25 more than 44 billion francs' worth of bonds were issued specifically to pay for war damages and by the end of 1926 the government had paid out a total of 85 billion francs for the repair of war-damaged property. Total net borrowings during the period amounted to 159 billion francs, while the internal debt of France nearly doubled in the eight years after the Armistice.[43]

Despite the large public outlays on reconstruction the budgetary problem as such was not the major difficulty. For most of the period France's budgetary deficit was declining and by 1925 the deficit had fallen to 3 per cent of national income, which could easily have been met by the flow of savings.[44] The real problem was the structure of the public debt. Much of the increase consisted of short-term bonds held by the public and the banks, and as the financial demands of business increased from 1923 onwards the government encountered increasing difficulty in renewing the debt as it matured. Moreover, the prospects of funding were limited since a large slice of long-term debt was due for repayment in 1925. Consequently the government was forced to borrow heavily from the Bank of France which greatly increased the resources of the commercial banks, and this in turn affected prices and the exchanges adversely.[45]

The upshot of these developments was that public confidence in

43. W. F. Ogburn and W. Jaffé, *The Economic Development of Postwar France: A Survey of Production* (1929), pp. 60, 66; Eleanor L. Dulles, *The French Franc, 1914–1928: The Facts and Their Interpretation* (1929), p. 10.

44. Though the complexity of French budgetary procedure with its double budget device makes it difficult to determine the exact position. See G. Wright, *France in Modern Times: 1760 to the Present* (1962), pp. 454–5.

45. J. H. Rogers, *The Process of Inflation in France 1914–1927* (1929), p. 350; A. G. V. Peel, *The Financial Crisis of France* (1925); H. E. Miller, 'The Franc in War and Reconstruction', *Quarterly Journal of Economics*, vol. XLIV (May 1930).

the franc steadily waned after 1923 and the reactions of investors and speculators made things worse. On the expectation that the franc would depreciate further there was heavy speculation against the franc which drove it down well below the level justified by the cost-competitiveness of French goods; in turn this added to the inflationary pressure through higher import costs and the need to generate an export surplus to finance the short-term capital outflow.[46] It was not until the speculative pressure reached almost panic proportions in July 1926, when the franc sank to its lowest point, that action to remedy the situation was taken.[47]

The delay in dealing with the situation may be explained by several factors. France continued to believe that she would eventually return to the gold standard at pre-war parity. The difficulties were considered only temporary and it was genuinely believed that the automatic functioning of monetary laws would ensure the re-emergence of the franc germinal as had happened in 1848 and 1870 when the gold standard had been abandoned temporarily.[48] For a time, moreover, the government seriously believed that the financial position would soon be restored by reparations payments. An additional factor was the politicial instability of France. Ministries came and went in quick succession – no less than eleven between March 1924 and July 1926 – and in the ten months before Poincaré came to office eight finance ministers had tried unsuccessfully to deal with the problem. Needless to say there was a serious division of opinion as to the

46. R. Z. Aliber, 'Speculation in the Foreign Exchanges: The European Experience, 1919–1926', *Yale Economic Essays*, vol. II (Spring 1962), pp. 242–3.

47. By 1925–6 concern about the value of the franc had spread far outside the range of the professional speculators: 'Every groceryman was considering the effect of the exchange rate on coffee, every stenographer was trying to build up a savings account in a gold standard country. It is hardly possible to exaggerate the extent to which the general public concerned themselves with such matters. The cost of the dollar was the subject of conversation in every corner café and one could hardly make a purchase without some discussion of the exchange rate. There was, in fact, a general increase in money consciousness, which made the situation peculiarly hard for the government to handle, and this growing feeling of uncertainty as to the future of all kinds of wealth on the part of all classes of people led eventually to the hysteria of July 1926.' Dulles, *The French Franc, 1914–1928*, pp. 45–6.

48. M. Wolfe, *The French Franc Between the Wars, 1919–1939* (1951), pp. 207–8.

measures which should be taken and the rate at which stabilization' should be effected.[49]

Fortunately the franc did not collapse. The right-wing Poincaré government of July 1926 restored confidence quickly by a series of rigorous measures which included increases in taxation, reductions in government spending, and the funding of a large part of the floating debt at an attractive rate of interest.[50] In August the Bank of France announced a fixed buying rate for the pound sterling. This package soon re-established financial confidence, and refugee capital returned to France. By the end of the year *de facto* stabilization of the franc was declared and in June 1928 France completed her currency reform with a return to the gold standard at the existing rate of exchange, that is equivalent to 20 per cent of the pre-war franc. This rate undervalued the franc and, for a time, gave a stimulus to exports.

Belgium's experience in many ways was rather similar. One difficulty in this case was that the Belga franc became seriously undervalued by speculative pressure, partly because it was closely linked with the French currency in the minds of speculators who expected it to exchange on a one-for-one basis with the French franc. Hence, despite any success on the domestic front, it was difficult for Belgium to pursue an independent stabilization policy.[51] But Belgium's own financial problems made stabilization difficult. The Belgian government undertook almost the entire cost of reconstruction on the optimistic assumption that Germany would pay for all the damages. This and other post-war expenditures involved a large increase in the public debt and heavy budgetary deficits, which averaged one-third of total government spending between 1919 and 1926. At first this caused no great concern but when reparations failed to come up to expectations and the Germans defaulted alarm was expressed both at home and abroad over unbalanced budgets and the rising volume of debt. This was reflected in a fall in the exchange rate as speculators sought to cover themselves and a disinclination of investors to

49. Kemp, 'The French Economy under the Franc Poincaré', pp. 83–4; J. Schmitz, *Inflation und Stabilisierung in Frankreich, 1914–1928* (1930).

50. A. Sauvy, 'L'inflation en France jusqu'à la dévaluation de 1928', in *Mélanges d'histoire économique et sociale en hommage au professeur Antony Babel*, vol. II (1963), p. 392.

51. Aliber, 'Speculation in the Foreign Exchanges', p. 242.

take up long-term government debt. This forced the government increasingly into short-term financing and, as in France, the rise in floating debt simply added to the inflationary process and in turn to the depreciation of the franc.

An unsuccessful attempt at stabilization was made between October 1925 and March 1926. The failure to improve the fiscal position, and particularly to deal with the large floating debt, was the main problem. The National Bank, as agent for the Treasury, began to buy up franc notes in exchange for foreign currencies (mainly dollars), but the notes were simply put back into circulation by the Treasury in meeting redemptions of maturing obligations. Hence no contraction took place in the total note issue. Doubts about the size of the public debt and near-record budget deficit in 1925 led to fears of further recourse to the printing press so that the Treasury found difficulty in renewing its maturing obligations.[52] Finally, in the spring of 1926, it was made known that attempts to secure an international loan to stabilize the franc at 107 to the £ had failed. This created near panic and the franc plunged to 230 to the £, a fall far greater than was warranted by the underlying economic conditions. A coalition ministry under Emile Franqui was immediately formed with full powers to deal with the crisis.[53] Drastic monetary and fiscal reforms, on the basis of which an international loan of $135 million was raised in October 1926, were introduced and the franc stabilized at one-seventh of its pre-war value. It too was undervalued.

Both Belgium and France suffered from over-speculation which eventually forced them to stabilize at an undervalued rate. In each case a large floating debt rendered monetary conditions sensitive to public confidence and at times magnified the inflationary influences of the government's fiscal activities. The control of the money supply was made especially difficult by the public debt structure, while confidence was closely related to domestic political conditions.

The Italian case provides a contrast. Here the budgetary problem was hardly an issue after the advent of the Fascist

52. H. L. Shepherd, *The Monetary Experience of Belgium, 1914–1936* (1936), pp. 30–31, 46, 233–5.

53. W. H. Pringle (ed.), *Economic Problems in Europe Today* (1927), pp. 140–41; F. Baudhuin, *Histoire économique de la Belgique, 1914–1939*, vol. I, 2nd edition (1946), pp. 152–72.

government in 1922 which brought drastic economy measures: the deficit of the early 1920s was sharply reduced and by 1924 the budget was in balance.[54] However until the debt owed to the Allies was settled an active stabilization policy proved difficult to pursue. Agreements reached late in 1925 and early 1926 with the U.S.A. and U.K. settled the terms of repayments and made stabilization easier to tackle. By this time, however, the currency showed signs of serious weakness partly as a result of rapid credit expansion between 1922 and 1926 designed to hasten industrial development. Political factors soon came to dominate the situation. Mussolini, determined to demonstrate his absolute authority and enhance the prestige of his regime, pledged support for the currency. In a speech to the populace in August 1926 he promised to 'defend the lira to the last breath, to the last drop of blood'.[55] In his eagerness to do the best possible for Italy he pushed through sharp deflationary measures and ended up by overvaluing the lira.[56] The rate was fixed at 19 lira to the dollar in December 1927 (that is around 25 per cent of its pre-war value) as against 25-6 lira to the dollar which had prevailed in the market over the previous two years. The overvaluation checked industrial expansion and exports and unemployment rose. But then Mussolini had more political freedom to enforce a deflationary adjustment policy than his counterparts in the pre-war parity countries.[57]

The restoration of the gold standard was no less an aim outside Europe, though again the war had left a legacy of problems. Latin American countries had fared well during the wartime boom in demand for their products and in most countries currencies had strengthened against sterling. When the post-war boom broke many were left prostrate, the victims of inflation and depreciating exchanges.

The task of achieving exchange stability was complicated by political upheavals, the heavy dependence on exports of primary

54. W. G. Welk, *Fascist Economic Policy* (1938), pp. 159–62. Though the high volume of short-term debt remained a problem. C. E. McGuire, *Italy's International Economic Position* (1927), p. 97.

55. J. S. Cohen, 'The 1927 Revaluation of the Lira: A Study in Political Economy', *Economic History Review*, vol. xxv (November 1972), pp. 647–69; R. Sarti, 'The Battle of the Lira 1925–27', *Past and Present*, vol. xlvii (May 1970).

56. The appreciation was also assisted by speculative activity.

57. Cohen, 'The 1927 Revaluation of the Lira', pp. 651–2.

products and the lack of adequate monetary institutions, notably central banks. Creation of central banks, together with a strengthening of the banking systems in general, became the instrument by which exchange stability was carried out. During the 1920s a Princeton University don, Dr E. W. Kemmerer, headed several missions to Latin America and was responsible for setting up central banks in several of the republics, including Peru (1922), Colombia (1923), Uruguay (1924), Chile and Guatemala (1925), Ecuador (1927) and Bolivia (1929). These banks were to function within the framework of the gold exchange standard; they were to have a monopoly of note issue, determine the bank rate, undertake open-market operations and operate as lenders of last resort. By these means it was hoped to regulate the governments' discretionary power of note issue, to check budgetary deficits which caused inflationary pressures, and force governments to finance their requirements by sounder methods.

The experiment was not an unqualified success. The rigidity of the gold standard rates circumscribed the activities of the banks. They lacked the requirements for controlling interest rates by classical means (e.g. attracting foreign funds) and in practice they were limited to controlling note issues. The mechanism of adjustment was difficult in economies specializing in the export of primary products and when export receipts fell (as in 1929) reserves rapidly dwindled. Under the rules of the game the banks were faced with the choice of either enforcing a sharp contraction or abandoning the gold standard.[58] Needless to say they chose the latter.

The pre-war parity brigade

Most countries would have liked to restore their currencies to their pre-war parities, but few were in a position to do so. In the end it was a question of whether they could stabilize at all and the rate at which they did it became of secondary importance. But a small number of countries grimly persisted and managed to return to par. These included the U.K. (and Dominions), Denmark, Sweden, Norway, Switzerland, the Netherlands and last of all

58. This account is based on D. Joslin, *A Century of Banking in Latin America* (1963), pp. 229–31, and C. Furtado, *Economic Development of Latin America* (1970), pp. 68–72.

Japan. Since each of these countries shared a fairly common cause we shall not tire the reader with individual case studies but simply outline the salient features.

None of these currencies had lost value to the extent experienced by continental countries, but all depreciated by some 10 to 20 per cent between 1914–20,[59] while none could look the dollar squarely in the face in subsequent years. But whether the parity rates should be changed was rarely entertained let alone seriously discussed.[60] The pre-war rates were sacrosanct and immutable, and should be restored at all possible speed and cost. 'The exchange rate was a sacred cow, to be worshipped in the market place and not to be milked. It was a symbol of Australia's sacrosanct commercial bond with Britain.'[61] Moreover, returning to the gold standard at pre-war rates symbolized the complete return to 'normalcy' after which everything would once again be in equilibrium.

The effort required to effect the return was considerable since prices and costs had risen faster in these countries than in America. Severe deflation was required to bring about an adjustment. Thus in Sweden there was violent deflation between 1920 and 1922 in preparation for the return, intermittent deflation in the U.K. in the years prior to 1925, and sharp deflation in Norway and Denmark between 1925 and 1928. Norway in fact was probably more severely affected than in 1929–32.[62] Moreover, once the decision to return to parity was taken speculators moved in and drove the currencies up to the pre-war level which virtually forced governments to honour their commitments.[63] The appreciation

59. Some by very much more. The Danish had dropped to 70 per cent of its par value.

60. See D. E. Moggridge, *The Return to Gold, 1925: The Formulation of Policy and Its Critics* (1969) and *British Monetary Policy 1924–1931: The Norman Conquest of $4·86* (1972).

61. G. Blainey, *Gold and Paper* (1958), p. 313; for New Zealand see G. R. Hawke, 'New Zealand and the Return to Gold in 1925', *Australian Economic History Review*, vol. XI (March 1971).

62. See D. H. Aldcroft, 'British Monetary Policy and Economic Activity in the 1920s', *Revue Internationale d'Histoire de la Banque*, vol. V (1972), pp. 283–5; E. Lundberg, *Business Cycles and Economic Policy* (1957), pp. 8–10, 95; R. A. Lester, 'The Gold-Parity Depression in Norway and Denmark 1925–1928 and Devaluation in Finland, 1925', Chapter 9 of R. A. Lester (ed.), *Monetary Experiments* (1939; 1970 reprint), pp. 221–2.

63. Aliber, 'Speculation in the Foreign Exchanges', p. 241.

of the Norwegian and Danish currencies, for example, from 50 and 60 per cent respectively to 95–100 per cent of par between 1924 and 1926 was largely due to an influx of speculative funds in anticipation of the return to parity.[64]

In the event most countries could not in effect adjust their costs and prices rapidly enough despite the deflationary policies so that they ended up with overvalued currencies. Deflation and subsequent overvaluation meant that their economies did not achieve their full growth potential in the 1920s, though the impact varied. Norway and, to a lesser extent, Denmark were badly hit in contrast to the rapid progress in Finland, a country which devalued significantly.[65] After initial difficulties Sweden made steady progress thanks largely to her highly adaptable economy.[66] The U.K. recorded a patchy performance but structural difficulties were the chief problem and these were scarcely a product of overvaluation.[67] Japan jumped back to parity very late in the day, January 1930, and for a very short time, so that no assessment is required. But the spasmodic deflation of the 1920s, partly with an eye to return to parity, certainly did not enable the economy to realize its full growth potential.[68] Perhaps the overall results were not too disastrous but was it really worth it for the sake of prestige ? Each country would certainly have benefited by choosing a lower parity and few problems would have been raised since virtually everyone else was at the same game.

64. League of Nations, *International Currency Experience: Lessons of the Inter-War Period* (1944), p. 121.

65. Lester, 'The Gold-Parity Depression in Norway and Denmark 1925–1928 and Devaluation in Finland, 1925', p. 222.

66. Unemployment among trade union members was nearly one-third in December 1922. Jack, *The Restoration of European Currencies*, p. 69; B. Thomas, *Monetary Policy and Crises: A Study of Swedish Experience* (1936), pp. 158–61.

67. R. S. Sayers, 'The Return to Gold, 1925', Chapter 12 of L. S. Pressnell (ed.), *Studies in the Industrial Revolution* (1960), pp. 322–6. Keynes's estimate that the pound was overvalued by 10 per cent has gained wide acceptance though it has never been conclusively proved. Few writers have challenged the view that it was overvalued, but see J. T. Walter, *Fixed Exchange Equilibrium* (1951), pp. 14–16.

68. H. T. Patrick, 'The Economic Muddle of the 1920s', in J. W. Morley (ed.), *Dilemmas of Growth in Prewar Japan* (1971), p. 260.

Conclusion

The process of currency stabilization cannot be regarded as a success story. It took most of the decade for all countries to bring some semblance of order to their currency and financial affairs in a piecemeal process carried out by one country after another in an entirely uncoordinated manner. By and large exchange stabilization was carried out as an act of national sovereignty, with each country acting independently with little regard to the resulting interrelationship of currency values in comparison with cost and price levels. After the violent currency disorders of the first half of the 1920s countries were so anxious to stabilize at any level that they did not pay much attention to what that level was in relation to those of other countries or to prices at home and abroad. Moreover, stabilization of a currency was conceived of in terms of gold rather than other currencies, and the level of stabilization was frequently expressed as a function of the previous gold content of the national currency. Each country thought of itself as attached to gold rather than attached to other countries' currencies through gold.

Not surprisingly the outcome was not stable or workable. International exchange rates were often fixed under the influence of abnormal short-term capital movements or speculation with the result that some countries emerged with overvalued currencies, others with undervalued ones. In both strong and weak currencies alike overtracking speculation caused actual rates to deviate from the equilibrium rates as determined by purchasing power parity relatives.[69] However, it should not be assumed that freely fluctuating exchange rates in the early 1920s necessarily led, as a general rule, to cumulative depreciation through self-aggravating speculative capital movements since, as Tsiang has pointed out, the underlying instability of the exchanges in many cases can be traced to a supply of money and credit which was extremely elastic with respect to the interest rate.[70] Nevertheless, a solution to the stabilization problem was often conditioned by the overplay of market forces rather than regulated by coordinated agree-

69. On this point see Aliber, 'Speculation in the Foreign Exchanges'.
70. S. C. Tsiang, 'Fluctuating Exchange Rates in Countries with Relatively Stable Economies: Some European Experiences after World War I', *International Monetary Fund Staff Papers*, vol. VII (1959–60), pp. 245, 273.

ment. Into an already complicated situation were introduced a new set of difficulties in which currencies diverged from their true equilibrium rates. From the start the new gold standard system was subject to various stresses and strains, the two most important sources of disequilibrium being the pound and the franc. Such a system could scarcely survive without adjustment for long; it ended without such adjustment and sooner than even the pessimists anticipated. As the League of Nations, with the benefit of hindsight, observed: 'The piecemeal and haphazard manner of international monetary reconstruction sowed the seeds of subsequent disintegration. It was partly because of the lack of proper coordination during the stabilization period of the 'twenties that the system broke down in the 'thirties.'[71] The working of the new standard and its weaknesses form the subject of the next chapter.

71. League of Nations, *International Currency Experience: Lessons of the Inter-War Period* (1944), p. 117.

7

What went wrong with the 'New' Gold Standard?

During the 1920s the dominating force in economic policy was the currency question: first the effort of stabilizing exchange rates and returning to gold, and then the struggle to maintain the new standard. For rich and poor nations alike the monetary ideal took precedence over all other matters of economic policy. Any short-term costs entailed in its restoration were considered worthwhile since much was expected from it.[1] Most countries faithfully believed that its resurrection would solve the economic problems left outstanding from the war. 'Before 1925 concentration upon the goal of a return to normal and upon the achievement of stable exchange rates, and after 1925 the splendours of a stable exchange standard blinded the eyes of bankers and of the world in general. The illusion that the economic maladjustments would be corrected by automatic forces was dominant in the world's financial thinking.'[2]

1. Thus Cassel, referring to the return to gold by Britain, felt that 'the relatively small sacrifices involved in that step were much more than counterbalanced by the restoration of international confidence and by the stimulus given to international trade through the replacement of the pound sterling in its old position as the principal currency of the world's trade'. G. Cassel, *The Downfall of the Gold Standard* (1936), p. 40. Cassel believed that the moderate degree of deflation which this entailed was a price well worth paying.

2. W. A. Brown, Jnr, *The International Gold Standard Reinterpreted, 1914–1934*, vol. II (1940), p. 801.

Such cherished illusions were quickly shattered however. Far from correcting the underlying maladjustments the revised gold standard itself was subject to serious strains from the start, and soon disintegrated. Like a damp squib rekindled it sputtered for a while and then fizzled out. One of the most intriguing and complex problems is to explain why it did not live up to previous expectations. How was it that a system which apparently served so well before 1914 failed to function 'properly' after the war? An answer to this question will go far towards explaining why the system collapsed in the early 1930s. A second point of considerable relevance for this study is how the gold standard affected the major business recession which set in at the end of the 1920s.

Few subjects have attracted so much attention as the gold standard. Contemporaries wrote profusely on various aspects though much of the writing was of mediocre quality and it tended to portray a stereotyped ideal which had never really existed in practice. Later writers have done much to correct or modify some of the popular notions regarding the operation of the system prior to the First World War though several aspects still require further clarification.[3] To appreciate the post-war developments it is essential to sketch briefly the pre-1914 background to the system, and particularly the reasons for its apparent success.

The pre-war gold standard

The international gold standard was essentially a creation of the latter half of the nineteenth century. Before that time most countries were on either silver or bimetallic standards of one sort or another and silver exceeded gold in active circulation until well into the second half of the nineteenth century. Several countries, including Russia, Italy, Austria–Hungary and the United States, were forced onto irredeemable paper systems by wars and revolutions in the period 1848–71. It was not until the 1870s that silver began to lose its role as a currency of international acceptability. Gold replaced silver as the standard money in most European countries, with the exception of one or two like Italy which had difficulties with their irredeemable paper, while the United States gradually moved in the same direction. The worldwide transition

3. Surprisingly there has been no recent full-scale study of the post-war gold standard. The standard work remains that of Brown cited above.

to gold came in the 1890s when the discovery of new gold supplies did much to ease the process. The United States completed the transition to a monometallic standard, while several other important countries, notably Austria–Hungary, Russia, Japan and India, adopted gold.[4] By 1914 China was the only major country still on silver though several smaller nations practised bimetallism and some Latin American countries retained inconvertible paper.[5] But for the most part gold had emerged as the prime unit of international exchange and the guarantor of exchange stability between nations.

Even in the heyday of the gold standard gold was by no means the chief unit of exchange. True, gold coin or bullion circulated freely both within and across national boundaries and paper instruments of exchange were readily convertible into commodity money.[6] But commodity money (gold and silver) rapidly diminished in importance as a medium of exchange in the latter half of the nineteenth century with the vast expansion in credit money (paper money and bank deposits). In the first half of the nineteenth century credit money constituted little more than one-third of the total money supply of the major nations while silver at its peak accounted for one-half. Thereafter gold began to replace silver but its importance also soon dwindled in relation to the total money supply. Between 1850 and the early 1870s two-thirds or more of total monetary expansion in the major developing nations was derived from credit money, and no less than 95 per cent in the years up to 1914. By that date paper and bank money had completely dwarfed commodity money; they accounted for some 85 per cent or more of total world monetary circulation, while gold constituted a mere 10 per cent and silver the rest.[7] Such dramatic changes were of course essential for ensuring high rates of economic expansion in the nineteenth century since these

4. India in fact adopted a gold exchange standard, the rupee being pegged to the pound sterling. A number of smaller countries adopted this form (e.g. the Philippine peso was pegged to the U.S. dollar) which gained wide acceptance after the war.

5. L. B. Yeager, *International Monetary Relations* (1966), pp. 252–4.

6. Indeed the essence of the gold standard was that countries maintained ready convertibility between gold and their national monetary units at fixed rates of exchange and the movement of gold across national boundaries was left free of restriction.

7. R. Triffin, *Our International Monetary System* (1968), pp. 20, 26.

could hardly have been achieved under the rigid metallic systems of monetary creation of earlier centuries. On the other hand, these developments clearly put a different complexion on the nature of the gold standard itself. Not only was it far less rigid and automatic as many writers have led us to believe but one may question the very nomenclature 'gold standard'. For, as Triffin observes, 'the nineteenth century could be far more accurately described as the century of an emerging and growing credit-money standard, and of the euthanasia of gold and silver moneys, rather than as the century of the gold standard'.[8]

Nevertheless, the facts that gold commanded universal acceptance as a means of clearing international payments and that most currencies were readily convertible into gold were sufficient reasons for regarding the gold standard as the guarantor of economic stability. However, though the system appeared to work reasonably well, this was partly the result of accident or fortuitous circumstance rather than conscious design; and, in any case, probing more deeply into the matter makes it clear that the benefits were partly offset by costs or frictions created by its operation. Moreover, it is equally clear that the mechanism of adjustment involved never worked as smoothly or as automatically as the classical supporters of the system believed, or for that matter it probably never operated in quite the manner they imagined. It would be impossible here to do full justice to these points but it is useful to discuss certain facets of the pre-war system in order to avoid misconceptions about the nature of the revised system in the 1920s.

The classical view of the automatic adjustment process under the international gold standard was stated explicitly in the influential report of the Cunliffe Committee in 1918.[9] Primary emphasis was placed on adjustment through the trade balance. Given a disequilibrium between countries the money flows arising from such imbalance would tend to bring about downward price adjustments in the deficit countries and upward price movements in the surplus countries. These would restore the former price and cost relationships and hence make for equilibrium again in their balance of payments. This 'automatic' adjustment

8. ibid., p. 21.
9. This committee had been set up to consider the question of Britain's maintenance of the gold standard after the war.

process was facilitated by the 'rules of the game' which the monetary authorities (central banks) supposedly adhered to. Discount rates were raised and credit tightened in countries losing gold while the opposite policies came into force in surplus countries. Their effect was twofold: interest rate changes stimulated short-term compensatory capital movements from surplus to deficit countries, while the variations in interest rates and credit policy reinforced the price and cost adjustments necessary to restore equilibrium.

This interpretation of the process was far too simplistic for practical purposes. It stressed price relationships and ignored the income adjustment effects, while it placed undue emphasis on the rectification of the current account balance (and primarily the trade balance) almost to the exclusion of the compensating mechanism operating within the capital account of the external balance sheet. In fact many developing countries along the periphery, for example Canada, Australia, the Argentine and even the United States, were able to pile up large deficits on current account without visible correction except in the long run simply because these were financed by large capital inflows derived from the main surplus nations, Britain, France and Germany. Such capital flows fulfilled a similar role in the 1920s, at least until they were suddenly curtailed.

The automatic nature of the adjustment process under the gold standard system has been questioned on several grounds. In the first place, instead of divergent movements in prices, imports and exports among the major trading nations one finds a remarkably high degree of parallelism.[10] A similar conformity is noticeable in the movement of interest rates.[11] Yet if gold standard countries were supposed to meet each other half-way one would expect a greater divergence in the movement of these variables.[12] Secondly, some writers have expressed scepticism regarding the second channel of adjustment, involving prices, incomes and employment. Bloomfield maintains that there is not much evidence that

10. Triffin, *Our International Monetary System*, pp. 5–6.

11. O. Morgenstern, *International Financial Transactions and Business Cycles* (1959).

12. Though such parallelism could be a source of strength for the system. See A. G. Ford, 'The Truth about Gold', *Lloyds Bank Review*, vol. LXXVII (July 1965), p. 8.

discount policies were heavily deflationary or that they caused severe unemployment. Restrictive credit policies slowed down the rate of economic expansion rather than imposed an absolute deflation of prices and incomes.[13] Prices and wages, especially the latter, were less flexible in a downward direction than often supposed and such adjustments rarely reached sizable proportions, while in cases where severe inflation was allowed to develop, for example in some Latin American economies, equilibrium was more often than not restored by devaluation rather than through price and wage compression. Thirdly, it has been argued that the monetary authorities played the 'rules of the game' just as badly before 1914 as afterwards. In particular, central banks appeared more often than not to offset or neutralize the internal effects of gold inflows and outflows.[14]

While it is probably correct to question some traditional notions about how the gold standard worked before 1914 it would be wrong to assume that these revisions preclude the operation of the classical forces of adjustment in some degree. If not, then it is difficult to conceive how equilibrium was maintained in the major industrial economies unless the burden of adjustment was thrown elsewhere. This, as we shall see, was partly the case but reservations must be expressed about recent research based largely on annual data which may well obscure the mechanism of adjustment to some extent. For example, it is quite possible that the traditional reinforcement of gold movements did occur but with such a lag as to be concealed by the year-to-year changes in the data. Alternatively apparent neutralization of gold flows may simply have been an automatic response to the influence of the business cycle, in that domestic and international assets moved in opposite directions, rather than the result of deliberate policy.[15] Perhaps more important, Bloomfield, following Nurkse's method for the inter-war years, adopts a definition of neutralization which includes any offsetting action, however small, by central banks of

13. A. I. Bloomfield, *Monetary Policy under the International Gold Standard, 1880–1914* (1959), pp. 43–4.

14. ibid., pp. 48–50. Though at the same time Bloomfield doubts whether the 'rules of the game' were ever explicitly formulated by central banks. See his 'Rules of the Game of International Adjustment', in C. R. Whittlesey and J. S. G. Wilson (eds), *Essays in Money and Banking in Honour of R. S. Sayers* (1968), pp. 27–30.

15. Yeager, *International Monetary Relations*, p. 288.

the changes in their international assets. It may well be therefore that a positive correlation frequently existed between changes in the central bank's international and domestic assets which would be sufficient to exert a considerable impact upon the domestic money supply – though not as great as that which would accrue from a one-to-one relationship under a pure gold coin system.

Moreover, the revisionists may have understated the domestic repercussion of monetary flows just as much as the classical proponents of the system chose to ignore the income effects. After all, even if the rules of the game were never explicitly stated, central bankers certainly followed certain implicit procedures, the most obvious being that primary consideration was given to maintaining convertibility and external stability. In effect when gold moved in or out appropriate action was taken regardless of whether or not this accorded with the needs of domestic economy. Thus even if some neutralization of gold flows did take place the economy remained subject to variations in interest rates which at that time were regarded as an important psychological barometer for the state of trade. As Sayers has noted: 'There is some reason to believe that both lenders and borrowers looked to Bank Rate as an important "Index" of economic prospects, and both sides would probably become more wary when Bank Rate rose, more adventurous when Bank Rate fell'.[16] Fortunately however, although policy was geared to external considerations its domestic impact was modified by the fairly close correspondence between changes in central bank discount rates and business reference cycles, especially in Britain and France.[17] This was because the reserves tended to move inversely with the cycle so that discount rate changes tended to move countercyclically – rising in booms and falling in recessions, though with a lagged reaction; they were therefore potentially stabilizing,[18] though at

16. R. S. Sayers, *Central Banking after Bagehot* (1957), p. 64.

17. Morgenstern, *International Financial Transactions and Business Cycles*, pp. 397–8.

18. Actually it was partly fortuitous that discount rates moved countercyclically since, at least in the case of Britain, the balance of payments tended to improve in booms and deteriorate in slumps. On normal expectations this should have resulted in a high Bank rate in recessions and a low one in booms. But in fact the Bank of England's reserves varied inversely with the cycle because of internal drains of currency in the boom and external drains

times the maintenance of high rates once the cycle had passed its peak tended to aggravate the downswing.

The relative absence of conflict between internal and external needs was one reason why the system worked fairly well before 1914. The adjustment mechanism was not completely smooth since fluctuations in output and employment were quite frequent, but the need for extreme deflationary or inflationary measures rarely arose.[19] It was only after the war that domestic and external needs came into serious conflict, a situation which eventually contributed to the collapse of the gold standard.

Developing this point further it can be argued that the gold standard worked, at least for the major industrial economies, largely because it was never subject to serious strain. Indeed any system of fixed exchange rates only operates smoothly so long as the countries which adhere to it are in fundamental equilibrium. Any severe disparity in costs and prices between countries requires domestic adjustment in order to preserve exchange parities intact. Fortunately exchange rate stability was never threatened by serious exposure to disequilibrium of this sort, partly because national rates of monetary and credit expansion among gold standard countries were harmonized in such a way as to prevent large surpluses or deficits in the balance of payments from occurring. Domestic monetary and credit policies were adjusted in accordance with both internal and external monetary flows to bring about, through income, price and cost adjustments, a tenable equilibrium in overall transactions. But as Triffin points out, 'the residual harmonization of national monetary and credit policies depended far less on *ex post* corrective action, requiring an extreme flexibility, downward as well as upward, of national price and wage levels, than on *ex ante* avoidance of substantial disparities in cost competitiveness and the monetary policies that would allow them to develop'.[20] Furthermore, the maintenance

---

associated with British lending abroad which exceeded the current account surplus. On this point see F. V. Meyer and W. A. Lewis, 'The Effects of an Overseas Slump on the British Economy', *The Manchester School*, vol. XVII (1949); I. Mintz, *Trade Balances during Business Cycles: U.S. and Britain since 1880* (1959).

19. Ford, 'The Truth about Gold', p. 9.

20. Triffin, *Our International Monetary System*, p. 14. Large disparities between internal and external price and cost levels were prevented by import and export competition.

of equilibrium was assisted by the ability of central banks to accumulate sufficient gold reserves[21] to guarantee convertibility, and the adaptibility of banking systems which enabled the monetary needs of an expanding economy to be met.

If the international monetary system suited the needs of the centre, that is the industrialized countries of the West and their closest affiliates notably the British Empire, the same could not be said for some countries on the periphery. Latin American countries in particular experienced wide fluctuations in their exchange rates with frequent devaluations. In fact there are grounds for arguing that some of the countries on the periphery bore the costs of the system and made it more acceptable to the countries of the centre. These adverse repercussions were transmitted through both the current and capital accounts of the balance of payments. Developing countries had little control over the rate of capital imports which followed a cyclical pattern determined by the needs of the creditor countries. Thus when pressure on reserves developed in the creditor countries a rise in interest rates would slow down the pace of capital exports and help relieve the strain, but at the same time borrowing countries would be subject to pressure as capital imports dried up. Rising interest rates at the centre also affected current balances through shifts in the terms of trade between industrial and primary producing countries. Britain in particular gained by her dependence on imported primary products and because the London money market played such a predominant role in financing the exports of the less developed countries. A rise in the London discount rate, though it tended to reduce British export prices, had a more dramatic impact on the prices of primary products thereby improving Britain's terms of trade and relieving the pressure on the current account balance at the expense of her suppliers. Thus on both current and capital accounts the primary producing countries were to pay for their dependence on the centre and in a sense they provided a safety valve for the maintenance of a stable monetary standard among the developed nations.

However, the perverse effects of the adjustment process on the less developed countries should not be pressed too hard for, as Williams has pointed out, it would be incorrect to conclude that Britain and western Europe boomed while the rest of the world

21. By increasing transfers from public circulation into centralized banking institutions.

languished in recession.[22] Over the longer term incomes and prices in most countries tended to move in unison though short-term divergencies left room for some adjustment. Moreover, even when long-term capital exports dwindled overseas countries were rarely left to face financial difficulties unaided. An outstanding feature of the pre-war system was that London's financial centre was always ready to alleviate strain by allowing countries in distress to borrow on short term. This in turn depended on London's ability to mobilize reserves from abroad, mainly Europe, or to retain overseas sterling balances, by the discount rate weapon. In this way 'London not only helped to finance the various upswings in economic activity but made a vital – perhaps more significant – contribution to the international economy by helping to cushion downswings in economic activity. London was always a source of finance for developing countries. When her own funds were fully stretched she was able to draw on – through the mechanism of interest rates – the liquid resources of other countries – outstandingly European – not normally engaged in extensive international short-term lending.'[23]

Indeed much of the strength of the gold standard system was that it virtually revolved around one strong financial centre, London. Other international financial centres were developing in this period (notably in Paris and Germany) but it was not until after the war that they became a threat to London's predominance.[24] The main financial and produce markets were located in London and most international payments were cleared in sterling. Sterling and gold were virtually interchangeable and this gave the Bank of England 'not only the role of regulator of the British monetary system but, in great part, that of regulator of the gold standard and the international payments system'.[25] Though the Bank of England operated on a very slender gold reserve (rarely

22. D. Williams, 'London and the 1931 Financial Crisis', *Economic History Review*, vol. xv (1962–3), p. 515.

23. ibid., p. 517.

24. Though in a recent and very informative monograph Lindert suggests that London's role as the only major reserve centre has been exaggerated. By 1913 Germany in particular was challenging London's position and the mark was already a more popular official reserve asset on the Continent than sterling. P. H. Lindert, *Key Currencies and Gold, 1900–1913* (1969), pp. 76–7.

25. W. M. Scammell, 'The Working of the Gold Standard', *Yorkshire Bulletin of Economic and Social Research*, vol. xvii (1965), p. 33.

more than about £40 million or 2–3 per cent of the country's total money supply) such was the confidence in sterling that its strength was never called into question in a way that would threaten the system. Convertibility of sterling was taken for granted and this in itself helped to keep gold demands to a minimum. Since sterling was universally acceptable countries were prepared to accept payment in sterling or build up balances in London and serious or sustained runs on the reserves were rare. And when temporary pressures did occur the Bank of England was always able to call upon support from abroad. Sterling currency never ran short, it had no competitors[26] and was accepted as almost as good as gold. Little wonder therefore that the pre-war international monetary system has been regarded as a sterling standard as much as a gold one.

The pre-war gold standard was therefore a complex and delicate mechanism. The intricate manner in which it operated still requires further investigation. But one can safely say that it worked well up to 1914 largely because of a fortuitous combination of favourable circumstances which ensured that no serious disequilibrium developed within the international payments mechanism. The monetary arrangements were viable because they were not subjected to persistent strains. In other words, although the operation of the gold standard system helped to maintain international equilibrium, the system itself was in turn dependent for its survival upon underlying forces making for a measure of equilibrium in the international economy. As Williams notes: 'The pre-1914 international gold standard gave an added stability to a world already in fundamental economic harmony.'[27] The inability to restore these

26. This is quite a crucial point and therefore requires brief elaboration. Sterling was strong enough to be a key currency largely because the economic circumstances of Britain made it so. Hence it could function without a large reserve backing. Had there been competitors of equal or near equal rank (say the franc or dollar) then sterling's position would have been quite different. Any temporary strains on sterling would have been magnified since speculators and financiers would have had alternative currencies to switch into, while London's ability to attract funds and resist departures would have been impaired. Under these circumstances sterling's reserve backing would probably have been inadequate and it is debatable whether the gold standard could have functioned as well as it did. This is important in the light of post-war events.

27. Williams, 'London and the 1931 Financial Crisis', p. 517.

ideal conditions in the post-war period was one of the main reasons for the failure to recreate a viable gold standard in the 1920s.

Disruption and resurrection of the gold standard

The war completely disrupted the pre-war international monetary system. The gold standard was suspended piecemeal since it was found impossible to maintain convertibility of currencies and the free export of gold when gold reserve covers fell drastically on account of the vast inflation in the monetary liabilities of national banks. But currencies were not allowed to float freely. The major countries resorted to extensive artificial pegging operations in an effort to maintain the pre-war pattern of exchange rates. This was remarkably successful since by the close of the war exchange rates were little different from those of pre-war.

However, this artificial pattern of exchange rates could not be maintained indefinitely given the varying degrees of price inflation during the war and the distortions in national cost and price levels through controls and shifts in economic power relationships. The increased strength of the American economy *vis-à-vis* most others meant that many currencies were overvalued in terms of the dollar. Hence the pegging operations were allowed to lapse soon after the war, whereupon most currencies declined against the dollar which had been restored to full gold strength in June 1919. During the next few years extreme instability ensued in the exchanges as currencies were allowed to float freely. Some currencies bounced backwards and forwards against the dollar while others, particularly those in central and eastern Europe, depreciated long and hard under the influence of extreme inflation. Given the unsettled economic conditions and uncertainty, together with frequent speculative movements of hot money, there seemed little likelihood that the exchanges would find a stable equilibrium level which reflected the changed pattern of price and competitive relationships among nations.

The failure of flexible exchange rates undoubtedly occasioned a move towards restoration of a more orderly system. Indeed the collapse of some currencies, notably the Austrian, German and Hungarian, forced the question of stabilization to the forefront, though it should not be forgotten that the authorities in most countries were resolved to return to the gold standard regime and if possible to restore their currencies to pre-war parity. The latter ideal was rarely attained but during the 1920s one country after another stabilized and returned to gold. By 1928, with a few notable exceptions, the process was complete.[28] The restoration of the pre-war monetary standard was regarded as the final task of reconstruction which would assure equilibrium. Yet within a matter of three or four years the whole edifice, so laboriously and painfully constructed, had collapsed in ruins. And largely because of the failure to recognize that the restored system was but a pale reflection of the old and that the environment in which it had operated successfully before 1914 no longer existed.

Characteristics and weaknesses of the restored gold standard

The gold standard system of the 1920s differed considerably from the 'classical' system of the pre-war period. It was not a full gold standard since gold coins disappeared from circulation almost everywhere, except in America and one or two other countries. Withdrawal of the remaining domestic coinage did help to swell the reserves of central banks but it also made the process of money creation entirely dependent on the fiduciary issues of national banking systems, though the rate at which these were expanded was obviously determined by the availability of central bank reserves for offsetting balance of payments fluctuations. Nor could the gold standard be regarded as a proper bullion standard by which currencies were directly convertible into gold. Many countries, through lack of gold reserves and other factors, were forced onto a gold exchange standard under which they held their legally required reserves wholly or partly in foreign exchange. This system was not unknown before 1914 when several countries had operated a gold exchange standard, but during the 1920s it became widespread throughout Europe and was also adopted by several countries overseas. It had been recommended by the Financial Committee of the Genoa Conference in 1922 as a way of economizing on gold which was thought to be in short supply. The effect was to increase considerably the foreign exchange component of central bank reserves; by 1927 foreign exchange accounted for 42 per cent of the total reserves (gold and foreign

28. The process of stabilization is dealt with fully in the previous chapter.

exchange) of twenty-four European central banks compared with 27 per cent in 1924 and around 12 per cent in 1913.[29]

The gold exchange standard may have eased the pressure on gold supplies but it only transferred the problem by one remove. Indeed it was a source of weakness rather than strength. The system led to a 'pyramiding' of claims on gold centres since more than one currency was built on the common foundation of a convertible currency, so that a crisis in one country might affect a whole series of currencies with serious consequences for the reserve currency.[30] Gold exchange standard countries built up their exchange reserve holdings by short-term claims on key currencies, notably sterling and the dollar. The accommodation of large holdings of foreign claims put a severe strain on the central money markets because these funds proved highly volatile and moved from centre to centre with shifts in relative interest rates and changes in confidence. The existence of more than one international financial market of importance (New York as well as London, and later Paris) provided ample opportunity for fund switching, whereas sterling's unchallenged supremacy and strength before the war provided little incentive for it. Moreover, there was always the possibility that funds might be withdrawn in the form of gold at short notice. Nor was the danger of conversion contingent solely upon a crisis of confidence. Many regarded the gold exchange standard as a temporary expedient or transitional phase prior to the adoption of the real thing. France in particular was very loath to sacrifice national prestige by remaining on an exchange standard. After the *de facto* stabilization of the franc in 1926 the Bank of France acquired the largest stock of foreign exchange (mainly in sterling and dollars) in the world. This was partly to prevent unnecessary appreciation of the French currency but there was the ever-present threat, which in the later 1920s became a reality,[31] that these holdings would be converted into gold to realize French dreams. Germany followed a similar policy. Soon after the stabilization of the mark the Reichsbank changed its foreign exchange reserves into gold. By 1928 foreign exchange

29. League of Nations, *International Currency Experience: Lessons of the Inter-War Period* (1964), pp. 29, 35.

30. Royal Institute of International Affairs, *The Future of Monetary Policy* (1935), pp. 152–4.

31. See below, pages 173–4.

accounted for a mere 8 per cent of total reserves (foreign exchange plus gold) as against 59 per cent in 1924.[32]

Inevitably therefore the gold exchange standard put greater pressure on the key centres, London and New York. They needed to hold larger gold stocks than were required to meet normal trading transactions for the eventuality that foreign claims might be withdrawn as gold at short notice. In this respect New York, with its large gold stocks and relatively small liabilities, faced no real problem. London was the weak link since this centre had large claims against it but little with which to meet them since gold stocks were low. Had sterling been a strong currency with no competitors as before the war there probably would have been little difficulty in operating with a low gold reserve. But sterling was continually under strain in the 1920s and the gold exchange standard merely increased the pressure.[33] Indeed, as we shall see below, Britain's inability to exercise control over the international monetary system as she had formerly done was an important factor in the collapse of the gold standard.

A second major source of weakness sprang from the stabilization process itself. The piecemeal and uncoordinated manner in which it was accomplished meant that little attention was paid to the crucial question of parity values. The haphazard choice of exchange rates, often under the influence of speculation and political motives, invariably meant that countries ended up with the wrong parities. Some were overvalued, others undervalued and it was a stroke of luck if a country made the right selection. Thus currencies which were restored to their pre-war value were generally overvalued; this was particularly true of sterling and probably also in the case of the Swedish, Danish and Norwegian currencies, while Italy went too far in the same direction. Conversely, the dollar, which was used as the yardstick for stabilization purposes, could be said to be undervalued in terms of several currencies.[34] Thus the system started off from a point of disequili-

32. J. Néré, *La Crise de 1929* (1968), pp. 53–6.

33. This was rather ironic in view of the fact that Britain had encouraged the adoption of the gold exchange standard as a means of relieving the strain on her slender gold reserves.

34. See S. Glynn and A. L. Lougheed, 'A Comment on United States Economic Policy and the "Dollar Gap" of the 1920s', *Economic History Review*, vol. xxvi (1973), p. 694.

brium and once the pattern was set there was little chance of adjustment. The new parities were regarded as sacrosanct in much the same way as those under the pre-war gold standard had been so that countries were reluctant to adjust them even when they were seen to be incorrect. Those countries which had undervalued their currencies were unwilling to forego the benefits of a depreciated exchange; France in particular did her best to neutralize the impact of the inward flow of funds immediately following stabilization by acquiring large amounts of foreign exchange.[35] But countries which overvalued their currencies, especially those which returned to pre-war parities, faced a more difficult problem. To devalue soon after stabilization was out of the question since this would have involved a serious loss of prestige. In any case, the currency most out of alignment was the British and a devaluation of sterling might well have undermined the whole process of stabilization. The alternative therefore was to adjust the domestic economy to accord with the exchange rate, which involved compressing domestic cost and price levels. One or two countries managed to do this fairly well though at the expense of employment and wages. Sweden, for example, acted early and achieved a very sharp deflation in the downswing of 1920–22 that almost did the trick, while Italy was able to do the same in the later 1920s in a favourable political climate. But for other countries the task was impossible. Britain especially was unable to deflate to the necessary extent. In part this may have been because prices and wages were less flexible in a downward direction than before the war.[36] However, one should not make too much of this point since both prices and wages had taken a fairly severe battering following the post-war slump and there was little scope for further compression. The British economy remained a high-cost one because of structural and technical inefficiencies rather than high wages. But perhaps more important, the authorities were reluctant to press deflation too hard given the high level of unemployment. Thus domestic and external objectives came into conflict in a way they had never done previously and in an effort to attain a

35. M. Wolfe, *The French Franc between the Wars 1919–1939* (1951), pp. 96–7.

36. A. D. Gayer, 'The Nature and Functioning of the Post-War Gold Standard', in R. M. McIver *et alia* (ed.), *Economic Reconstruction: Report of the Columbia University Commission* (1934), p. 135.

compromise neither goal could be achieved.[37] Sterling therefore could not regain its former strength and Britain's economic resources remained underemployed.[38]

Given the initial parity disequilibrium it is not surprising that the gold standard functioned less smoothly than before 1914. The choice of the wrong exchange rates magnified balance of payments problems and so the system was called upon to make adjustments on a scale far greater than previously and for which it was never designed, and at a time when the adjustment mechanism was less easy to operate. Few countries were prepared to sacrifice the stability of their domestic economies completely for external equilibrium. Thus countries with overvalued exchanges were reluctant to carry through the necessary adjustments to their internal economies, while surplus countries were equally unwilling to meet the former half-way. This is shown clearly by the frequency with which central banks neutralized the domestic monetary effects of gold flows which had formerly been the traditional mechanism for dealing with balance of payments disequilibria. Gold surplus countries in particular were active in this respect. For much of the 1920s the United States Federal Reserve took measures to offset the domestic impact of gold inflows. Initially, in the early 1920s when the U.S.A. accumulated large amounts of gold, a policy of stabilization could be justified on the grounds that the inflow was temporary and likely to be reversed once the gold standard was restored elsewhere.[39] The U.S.A. also required larger gold stocks because of the increase in short-term foreign balances deposited there. Moreover, the authorities were not prepared to countenance the inflationary consequences of gold inflows. However, this action was only justified so long as most other countries were off gold and there was prospect of some returning with undervalued currencies which would have led to a reversal of the inflow. But stabilization was continued for most of the 1920s, though its implications were probably less serious than often imagined since the United States

37. See A. E. Feavearyear, *The Pound Sterling*, revised edition by E. V. Morgan (1963), p. 361.

38. Though one should not conclude from this that overvaluation of sterling was solely responsible for the depressed nature of certain sectors of the British economy.

39. D. Davidson, *The Rationalization of the Gold Standard* (1933), p. 20.

did not accumulate gold again on a large scale until 1929. Rather it was France which experienced a 'golden avalanche'[40] in the later 1920s when the Bank of France's gold holdings, under the influence of a favourable balance of payments and liquidation of foreign exchange balances, rose dramatically.[41] Though the Bank discontinued its conversion of exchange holdings after 1929 the commercial banks kept up the pressure and hence France absorbed more gold. More to the point, the domestic impact of these large gold inflows was partly neutralized by offsetting action.

Stabilization procedures may have been justified to insulate the internal economy from monetary movements but they were not compatible with the maintenance of the gold standard. Had all countries followed a similar course of action the gold standard would have been rendered unworkable almost from the start. As it was, the neutralization of gold flows by the major surplus countries placed a severe strain on the system and threw the major burden of adjustment on the countries experiencing gold outflows.[42] This was a particularly serious problem for Britain, with her persistent tendency to lose gold, and one she was not fully prepared to accept given the state of her domestic economy. The Bank of England therefore attempted to minimize the domestic impact of gold losses.

The failure of surplus and deficit countries to meet each other half-way meant that the pre-war adjustment mechanism was largely inoperative, a situation all the more serious given the initial disequilibrium arising from the fixing of exchange rates. This accentuated the maldistribution of the world's monetary reserves which had been in process since 1914. Gold was the operative medium since, though reserve currencies were used to make the existing gold stocks 'go further', it was gold that mattered in the final analysis. This is borne out by the fact that countries regarded the gold exchange standard as a temporary expedient; they were anxious to build up their gold holdings and transfer to a

40. Wolfe, *The French Franc between the Wars 1919–1939*, p. 96.
41. W. H. Wynne, 'The French Franc, June 1928–February 1937', *Journal of Political Economy*, vol. xlv (1937), pp. 484–90. Hawtrey, rather disparagingly, likened the Bank's action to a boa-constrictor swallowing a goat – it cannot stop. Royal Institute of International Affairs, *The International Gold Problem* (1932), pp. 208–9.
42. M. Friedman and A. J. Schwartz, *A Monetary History of the United States, 1867–1960* (1963), pp. 283–4.

fully convertible standard. Moreover, most countries were only prepared to retain balances in a reserve currency so long as that currency remained sound. Once difficulties arose then gold conversion of the balances was requested.

As regards the actual distribution of the world's gold stocks the trends are quite clear. The United States, France, the European neutrals and a few countries on the periphery, notably Japan, absorbed an increasing share of the world's gold reserves. The United States' share rose rapidly, from just over one-quarter to 48 per cent between 1913 and 1924, after which it declined slightly; France's stock declined over the same period but she then increased her share rapidly in the later 1920s; the European neutrals tended on balance to increase their holdings throughout the 1920s while non-European countries did so until 1928. The net result was that by the end of the 1920s the United States, France and the European neutrals accounted for nearly 68 per cent of the total compared with 54 per cent in 1913, while eight countries (United States, France, Japan, Germany, Britain, Italy, Spain and Argentina) owned over 80 per cent. Britain's gold stock, on the other hand, declined slightly and accounted for less than 7 per cent of world reserves by 1929.[43]

However, the crucial significance of these shifts in gold reserves remains to be stated. Much of the gold moved to those countries which did not need it, either because their currencies were not used as an additional reserve base (e.g. those of the neutrals and Japan) or because they had more than enough gold for current liabilities. In the latter context the United States was clearly the prime example. Her gold stocks amounted to over $4 billion in the later 1920s whereas dollar liabilities (central bank holdings of dollar exchange) were only $0·6 billion. In other words, America could have coped with a wholesale liquidation of foreign dollar balances and a deterioration in her balance of payments and still have had ample reserves. By contrast, Britain's position was the reverse since gold reserves fell short of sterling liabilities by a large amount. In 1928 central bank holdings of sterling exchange amounted to some $2½ billion, or nearly four times the Bank of England's gold reserves.[44] Even when allowance is made for the

43. Davidson, *The Rationalization of the Gold Standard*, p. 33; *Report of the Committee on Finance and Industry*, Cmd. 3897 (1931), p. 63.
44. Triffin, *Our International Monetary System*, pp. 31, 46–7.

short-term assets on which Britain could theoretically call in an emergency,[45] and also that part of the gold reserve which was earmarked as backing for the domestic note issue, liabilities still amounted to some three times the Bank's free reserve.[46] Clearly Britain was the weak link in the system. She had the largest liabilities and the smallest gold reserves of any major country, while her balance of payments position was far from strong. Any deterioration of the latter or loss of confidence in sterling was bound to bring more pressure to bear than the reserves could meet. It is true that Britain had operated with a very small gold reserve before the war but then her liabilities were smaller, her quick assets could be easily recalled, the balance of payments was much stronger and confidence in sterling remained firm.

Before looking at the position of London in more detail we should take up a matter which bothered contemporaries a great deal, namely the alleged world gold shortage. Several writers then and since have argued that world gold supplies were insufficient to support the current level of prices and activity,[47] while others have maintained that the problem was of a maldistribution of reserves rather than general shortage.[48] It is true that gold production increased less rapidly in this period than in the nineteenth century: world gold stocks rose by about 2·5 per cent

45. Though in practice these became 'locked in' during a crisis, as in 1931.

46. S. V. O. Clarke, *Central Bank Cooperation, 1924–31* (1967), pp. 141, 183.

47. The main proponents were Cassel and Kitchen. See G. Cassel, *The Downfall of the Gold Standard* (1936), and J. Kitchen, 'Gold Production', in Royal Institute of International Affairs, *The International Gold Problem: Collected Papers* (1932). They also presented memoranda to the League of Nations, *First Interim Report of the Gold Delegation of the Financial Committee* (1930), Annexes x, xi. See also G. F. Warren and F. A. Pearson, *Prices* (1933); J. R. Hicks, *A Contribution to the Theory of the Trade Cycle* (1950), p. 163; C. Rist, *La Défense de l'or* (1953); P. Jacobsson, *Some Monetary Problems: International and National* (1958), pp. 18–19.

48. W. A. Berridge, 'The World's Gold Supply Again Considered', *Review of Economic Statistics*, vol. xvi (1934); F. Mlynarski, *The Functioning of the Gold Standard* (1931), p. 68; League of Nations, *Reports of the Gold Delegation of the Financial Committee* (1930–32); C. O. Hardy, *Is There Enough Gold?* (1936); M. Palyi, *The Twilight of Gold, 1914–1936* (1972), pp. 123–32. There is also a useful summary of the contemporary debate in A. D. Gayer, *Monetary Policy and Economic Stabilization: A Study of the Gold Standard* (1937).

per annum between 1913 and 1929 as against 3·1 per cent in the half century before 1914. However, centralized gold reserves increased much more rapidly, possibly by as much as 5–6 per cent per annum, largely because of a concentration of gold stocks within central banks and treasuries.[49] By 1929 the latter held some 92 per cent of all gold stocks as against just over 50 per cent in 1913. In addition, these gold reserves were augmented, or used more effectively, because they were supplemented by foreign exchange holdings which, according to some authorities, were regarded as good as gold until 1930.[50] We would express some serious reservations about the last point since it is doubtful if foreign exchange was regarded as a viable alternative in the final analysis. Moreover, with regard to centralized gold holdings one must also bear in mind that most countries had higher legal cover requirements for domestic liabilities (usually notes and sight deposits) than previously. By the late 1920s the great majority of central banks were subject to legal reserve ratios ranging from 30–50 per cent, while some countries exceeded the legal cover requirements.[51] The League of Nations estimated that as much as one-half the total gold and exchange reserves of the monetary authorities was tied up as 'cover', and the effect was to withhold an increasing proportion of gold from the international currency function.[52]

It is difficult to estimate the exact impact of these conflicting trends, but any serious absolute shortage of gold during the 1920s seems unlikely. And as far as gold's international function was concerned, the cover ratios could easily have been relaxed to provide additional liquidity for international purposes. The cover requirements were only necessary as a token confidence factor and even this was of dubious consequence since 'a paper currency in normal times gains little if anything by having a legal "backing" of gold or foreign assets; while in abnormal times the cover

49. Much of the increase being derived from the withdrawal of gold coins from circulation.

50. A. D. Gayer, *Monetary Policy and Economic Stabilization: A Study of the Gold Standard*, 2nd edition (1937), pp. 96–7.

51. Practice varied as to the proportions of gold and foreign exchange employed and as regards the composition of the liabilities to be covered.

52. League of Nations, *World Economic Survey, 1931–32* (1932), p. 200, and *International Currency Experience: Lessons of the Inter-War period* (1944), pp. 94–6, 215.

regulations have usually had to be suspended, repealed or relaxed in any case'.[53]

London and the 'new' financial centres

No one would deny that the pre-war gold standard required a certain amount of management even though there might be debate as to the precise rules of the game. Much of the control was informal and directed by the one dominant financial centre, London. The weakening of Britain's economic and financial strength during and after the war and the emergence of New York and Paris as important financial centres completely transformed the situation. These two centres competed with London for the employment of funds the flow of which 'ceased to be under any single, centralized control'.[54]

The dispersal of control was not in itself fatal to the post-war gold standard. But it was clear, as the Genoa Conference of 1922 noted, that concerted action among the main financial centres was necessary if the system was to be preserved.[55] And, more particularly, it was essential that sterling, given its weakened condition, should be supported by New York and Paris in times of strain. The alternative was for one of these two centres to have taken over London's pre-war role of 'managing' the system. In the event none of these conditions was satisfied fully.

It would be wrong to say that there was no cooperation among the chief monetary centres in the 1920s. Indeed central bankers were probably in closer and more frequent contact than before the war since currency stabilization itself inevitably involved a measure of collaboration. Moreover, Norman and Strong, of the Bank of England and Federal Reserve respectively, worked in close harmony for much of the time, while even the Bank of France was prepared to toe the line on occasions.

On the other hand, it can hardly be said that collaboration among central bankers in the international monetary field was

53. League of Nations, *International Currency Experience: Lessons of the Inter-War Period* (1944), p. 96.

54. E. Nevin, *The Mechanism of Cheap Money* (1955), p. 15.

55. H. Strakosch, 'The Money Tangle of the Postwar Period', in A. D. Gayer (ed.), *The Lessons of Monetary Experience: Essays in Honour of Irving Fisher* (1937), p. 162.

free of friction. This is perhaps not surprising since the major central banks were dominated by powerful and independent governors.[56] But there was more to it than that. In part the problem was political, and this probably explains why France was an unwilling partner. The general French belief that the Anglo-Saxons had cheated France over Germany and the fear that they might dominate the international monetary system left its mark on the Bank of France. Emile Moreau, Governor of the Bank of France, was suspicious of Norman's alliance with Strong and his pro-German attitude. Since French interests could easily be threatened by this powerful team Moreau felt little compunction to work with the system. The strength of the franc after stabilization enabled France to assert her independence. As we have seen, sterling holdings were liquidated during the late 1920s, a policy which contributed to the collapse of the gold standard.[57] However, in all fairness it should be noted that the Bank of France relaxed its policy after 1929 and it did not contribute to pressure on the Bank of England in September 1931.[58]

The emergence of the Bank of France as a monetary leader also had repercussions in another direction. It offered an effective challenge to the Bank of England and the Federal Reserve and split the unity of leadership which had existed hitherto between the two banks.[59] According to Meyer, 'not only were there fundamental differences between the Bank of England and the Bank of France, but the unity of outlook on the part of the Bank of England and the Federal Reserve Bank of New York began to break down. Thus, the original unity of leadership disappeared, and at the same time no one of the three was strong enough alone to be accepted without question by the others as the leader'.[60] This, he argues, partly explains why cooperative efforts in defence of the system, namely the few desperate efforts to prop up sterling in the summer of 1931, were attempted too little and too late.[61]

Whether a more favourable political climate would have made

56. Norman, Strong, Moreau and Schacht.
57. S. Strange, *Sterling and British Policy: A Study of an International Currency in Decline* (1971), pp. 51–4.
58. Wolfe, *The French Franc between the Wars 1919–1939*, pp. 97–9.
59. A process no doubt exacerbated by the death of Strong in October 1928.
60. R. H. Meyer, *Bankers' Diplomacy: Monetary Stabilization in the Twenties* (1970), p. 14.
61. ibid., pp. 138–9.

much difference is debatable since the real challenge to effective international cooperation lay elsewhere. Once currency stabilization was restored the chief task was that of maintaining stable exchange rates and to do this central banks required complete freedom of action in monetary policy if they were to secure external equilibrium. But this they never had since domestic monetary objectives came increasingly into focus during the course of the 1920s, partly as a result of the unemployment problem and the growing interest of treasuries in economic affairs. In other words, it became increasingly difficult for monetary policy to serve central banks' international aims unless these happened to coincide, or at least did not conflict seriously, with domestic objectives. Thus in 1924 and 1927 the Federal Reserve was able to support sterling since both aims coincided. But in 1928–9, when sterling came under pressure during the U.S. boom, the Board favoured domestic over external objectives. Even the Bank of England, whose Governor was primarily concerned with maintaining external equilibrium,[62] was not entirely unmindful of the domestic consequences of its monetary policy, though usually only after prodding from the Treasury. For example, in May 1927, when Moreau requested the Bank of England to raise its discount rate to check the heavy influx of sterling into Paris, Norman felt unable to oblige 'without causing a riot'.[63] In fact there were only two occasions, 1919–20 and 1929–30, on which external and internal requirements coincided and the Bank was able to pursue a policy which met both.[64] The conflict between the two was much greater than before the war and central bankers everywhere were giving more consideration to the domestic needs of their economies.

That France and the United States followed policies inconsistent with maintaining the gold standard is partly understandable. Neither country had the experience of Britain in managing the payments system and neither was prepared to shore up a system

62. D. Williams, 'Montagu Norman and Banking Policy in the Nineteen Twenties', *Yorkshire Bulletin of Economic and Social Research*, vol. XI (1959), pp. 39–40, 51.

63. Clarke, *Central Bank Cooperation, 1924–31*, pp. 29–30.

64. Though it overdid the policy of restriction in 1919–20. See D. H. Aldcroft, 'The Impact of British Monetary Policy, 1919–1939', *Revue Internationale d'Histoire de la Banque*, vol. III (1970), p. 44.

which they had not created in the first place. Since even Britain was not prepared to concede complete priority to external equilibrium other countries could hardly be expected to do so. The conflict between domestic and external equilibrium had only arisen occasionally and in a comparatively mild form before the war, but in the post-war period this conflict became chronic and in 1931 it was critical.[65] Thus, although in some respects there may well have been greater cooperation among central bankers in this period it was insufficient to offset the effects of the growing weight attached by central banks to domestic policy objectives. And in any case, these cooperative efforts were 'wholly inadequate to sustain the gold standard in the face of the underlying disequilibria and major institutional changes of the 1920s that were fundamentally responsible for its collapse'.[66]

The gold standard under pressure

The new gold standard was restored against a background of unresolved economic problems, in particular the fundamental imbalance between the debtor and creditor nations of the world.[67] Given the manner in which it was restored and subsequently operated it was inconceivable that the gold standard could provide any solution to these problems. Indeed, it was only a matter of time before the new system itself disintegrated since it was powerless to withstand pressures as countries were not prepared to sacrifice their domestic economies on the altar of the exchanges.

65. Feavearyear, *The Pound Sterling*, p. 361.
66. Bloomfield, 'Rules of the Game', in *Essays in Money and Banking in Honour of R. S. Sayers*, p. 31. According to Clarke (*Central Bank Cooperation, 1924–31*, p. 27), 'The vision of a unified world economy, functioning according to accepted rules, could not be fitted to the circumstances of the 1920s. Yet, so influential was the gold standard vision that the few attempts to develop alternative conceptions of the working of the world economy were dismissed or ignored by the authorities. Rather than discard the cherished vision, each central banker sought to reinterpret the traditional theory to suit his country's particular needs. However, as these needs were seldom similar and often diametrically opposed, the reinterpretations resulted in conflicting views about the manner in which the gold standard should operate. The result was confusion and misunderstanding and in the end a failure to deal effectively with the economic difficulties of 1924–31.'
67. Brown, *The International Gold Standard Reinterpreted, 1914–1934*, vol. II, pp. 791–2.

Moreover, much of the strength of the pre-war system had been derived from the power of one financial centre which virtually controlled the international monetary framework. In the post-war period London was the weak link in the chain and no other country, despite the rivalry of New York and Paris, was prepared to hold the system together.

The new system might have been able to hobble along for several years had there been no severe strains and had American lending continued to paper over the cracks of disequilibrium in the international economy.[68] But no sooner had the gold standard been reestablished than pressures began to develop which undermined the system. The events leading up to the final crisis have already been the subject of detailed study so that only the salient features need be recounted here.[69]

As Williams has pointed out, the disastrous events of the summer of 1931 represented the culmination of a prolonged increase in the demand for liquidity which began as far back as the middle of 1928.[70] The first phase began when strains developed in some primary producing countries as their prices and incomes fell at a time when international lending was drying up. Consequently the debtor countries ran into balance of payments difficulties. They were forced to repay, rather than fund, earlier borrowings at a time when their foreign exchange earnings were dwindling. Accommodation from the main creditor countries was not forthcoming and so the only way to balance the accounts was to let funds flow out. Many debtors therefore faced a steady drain of their gold reserves from late 1928 onwards; total South American gold stocks declined from $927 million at the end of 1928 to $558 million at the end of 1930; Asia's fell from $738 to $601 million, while those of Oceania declined by 60 per cent between 1929 and 1930.[71] Some countries, notably Argentina, Brazil and Australia, lost most of their gold reserves in the process.[72] Rather

68. See Chapter 10, pages 249 et seq.

69. See, for example, D. Williams, 'London and the 1931 Financial Crisis', *Economic History Review*, vol. xv (1962–3), and 'The 1931 Financial Crisis', *Yorkshire Bulletin of Economic and Social Research*, vol. xv (1963).

70. Williams, 'The 1931 Financial Crisis', p. 101.

71. Williams, 'London and the 1931 Financial Crisis', p. 518.

72. L. Smith, 'The Suspension of the Gold Standard in Raw Material Exporting Countries', *American Economic Review*, vol. xxiv (1934), p. 431; V. P. Timoshenko, *World Agriculture and the Depression* (1933), pp. 76–8.

than face the full force of the severe deflationary measures required to restore their accounts to equilibrium several countries abandoned the gold standard. By April 1930, six Latin American countries together with Canada, Australia and New Zealand had abandoned gold and devalued their currencies. The first chink in the gold standard armour had been made.

Conceivably the initial crisis could have been staved off had the creditor countries been more willing to assist the primary producers before the international business depression raised the problem of world liquidity to quite a different order of magnitude. But the two strongest creditors, the United States and France, were not prepared to make sufficient funds available on either a long-term or short-term basis. Instead they added to the pressure on the one possible source of funds, namely London, since for much of 1929 funds were leaving London for New York (as a result of the stock market boom) and Paris which was liquidating its sterling balances. Thus both France and the U.S.A. were large gold importers in 1929, while Britain lost substantial reserves in the third quarter of the year,[73] and was in no position to cope with the problems of the debtor countries. Nor did the strain on London end with the collapse of the New York stock market in October 1929 since the financial needs of the debtor countries and the withdrawal of European balances from London continued through much of 1930 and 1931.

There was some easing of the pressure in the first half of 1930, partly as a result of a temporary revival in American foreign lending, but this proved short-lived. The decline in business activity soon began to sap international confidence which resulted in a renewed demand for liquidity. Moreover, the links forged by the fixed exchange rates of the gold standard assured that the decline would be world-wide since, as Friedman and Schwartz point out, no major contraction involving a substantial fall in prices could develop in any one country without those links enforcing its transmission and spread to other countries.[74]

73. League of Nations, *The Course and Phases of the World Economic Depression* (1931), pp. 228–9.

74. Friedman and Schwartz, *A Monetary History of the United States, 1867–1960*, p. 359. The significance of fixed exchange rates in the transmission process is shown by the case of China. This country was on a silver standard and so had the equivalent of a floating exchange *vis-à-vis* gold standard

Countries still on gold reacted to balance of payments deficits and unbalanced budgets with deflationary policies in an effort to regain external equilibrium, but this only aggravated the downward spiral. In turn the gold standard itself was rendered increasingly vulnerable not only because of the limit to which countries were prepared to go in deflating their domestic economies to maintain fixed exchange rates, but also because the gold exchange standard was much more sensitive to disturbances than the pre-war system because it raised the ratio of claims on the relevant high-powered money – gold – to the amount of high-powered money readily available to match those claims.[75]

By the middle of 1930 therefore, creditor countries were in no mood to increase their financial commitments to debtor countries. Indeed from then onwards there was a steady contraction of credits and withdrawal of funds from abroad as the deepening business depression further eroded confidence and gave rise to bankruptcies, exchange depreciation and bank failures. Banking crises in the two main creditor countries, France and the United States, in 1930–31 intensified the demand for liquidity which led to a withdrawal of funds from central and eastern Europe and further pressure on London as France liquidated her sterling holdings. The widespread foreign ownership of national bank deposits in Europe also aggravated the problem. Thus for much of 1930 and 1931 debtor countries were losing foreign exchange and gold at an accelerating rate and were finding it almost impossible to finance their overall deficits by borrowing or by expanding exports, while even severe deflation proved to be no panacea, at least in the short term, to the liquidity problem.

The final phase came in the summer of 1931, beginning with the failure of the Austrian Credit–Anstalt; this disaster had severe repercussions on the banking system of Europe as a whole. The German banking system collapsed and most other central and eastern European banks came under severe pressure. The crisis enormously increased the demand for liquidity and by July the scramble for cash and gold reached panic proportions. London,

---

countries. Thus China was able to maintain external balance without drastic internal deflation and avoid the severe contraction suffered elsewhere. China only began to experience depression when the gold standard countries abandoned gold and depreciated their currencies.

75. ibid., p. 359.

which had been losing funds steadily since the middle of 1930, bore the brunt of the panic since it was one of the few places still willing to grant accommodation. The rapid withdrawal of sterling balances and loss of reserves between July and September were largely occasioned by the continental financial crisis, but were undoubtedly aggravated by Britain's unfavourable liquidity position and the consequent loss of confidence in her ability to maintain solvency as her payments position deteriorated. The Macmillan Committee in its Report published on 13 July drew attention to Britain's large short-term liabilities, while the Report of the May Committee at the end of the month further undermined confidence by revealing the unsound state of the public finances. Thus despite last-minute lines of credit totalling £130 million from America and France the drain on London continued. The final blow came on the three days following the alleged naval mutiny at Invergordon (15 September) when £43 million was withdrawn from the London money market, making a total of nearly £200 million in two months.[76] The strain proved too much for the authorities and on 21 September Britain officially left the gold standard. This marked the effective end of the system since many other countries quickly followed Britain's action.

It is unlikely that Britain could have saved the gold standard system single-handed, and for that matter it is doubtful whether it was worth saving. Britain's weakened economic position after the war and her slender resources left her vulnerable. There was no problem so long as confidence in London was maintained and no severe strains were placed upon this centre. But events from 1929 onwards rapidly undermined that confidence and fears arose as to the liquidity of financial institutions and the convertibility of assets into gold. When the general demand for liquidity increased and London became the focal point of the pressure she could not withstand the strain without either depleting the reserves, realizing short-term assets or further borrowing. All these solutions entailed certain difficulties. The loss of gold reserves simply reduced confidence in sterling further, and there was a limit to the extent to which losses could be sustained. The Bank of England's reserves were only sufficient to offset a small part of the liabilities, while special measures to release additional reserves in support of the currency were more likely to aggravate than alleviate market

76. Clarke, *Central Bank Cooperation, 1924–31*, p. 216.

fears and uncertainties. The realization of Britain's short-term assets abroad was very difficult since many were locked up in European financial centres which were themselves in an illiquid state. Short-term assets in Germany alone amounted to £70 million, and the total assets in Europe as a whole, most of which were effectively frozen, were a good deal higher.[77] The only other solution was to borrow abroad to cover the outflow of funds. Since most countries were experiencing financial difficulties this was easier said than done, though, as we have noted, in the last stage of the crisis some £130 million worth of credits were scraped up in New York and Paris. This rescue operation was too little and too late; it emphasizes the limited nature of international cooperation in this period. Moreover, the effect of the assistance was weakened by the fact that it was made in two separate tranches instead of one single package, the second of which was not arranged until the first had been exhausted.[78] 'It was this inability to either retain previously invested funds in London or to attract further investment by foreigners that was the root cause of London's short-term difficulties.'[79]

Williams suggests that a rise in the Bank's discount rate early in 1931 might have eased the position, because higher interest rates would have attracted funds to London and/or prevented existing funds from leaving. It is true that the Bank of England's policy was weak and ineffective during the crisis, with no effort being made to push up interest rates. It is doubtful, however, whether this alone would have done the trick. Indeed, the loss of confidence and severity of the liquidity panic were so great that it is doubtful whether much could be done. Clarke believes sterling was beyond salvation whatever measures had been adopted.[80] The critical liquidity situation and the loss of confidence in London make it doubtful whether the Bank rate weapon would

77. Williams, 'London and the 1931 Financial Crisis', p. 524.
78. Clarke, *Central Bank Cooperation, 1924–31*, p. 204.
79. Williams, 'London and the 1931 Financial Crisis', p. 522.
80. Clarke, *Central Bank Cooperation, 1924–31*, p. 204. Palyi, on the other hand, believes that the position was not beyond redemption and that more could have been done to save the gold standard had the Deputy Governor of the Bank of England and the Treasury officials not lost their nerve. Norman was away ill throughout the crisis but due to return on 23 September. It is somewhat odd that they did not manage to hold out until his return. See Palyi, *The Twilight of Gold, 1914–1936*, pp. 266–77.

have produced its previous 'quick' adjustment effects. Moreover, raising the discount might have had a perverse effect by increasing distrust in sterling even further. On the other hand, it is not altogether clear why the Bank did not resort to the traditional remedy for dealing with a drain in the reserves. Possibly the awareness that higher interest rates would make the domestic situation even worse prevented the Bank from taking a stronger line.[81] During the 1920s use of the interest rate weapon as a flexible instrument to control the exchanges had been circumscribed, in part by domestic considerations, and it was becoming clear that the twin goals of domestic and external stability could not be pursued simultaneously. One or other had to go and in the end it was the gold standard. Devaluation, however distasteful to the authorities, was preferable to further internal deflation which would have been necessary to secure adjustment under the gold standard.[82]

81. W. A. Morton, *British Finance, 1930–1940* (1943), p. 44.

82. It is somewhat ironic that after gold had been abandoned Bank rate was raised to 6 per cent as a gesture of reassurance and to prevent inflation!

8

The Boom of the Later 1920s

By the middle of the 1920s economic and political conditions were much more stable than a few years earlier. The Locarno Pact of 1925, the revised reparations settlement of the previous year and the negotiated agreements regarding Allied war debts did much to boost international confidence and reduce political tensions and suspicions of war. Most of the great inflations had run their course and Britain's return to the gold standard in April 1925 paved the way for the completion of currency stabilization elsewhere. Primary commodity prices had firmed considerably after the disastrous drop which followed the post-war boom. Above all, reconstruction and recovery in Europe were virtually complete and 'real progress began to take the place of a painful struggle to regain a plateau of prosperity which had been lost . . .'.[1] If there were still signs of tension and weakness in the international economic system these were all but forgotten as the world looked forward to sustained prosperity.

Extent and nature of the boom

The expansion of industrial and primary production in the latter half of the 1920s was more rapid and more widespread than in the

1. A. Loveday, *Britain and World Trade* (1931), p. 47.

period from the beginning of the war to 1925. In the four years 1925–9 world industrial production rose by more than 20 per cent, a slightly larger absolute increase than in the whole twelve years prior to 1925. Total primary production increased by over 10 per cent, or 2·6 per cent per annum as against 1·4 per cent a year between 1913 and 1925. The pace here was set by raw materials, with a 27 per cent increase, since food production only recorded a fairly modest rise of about 6 per cent. At the same time the volume of international trade rose by nearly 21 per cent. On an annualized basis, rates of expansion work out at around 5 per cent which by historical standards was quite an impressive performance.

TABLE 7

INDICES OF INDUSTRIAL PRODUCTION FOR SELECTED REGIONS, 1925–9 (1925 = 100)

	1925	1926	1927	1928	1929
Industrial Europe *	100	95·6	113·2	116·5	123·1
Agricultural Europe †	100	105·6	112·2	113·3	122·2
United States	100	106·0	105·0	110·0	123·0
Canada	100	113·8	121·5	133·8	143·0
U.S.S.R.	100	143·8	168·4	205·3	256·1
Rest of world ‡	100	107·7	108·8	113·2	119·8
World Total §	100	102·2	108·7	113·0	120·7

* Austria, Belgium, U.K., Czechoslovakia, Denmark, France, Germany, Luxemburg, Netherlands, Sweden, Switzerland, and the Saar.
† Bulgaria, Estonia, Finland, Greece, Hungary, Italy, Latvia, Poland, Portugal, Romania, Spain, Yugoslavia.
‡ Includes ten countries in Latin America, Africa, Asia and Oceania: Argentina, Australia, Brazil, British India, Chile, Japan, Mexico, New Zealand, Peru, South Africa.
§ The world indices are probably on the low side since the League of Nations' estimates for the United States require some upward revision.

SOURCES: League of Nations, *World Production and Prices, 1925–1932* (1933), pp. 45, 49; for the United States, OEEC, *Industrial Statistics, 1900–1959* (1960), p. 9.

Most of the main regions of the world, whether industrial or primary-producing, shared in the prosperity, though some more than others. A regional breakdown of activity for industrial and primary production is given in Tables 7 and 8. All regions recorded substantial increases in industrial production and there was more

TABLE 8
INDICES OF WORLD PRIMARY PRODUCTION BY REGION, 1925–9
(1925 = 100)

	1925	1926	1927	1928	1929
Europe (excluding U.S.S.R.)	100	93·7	105·3	109·5	117·9
Europe (including U.S.S.R.)	100	97·9	106·4	109·6	118·1
North America	100	103·1	101·0	106·2	105·2
Latin America	100	101·1	106·3	109·5	109·5
Africa	100	100·0	103·2	108·4	114·7
Asia (excluding Asiatic Russia)	100	100·0	102·1	106·2	107·2
Oceania	100	108·6	105·4	112·9	109·7
World Total *	100	100·0	103·1	107·3	110·4
of which:					
Agricultural production	100	99·0	101·0	105·1	106·1
Non-agricultural production	100	102·2	111·1	116·7	126·7

* 62 commodities weighted by 1930 values.

SOURCE: League of Nations, *World Production and Prices, 1925–1932* (1933),
p. 17.

uniformity in rates of advance than in the first half of the 1920s.
Progress in Europe as a whole, for example, matched that of the
United States. The major exception was the U.S.S.R. which
registered a remarkable advance in output, but much of this only
served to recoup what had been lost in the war and the early years
of the new Bolshevik regime. Fairly widespread advance was also
apparent in primary production though here there was greater
diversity between the regions. Europe regained some of the
ground she had previously lost and eastern Europe did better than
countries to the west and north.[2] Africa also achieved an above-
average rate of advance which partly reflected the strong demand
for vegetable oils and fats. In general those countries or regions
which concentrated on minerals and raw materials did considerably better than those engaged in producing agricultural products
in which market conditions were deteriorating.

Such broad indicators of progress do however convey a
misleading impression of a pervasive boom. The boom was far
less extensive and sustained than one generally imagines. Virtually
all countries for which recorded data are available did show an
increase in economic activity in the years 1925–9 but the pace of
expansion varied considerably from country to country and it was

2. ibid., p. 49.

rarely free from interruptions. For example, the U.K., Denmark, Spain, Norway, Greece, Austria and Italy all recorded rather modest rates of growth,[3] whereas Belgium, Luxemburg, France, Germany, the Netherlands and Sweden grew fairly rapidly. Some east European and Baltic countries did even better, notably Hungary, Romania, Poland and Latvia. Outside Europe the boom was particularly noticeable in the United States, where the dramatic stock market speculation lent added colour, in Canada, South Africa and in some Latin American republics, especially Chile which enjoyed a sharp surge forward in industrial output, and in those countries producing raw materials. By contrast growth slowed down markedly in Australia, though New Zealand did quite well; Japan's progress, though significant, was below potential and India marked time. However, a slowing down in the rate of expansion was nothing very exceptional since most countries grew more slowly in this period compared with the early 1920s, though appreciably faster than during the war and through to 1925.

Nor was growth during the later 1920s free from interruptions. This is not all that surprising given the high degree of instability of the inter-war years as a whole. The major recessions of 1921 and 1929–32 were generally more severe than those before the war and they affected a large part of the world. But in addition, the growth trend was punctuated by minor cycles though here the degree of international synchronization was fairly limited. Thus the U.K. and Germany suffered setbacks in 1926 associated with the General Strike and the stabilization crisis respectively. In the following year the United States experienced a recession as did France, Italy and Denmark, while Japan was in the throes of a severe banking crisis. The U.K. experienced another dip, albeit modest, in industrial production in 1928 and so did India and Poland, while Germany's expansion showed signs of faltering later in the year. During the first half of 1929 and into the third quarter in many cases, there was a strong upsurge in activity; yet in several countries production either remained static or declined slightly on an annual basis in, for instance, Germany, Austria, Poland, Australia, Finland and Argentina. Generally speaking,

3. Kindleberger's suggestion that the boom was most pronounced in Italy and Australia is somewhat wide of the mark. C. P. Kindleberger, *The World in Depression, 1929–1939* (1973), p. 60.

these recessions were more moderate than those in the first half of the decade. Nevertheless, few countries, apart from Luxemburg and the Netherlands, escaped minor setbacks during this short period.

Despite these interruptions many countries did experience substantial growth in industrial output or primary production or both, but whether they enjoyed real boom conditions is another matter. In few countries, with the possible exception of France, was there any of the serious pressure on real resources which one normally associates with boom conditions. Indeed rather the opposite since indicators for unemployment, prices, wages and capacity suggest there was still considerable slack to be taken up. Swedish industrial output rose by over a third between 1925 and 1929 yet wholesale prices fell by 13 per cent, average hourly earnings in industry rose by a mere 7 per cent, while unemployment even at the peak of prosperity, 1928-9, remained at around 10 per cent.[4] The position was no better in Germany. Unemployment throughout the later 1920s averaged well over 10 per cent, wages rose slowly and prices drifted downwards; even by 1929 she barely managed to attain her pre-war level of per capita income.[5] Unemployment rates of around 10 per cent were by no means uncommon in the 1920s and in some countries, notably those with a poor growth record such as Norway and Denmark, the rate was a great deal worse. If anything the absolute magnitude of the problem increased during the course of the decade. Landes suggests that in Europe as a whole the number of unemployed rose from 3½-4 million in the years 1921-5 to 4½-5½ million in 1926-9.[6] However, too much should not be read into these figures. Inter-war unemployment data are notoriously incomplete and most of the unemployment figures refer to that part of the labour force with a higher incidence of unemployment than the labour force as a whole, including self-employed. Attempts at standardization on a more meaningful and comprehensive basis suggest that

4. E. Lundberg, 'Business Cycle Experiences in Sweden with Special Reference to Economic Policy Issues', in E. Lundberg (ed.), *The Business Cycle in the Post-War World* (1955), p. 56.

5. G. Bry, *Wages in Germany 1871–1945* (1960), pp. 326–7.

6. D. S. Landes, *The Unbound Prometheus: Technological Change and Industrial Development in Western Europe from 1750 to the Present* (1969), p. 369.

the problem was not quite so severe but such calculations are subject to wide margins of error and may even introduce a downward bias.[7]

Even allowing for the unsatisfactory statistics there seems little doubt that unemployment in Europe was considerably higher than pre-war, in some sectors appreciably so. Persistent heavy unemployment was especially noticeable in the older staple sectors – textiles, leather, coal, iron and steel, and ship-building – which faced increasing competition in world markets at a time when the demand for their products was either stagnant or declining. This resulted in severe overcapacity, a problem accentuated by the too-rapid expansion in wartime in some cases and the growth of import-competing industries in less developed countries. The experience of the coal industry provides a good illustration. By 1928 world coal consumption was only some 4 per cent up on 1913 whereas before the war it had expanded by this amount on average every year. Yet capacity was very much greater by the end of the decade as countries cut off from supplies during hostilities rapidly expanded, and there were also productivity improvements and natural growth elsewhere. Between 1913 and 1928 production in Spain rose by 50 per cent, in Japan by 46 per cent, in India by 30 per cent and in the Netherlands from 1·9 to 10·7 million tons. Excess capacity in the main European coal-producing regions was therefore widespread, upwards of one-quarter and as much as one-half in Holland, and even without further additions to capacity the gap between demand and supply would have taken decades to close.[8] Textiles, shipbuilding, iron and steel showed the same difficulties, to a greater or lesser degree.

Attempts to deal with excess capacity were not particularly extensive in the 1920s except in Germany where rigorous rationalization programmes in several industrial sectors were carried through after the currency stabilization. Perhaps this was as well since the elimination of redundant capacity only aggravated the unemployment problem as did the fairly strong rise in productivity stemming from technical innovation. The new growth industries, e.g. electricity and electrical engineering, chemicals, motor manu-

7. On this point see E. Lundberg, *Instability and Economic Growth* (1968), pp. 30–32.

8. League of Nations, *The Problem of the Coal Industry: Interim Report on its International Aspects* (1929), pp. 6–9.

facturing and consumer durable trades, developed quite rapidly but they could not possibly absorb all the labour displaced from the declining sectors which had in any case been overmanned in the past. The employment situation was further aggravated by the fact that European agriculture was none too healthy. Competition from overseas suppliers, improvements in productivity and the slow growth in demand for certain products, especially cereals, meant that agriculture was tending to discharge rather than absorb labour. And in many east European countries with fast-rising populations the amount of concealed unemployment in agriculture must have been considerable.

Nor is there much evidence outside Europe that the boom was associated with severe pressure on resources. If anything the statistical indicators point in the opposite direction. For the most part primary production was booming but prices were either levelling out or declining slowly and industrial activity in the U.S.A. and western Europe was never hampered by a shortage of raw materials. Indeed in primary producing countries, especially those specializing in foodstuffs, there was still slack capacity. Even in America, the country one readily associates with boom conditions, prices were falling gently and wages barely rising in the years preceding the collapse.[9] The cyclical expansion of 1927-9 is one of the few on record during which prices were a shade lower in the three months centred on the peak than they had been in the three months centred on the initial trough. U.S. unemployment too, though lower than in many European countries, was still around 3 per cent. The boom then was hardly spectacular in terms of the use of resources and one must agree with Friedman and Schwartz that 'Far from being an inflationary decade, the twenties were the reverse.'[10]

The fact that production fell below potential in many countries does not preclude an explanation of the turning-point of the cycle in terms of real rather than monetary forces. The particular features of the boom itself would permit a causal sequence based

9. Royal Institute of International Affairs, *Monetary Policy and the Depression* (1933), p. 7.

10. M. Friedman and A. J. Schwartz, *A Monetary History of the United States, 1867–1960* (1963), p. 298. But for the opposite view see M. Palyi, *The Twilight of Gold, 1914–1936: Myths and Realities* (1972), pp. 218, 243, 304, 310–11, 337, and the comment in Chapter 11 of this volume.

on real forces. Kindleberger's notion of structural deflation, by which excess supply or capacity in certain sectors imposed a drag on the system, is one possible approach.[11] Alternatively, since the boom was dominated by investment in producer goods, consumer durables and to a lesser extent social overhead capital, especially residential construction and urban development, one can argue for an exhaustion of investment opportunities with Schumpeter's innovations thesis thrown in for good measure. This explanation is particularly applicable to the American economy and it would be compatible with explaining the international scope of the depression, given the important influence that economy exerted in the initial phase of the downswing. A third possibility centres on the distribution of the gains from the upswing. Though adequate data for a cross-section of countries are lacking what information is available suggests that business profits were expanding much more rapidly than incomes, particularly wages. The net profits of 536 business corporations in America rose by 42 per cent between 1925 and 1929 whereas wages over the same period increased by less than 5 per cent.[12] For the U.K., Hart's profits figures suggest a rise of nearly 14 per cent between 1926 and 1929 at a time when wage earnings were static.[13] This skewed distribution of the income gain, by which the wage-earner did not share fully in the fruits of development, may well have depressed the level of consumption which ultimately contributed to breaking the boom. For the moment we offer no commitment to these possibilities since they come up for discussion in this and subsequent chapters.

Clearly the boom of the later 1920s was unusual. It differed from those of the past and those which were to follow, especially post-1945, in several respects. There was no significant pressure on real resources at the peak of the cycle – indeed there was still considerable slack to be taken up. Prices were drifting downwards slowly

11. Kindleberger, *The World in Depression, 1929–1939*, p. 106, though his reference is mainly to the primary product world.

12. Royal Institute of International Affairs, *Monetary Policy and the Depression* (1933), p. 7; League of Nations, *The Course and Phases of the World Economic Depression* (1931), p. 125.

13. The profit figures cover extractive industry, manufacturing, construction, public utilities, transport and distribution but *not* finance and the professions. P. E. Hart, *Studies in Profit, Business Saving and Investment in the United Kingdom, 1920–1962*, vol. I (1965); for wages data see D. H. Aldcroft, *The Inter-War Economy: Britain, 1919–1939* (1970), p. 352.

and wages were subject only to marginal upward adjustments. For want of a better term one might describe this condition as structural deflation within a cyclical boom.[14] The main point of similarity was the significant rise in output, together with the upsurge in business profits in industrial countries.[15] But the rises in output and income were by no means as spectacular as some in similar phases of past cycles and it is surely an exaggeration to say, as Rees has done with reference to America in the later 1920s, that 'at no time in human history had wealth increased so rapidly, or on so vast a scale. . .'.[16] What marked this boom out was the intense stock market speculation in America,[17] and to a lesser extent in some European countries, and for this reason, together with the dramatic collapse which followed, the boom has attracted more interest than it would otherwise deserve. It is appropriate, therefore, that we examine first the American upswing.

The American boom

The intense stock-market activity of the later 1920s has been the main feature of attention in many writings. To a large extent it is a side-issue, though a very dramatic and interesting one, since the bull market itself had little bearing on the character of the upswing nor did it contribute in any significant way to the collapse. Indeed the turning-point in the share cycle lagged behind the peak in business activity[18] and so proved for once a particularly bad predictor of future business conditions: by the later 1920s specula-tion had moved into the realms of fantasy – a gamblers' paradise seemingly without end – which bore little relation to current or prospective business conditions or to the level of profits. Between the end of 1925 and the peak in September 1929 average share

14. The reverse process, structural inflation within a cyclical recession, is a post-war phenomenon and was particularly marked in the early 1970s.

15. Though in the latter respect agricultural producers fared much less well.

16. G. Rees, *The Great Slump: Capitalism in Crisis 1929–33* (1970), p. 18. The rest of the sentence, 'and at no time had man seemed to have come so near to solving the fundamental problems of production', seems to have little meaning.

17. See R. Sobel, *The Great Bull Market: Wall Street in the 1920s* (1968).

18. The common share index peaked in September whereas the National Bureau of Economic Research gives the reference cycle peak as June.

prices more than doubled whereas industrial output rose by less than one-quarter and business profits by under one-half. Probably the share market mania can only be satisfactorily explained in psychological terms, though the disastrous experience of the Florida land boom in the mid 1920s makes it difficult to believe that the episode could be repeated again on an even grander scale.

Be that as it may it still remains true that the United States achieved considerable economic expansion in the later 1920s. This was very much a continuation of the upswing following the slump of 1921; apart from two minor recessions in 1923–4 and 1927, which hardly show up in the smoothed national income data, the period was one of continuous progress. Industrial output rose by 45 per cent (1922–9) and real gross product by 40 per cent, while capital formation remained at a constantly high level of between 18 and 20 per cent of G.N.P.

The prosperity was dominated by certain sectors. First there was an enormous construction boom which was particularly marked in the first half of the period as a result of the housing backlog following the war. This was soon intensified by the need for additional factory space to meet the demand for new consumer products. Secondly, there was a noticeable shift of resources away from the semi-depressed agrarian sector towards manufacturing and certain service trades, particularly financial services and those related to new consumer products. Manufacturing investment in particular was stimulated by 'a concentrated flowering of investment opportunities' created by the rapid maturing of a series of new industries, services and innovations.[19] The most spectacular was the motor car which provided the basis of the consumer durable boom. Passenger car production tripled in the 1920s and by the end of the decade more than 26 million vehicles were registered in the United States. The purchase of cars and also other consumer durables was greatly facilitated by easy credit facilities and some 50 per cent of the cars sold in this period were paid for by instalments. By 1929 the auto industry was one of the largest in America and accounted for about one-eighth of the value of all manufactures. Moreover, it stimulated a whole range of other industries including steel, petroleum, glass, rubber and the metal

19. R. A. Gordon, 'Cyclical Experience in the Interwar Period: The Investment Boom of the Twenties', in National Bureau of Economic Research, *Conference on Business Cycles* (1951), p. 210.

trades. The rapid spread of car ownership was responsible for a massive programme of highway construction; it encouraged suburban development which in turn contributed to the residential construction boom.[20]

Another sector which made an important contribution was electricity. The generation of electric power doubled between 1923 and 1929 and a whole range of new industrial and domestic electrical appliances, e.g. refrigerators, vacuum cleaners, washing machines, was foisted on the American public. At the same time as new products were being marketed on a massive scale new innovations were applied to old products and mechanization was advancing rapidly throughout the industrial sector. Horsepower per worker increased by 50 per cent between 1919 and 1929 and productivity (output per man-hour) advanced by more than 60 per cent in manufacturing. Such improvements brought down costs which enabled business firms to increase profits and hold prices stable.[20]

Thus American prosperity of the 1920s was largely based on interrelated developments, in road transport, electricity and residential development, which provided such powerful investment stimuli that for nearly a decade the economy was fairly immune to reversals in short-term business expectations.[22] A strong and sustained revival in foreign trade also contributed to prosperity. From the trough in 1922 exports rose every year to 1929 at which date they were some 48 per cent greater in volume. A large surplus on the trade balance was financed by the outflow of American capital which helped the rest of the world to share in the prosperity.

Not all sectors of the American economy were buoyant during the 1920s. Agriculture languished and some older consumer trades, e.g. textiles and leather products, did rather badly. Producer goods and consumer durable products held the centre of the stage. But the prosperity was sufficiently widespread and visible that many began to feel that the economy had entered a new era of permanent prosperity. Yet by the summer of 1929 expansion ground to a halt. In the latter half of that year business

20. M. W. Lee, *Macroeconomics, Fluctuations, Growth and Stability*, 5th edition (1971), pp. 145–6.
21. ibid., pp. 141–2.
22. Gordon, 'Cyclical Experience in the Interwar Period', p. 210.

activity declined sharply and the stock market boom blew up. Why did it all end so dramatically?

Past experience might have indicated a major turning-point towards the end of the 1920s. Major or Juglar cycles of some seven to nine years' duration had been a common feature of the nineteenth century and since the previous peak had been in 1920 it was reasonable to expect a turning point sometime in 1928 or 1929. However, it has never been satisfactorily demonstrated whether the tendency towards regular periodicity was the result of accident or whether it can be explained in terms of a self-generating model. For this reason explanations of particular turning-points have often been couched in more eclectic terms.

There is little doubt that the American downturn was internally generated but there remains considerable disagreement as to the approximate cause between the monetary school and those who support real forces. The former, led by Friedman and Schwartz and Pedersen, argue that monetary policy was largely at fault. Anxious to curb the stock market speculation, the monetary authorities adopted a restrictive credit policy in 1928-9. Unfortunately this action failed to curb the bull market but was restrictive enough to shock business confidence and cause a downturn in investment. Pedersen therefore believes that the Federal Reserve Board was directly responsible for the outbreak of depression in 1929 and its world-wide repercussions.[23] Friedman and Schwartz are more circumspect though their ultimate line of argument is much the same. Restrictive action was maintained too long partly because of a policy stalemate within the Federal Reserve following the death of Benjamin Strong, the Governor, in October 1928. During the cyclical expansion of 1927-9 the stock of money failed to rise and even fell slightly during most of the upswing – in distinct contrast to movements in previous cyclical expansions.[24] The subsequent contraction of the monetary stock, due to the failure of the Federal Reserve to reverse its policy, certainly exerted a powerful effect on nominal incomes. The authors admit

23. J. Pedersen, 'Some Notes on the Economic Policy of the United States During the Period 1919–1932', in H. Hegeland (ed.), *Money, Growth and Methodology: Essays in Honour of Johan Åkerman* (1961), pp. 488–9.

24. Friedman and Schwartz, *A Monetary History of the United States, 1867–1960*, p. 298. See also E. R. Walker, *Federal Reserve Monetary Policy 1917–1933* (1966), p. 143.

that the contraction could still have been fairly severe even with a different monetary policy 'but it is hardly conceivable that money income could have declined by over one-half and prices by over one-third in the course of four years (1929–33) if there had been no decline in the stock of money'.[25]

There is no doubt that the Federal Reserve maintained a restrictive monetary policy far too long and that it contributed to the severity of the depression.[26] On the other hand, it is difficult to believe that it played such a crucial role at the initial turning-point. Until then monetary policy was not unduly severe and could not have exerted such a strong impact if the real forces which underpinned the boom had not been beginning to peter out. There was no severe pressure on real resources at the peak of the boom so that one cannot argue that full employment bottlenecks were responsible for the turning-point. On the other hand, there is evidence that investment opportunities were drying up. Several years of rapid expansion had exhausted the investment backlog both in residential construction, which peaked in the mid 1920s, and in the new consumer durable trades. The gestation period for the latter was relatively short and for the time being the market for new products had been saturated. That this was so may be borne out by the limited recovery in demand for both houses and consumer durables in the 1930s. Given the exhaustion of the market it is not surprising that investment would be vulnerable to policy shocks.[27] Thus restrictive monetary policy in 1928–9 probably only accentuated a decline in business expectations that was already imminent.

Wilson some years ago described a similar argument with under-consumption thrown in for good measure. 'The collapse occurred only because the development of under-consumption was accompanied by a declining demand for houses and a serious exhaustion of investment opportunities.'[28] Under-consumptionist

25. Friedman and Schwartz, *A Monetary History of the United States, 1867–1960*, p. 301.

26. Much the same point was made by Currie in the early 1930s. L. Currie, 'The Failure of Monetary Policy to Prevent the Depression of 1929–32', *Journal of Political Economy*, vol. XLII (1934), p. 176.

27. Gordon, 'Cyclical Experience in the Interwar Period', pp. 208–11; see also A. H. Hansen, *Business Cycles and National Income* (1951).

28. T. Wilson, *Fluctuations in Income and Employment*, 3rd edition (1948), p. 156.

theories have never attracted widespread support and Wilson himself was inclined to discount the prospect initially.[29] Under-consumption in earlier years had not produced a collapse largely because of strong compensating factors, namely the building boom and new consumer goods. Had these not dried up in the later 1920s the fall in the rate of growth in consumption between 1928 and 1929 would not itself have caused the collapse.[30] However, one wonders whether, *ceteris paribus*, consumption would have regained its former growth track in the following years given the skewed distribution of the income gains. Business profits, as we have seen, were rising rapidly in the later 1920s while money wages were relatively static; real wages were rising slowly largely because of the gentle downward trend in prices. Under these conditions it seems probable that consumption was likely to continue at a permanently lower level,[31] which would have exerted a powerful deflationary impact on the economy.

There are still some obscure points to be clarified but there is no basic mystery about the causes of the U.S. downturn. Stabilization policy may have much to answer for in the 1920s but it was not crucial at the turning-point of the cycle. The boom broke because the forces that had powered it throughout the 1920s eventually weakened, thereby removing the props to prosperity.[32] It is unlikely that policy changes could have prevented this happening though they would have alleviated the situation. Moreover, it was certainly a mistake to maintain a restrictive policy once the downturn was under way and there seems little doubt that the severity of the depression was very much a product of inept monetary policy.

The European experience

Europe as a whole progressed more rapidly than most major regions of the world in the later 1920s. Industrial production kept pace with the world average while the output of crude products advanced considerably faster. By 1929 Europe had recovered part of the ground lost earlier, though the League's comment that the pre-war equilibrium between Europe and the rest of the

29. ibid., p. 125.
30. ibid., p. 156.
31. The rise in the consumer debt burden would point in the same direction.
32. A. G. Hart and P. B. Kenen, *Money, Debt and Economic Activity*, 3rd edition (1961), p. 406.

world had largely been restored now appears somewhat wide of the mark.[33] If there was an equilibrium it was more apparent than real. Below the surface there were plenty of signs of maladjustment, notably large areas of underemployed resources in certain sectors, the rise in primary inventories, the dependence of some countries on foreign capital and the patched-up nature of the international currency system. But despite these difficulties Europe enjoyed some real progress and by 1929 income per head of population was greater than in 1925 or 1913 even though it remained unevenly distributed.

The rate of progress was very uneven. It ranged from the dramatic, with Russia surging ahead in the last year or two under the impetus of the first five-year plan, to near stagnation in Denmark and Norway which were both suffering from gold parity deflation.[34] Italy, the U.K. and Austria performed a little better but in the West the best achievements were recorded in Belgium, Sweden, Luxemburg, France and Germany. On balance eastern Europe probably did even better – Hungary, Romania and Czechoslovakia in particular had quite impressive rates of industrial growth together with a good recovery in primary production – though the East was only recovering much of the ground lost during the war and up to 1925. Cyclical experience in Europe also varied a great deal especially at the final turning-point. Poland hit the peak as early as February 1929, followed by Belgium in March and Germany in April. The Swedish downturn came in the second quarter of the year, then the British in July 1929, but France hung on until March 1930. The spread is wide and there is some evidence of independent recessionary tendencies within Europe before the U.S. downturn. Some were prompted by the withdrawal of American lending, while the U.S. collapse in activity in the summer of 1929 made certain that a severe depression would develop.[39]

The varied European experience can best be illustrated by examining selected countries in greater detail.

33. League of Nations, *The Course and Phases of the World Economic Depression* (1931), p. 17.

34. R. A. Lester, 'The Gold-Parity Depression in Norway and Denmark 1925–1928, and Devaluation in Finland, 1925', Chapter 9 of R. A. Lester, *Monetary Experiments* (1939), pp. 221–2.

35. See Chapter 11, pages 281–2.

Britain's performance has been painted in very uncomplimentary terms. Lewis notes that there was not even an interlude of prosperity,[36] while Kindleberger maintains that the country spent most of the time in the doldrums.[37] Such judgements may be too harsh. It is true that unemployment remained high throughout and there were severely depressed sectors. The boom was feeble in comparison with North America and many European countries but Britain was not the worst performer. Progress however was very erratic. Industrial production and exports dipped twice, in 1926 and 1928, but some notable advances were recorded over the period as a whole and there was even a minor stock exchange boom. The recession of 1926 requires little explanation. It was comparatively mild in comparison with 1921 and largely a product of the industrial troubles of that year. The main burden was borne by the heavy trades whereas some newer sectors continued to expand, though at a reduced rate. The 1926 recession therefore can be regarded as a temporary interlude caused by a random shock since had the General Strike not taken place it is very likely that economic activity would have continued its upward trend through 1926. From 1926 to 1929 the record was not too bad despite the slight recession in 1928; industrial production rose by 17·6 per cent, the volume of exports by 20·5 per cent and real income by 15·6 per cent.[38] Even so the performance was far from brilliant especially if measured on the basis of 1925; at best it was a dampened boom.

The stock explanation is that exports were at the root of the trouble. Export growth was weakened by high and inflexible wage costs and an overvalued currency. There is some truth in the export thesis but its importance should not be overstressed: exports rose more rapidly than industrial production between 1926 and 1929, although export growth was not entirely satisfactory – the volume of exports was still some way below the immediate pre-war level. But it is unlikely that the overvalued currency was very important in restraining Britain's export potential, though a lower rate of exchange would have made things slightly easier.[39] It is far from clear, moreover, whether high

36. W. A. Lewis, *Economic Survey, 1919–1939* (1949), p. 41.
37. Kindleberger, *The World in Depression, 1929–1939*, p. 38.
38. Aldcroft, *The Inter-War Economy*, p. 34.
39. ibid., Chapter 8, for a full analysis of this point.

wage costs were the real trouble. Though money wages remained relatively stable in the later 1920s, at roughly double the pre-war level, wages in the United States followed a similar course. In fact wages in U.S. manufacturing were more than double those of pre-war and they rose slightly in the latter part of the decade.

Alternative explanations of the export lag are not difficult to find. International competition in manufactures increased sharply in the later 1920s as a result of the revival in European countries, including Germany after her currency stabilization, and France and Belgium, both of which were assisted by undervalued rates of exchange. The delayed recovery of Europe after the war had lulled Britain into a false sense of security. Secondly, many British exports consisted of staple products the demand for which was either declining or rising very slowly. Moreover, many staple products were becoming uncompetitive in world markets because technical inefficiency in their production made them expensive. The structure and composition of Britain's export trade and markets also worked to her disadvantage. To a large extent Britain specialized in exporting staple products to primary producers. This had a twofold effect. Britain was severely hit by industrialization in these countries, while the tendency for incomes of primary producers to sag in the later 1920s under falling commodity prices reduced the propensity of these countries to import British goods. It is noted elsewhere that some of her main markets peaked out at a relatively early date and exports as a whole tended to lead at the turning-point of the cycle.[40]

Vigorous export-led growth in the late 1920s was therefore out of the question. But the failure of the economy to generate a strong boom cannot be explained away simply in terms of exports. The American experience is instructive. The industries which led the boom in the United States, construction, services, transport and the new consumer durable trades, were much less buoyant in Britain. The rise in investment was very modest, especially after 1927, while many potential growth industries exerted only a moderate impact on the economy. Building, for example, collapsed in 1927–8 as a result of the cut-back in the subsidy programme and over the years 1926–9 the construction industry shrank. Most service industries, including transport and distribution, only recorded modest expansion, while growth in some

40. See Chapter 9, pages 233–4.

newer industries, electricity, electrical engineering and vehicles in particular, was no greater than the average for all industry and considerably lower than in the first half of the 1920s.

Nevertheless the failure to participate fully in the upswing of the later 1920s had its compensations. The weak boom helped to soften the impact of the subsequent depression in Britain and left something in reserve for recovery. The economy did not over-shoot itself leaving exhausted sectors in its wake as it did in America, so the chances of an early and sustained recovery were greater.

Several other countries besides Britain suffered the adverse affects of currency policy, and in most cases to a greater degree. The deliberate appreciation of the lira by Mussolini in 1927 was clearly a mistake since it involved severe domestic deflation and high unemployment. Unemployment nearly tripled between 1926 and 1929, industrial production stagnated and the growth of exports was checked.[41] The Italian economy made very limited headway compared with the first half of the 1920s, though some slowing down was probably inevitable after over-vigorous expansion prior to 1927 and because many of the favourable circumstances were disappearing by the middle of the decade.[42] On the other hand, under the Italian political system it was easier than, say, in Britain, to adjust domestic policy to accord with the exchange rate. Whereas political and social pressures in Britain prevented any real solution through intensive deflation Mussolini was able to force the Italian populace to accept, albeit reluctantly, deflation, unemployment and severe wage cuts in an effort to reduce industrial costs.[43] Public works and subsidies to agriculture were used to offset unemployment, though they only scratched the surface of the problem; while agricultural policy, especially the Battle of the Grain, simply shored up an inefficient sector of the economy. Industrial reorganization and rationaliza-tion of production techniques, though in evidence, were never anywhere near as extensive as in Germany, and the common opinion that these were carried out in a grandiose Fascist corporate state, under which large sectors of the economy came under the

41. W. G. Welk, *Fascist Economic Policy* (1938), p. 164.

42. W. H. Pringle (ed.), *Economic Problems in Europe Today* (1927), p. 34.

43. J. S. Cohen, 'The 1927 Revaluation of the Lira: A Study in Political Economy', *Economic History Review*, vol. xxv (1972), p. 652, note 2.

control of the official party, is very misleading. Certainly the government played a more active role in economic affairs than previously but the corporate state, as conceived by Alfredo Rocco, did not come into existence until the early 1930s, and even then it was little more than a paper entity.[44] Moreover, the Fascist corporations which were set up were more akin to medieval guilds which the business world regarded 'as decorative legal props for existing capitalist arrangements' rather than forces of innovation.[45]

Norway and Denmark also fared rather badly at this time. Stagnation in these countries, which was particularly severe in Norway, was largely caused by official monetary policy intended to increase the exchange value of their currencies prior to stabilization (1927–8) at the pre-war parity. The experience of Finland, which achieved rapid economic progress throughout the 1920s, suggests that Denmark and Norway could have avoided severe compression and disequilibrium by allowing their currencies to depreciate.[46] Sweden went through a similar experience somewhat earlier but managed to adjust more rapidly partly thanks to a massive industrial transformation which had been started during the war and buoyant demand for her exports. Thus in the later 1920s Sweden's economy was expanding vigorously despite a return to pre-war parity in 1924, though much of the domestic adjustment required to carry through the stabilization had been accomplished in the violent contraction of 1920–22.[47]

Two countries in western Europe which did particularly well in the 1920s were France and Belgium and partly by following rather different policies to those of the countries already discussed. Both countries faced a big reconstruction task at the end of the war but they had made the most of government reconstruction payments, inflationary financing and disrupted exchanges to recoup lost ground. Currency stabilization did not halt expansion since neither country made the mistake of restoring the former parity,

44. E. R. Tannenbaum, *The Fascist Experience: Italian Society and Culture, 1922–1945* (1972), pp. 90, 93, 111.

45. ibid., pp. 90, 92–3. See also R. Sarti, *Fascism and the Industrial Leadership in Italy, 1919–1940* (1971).

46. Lester, 'The Gold-Parity Depression in Norway and Denmark 1925–1928, and Devaluation in Finland, 1925', pp. 219–22.

47. E. Lundberg, *Business Cycles and Economic Policy* (1957), pp. 9–23; E. Dahmén, *Entrepreneurial Activity and the Development of Swedish Industry, 1919–1939* (1970), pp. 393–8.

much though it was desired. In fact both currencies were somewhat undervalued in the later 1920s, though the gains on this account were probably less marked than in the first half of the decade. Indeed French exports rose hardly at all after 1927, though the booming tourist trade provided substantial invisible earnings. Nevertheless, apart from a recession in France in 1927, both countries experienced fairly rapid expansion and France did not slide fully into depression until 1931.

Kemp feels that France put up a brilliant performance in the 1920s.[48] This is probably an exaggeration, reflecting the contrast with the depressed decade of the 1930s. Even so it was highly commendable given the setback engendered by war. The recovery process was more or less complete by the mid 1920s when production levels exceeded those of pre-war. Much of the momentum was maintained for the rest of the decade. Industrial production rose by over one-quarter between 1925 and 1929 while income per head increased by nearly 17 per cent. By the end of the period industrial production was some 35–40 per cent greater than pre-war, income per head higher by one-quarter or more, while the volume of exports was nearly 50 per cent larger.[49] Even agricultural production surpassed the pre-war level by some 10 per cent.

On the industrial front France made significant strides. Capacity in some sectors, notably chemicals, engineering and metallurgy, expanded rapidly and the technical standards of the new equipment were often very high. Iron and steel and coal-mining experienced significant advances, helped by the recovery of Alsace–Lorraine. France also made significant headway in the newer industrial sectors, rayon, electricity, rubber and motor-car manufacturing. The automobile industry in particular exemplified modern mass-production techniques and France had the largest

48. T. Kemp, 'The French Economy under the Franc Poincaré', *Economic History Review*, vol. XXIV (1971), p. 99.

49. The figures are approximate orders of magnitude since the estimates vary somewhat. See OEEC, *Industrial Statistics 1900–1959* (1960), p. 9; A. Sauvy, *Historie économique de la France entre les deux guerres (1918–31)* (1965), pp. 282, 465; T. J. Markovitch, 'L'industrie francaise de 1789 à 1964 – Conclusions générales', in *Histoire quantitative de l'économie française* (1966), p. 170; L. J. Zimmerman, 'The Distribution of World Income, 1860–1960', in E. de Vries (ed.), *Essays on Unbalanced Growth* (1962), pp. 52–3; A. Maddison, 'Growth and Fluctuation in the World Economy, 1870–1960', *Banca Nazionale del Lavoro Quarterly Review*, vol. XV (1962), p. 186.

production and export of cars in Europe, second only to the United States. André Citroën, inspired by Henry Ford, did much to streamline the manufacture of cars and his large-scale marketing methods were aimed at the mass market.[50] But it is easy to exaggerate, by such examples, the extent of progress as a whole. A large part of industry was hardly touched by modern methods or indeed by reorganization in any form. Much production still remained in the hands of small-scale or traditional firms, using relatively inefficient methods of production and sheltered by market-sharing cartel arrangements. French agriculture also continued in much the same old way – small inefficient farms using traditional non-mechanized methods. Overall farming efficiency increased but much of the improvement was concentrated in the wheat and sugar-beet country of the north-east where large-scale mechanized farming was making substantial headway. By 1929 average wheat yields were some 30 per cent higher than in 1913. But this was exceptional and far too many resources remained locked up in low productivity sectors. Over one-third of all Frenchmen were still tied to agriculture but they received only 18 per cent of the total national income.[51]

Modernization of agriculture could have solved France's labour problems. Manpower was in short supply for most of the decade even with a large inflow of immigrants from all over Europe. Despite the tight labour market French employers were very successful at keeping down costs at the expense of wages. Real wages advanced by a mere 10 per cent between 1914 and 1929 as against an increase of one-third or so in industrial production. As in other countries, profits probably advanced more rapidly than wage incomes which inevitably dampened the growth of consumer demand.

Belgium's experience was somewhat similar. There was no severe post-stabilization crisis, as in the central European countries, and Belgium launched quickly into the 'boom era'. Production gains were impressive, especially in steel, metallurgy and textiles; industrial production as a whole advanced by about one-third (1925–9) while exports surged forward. On balance Belgium probably slightly outperformed her neighbour in these years. Agriculture too was fairly prosperous down to 1930. Baudhuin

50. G. Wright, *France in Modern Times: 1760 to the Present* (1962), p. 459.
51. ibid., p. 458.

regards the achievements as highly commendable and labels the years 1926–30 *'une grand époque'*, though he has reservations. In particular, he suggests that the prosperity of the late 1920s was perhaps a little 'overdone' by premature stabilization at too low a rate.[52] But in view of subsequent events, which one small country was powerless to control, this hardly mattered much. Undervaluation possibly delayed Belgium's entry into the depression since exports held up till the end of 1929, though French experience hardly supports this contention. Actually Belgium beat France into depression since industrial production began to level out in the spring of 1929 though only in the first few months of 1930 did the downward trend become really apparent. Happily the stock market, which began to weaken visibly in 1928–9, was a better precursor of subsequent events than its U.S. counterpart.[53]

Germany by contrast had to reconstruct again since the explosive inflation of 1923 wreaked havoc. True it did not destroy fixed assets – indeed it brought into being much new plant and equipment albeit not entirely suitable for future needs – but it did severely check the expansion of the early 1920s, so much that the level of activity was little better than at the end of the war. Most fixed debts were wiped out but this was offset by a severe loss of working capital. For a short time stabilization itself exerted a deflationary impact and led to the collapse of some cumbersome industrial empires which had been formed during the inflationary period. Doubts about whether stabilization would hold led to a minor crisis in 1926 with deflationary implications.

The tasks ahead were formidable. Apart from the critical liquidity problem much industrial plant and equipment required renovating or reorganizing to make it more efficient. Productivity had sunk to a low level in 1923 and the large amount of new capacity did little to improve the situation. Moreover, given the reparations bill Germany needed a large boost to exports which could only be achieved by improving her competitive position.

Despite the difficult situation the German economy achieved a remarkable rejuvenation in the later 1920s. Heavy reliance was placed on foreign borrowing the consequences of which are dis-

52. F. Baudhuin, *Histoire économique de la Belgique, 1914–1939*, vol. I, 2nd edition (1946), pp. 172–3, 184–5, 187–9, 191.
53. ibid., pp. 229, 231, 234.

cussed elsewhere.[54] It is to be doubted whether much of this found its way directly into 'productive' enterprise but the inflow of funds certainly eased the capital shortage and released domestic resources for internal development. Whatever the precise direction of the capital flow the record of achievement is certainly impressive. Progress was especially marked in the heavy capital goods sectors and the newer science-based industries, and much less apparent in the consumer goods trades. Large additions to capacity were accompanied by extensive mechanization and rationalization in many key sectors such as the coal, iron and steel, chemical and electrical industries. The loss of hard coal reserves in Silesia and the Saar was offset by the rapid exploitation of lignite the production of which doubled. Mining operations were extensively mechanized and by 1928, 78 per cent of the Ruhr coal output was cut mechanically.

A striking feature of the period was the extensive rationalization of productive facilities which eliminated both jobs and plant. The rationalization movement caused the loss of some 2 million jobs between 1925 and 1930 including many handicraft or semi-handicraft occupations.[55] To a large extent the process was dominated by the giant trusts, combines and cartels; many of these had a long history but even more spectacular groupings emerged in the 1920s including Carl Duisberg's giant chemical complex, I. G. Farben, Albert Vögler's equally monster Vereinigte Stahlwerke A.G. and the monopoly control exercised by Siemens Konzern in the electrical field. Thomson's remark that 'a feudal oligarchy was built into the democratic Weimar Republic'[56] may not be wide of the mark. Such concerns certainly exercised considerable power and influence, and subsequently formed the backbone of the Nazi economic machine. But they also had some creditable achievements to their name. A chief beneficiary was the iron and steel industry a good part of which had been lost through the Versailles settlement. Much new and technically advanced capacity was built to replace that lost, while plant operations were drastically streamlined. For example, in the smelting process in 1924, 55 plants with 138 blast-furnaces produced an average of

54. See Chapter 10, pages 254–7, 265–6.
55. R. Knauerhase, *An Introduction to National Socialism, 1920 to 1939* (1972), pp. 27, 32.
56. D. Thomson, *Europe Since Napoleon* (1966), p. 657.

1,655 tons of molten metal per furnace per week; by 1929 the number of plants and furnaces was down to 45 and 115 respectively and each furnace turned out, on average, 2,567 tons a week. Similar rationalization schemes were carried through in other branches of the trade which resulted in large savings in labour, energy consumption and other inputs.[57]

By such efforts German industry had been placed on a more secure footing at the end of the decade. But one must get the perspective right. Much of the considerable expansion achieved between 1925 and 1929 only made up ground lost earlier. Only in the last couple of years of the decade did levels of economic activity and real income regain or surpass their pre-war dimensions,[58] and by then there were signs that the economic prosperity was ending as the inflow of foreign capital diminished. There were, too, several weak spots. Certain sectors remained depressed, particularly agriculture despite substantial protection, and unemployment was still far too high. Exports barely managed to regain their pre-war level, a performance hardly in keeping with Germany's heavy external commitments. Indeed, one cannot but conclude that Germany's prosperity was very precariously based and, as we have noted, the economy was literally kept in motion by the influx of foreign funds.

It is far more difficult to generalize about the rest of Europe and the Baltic countries owing to a paucity of information. What evidence there is suggests that eastern Europe as a whole did slightly better in terms of absolute growth than the West in the later 1920s. Certainly primary production increased more rapidly and there were some impressive gains in industrial production, particularly in Hungary, Romania, Latvia, Czechoslovakia and Poland. After the lean years of reconstruction, the whole area, according to Spulber,[59] registered an expansion of capital formation and a diversification of output with notable gains in coal, iron

57. Knauerhase, *An Introduction to National Socialism, 1920 to 1939*, pp. 27–8.

58. Bry, *Wages in Germany 1871–1945*, p. 327; H. Mendershausen, *Two Postwar Recoveries of the German Economy* (1955), Chapter 1; E. H. Phelps Brown and M. Browne, *A Century of Pay* (1968), p. 436.

59. N. Spulber, *The State and Economic Development in Eastern Europe* (1966), pp. 28–30. On eastern Europe generally see J. Rothschild, *East Central Europe between Two World Wars* (1974), and I. T. Berend and G. Ranki, *Economic Development of East-Central Europe in the 19th and 20th Centuries* (1974).

and steel, cement and oil production. Adaptation was assisted by the influx of foreign capital and systematic encouragement of industry by State subsidies, tax reliefs, import controls and high tariffs. The drive towards self-sufficiency was also accompanied by an extension of state enterprise. Even so, the gains in per capita income were often very modest, partly because of rapid population growth in some of the countries, while in Poland and Bulgaria real income per head at the end of the decade was still below that of pre-war. Income levels generally were much lower than in western Europe.

For virtually all the countries in agrarian Europe the 1920s as a whole was a period of reconstruction and fundamental adjustment to new conditions both internally and outwith these countries. New markets had to be sought, new products developed, agricultural methods were in urgent need of improvement, while industrial expansion was required to cater for the growing population and the resources released from the land. Most countries managed to make some, though slow, progress in all respects. Given the high agricultural content of these economies and their dependence on imported supplies for industrial diversification, probably the first and most essential step was to reform agriculture and improve its efficiency so as to permit an increase in exports and provide much-needed foreign exchange. Some post-war land reforms impeded progress in this respect since they led to a greater fragmentation of holdings which was inimical to innovation and enhanced efficiency. On the other hand, several countries did make considerable progress which helped to strengthen their economic position. An enlightened agricultural policy in Czechoslovakia did much to support the prosperity of industry. Land reform was accompanied by technical and financial assistance to farmers who improved their methods of production and concentrated on the more profitable crops such as sugar-beet. The large estates in Lithuania were replaced by a progressive co-operative movement the leaders of which recognized that the peasantry would be condemned to subsistence farming unless old practices were changed. Within a decade Lithuania, like Denmark, had shifted from cereals to dairy and livestock products which could be sold at excellent prices abroad.[60] The other Baltic states also proved highly successful in adapting their primary sectors by

60. P. Alpert, *Twentieth Century Economic History of Europe* (1951), p. 114.

exploiting their forest resources, and Estonia and Latvia developed foreign markets for butter and bacon.[61]

Evidence of progress is not difficult to find but it hardly amounts to a revolution. At the end of the 1920s eastern Europe remained backward and economically vulnerable. Standards of living were low and both agriculture and industry were highly inefficient by western standards. A policy of economic nationalism, while not without effect, tended to foster inefficiency and high-cost enterprises. The area remained very sensitive to events in the outside world because of its heavy dependence on exporting primary products, especially agricultural commodities, at favourable prices and its reliance on imported capital. Only for as long as these conditions held could its shaky equilibrium be maintained.

Expansion along the periphery

Conditions outside Europe and America varied a great deal in the later 1920s, from slow or no growth at all to rapid advance, though expansion predominated. Most countries still depended heavily on primary production though manufacturing activity was increasing. Probably the most dynamic economy was the Canadian which outperformed most other countries. We have noticed that Canada achieved a considerable advance during the war and in the first half of the 1920s, when the development of new sectors and a sharp upsurge in exports set the stage for the remainder of the decade. Between the third quarter of 1924 and the first quarter of 1929 industrial output almost doubled, while there was a rapid growth in many service industries. Gross domestic capital formation was 60 per cent higher in 1926–30 than in the first half of the twenties and was concentrated in construction, in the newer sectors such as machinery, electricity, chemicals and motor manufacturing, and in industries enjoying a buoyant export demand such as pulp and paper and non-ferrous metals which accounted for 30 per cent of total exports in 1929 compared with only 19 per cent in 1920.[62]

The boom was predominantly internally-generated rather than

61. Royal Institute of International Affairs, *The Baltic States* (1938), pp. 104, 143.

62. R. E. Caves and R. H. Holton, *The Canadian Economy: Prospect and Retrospect* (1959), pp. 101–3.

based on exports. Exports continued to be important but their growth slackened off appreciably compared with the early 1920s. Indeed, apart from a temporary upswing in 1928, exports remained almost static between 1926 and 1929 though this is largely attributable to the lag in newsprint and wheat and flour exports. Nor does proximity to the large American market readily explain the buoyancy of the Canadian economy although it absorbed over one-third of her exports. Canada expanded very much more rapidly than the U.S.A. in this period and by 1929 the investment ratio had reached nearly 25 per cent as against 19 per cent for the United States.[63]

The turning-point of the Canadian upswing developed partly independently of cyclical impulses from abroad. In particular, American cyclical developments cannot fully explain the initial downturn in Canada since the peak in activity occurred between April and May of 1929, just before the peak in the United States. Moreover, the inflow of capital from the U.S.A. did not suffer a sharp reversal until the July, while exports to the United States turned down after the Canadian peak. However, there were weaknesses on the export front. Though total exports remained high in the first few months of 1929 the deseasonalized export peak occurred in July 1928. Certain export sectors experienced difficulties at an early stage. The paper and pulp industry was affected badly by the downturn in the American newsprint industry and threatened competition from Swedish pulp, while the 'holdback' of wheat in the 1928–9 crop year to secure better prices lost markets as buyers switched to other suppliers. This largely accounts for the early decline in exports to Britain and Germany in the latter half of 1928. But though these developments created temporary exchange difficulties they were insufficient to halt domestic expansion. This was brought about mainly, as in the American case, by the drying up of investment opportunities following the very rapid expansion of the 1920s. In several sectors, particularly residential construction, metals and newsprint, there was evidence of temporary overexpansion and saturation of the market.[64]

Thus even if world business conditions had not deteriorated

63. A.E. Safarian, *The Canadian Economy in the Great Depression* (1959),p. 40.
64. ibid., p. 42; E. Marcus, *Canada and the International Business Cycle, 1927–1939* (1954), pp. 196–205.

there would have been some slowing down in Canada's expansion. According to Malach, 'The deadlock in wheat and the decline of investment opportunities seem to be the major causes of Canada's early downturn. Before these two problems could be solved the rest of the world had also suffered set-backs so that what might have been but a minor recession for Canada developed into a major depression.'[65] Once the export crunch came, with the collapse of the British and American markets which absorbed about 60 per cent of Canada's exports, there was little to take up the slack and few domestic investment opportunities to exploit.[66]

Of the other British Dominions only South Africa made a really notable advance. National income rose by no less than 7·6 per cent per annum between 1922 and 1929, largely because the manufacturing sector continued its rapid development at the expense of mining and agriculture. Even so, per capita income remained well below that of the other Dominions.[67] By comparison Australia turned in a very disappointing result. A slowing down in the rate of industrial growth was accompanied by difficulties in wool and wheat towards the end of the period. Industrial investment was almost halved in the later 1920s, partly a reflection of the over-expansion of capacity earlier in the decade when imports were low and domestic demand buoyant. Moreover, despite further protection foreign competition tended to increase as import prices fell, and since Australian manufacturers found it difficult to reduce costs correspondingly their profit margins were squeezed.[68] Nevertheless, industrial expansion was by no means negligible, though insufficient to make up for the slack elsewhere, and for most of the 1920s unemployment remained high (around 10 per cent). After 1925–6 total national income was static while in per capita terms there was a moderate fall.[69] A number of writers

65. V. W. Malach, *International Cycles and Canada's Balance of Payments, 1921–33* (1954), p. 32.

66. E. Marcus, 'The Cyclical Adjustment Pattern of an "Open Economy": Canada, 1927–1939', *Economic Journal*, vol. LXII (1952), p. 307.

67. C. G. W. Schumann, *Structural Changes and Business Cycles in South Africa, 1806–1936* (1938), pp. 223–5; and 'Aspects of Economic Development in South Africa', Chapter 1 of M. Kooy (ed.), *Studies in Economics and Economic History: Essays in Honour of Professor H. M. Robertson* (1972), pp. 7–9.

68. C. B. Schedvin, *Australia and the Great Depression* (1970), p. 53.

69. Calculated from N. G. Butlin, *Australian Domestic Product, Investment and Foreign Borrowing 1861–1938/39* (1962), pp. 7, 34.

have stressed the inherent weaknesses of the Australian economy at this time, in particular the growing burden of external debt, the increasing dependence of industry on tariff protection, sagging export prices and a high wage level.[70] Copland suggested that the stresses were partly due to pushing development too rapidly and some readjustment would have been necessary even had external conditions remained favourable. But there was nothing to suggest a major economic crisis was at hand,[71] at least not in the short term, but on a longer view the matter is more debatable. New Zealand's position, on the other hand, was less problematical. Though growth decelerated in the later 1920s she did better than her neighbour partly because of the strong demand for dairy and livestock products. Both in volume and value terms New Zealand's exports were well maintained until 1930.[72]

Elsewhere the gains were spotty and irregular. Japan in particular was a mixture of contrasts. In the 1920s the overall growth of her economy slowed considerably, though still at a respectable rate of over 3 per cent per annum. Agriculture, which still absorbed around half the gainfully employed population, was relatively depressed however, partly because of a compression in prices especially after the post-war boom and again in the later 1920s. On the other hand, the growth in manufacturing output accelerated in the latter half of the decade, to an annual rate of 7 per cent. Some sectors did very well, notably the silk industry which benefited from the United States boom, while there was considerable diversification into more sophisticated branches of production such as steel, chemicals and machinery. But the growth record was very jerky. Expansion was checked by the severe earthquake of 1923 and followed by a violent reconstruction boom which led to an overexpansion of credit and the banking crisis of 1927. Not long after expansion had been resumed it was

70. D. B. Copland, *Australia in the World Crisis 1929–1933* (1934), pp. 15–17; E. R. Walker, *Australia in the World Depression* (1933), pp. 92, 100, 114.

71. D. B. Copland, 'The National Income and Economic Prosperity', *Annals of the American Academy of Political and Social Science*, vol. CLVIII (1931), pp. 259, 261.

72. M. F. Lloyd Prichard, *An Economic History of New Zealand to 1939* (1970), pp. 372–3; G. R. Hawke, 'The Government and the Depression of the 1930s in New Zealand: An Essay Towards a Revision', *Australian Economic History Review*, vol. XIII (1973).

cut short again by the world depression and the deflationary policy of the Minseito government of 1929, which was aimed at getting Japan back onto the gold standard. Patrick argues that the muddled and intermittent deflationary policy of the government was primarily responsible for Japan's relatively poor performance in the 1920s.[73]

But Japan was more fortunate than many other countries in the East. Few, apart from China, enjoyed anything approaching an industrial boom. In the Malayan territories prosperity depended on the continued demand for the raw materials of the region rather than on diversification into secondary industry. The boom virtually by-passed India. The flourish of industrial activity during and shortly after the war soon lost its momentum and there is even a suggestion of 'deindustrialization' as revived foreign competition made many industrial and handicraft workers redundant.[74] Cotton textiles was the one reasonably bright spot but this could hardly compensate for stagnation in agriculture and the export trade.[75] Indeed, measured by any indicator, 'India remained industrially backward and almost stagnant'.[76] Apart from the obvious handicaps of its traditional economy, India suffered from an overvalued exchange, falling primary product prices in her main markets and widespread labour unrest in 1928–9. Even Vera Anstey, who takes a slightly more favourable view of the 1920s, is inclined to regard the Indian economy as somewhat unstable and unbalanced which inevitably made it vulnerable to external shocks.[77]

In industrial development many Latin American republics had a far better record than their Asian counterparts. By the 1920s some, notably Argentina, Mexico and to a lesser extent Brazil, already had sizeable industrial sectors, while several others benefited appreciably from demand for their raw products, especially tin and crude oil. It was principally the countries

73. H. T. Patrick, 'The Economic Muddle of the 1920s', Chapter 7 of J. W. Morley (ed.), *Dilemmas of Growth in Prewar Japan* (1971), p. 213; W. W. Lockwood, *The Economic Development of Japan* (1968), pp. 42–4, 55–62.

74. K. L. Mitchell, *Industrialisation of the Western Pacific* (1942), p. 227.

75. A. K. Bagchi, *Private Investment in India, 1900–1939* (1972), pp. 85–7.

76. D. R. Gadgil, *The Industrial Evolution of India in Recent Times*, 5th edition (1971), p. 167, and V. B. Singh, *Economic History of India 1857–1956* (1965), pp. 656–60, 700–702.

77. V. Anstey, *The Economic Development of India*, 4th edition (1952), pp. 469, 491, 495.

supplying raw materials which enjoyed boom conditions in the later 1920s since export-led industrialization was showing signs of exhaustion well before 1929, particularly in those countries, such as Brazil and Argentina, which depended on the export of food products, but industrial activity also stagnated in Mexico after the mid 1920s.[78] In part this general slowing down can be attributed to the intrinsic limitations of the form which industrialization took. It was based primarily on a nucleus of industries producing non-durable consumer goods, e.g. textiles, leather, clothing, processed foods, building materials – industries which could not easily generate sustained growth on a wider front once the import replacement demand had been met. Moreover, an industrial structure geared to producing relatively unsophisticated consumer products had little need of the modern technology associated with capital goods industries even if foreign assistance had been readily available.[79]

As a whole the Latin American economies continued to depend heavily on primary production and the export of one or two commodities. Moreover, their development was propped up to a considerable extent by the influx of foreign funds. Not surprisingly their position remained unstable and vulnerable to a change in external conditions the details of which are outlined more fully in subsequent chapters.

In sum there was a boom of sorts in the later 1920s but it was certainly not as strong or as pervasive as some commentators would have us believe. It was patchy and lacked some of the features of previous cyclical booms. The foundations of prosperity, in Europe and probably elsewhere, remained 'fragile and precarious'.[80] There were signs of weaknesses within particular countries and with the international economy as a whole. And these became all too apparent once the basis of prosperity was undermined. But for the time being expansion was sufficient to conceal the sources of instability which in turn reduced the urgency of making the necessary adjustments.[81]

78. W. Baer, *Industrialisation and Economic Development in Brazil* (1965), pp. 19–20; S. J. Stein, *The Brazilian Cotton Manufacture: Textile Enterprise in an Underdeveloped Area 1850–1950* (1957), p. 114.

79. C. Furtado, *Economic Development of Latin America* (1970), pp. 82–3.

80. Thomson, *Europe Since Napoleon*, p. 658.

81. J. B. Condliffe, *The Commerce of Nations* (1951), p. 440.

9

The Problems of Primary Producers

There are several reasons why particular attention should be devoted to the primary producing countries in the 1920s. For one thing the larger part of the world's population was engaged either directly or indirectly in the production or processing of agricultural or raw material products. Secondly, many countries were heavily dependent on one or two products, the unstable demand and supply conditions of which often gave rise to serious difficulties. Over-supply and falling prices could seriously strain their economies since most depended heavily on external finance, and servicing the foreign debt became increasingly difficult as incomes fell. Thirdly, and particularly relevant to the theme of this volume, it has frequently been suggested that primary producing countries played a critical role in the downturn of 1929 for they faced falling prices and incomes and rising debt payments even before the turning-point occurred in the major industrial countries. And even if their critical situation was not crucial to the initial downturn, it aggravated appreciably the course of the downswing. Finally, as Asa Briggs has intimated, too little attention has been paid to the primary producers in these years in comparison with, say, war debts and reparations.[1]

1. A. Briggs, 'The World Economy: Interdependence and Planning', Chapter 3 of C. L. Mowat (ed.), *The Shifting Balance of World Forces, 1898–1945* (1968, vol. XII of the *New Cambridge Modern History*), p. 59.

This and to some extent the following chapter go some way towards repairing this neglect.

The importance of the primary sector

At the end of the 1920s the greater part of the world's population was still engaged in producing primary commodities, either foodstuffs or raw materials. Nearly two-thirds of the total population was attached to agriculture and related activities, and even this proportion probably understates the dependence on primary production since it excludes the extraction of certain raw materials such as crude oil. The highest concentrations were in the low income countries of Asia, Africa, parts of Latin America and eastern Europe where between 70 and 80 per cent of the population lived off the land. By contrast, in North America and parts of western Europe the proportion of population employed in agriculture was one-quarter or less, though in some cases, notably Italy, France, Denmark, Sweden and Norway, it was still one-third or more.[2]

Primary commodities also featured significantly in international trade. Nearly two-fifths of the world's trade consisted of foodstuffs and agricultural products and raw materials accounted for perhaps another fifth. The majority of underdeveloped countries depended heavily on these products for their export earnings. Triantis lists no less than forty-nine countries in which farming, forestry, fishing and mining products, in a raw or semi-processed state, accounted for at least one-half the value of merchandise exports; these countries contributed 36 per cent of world trade.[3] At the other end of the spectrum a small band of industrial

2. Royal Institute of International Affairs, *World Agriculture: An International Survey* (1932), p. 4 and League of Nations, *Industrialization and Foreign Trade* (1945), pp. 26–7.

3. The forty-nine countries were: Argentina, Australia, Bolivia, Brazil, Bulgaria, Canada, Ceylon, Chile, China, Colombia, Costa Rica, Cuba, Denmark, Dominican Republic, Dutch East Indies, Ecuador, Egypt, Estonia, Finland, Greece, Guatemala, Haiti, Honduras, Hungary, India, Irish Free State, Yugoslavia, Latvia, Lithuania, Malaya, Mexico, Netherlands, New Zealand, Nicaragua, Nigeria, Norway, Panama, Paraguay, Persia, Peru, Philippines, Poland, Portugal, Romania, Salvador, Siam, Spain, Turkey, Venezuela. S. G. Triantis, *Cyclical Changes in Trade Balances of Countries Exporting Primary Products, 1927–1933* (1967), p. 5.

countries, accounting for over one-half of world trade, had more than 50 per cent of their exports in manufactures.[4]

In many regions dependence on primary commodities was very high indeed. They accounted for the bulk of the export earnings and the latter in turn constituted a large proportion of national income – as much as one-half in certain countries. Thus in Africa, Oceania, much of Latin America and south-east Asia foodstuffs and materials accounted for over 90 per cent of total exports, while in India, Burma and Ceylon and eastern Europe the proportion was three-quarters or more.[5] Furthermore, many countries secured the bulk of their export earnings from one or two commodities. For example, 77 per cent of Ceylon's exports consisted of rubber and tea, 71 per cent of Brazil's were coffee, 70 per cent of Cuba's sugar, 61 per cent of the Argentine's wheat, maize and meat, 63 per cent of India's cotton, jute, rice and tea, and 47 per cent of Malaya's rubber. High export concentrations were not confined to underdeveloped countries; a number of high income countries had a similar pattern. No less than 86 per cent of New Zealand's exports consisted of wool, meat and dairy produce, 63 per cent of Denmark's were butter and meat and over half of Australia's were wool and wheat products.[6]

Clearly then the primary sector of the world economy was important. Non-industrial countries accounted for about one-half or more of exported primary produce some 84 per cent of which went to industrial countries, while the non-industrial countries also accounted for one-half of the total imports of manufactures, mostly from the industrial countries of the west.[7] Conceivably the primary sector was large enough to act as an independent force in the depression, and its difficulties certainly aggravated the 1929 downswing once it was under way. The main problem however is to determine how far the primary sector, and in particular agriculture, exerted an initiating role. Did the business downturn of 1929 originate in the overseas primary sector?

This is by no means an easy problem. One difficulty is that there is

4. The U.K., U.S.A., Belgium, France, Germany, Italy, Sweden, Switzerland.

5. W. S. and E. S. Woytinsky, *World Commerce and Governments* (1955), p. 118.

6. J. H. Kirk, *Agriculture and the Trade Cycle* (1933), pp. 80–81.

7. P. L. Yates, *Forty Years of Foreign Trade* (1959), p. 58.

much conflicting evidence and comment, and yet at the same time there is still insufficient data and analysis. Most authorities concede that many primary producers were in difficulties during the latter part of the period and point to the fall in prices and accumulation of stocks in key commodities. But the significance attached to these developments varies. Lewis in particular is sceptical of the overproduction thesis and rejects the notion that the depression originated in the agrarian sector. Yet he suggests that the level of trade in primary products was lower than it should have been largely because industrial countries 'were buying too little of primary products and paying so low a price for what they bought'.[8] Similarly, the Royal Institute of International Affairs in their survey of world agriculture doubted the existence of serious overproduction (except in cereals), certainly not enough to account for the price fall in primary products. They too felt that oversupply was a symptom of diminished demand and then, rather irrelevantly, attacked theories of overproduction on the grounds that there were millions of people whose potential demand for foodstuffs was not yet satisfied.[9] More recently, Fleissig, in a very informative paper, has questioned the theory of overproduction.[10]

Several contemporary writers attached considerable importance to overproduction.[11] Ohlin, Condliffe and Timoshenko, especially the latter who argued a very persuasive thesis, regarded the primary sector as an independent element in the depression as a result of tendencies to overproduction.[12] According to their interpretation a depression would have occurred even without a recession in the major industrial countries. Copeland, on the other hand, did not assign an independent causal role to the primary

8. W. A. Lewis, *Economic Survey 1919–1939* (1949), pp. 46, 150–55.

9. Royal Institute of International Affairs, *World Agriculture: An International Survey* (1932), pp. 9–12, 27.

10. H. Fleissig, 'The United States and the Non-European Periphery during the Early Years of the Great Depression', in H. van der Wee (ed.), *The Great Depression Revisited* (1972), p. 161.

11. For a useful review of contemporary opinion on this matter see S. D. Neumark, 'The World Agricultural Crisis: A Review of Recent Economic Literature', *South African Journal of Economics*, vol. II (1934).

12. League of Nations, *The Course and Phases of the World Economic Depression* (1931, Ohlin Report), pp. 38–59; J. B. Condliffe, *The Commerce of Nations* (1951), p. 481; V. P. Timoshenko, *World Agriculture and the Depression* (1933); also H. W. Arndt, *The Economic Lessons of the Nineteen-Thirties* (1944), p. 11.

sector, but maintained that the raw commodity situation helped to turn the business slump which began in 1929 into a major economic disaster.[13] More recent writers have also acknowledged the existence of a supply problem but have been more cautious in attributing a key role to the primary sector.[14] Lee suggests that even without the depression the position of the primary producers would have been just as desperate in the 1930s,[15] while Kindleberger gets the best of both worlds when he argues a case for structural deflation in the primary product economy but suggests that this could have been alleviated by the absence of monetary deflation. 'Surpluses and deflation provided the fateful mixture.'[16]

That the debate has reached such an inconclusive stage can be attributed to two factors. The difficulty of obtaining data on key variables has limited the level of analysis. In particular, the inadequate figures on national income and export earnings for a reasonable cross-section of primary producers have made it difficult to determine exactly how they fared in the 1920s. Prices and stocks have been used as proxies but may not reflect the true position. Secondly, the mode of analysis has left much to be desired, since most writers have been very unsystematic in using the data available. Basically the issue must be examined in three stages. First, it is necessary to determine how extensive overproduction was and whether it had a significant effect on the earnings and incomes of primary producers. Secondly, what impact did the fall in incomes have on the demand for imports from industrial countries? Was the decline in primary incomes early enough and large enough to affect the exports of say the U.S.A. and U.K. sufficiently to induce an externally-generated downturn? And finally, why was the deflationary impact of

13. M. T. Copeland, *A Raw Commodity Revolution* (1938).

14. Though Alpert suggests that the world depression began in the primary producing countries and it was this that destroyed the unsteady balance of U.S. prosperity. He also uses a similar explanation for the 1921 depression. P. Alpert, *Twentieth Century Economic History of Europe* (1951), pp. 50, 122.

15. C. H. Lee, 'The Effects of the Depression on Primary Producing Countries', *Journal of Contemporary History*, vol. IV (1969), p. 141.

16. C. P. Kindleberger, *The World in Depression, 1929–1939* (1973), p. 107. Other writers have noted the existence of overproduction but declined to comment on its significance in terms of the 1929 downturn. See J. W. F. Rowe, *Primary Commodities in International Trade* (1965), pp. 79–84; P. L. Yates, *Commodity Control: A Study of Primary Products* (1943), especially pp. 212–13.

falling primary prices and earnings not offset by increased consumer spending in the industrial countries as falling import prices
made real incomes rise?

Was there an oversupply problem?

The large number of products involved make it difficult to generalize since demand and supply relationships varied considerably
from one commodity to another. An exhaustive treatment would
therefore require detailed examination of each commodity
separately. Moreover, it is not always easy to determine oversupply, or given oversupply that the export earnings of the
countries concerned are reduced. Falling prices do not necessarily
indicate overproduction: they may simply reflect a reduction in
costs through technical innovation and improvements in productivity. Similarly, temporary stockpiling of unusually good crops in
certain years does not necessarily indicate long-run overproduction.
Conversely, overproduction may exist even though prices and
export earnings are maintained if the market is rigged in the producers' favour by a restriction scheme. Alternatively, a decline in
prices may be offset by higher export volumes. However, generally
speaking, one would be normally inclined to conclude that
continuously falling prices and rising stock levels indicate increasing oversupply and a tendency towards depressed earnings.

Technically there were several good reasons why oversupply,
especially in foodstuffs, might have been expected in the 1920s.
The war and post-war boom gave an enormous boost to primary
production outside Europe. The two most notable examples were
cereals (wheat especially) and sugar. Moreover, because the
production cycle in many primary commodities responds exces-
sively but slowly to demand stimuli, part of the increased production came on stream after the boom had petered out. This
expansion was often maintained or even augmented after the war
even though European production had fully recovered by the
later 1920s, in part because primary supply is inelastic in the short
run since it is difficult to cut back quickly. Supply is surprisingly
inelastic with respect to price changes and in some cases even
reacts in a perverse manner. When prices fall agrarian producers
often increase production for a time to maintain their aggregate
incomes. Thus the sharp fall in prices after the post-war boom

reduced farm incomes and increased the burden of agrarian debt considerably and in an attempt to maintain gross earnings and reduce unit overheads farmers tended to produce more rather than less which simply aggravated the situation.[17] Declining prices for some products in the later 1920s called forth a similar response. The most notable example is perhaps Japanese silk production; from 1925 to 1931 cocoon prices fell by more than two-thirds but output rose by 25 per cent.[18] The recovery in primary prices during the middle of the 1920s, together with restriction schemes for certain commodities which maintained prices above the equilibrium level, had a similar effect by encouraging producers to be optimistic. In other words, whichever way prices moved in the short term the effect was basically the same – producers were encouraged to increase their output.

Technical factors were also important in two respects. First, synthetic substitutes, for example, nitrates and rubber, together with increased reclamation or recycling of scrap materials, cut down the demand for some original base products. Secondly, and more important, rapid technical progress over a fairly wide area of primary production seems to have occurred. This included not only the mechanization of farming practices, especially in the U.S.A., but also new plant strains, increased use of fertilizers, better methods of disease control and a host of other improvements. The rate of progress varied from commodity to commodity but most authorities agree that technical progress was more rapid in this period, and Copeland even describes the process as a raw commodity revolution.[19] These developments increased considerably the productive potential of the primary producing regions and at the same time lowered the costs of production. This cost-reducing effect makes it difficult to determine how far the fall in prices was due to oversupply.

Finally, demand forces also worked in the same direction for some commodities. The development of substitutes and the reclamation of scrap reduced the demand for certain products. The most obvious instance is the rapid shift towards oil as a fuel in place of coal, and the examples of nitrates and rubber already

17. J. P. Day, *An Introduction to World Economic History since the Great War* (1939), p. 47.
18. W. W. Lockwood, *The Economic Development of Japan* (1968), p. 57.
19. Copeland, *A Raw Commodity Revolution*.

mentioned. In addition, some food products, notably cereals, faced an inelastic demand schedule as a result of a slowing down of population growth and a change in dietary patterns in the main consuming regions. This was particularly true of north-west Europe where population growth slowed down very sharply over the period 1913 to 1929.

The above factors suggest a tendency towards overproduction in primary commodities during the 1920s. It remains to be seen whether this expectation was realized.

The global data hardly suggest severe oversupply. Food production as a whole increased more rapidly than population between 1913 and 1929 (18 per cent as against 11–12 per cent); world food exports outstripped this rate of production partly because deficiencies in certain areas continued and partly as a result of the increased demand for more sophisticated foods such as meat, fruit and vegetables etc., in the high-income countries. The only real problem commodity in this respect was cereals where exports rose slightly less than world production. Output of raw materials over the same period expanded by approximately 60 per cent, a rate only slightly higher than the growth in world manufacturing production and trade.[20] However, this does not prove conclusively that oversupply conditions did not exist. For one thing measurement between initial and terminal years only may conceal several intermediate years of abundance which resulted in stockpiling and falling prices. Secondly, the aggregate data do not reveal the wide variations in supply conditions between different commodities.

For this reason the statistics on stocks and prices for individual commodities provide a better assessment. These show that for several important commodities (notably wheat, sugar, coffee, cotton, rubber, natural silk, lead, zinc and mineral oil) stocks were rising steadily and prices falling from around the mid 1920s. On average stocks nearly doubled between 1924 and 1929 while prices fell by between 25 and 30 per cent, and for particular commodities the changes were even more dramatic.[21] Timoshenko gives a list of fifteen commodities, ranked on the basis of

20. Based on data in A. Loveday, *Britain and World Trade* (1931), p. 49 and P. L. Yates, *Forty Years of Foreign Trade* (1959), pp. 39, 62, 63.
21. See the data in League of Nations, *World Production and Prices, 1925–1932* (1933), p. 34; Timoshenko, *World Agriculture and the Depression*, p. 122

their value in international trade, whose prices were falling before 1929 and which accounted for nearly one-quarter of world exports.[22] Exports of these commodities comprised about one-half the total exports by value of sixteen principal agrarian countries outside Europe, namely Argentina, Brazil, Uruguay, Cuba, Canada, Australia, New Zealand, South Africa, Algeria, Egypt, British India, the Dutch East Indies, British Malaya, French Indo-China, China and Siam.[23]

For a number of the commodities listed above serious difficulties did develop during the 1920s. Most authorities agree that the wheat market was becoming glutted, though the problem really only became acute in the late 1920s. During the war and early post-war years there was an enormous expansion of wheat acreage in Canada, Australia, the U.S.A. and Argentina which made up the deficiency in Europe including Russia. Even with the expansion in the newer regions world wheat production in the early 1920s was still slightly below pre-war, and given the increase in population, per capita consumption was somewhat less.[24] By the late 1920s however the position had changed considerably. The recovery of European production, bumper crops in Europe and Canada in 1928–9,[25] and the subsequent re-entry of Russia into the world wheat market, pushed production well above the increase in population. Moreover, the consumption of wheat per head in the more advanced countries was declining during this period with dietary changes. Thus for the period 1924–9 world wheat production (excluding U.S.S.R.) rose by nearly 17 per cent above the pre-war average (1909–14), whereas world consumption was less than 11 per cent greater.[26] Stocks in all the main producing

---

and the graph for nine commodities in P. L. Yates, *Commodity Control: A Study of Primary Products* (1943), p. 213.

22. The commodities were cotton, wheat, sugar, wool, coffee, silk, rubber, hides, rice, tea, copra, cocoa, jute, flax and hemp.

23. These countries accounted for around one-quarter of total world exports in 1929.

24. League of Nations, *The Agricultural Crisis* (1931), vol. I, pp. 22–5; W. Malenbaum, *The World Wheat Economy 1885–1939* (1953), Appendix tables.

25. The maintenance of wheat prices by the Canadian Wheat Pool helped to encourage production in Canada; see W. L. Holland (ed.), *Commodity Control in the Pacific Area: A Symposium on Recent Experience* (1935), pp. 132–6.

26. Malenbaum, *The World Wheat Economy 1885–1939*, Appendix tables.

regions were rising steadily from 1925 onwards when prices began to fall. By 1929 stocks of wheat were twice the average for the early 1920s, and the total world stocks of 28 million tons in the middle of 1929 were equivalent to more than a year's exports by all the major exporting countries.[27] Even so, this was still only a relatively small proportion of one year's output and the position might well have been relieved had it not been for further big crops in 1930 and the large-scale entry of the U.S.S.R. into the world wheat market.

Sugar is a more interesting situation since demand was growing much more rapidly than before the war and yet the price of sugar fell almost continuously from 1923 onwards. After the war world consumption increased at $4\frac{1}{2}$ per cent per annum compared with 3 per cent before 1914, while the price of sugar by 1929 was little more than one-third what it had been in 1923.[28] In many respects the production pattern in sugar was like that of wheat. The setback to European beet production during the war called forth a significant increase in cane output in Cuba, Java and Mauritius so that by the end of the war these three accounted for nearly 80 per cent of the world's sugar output. Cane production continued to increase rapidly in the 1920s as a result of fresh plantings of new varieties giving improved yields. By the end of the decade yields per hectare in Java were nearly twice those of 1919–21. But the European beet sugar industry, under the stimulus of tariffs and subsidies, recovered rapidly and by the late 1920s output was slightly above pre-war.[29] The upshot was that world production outstripped demand and stocks rose sharply in the late 1920s though they constituted only a small proportion of world consumption. By all accounts most sugar producers were finding the going unprofitable after 1925 and incomes in the overseas producing countries were falling.[30] However, it is easy to exaggerate the position. The level of stocks was not unduly high while much of

27. M. Tracy, *Agriculture in Western Europe: Crisis and Adaptation Since 1880* (1964), p. 118: Joint Committee of Carnegie Endowment and International Chamber of Commerce, *International Economic Reconstruction* (1936), p. 112.

28. By 1929 sugar prices were about the same as they had been in 1913. League of Nations, *The World Sugar Situation* (1929), p. 9.

29. ibid., p. 6; L. B. Bacon and F. C. Schloemer, *World Trade in Agricultural Products* (1940), Chapter 14.

30. P. L. Yates, *Commodity Control: A Study of Primary Products* (1943),

the fall in prices during the 1920s must surely have reflected the significant drop in cane production costs.

Several commodities in the 1920s were the subject of control schemes with the basic aim of maintaining prices above the free market level. Two of the most successful in terms of inducing an increase in output were those for coffee and rubber the production of which is subject to long gestation lags. Thus large-scale rubber plantings in the period just prior to, and during, the war did not come into full production until about 1918 when the market was becoming glutted. Prices dropped sharply and the industry faced a severe crisis.[31] At this point the British government rescued the industry by establishing a restriction scheme (the Stevenson Plan) in the British rubber-growing regions of Malaya and Ceylon. The main objective was to raise prices by restricting exports, though ultimately it was hoped that it would lead to a limitation of production. For a time it did lead to a modest cut-back in production but the subsequent rise in prices was so dramatic that this was soon reversed. The spot price of rubber rose from under 25 cents late in 1922 to over 100 in November 1926 and then fell away sharply to a level similar to that when the restriction scheme was instituted. Much of the temporary increase in rubber prices can be attributed to speculation and buyer psychology anticipating rubber shortages induced by the restriction scheme, but it was sufficient to stimulate considerable new plantings, especially in the non-restricted areas outside British control, and the tapping of old plantations. Moreover, the high price encouraged much greater use of reclaimed rubber, especially in the United States. In other words, the scheme induced a much greater expansion of rubber acreage than was warranted since stocks of rubber were already on the increase by 1926. By the late 1920s stocks were nearly twice those of the early 1920s and prices had fallen to almost the post-war depression levels.[32] Even so, most rubber growers, who had made fat killings in the period of high prices,

---

p. 31; League of Nations, *Economic Stability in the Post-War World. Report of the Delegation on Economic Depressions*, part 2 (1945), p. 35.

31. K. E. Knorr, *World Rubber and its Regulation* (1945), p. 68; Lim Chong-Yah, *Economic Development of Modern Malaya* (1967), pp. 76, 322; J. H. Drabble, *Rubber in Malaya, 1876-1922* (1973), pp. 184-92.

32. The Stevenson Plan was abandoned late in 1928 owing to increasing opposition from consumers of rubber and its growing ineffectiveness.

were still making profits since costs of production had fallen substantially. But the full force of the new plantings was still to come, in the early 1930s, when the planters reaped the harvest of their over-expansion in the mid 1920s.[33]

Since the early twentieth century the Brazilian government had sought, with varying degrees of success, to regulate the coffee market. In an effort to stabilize prices it had instituted several valorization schemes which bought up part of the coffee crop and withheld it from the market. When the federal government abandoned the process of control in 1924, Sao Paulo, the largest producing state accounting for three-quarters of Brazil's output and two-thirds of the world supply, established a permanent defence programme.[34] A Coffee Institute was set up to maintain prices by regulating supplies coming onto the market, a process financed by heavy borrowing abroad. The defence scheme was quite successful since prices were maintained at a fairly high level for several years up to 1929. But it also had unfortunate consequences. It stimulated excessive planting both in Brazil and elsewhere, far in excess of immediate requirements. By 1929 Brazil's productive capacity was nearly double what it had been five years earlier, and nearly twice the amount exported.[35] But even before these extensions had reached their full effect production was racing ahead of demand with bumper crops derived from earlier plantings and expanded production in other countries, notably Colombia. Not surprisingly world coffee stocks rose rapidly in the later 1920s to reach a level not far short of one year's consumption. Most of the stocks were in Brazil and, with the prospect of further massive crops in 1929–30, the resources of the Sao Paulo Coffee Institute were severely strained. When foreign finance dried up in the autumn of 1929 the Institute ran out of funds, market intervention was withdrawn and coffee prices collapsed.[36]

Both the coffee and rubber control schemes brought short-term gains to the producers but the long-term consequences were disastrous. They did not restrict production facilities; in fact the

33. B. B. Wallace and L. R. Edminster, *International Control of Raw Materials* (1930), pp. 182–210.

34. ibid., pp. 150–52.

35. J. W. F. Rowe, *The World's Coffee* (1963).

36. V. D. Wickizer, *The World Coffee Economy with Special Reference to Control Schemes* (1943), pp. 146, 161–2, 248.

higher prices induced enormous expansions of capacity, the fruits of which came at the worst possible time. By 1930 the productive capacity in coffee and rubber was far in excess of consumption requirements for many years to come. Had new plantings been restricted it might have been possible to support the high price levels, though it would not have prevented expansion in those areas outside the restriction schemes. One difficulty was that not all producing interests were included and those outside took advantage of their freedom. Thus British rubber growers lost out to Dutch interests, while Brazil's monopoly in coffee was steadily undermined by Colombia, Costa Rica, Haiti, Guatemala and Nicaragua. By 1928–9 Brazil accounted for 61 per cent of total world coffee exports compared with 74 per cent just before the war.[37]

Overproduction most affected the four commodities discussed above. Elsewhere the record was mixed. Several commodities experienced falling prices and rising stocks before 1929 but only in a few cases was production threatening to become excessive by the end of the decade.[38] Tin falls into this category as a result of the rapid exploitation of low-cost mines in the mid 1920s.[39] After 1927 productive capacity was excessive, prices were declining and visible stocks were increasing with the result that voluntary attempts at restriction were being attempted before the crash came. Part of the tin problem arose from the fact that in the post-war slump the Malay States and the Netherlands East Indies had formed a stock pool to take excess supplies off the market for sale when prices recovered. These were released in 1923–4, and so disguised the fact that tin consumption was then outstripping production. Thus tin prices did not react fully until the stocks were exhausted and then they soared to extremely high levels. This in turn overstimulated investment and led to subsequent excess capacity.[40] Lead, zinc, cotton and wool were also experiencing

37. Wallace and Edminster, *International Control of Raw Materials*, pp. 165–7.

38. Rice is an interesting case, since although prices were falling from 1926 there was no real sign of overproduction and most small rice mills made good profits until the depression of 1929. See S. Cheng, *The Rice Industry of Burma, 1852–1940* (1968), p. 95 and V. D. Wickizer and M. K. Bennett, *The Rice Economy of Monsoon Asia* (1941), Appendix tables.

39. J. W. F. Rowe, *Markets and Men: A Study of Artificial Control Schemes in Some Primary Industries* (1936), pp. 158–9.

40. P. P. Courtenay, *A Geography of Trade and Development in Malaya* (1972), pp. 118–19; K. E. Knorr, *Tin Under Control* (1945), pp. 79–80.

difficulties, the latter two partly because of the early downturn of the textile cycle in the major industrial countries. Activity in the woollen industry, for example, declined in 1927–8 in a number of countries and though there was some recovery in 1929 the setback put pressure on Australia, the largest producer of raw wool.[41] On the other hand, demand for an equally large number of commodities was growing steadily and there was little weakness in prices as a result of stockpiling. This category includes meat and dairy products, vegetables and fruits, vegetable oils and fats, cereals other than wheat, timber and wood pulp, cocoa, copper, petroleum and minor products.

Although the statistical data are incomplete, and further study is certainly required before definite conclusions can be drawn, the available evidence does not indicate that sheer excess production existed throughout the primary producing world. Certainly supplies of some products outran demand but changes in stocks showed no general trend towards either shortage or surplus, only great variations. Taking all primary commodities together there was a steady fall in prices in the later 1920s, but again there was considerable variation from one commodity to another and much of the decline was in raw material prices. But the fall in prices was not necessarily a result of excess production since cost-reducing innovation was rapid in all the important raw material industries.[42] On the other hand, primary producers suffered a considerable deterioration in their terms of trade from those of pre-war, so that by 1926–9 these countries were having to exchange perhaps 20 to 30 per cent more exports than in 1913 to obtain the same quantity of imports of manufactures.[43]

The primary sector and the business depression

We cannot conclude so far that the primary producers were crucial to the business downturn of 1929 in the advanced industrial countries. Though primary prices as a whole were declining it does

41. E. R. Walker, *Australia in the World Depression* (1933), pp. 91–2.

42. League of Nations, *The Course and Phases of the World Economic Depression* (1931), pp. 55, 64.

43. J. W. F. Rowe, *Primary Commodities in International Trade* (1965), p. 83.

not necessarily follow that the incomes and export earnings of the primary producers were also declining and that their demand for manufactured imports fell. Some price falls, especially in raw materials, were the result of cost-reducing innovations. Secondly, price declines were partly offset by rising export volumes. If this were not so why did declining prices not have an impact earlier, given that they were trending downwards from the mid 1920s? Thirdly, there is the curious paradox that many commodity prices remained quite firm in the crucial period June to September of 1929.

Unfortunately data on incomes and foreign currency earnings of the primary producers are fragmentary so that it is not easy to see what was happening at the critical time. Timoshenko suggests that the credit balances on merchandise trade of many primary producers were falling rapidly after 1925. For fifteen countries outside Europe they were reduced by one-half between 1926 and 1928, and then fell again in 1929 to $233 million compared with $1,700 million in 1925.[44] On the other hand, the decline in credit balances does not necessarily indicate these countries had a reduced capacity to import since the narrowing of the surplus may be the result of a rising volume of imports rather than a fall in the value of exports. Figures given by Kirk for a selection of countries indicate considerable variation in the movement of export earnings. In Canada, Cuba, Ceylon and Malaya export receipts were falling quite markedly between 1927 and 1929. But in Argentina, Brazil, New Zealand, Denmark, Greece, Hungary, Poland and Ireland they were still rising, while in Australia, China and India they were more or less stationary.[45] Fleissig even contends that the periphery as a whole[46] suffered no contraction of incomes and exports between 1925 and 1929. Export earnings rose slightly, and though the value of primary production fell by 3·2 per cent most of this was accounted for by the reduced value of cereals and other food crops. Furthermore, this reduction was less than the

44. The countries were Argentina, Brazil, Uruguay, Cuba, Canada, Australia, New Zealand, British India, China, Dutch East Indies, British Malaya, Siam, Algeria, Egypt and South Africa. Timoshenko, *World Agriculture and the Depression*, p. 45.

45. J. H. Kirk, *Agriculture and the Trade Cycle (1926–1931)*, (1933), p. 84.

46. Asia, Oceania, Africa and Latin America.

fall in the price of manufactures so that on balance the purchasing power of the primary producers in terms of industrial goods probably rose.[47] However, in 1929 the position of the primary producers deteriorated as a result of a further fall in export prices, a decline in U.S. and European lending, rising debt service payments and some weakening in the demand for primary products from the industrial nations. Hence exchange earnings and balance of payments surpluses in most peripheral countries of Latin America, Asia, Africa and Oceania declined during the year.[48] And since an increasing proportion of export proceeds were required to service their external debt it seems that the amount remaining for import purposes was reduced. For most of these countries, with a few exceptions such as Canada, the credit balance on merchandise trade was practically the only means of meeting their financial obligations.

Thus we may conclude that the incomes and exchange earnings of the periphery as a whole were maintained reasonably well until 1929. In that year many countries were running into serious difficulties. Export revenues and incomes were declining, debt servicing costs were still rising, the inflow of foreign capital fell below payments of amortization, interest and dividends, and the overall deficit had to be financed from the limited reserves of gold and foreign exchange. Hence the capacity of the periphery to import manufactures declined. It therefore remains to determine to what extent this weakness contributed to the turning-point of the business cycle in the main industrial countries. For this purpose we can confine our attention to four countries, the U.S.A., U.K., Germany and France, which together accounted for virtually 70 per cent of world manufacturing production in the late 1920s, while the first two countries alone were responsible for over half the total.

Pressure on the primary producers was likely to be more readily transmitted to the U.K. than to the U.S.A. given Britain's heavy dependence on exports and her reliance on the primary producing countries as markets. The latter absorbed nearly 58 per cent of all British exports in 1929, compared with 33 per cent of American exports, while low-income countries took nearly 38 per cent of the

47. Fleissig, 'The United States and the Non-European Periphery during the Early Years of the Great Depression', p. 161.
48. ibid., pp. 156–8.

total. U.K. exports as a whole led the downturn in domestic activity by some six months and exports to low-income primary producers turned down earlier than those to other markets. Thus Britain's exports to South America, British India, the British colonies, the Far East, South Africa and Canada preceded the general downturn in exports by six months to a year. In particular, the low-income importers of consumer non-durables curtailed their import demand first, which in turn reduced U.K. demand for imported raw materials.[49] The chief industry which led into depression was cotton, which provided a large share of the imports of those countries where British exports declined first. On the other hand, exports to high-income countries, European and Scandinavian, the United States, Australia and New Zealand, lagged at the upper turning-point.

Corner suggests that this premature fall in foreign demand reduced U.K. national income by 2 per cent on a quarterly basis and that this factor would have caused some recession even if the domestic markets of the U.K. and U.S.A. had remained more buoyant. In the event, the contraction of American domestic activity and the consequent decline in its imports aggravated the downturn in the U.K., Europe and elsewhere.[50]

It is unlikely that the same causal sequence could apply in the United States since, though exports as a whole led the cycle, the foreign trade component and dependence on primary producing markets was much less than in Great Britain. Fleissig has shown that the quantitative impact of the initial fall in imports of the periphery was very small. The total fall in imports between 1929 and 1930 amounted to 55 per cent of the combined drop in exports of Europe and the United States, or some 1 per cent of their G.N.P. This assumes that all the imports of the periphery were derived from the centre. In fact the proportion from this source was only about one-third and the decline in U.S. exports to the periphery amounted to $600 million (or 29 per cent of the total decline in imports of the periphery), equivalent to $4\frac{1}{2}$ per cent of the $13·3 billion drop in U.S. G.N.P. in that year. The fall in American domestic gross investment in 1930 was $5·2 billion and, as Fleissig

49. Imports into both the U.K. and U.S.A. turned before the peak in economic activity.

50. D. C. Corner, 'Exports and the British Trade Cycle: 1929', *Manchester School*, vol. xxiv (1956).

observes, a simple static comparison suggests that the fall in investment was by far the more important.[51]

If reduced foreign demand on the U.S. economy had relatively minor effects in the early stages of depression, the ability of America to inflict damage on the rest of the world was far greater. At the end of the 1920s the U.S.A. accounted for more than 12 per cent of world imports, over one-half of which were raw materials, while she was the predominant consumer of many important primary products.[52] Moreover, she was also the world's largest foreign lender in the 1920s and much of her foreign investment was directed to underdeveloped areas and central Europe. On both counts the position of the primary producers was weakened during the course of 1928 and 1930. Lending contracted between 1928 and 1929 while the slackening of domestic activity in 1929 was preceded by a peak in retained imports in the late spring of 1929, though the real impact of declining import demand was felt from 1930 onwards. It is probable that these two factors combined were more important initially than overproduction in squeezing primary producers. The reduction in U.S. foreign lending and trade spread to the periphery both directly and through Europe, in that Europe's propensity to import from and lend to the periphery was adversely affected.[53] On the other hand, the U.K. probably only exerted a marginal impact on the periphery in the initial stages of the downturn. There was hardly any significant downward shift in Britain's retained imports until after the fourth quarter of 1929, while the decline in overseas investment was limited.

In the other two major industrial countries, France and Germany, the repercussions either way were fairly limited. The impact in France was negligible since she entered the depression

51. Fleissig, 'The United States and the Non-European Periphery during the Early Years of the Great Depression', p. 166.

52. The U.S.A. consumed over 60 per cent of the world output of asbestos, molybdenum, petroleum, platinum, silk, sulphur, rubber and vanadium, over 40 per cent of the world output of aluminium, coal, copper, chromite, camphor, nickel, iron, mica, sisal and tin, and over 20 per cent of antimony, bauxite, coffee, cotton, jute, manila, hemp, lead, manganese, mercury, phosphates, sugar, tungsten and zinc. In many cases she was of course an important producer. E. Staley, *Raw Materials in Peace and War* (1937), p. 14.

53. International lending and its ramifications are dealt with separately in the next chapter, pages 239–67.

fairly late and in any case her trade links with the periphery were much less important than those of either the U.K. or the U.S.A. The German position was more complicated. Germany was an important consumer of primary products and an important exporter to the periphery, especially to Latin America. But it is more than likely that the line of causation in this case ran from Germany to the periphery rather than the other way round. The hiatus in German domestic activity towards the end of the decade, partly through the contraction of U.S. lending,[54] reduced Germany's demand for imported commodities. The impact was not large and was geographically localized but it added to the difficulties of some primary producers.

The upshot of the above analysis is that independent developments in the primary producing world were not crucial to the business downturn of 1929. Only in Britain is there evidence prior to the decline in domestic activity of a significant easing of exports to the periphery of sufficient magnitude to induce recession. This is not to say that the increasing difficulties of the primary producers would not have caused a more widespread check to activity in the industrial countries. But before this happened developments in the United States were to dominate the situation. The decline in foreign lending and subsequent collapse of American import demand were sufficient to create overwhelming world-wide disturbances. At a time when the primary producing world was becoming increasingly vulnerable to outside shocks the effects were cataclysmic. Prices of commodities rocketed downwards, export proceeds declined sharply and the primary producers ran into overall deficit with the industrial nations. As a result their reserves rapidly dwindled and panic measures were taken to check the outflow. Once started the process was cumulative; it reverberated back to Europe and the United States and intensified the international downswing of the early 1930s.[55]

One final point remains to be considered. The massive fall in primary commodity prices made it axiomatic that industrial

54. Though this causal link has been questioned. See Chapter 10 (pages 263–6) and P. Temin, 'The Beginning of the Depression in Germany', *Economic History Review*, vol. XXIV (May 1971).

55. I have refrained from dealing with events after 1929 since these are covered fully by the subsequent volume in this series, C. P. Kindleberger, *The World in Depression, 1929–1939* (1973), especially Chapters 4–8. Some brief comments are also made in the next chapter, pages 261–7.

nations would benefit through cheaper imports and improved terms of trade since the price of manufactures fell much more slowly. In other words, losses in one sector were offset by gains in another and the net real income effects should not have been deflationary.[56] The increased spending power in the industrial countries would boost their activity, and lead to increased imports from primary producers. In practice things work out rather differently. Even if all the increased income of the consumers is spent the likelihood of this restoring equilibrium in primary producing countries is rather remote. Only a small proportion of the increased income is devoted to primary products, especially food, since the income elasticity of demand for such commodities is low. Thus the main beneficiaries of the increased spending are the nations in which the rise in incomes occurs and the transmission effects to the primary producers are weak and lagged. But even the industrial nations do not receive the full benefits of the rise in spending power. As incomes increase the marginal propensity to consume tends to fall. This is so even at relatively low levels of income in the short term, so that some of the rise in income leaks into savings. In a survey of eleven mainly industrial countries it was found that in all but France and Italy small-scale savings and food prices varied inversely. As food prices drifted downwards in the late 1920s and early 1930s savings increased, and the damage done to savings in the latter part of the period through unemployment and wage cuts was more than made good by the increased savings due to falling food prices.[57] Thus the trend of savings aggravated the downturn in both industrial and primary producing countries. In time, adjustments to the new level of income may well take place as consumers at their leisure 'learn' to utilize their greater spending power.[58] But by then the damage has already been done. Primary producers cannot wait for these adjustments and in the face of rapidly falling incomes are forced to take restrictive measures, for example tariffs, quotas, exchange

56. The same process can happen between sectors within the same country. This seems to be Lewis's argument though the line of reasoning is not followed consistently. Lewis, *Economic Survey 1919–1939*, pp. 46, 55.

57. Kirk, *Agriculture and the Trade Cycle (1926–1931)*, pp. 45–8.

58. In part this will depend on whether or not the income adjustment is considered to be permanent, though in Britain the propensity to consume seems to have reacted very quickly in an upward direction during the depression. H. W. Richardson, *Economic Recovery in Britain, 1932–39* (1967), p. 103.

depreciation etc., to check imports, while even some industrial countries are forced to protect their agricultural interests from the flood of cheap imports. This simply compounds the difficulties and makes the task of restoring international equilibrium even more difficult. In short, deflation once started is difficult to stop.

10

Debtor Nations and International Lending

The changing pattern of international lending

In the half century or so before 1914 there was a large and continuing stream of international investment and migration from Europe to the regions of recent settlement. The total value of foreign investments by the main creditor nations rose from under $4 billion in 1864 to around $42–4 billion in 1913, while over the same period some 60 million people left Europe to settle in the 'new world'. By far the largest contributor to this flow of capital was the United Kingdom; in the period 4 per cent of her national income and 40 per cent of her gross capital formation went overseas and by 1914 she accounted for 47 per cent of the total world long-term investment. France and Germany contributed much of the remainder, with 20·7 and 16·1 per cent respectively, and these three countries together accounted for nearly 84 per cent of the world total. At this stage the United States was still a very small lender on international account and her heavy capital imports made her a net debtor up to the outbreak of the First World War.[1]

The distribution of capital abroad was somewhat more even

1. N. S. Buchanan and F. A. Lutz, *Rebuilding the World Economy* (1947), p. 156; J. H. Dunning, *Studies in International Investment* (1970), pp. 16–18.

than the source of its dispensation. Europe was the largest recipient accounting for 27·3 per cent of the total, while the next largest debtor area, Latin America, absorbed 19·3 per cent. The United States accounted for 15·5 per cent, Asia 13·6 per cent while the remainder went to Africa, Oceania and Canada. By far the greater part was in fixed interest securities, particularly railway stocks and government bonds, and the proportion in equity stocks and direct investment was small.[2] Though one may debate the motives and the ultimate beneficiaries of this investment much of it was put to productive use and the earning power of the major recipients was enhanced considerably. Without international lending on this vast scale world economic progress would have been considerably less rapid.

The war had a dramatic effect on the pattern and character of international lending. For one thing it created a whole series of new international debts, the reparations and Allied war loans examined earlier. Secondly, western Europe's status as a creditor changed substantially. Most European countries were forced to relinquish sizeable portions of their foreign assets either in paying for the war or because debtors defaulted. France, for example, lost over one-half her foreign holdings, largely in Russian bonds which became valueless when the Bolshevik government assumed power in 1917. Britain gave up about 15 per cent of her investments mostly through sales of U.S. securities, while Germany relinquished virtually all her overseas holdings through either wartime sale or confiscation in the peace settlement. At the same time these countries contracted large war debts and France continued to import capital in the immediate post-war period.[3] By contrast the United States emerged as a strong net creditor. At the end of 1919 America had invested abroad, on private account, some $6·5 billion, that is approximately double the pre-war total, while her long-term liabilities were substantially reduced. The United States became a net long-term creditor of over $3·3 billion as compared with a net debtor status of similar amount before the war. If the wartime inter-governmental debts are included then America's net creditor status is very much

2. In 1914 some 90 per cent of all international capital investments were in the form of portfolio investment.

3. League of Nations, *The Course and Phases of the World Economic Depression* (1931), p. 29.

larger, amounting to over $12·9 billion in 1919,[4] but most of these were never paid.[5] Japan also emerged from the war a net creditor, mainly on short-term account, though the accumulated balances were subsequently used to finance her external deficits.[6]

During the 1920s international lending was resumed on a scale comparable to that before 1914 and by 1929 the total volume of foreign-owned assets was considerably larger than before the war. But there were several important changes in the characteristics of investments. The United States replaced continental Europe as the major creditor. Between 1919 and 1929 her long-term investments abroad rose by nearly $9 billion and accounted for about two-thirds of world new investment. This raised America's foreign stake to about $15·4 billion or nearly one-third of the world total, while her net long-term position, after allowing for the purchase of United States securities by foreigners, rose to over $9·5 billion.[7] No other country came anywhere near the scale of American lending. Britain resumed lending on a diminished scale after the war and her total overseas investments were less than one-half those of the United States. By the end of the decade she had just about managed to recover her pre-war position though her foreign assets now constituted less than 40 per cent of the world total. France, on the other hand, failed to recoup her large war-time losses, despite substantial lending in the latter half of the decade, and her share of the total fell to less than 8 per cent. Even so these three countries, America, Britain and France, accounted for over three-quarters of all foreign investments in 1929. Other significant lenders, notably Switzerland, Belgium, Sweden and the Netherlands, increased their shares marginally.[8]

Britain's loss of pre-eminence to America in capital exporting is not difficult to explain. After the war the surplus available for overseas investment was reduced considerably by the deterioration in the commodity balance of trade (mainly because of difficulties

4. The above figures exclude short-term investments. Cleona Lewis, *America's Stake in International Investments* (1938), pp. 447, 450.

5. In any case inter-governmental debts are discussed fully in Chapter 4, pages 92–6.

6. W. W. Lockwood, *The Economic Development of Japan* (1968), pp. 259–60. Despite long-term capital imports in the 1920s Japan was probably a marginal net lender.

7. Lewis, *America's Stake in International Investments*, p. 447, 450.

8. Buchanan and Lutz, *Rebuilding the World Economy*, p. 156.

in the export trade) and by the reduced value of overseas interest and dividend receipts. Indeed, given the relative weakness of the current account Britain's capital exports remained large, though in some years, notably 1924–7, these were only maintained by borrowing foreign currency to balance the external accounts.[9] During this period Britain was 'lending long and borrowing short', creating large foreign balances in London which became a potential source of danger to the whole financial structure.[10] The United States, on the other hand, maintained a large and positive balance on her current account throughout the 1920s so that financing the large capital outflow produced no undue strain.[11] Moreover, the United States became a more attractive source of funds for foreign borrowers since the cost of finance was on average lower in New York than in London, while American financial agencies made every effort to press loans on potential clients. Intermittent embargos on foreign lending in Britain and the narrowing of the yield gap between consols and foreign securities also diminished the importance of the London market.[12]

These latter factors, together with informal imperial pressure, were mainly responsible for the geographical shift of British investments towards the Empire. This area had always been a significant borrower in London but its importance increased both absolutely and relatively so that by 1931 it accounted for 59 per cent of all Britain's overseas investments as against 47 per cent in 1913. However, the increase in imperial indebtedness after the war was spread very unevenly. Australia, New Zealand, India and Ceylon received the lion's share of the new investments in the Empire, while Canada and South Africa declined in importance.

9. Actually in the early 1920s the positive balance was larger than the demand for new overseas issues so that capital had to be exported in other forms.

10. Royal Institute of International Affairs, *The Problem of International Investment* (1937), pp. 140–41; D. E. Moggridge, *British Monetary Policy 1924–1931: The Norman Conquest of $4·86* (1972), p. 200.

11. H. B. Lary, *The United States in the World Economy* (1943), pp. 151–2 and Appendix tables.

12. D. H. Aldcroft and H. W. Richardson, *The British Economy 1870–1939* (1969), pp. 89–90; D. E. Moggridge, 'British Controls on Long Term Capital Movements, 1924–1931', Chapter 4 of D. N. McCloskey (ed.), *Essays on a Mature Economy: Britain After 1840* (1971).

The second major shift took place in the United States, where British investments declined both absolutely and relatively, a reflection of both the newly found creditor status of the United States and the wartime liquidation of British investments to provide Britain with foreign exchange to purchase American supplies. By 1930 America accounted for only 5 per cent of British foreign investments compared with 20 per cent in 1913. Elsewhere the changes in shares were relatively insignificant. Latin America still absorbed one-fifth of Britain's investments, though the relative importance of different countries within this region changed. Europe increased her share slightly, from 6 to 8 per cent, with much of the new investment flowing to Germany.[13]

Germany was by far the largest borrower in the 1920s incurring a long-term debt of some $7·5 billion by the end of the period, a large part of which was owed to the United States. This was a striking contrast to the position before 1914 when Germany, along with Britain, had been a major creditor of the United States. The flow of American capital to Germany accounts largely for the significant rise in the European share of American overseas investment, from 13·4 to 31·4 per cent in the period 1913 to 1930. Though American investments to most areas outside Europe increased (the chief exception was Mexico whose importance declined sharply both absolutely and relatively), the major regions of attention were South America, the West Indies and Canada. In 1914 investments in the first two areas were insignificant but by the end of the 1920s they had absorbed over $4 billion of U.S. capital and accounted for more than one-quarter of all American holdings, with by far the larger part in South America. Canada also experienced a large absolute increase in American investment though her share of the total declined slightly to 25 per cent in 1930.[14]

Though the volume of foreign lending was substantial after the war it by no means follows that it was utilized or disbursed in the optimal way. Indeed the manner in which it was invested did more to destabilize the international system than to maintain equilibrium. There are several grounds for criticism. From a moral

13. Royal Institute of International Affairs, *The Problem of International Investment* (1937), pp. 144–5.
14. ibid., p. 166.

point of view the low-income underdeveloped countries came off badly since the bulk of the long-term lending went to developed or semi-developed countries not all of which were equally deserving. In the first instance funds flowed to the richer credit-worthy countries rather than to those areas most in need of development assistance. This reflected a lack of any coherent policy on the part of creditor nations as to what factors should determine the flow of funds to particular areas. The profit motive continued to dominate, as in the nineteenth century, the placement of funds, and faith in the efficacy of free enterprise and the pursuit of gain determined much American overseas lending, apart from government assistance for relief and reconstruction of Europe in the immediate post-war years. The increasing 'direct' investments in this period, that is investment in overseas companies or foreign subsidiaries particularly by American firms, indicates a greater concern for control over the use to which funds were put.[15] Much the same forces operated with respect to lending from other countries though one can detect a noticeable swing towards politically determined investment patterns, notably in the case of France and the United States,[16] but also in Britain where the emphasis was directed towards imperial connections.

The dominance of the profit motive did not prevent extravagant and unwise lending, the extent of which was probably more marked than in the pre-war period. The uncertain post-war conditions probably led to greater speculative activity in the hope of a quick 'turn', while the lack of controls over lending practices left the way open for imprudent investment. America, inexperienced in this field, had no discriminating policy and made several unwise investments, notably in Germany and parts of Latin America. In these cases and others loans were not used very productively, and failed to generate sufficient exchange proceeds to service the debt. In effect the borrowers were allowed to overextend themselves, the debt burden mounted and the only way out was to keep on borrowing. Once the flow of funds was checked

15. Though see below, page 259-60.
16. The United States government sought to supervise loans by private investment bankers in an effort to strengthen the Department of State's implementation of foreign policy, particularly in Latin America. See N. S. Kane, 'Bankers and Diplomats: The Diplomacy of the Dollar in Mexico, 1921-1924', *Business History Review*, vol. XLVII (1973).

and economic conditions deteriorated the burden became intolerable.

The flow of funds was far from steady from year to year and this instability gave rise to difficulties in the borrowing countries. Large swings in investment volume were quite common and partly due to changes in domestic conditions in the creditor countries. Thus in 1921, 1923 and again in 1926 the net capital outflow from the main creditors fell sharply only to rise equally sharply in the years following.[17] The contraction in the immediate post-war period was particularly serious since it delayed the European recovery, but the checks in the mid 1920s were less damaging since by then world economic conditions were much more buoyant. The really critical period came in 1928–30 when overseas lending almost dried up completely at the same time as many borrowers were showing signs of strain. The position was made worse by the increasing pressure on short-term funds, many of which had been employed unwisely in Central Europe. After 1925 especially a growing volume of short-term lending was partly used to finance long-term projects; these loans created an unstable situation in which the danger of default was serious. In addition, short-term capital movements in and out of the major financial centres added a further destabilizing influence.

In short, the international lending of the 1920s created an illusion of soundness and stability which did not exist.[18] So long as the flow of funds continued the cracks in the international economic structure remained concealed. But at the same time the lending widened the cracks so that once the flow was cut off the system was undermined completely. As Dunning notes 'a climate of investment so radically different from that of pre-war days, combined with substantial short-term capital movements, powerfully contributed to the world economic collapse of 1931 and its aftermath'.[19]

17. D. C. North, 'International Capital Movements in Historical Perspective', Chapter 2 of R. F. Mikesell (ed.), *U.S. Private and Government Investment Abroad* (1962), p. 43.

18. P. T. Ellsworth, *The International Economy*, 3rd edition (1964), p. 405.

19. Dunning, *Studies in International Investment*, p. 20.

The course of overseas lending in the 1920s

It is difficult to plot precisely the movement of foreign capital since the data on capital flows are none too reliable. Several estimates have been made but they all differ partly because of variations in coverage. Most of the annual figures have a derivative base, that is they are essentially residual estimates from balance of payments transactions which often include considerable errors and omissions, so the capital movements are at best tentative. The most difficult item is short-term capital transactions, the volume of which increased considerably in the 1920s. There is no really reliable series for short-term capital movements as a whole. But short-term funds moved frequently and in large quantities during this period and some were used for long-term purposes. Unlike the position before 1914, short-term capital movements often shifted in a destabilizing manner and their crucial role in the 1931 crisis has been the subject of considerable study. Here we shall not be concerned with the immediate events leading up to the international financial collapse of that year. The primary aim of this chapter is to look at the pattern and character of lending in the 1920s and to examine some of its weaknesses particularly with reference to the turning-point of 1929.

In the immediate post-war period virtually the only country in a position to service the world's capital and foreign exchange needs was the United States. The U.K. resumed foreign lending soon after the war but she was in no position to take on the burden alone. Most former creditor countries were out of commission for one reason or another. Germany, by virtue of her defeat, became a large debtor, while France, as a result of her reconstruction, was a capital importer on some considerable scale in 1919 and 1920. This left only possible minor participants, Belgium, Sweden, Switzerland and the Netherlands, and these too were importing capital in the immediate post-war years. Most of the rest of the world was traditionally a capital importer.

Her large favourable trade balance, derived principally from the strong demand for exports by countries unable to supply their own needs, enabled the United States to become the automatic source of finance for the debtor countries in the first two years after the Armistice. In 1919 and 1920 net capital movements from the United States totalled nearly $7·0 billion and most of this found its way into Europe where needs were most pressing. France alone recorded net capital imports of $2·3 billion in these years, Sweden imported $384 million while the rest was distributed in a somewhat haphazard fashion rather than in relation to specific needs. A considerable part of the flow – possibly $3 billion – consisted of inter-governmental credits of one form or another, while much of the remainder was short-term capital transactions on private account, often speculative funds attracted to Germany and European countries with depreciated currencies. Long-term privately floated capital issues were rare in these uncertain years. In one or two cases, notably Sweden and Switzerland, capital imports were partly derived from accumulated balances abroad. Though the United States was by far and away the largest lender in these years some small assistance was rendered from other sources, and sometimes unexpected ones at that. The U.K. resumed lending in 1920, while certain countries with marketable surpluses of primary products, for example the Argentine, granted credits to European countries until their terms of trade took a distinct turn for the worse.[20]

International lending was cut back sharply once the post-war boom broke. The U.S. government curtailed its aid programme to Europe quite abruptly, while the deterioration on the current account balance checked the outflow of private capital. Thus net movements of capital out of the United States fell from $2,912 million in 1920 to $878 million in the following year, and the amount continued to dwindle until 1923 when it reached insignificant proportions.[21] Private long-term capital flows increased for a time though the unstable political and monetary conditions in Europe in 1923 significantly restricted activity on this account. But this was offset in any case by sharp reductions in short-term lending. By 1921 both France and the U.K. were net lenders but were hardly in a position to offset the large drop in U.S. investment abroad. As a result aggregate net capital movements from the main creditor countries declined from $2,504 million in 1920 to $1,290 million in 1921 and to a low of $639 million in 1923.[22]

20. United Nations, *International Capital Movements during the Inter-war Period* (1949), pp. 9–10.

21. North, 'International Capital Movements in Historical Perspective', p. 40.

22. ibid., p. 43.

The check to overseas lending occurred at a most inopportune time for the debtor countries. Reconstruction in Europe was still far from complete and many countries, especially in central and eastern Europe, were desperately short of capital. The sudden drying-up of government aid hit hard since private investors were reluctant to risk lending to these countries. Under pressure they were forced to let their exchanges fall further in an effort to balance their external accounts. Moreover, the dramatic collapse in prices imposed a heavy burden on all debtor countries who had incurred debt at inflated prices. It created a severe transfer problem for primary producers who found difficulty in acquiring sufficient dollars to service their debts at lower prices, and this in turn encouraged them to increase output further in an effort to maximize their external earnings.[23] This aggravated the price fall and made matters worse so that in many cases restrictive action was taken in an attempt to balance the accounts.

Foreign lending on a large scale was resumed in 1924. Improved economic and political conditions, and particularly the progress towards currency stabilization achieved in central and eastern Europe, encouraged the movement of private capital. During the next few years nearly every country obtained capital from the main creditor nations – the United States, Britain and France. However, certain areas benefited much more than others. American investment was directed heavily towards Europe, Latin America and Canada, while Britain concentrated on the Dominions and Asia. Europe and Latin America took up almost 60 per cent of the net capital issues on foreign account in the U.S.A. and U.K. between 1924 and 1929.[24] Apart from 1926, when there was a sharp check to the export of capital, the net capital outflow from the major creditors rose from $639 million in 1923 to a peak of $2,241 million in 1928 after which it declined sharply. By 1930 the flow had been reduced to a trickle and in the following year the creditors were large capital importers on balance.[25]

This contraction was serious in itself but its real significance can only be appreciated by the difficulties created in debtor countries

23. H. B. Lary, *The United States in the World Economy* (1943), p. 146.
24. League of Nations, *The Course and Phases of the World Economic Depression* (1931), Appendix Table 1, p. 367.
25. North, 'International Capital Movements in Historical Perspective', p. 43.

as a result of profligate borrowing during the 1920s. Any interruption to the flow of capital was bound to induce economic and
exchange difficulties in the debtor countries but the position was
made very much worse by the fact that much of the borrowing
of this period was not self-liquidating. Debts piled up without a
commensurate increase in the external earnings needed to service
them and the only way to maintain equilibrium was to increase
borrowings still further. In other words, the maintenance of
international equilibrium came to depend on the continued
outflow of capital from the United States and to a lesser extent
from the U.K. and France. Even had domestic conditions in the
United States not determined the sequence of events a reaction
was bound to come in time since the situation was inherently
unstable. By the late 1920s many debtors were paying out more in
interest, dividends and amortization payments than they were
receiving in new borrowings (at least on long-term account),
while equilibrium was often only maintained by large short-term
capital flows which were themselves a source of future instability.
This precarious position could not be maintained: once lending
ceased and prices fell the debtors were in serious difficulties.

Overcommitment of the debtors

Many debtor countries overborrowed during the 1920s. They ran
up large commitments which they could not service properly,
partly because the borrowings were not always utilized in a
productive manner. But some of the blame for their increasing
difficulties can also be attributed to the creditor nations. Some of
the problems which arose from the lending process can best be
illustrated by the experience of particular regions.

Latin America was one of the largest borrowing regions in the
1920s. Nearly all the republics increased their long-term debts
considerably, with the United States superseding Britain as the
major source of finance.[26] The region absorbed 24 per cent of the
new capital issues floated for foreign account in the United
States between 1924 and 1928 and accounted for 44 per cent of
new direct American investment abroad. A large part (possibly
as much as 80 per cent) of the American investments were publicly

26. For a list of investments by country see P. Renouvin, *Les Crises du XX*e
siècle: I. De 1914 à 1929 (1957), pp. 326–7.

floated bonds of governments, municipalities and stocks of private corporations, with an average yield of around 7 per cent, or some 40 per cent higher than the yield on U.S. domestic bonds. U.S. direct investments were also important and concentrated in agriculture, especially sugar production, and minerals including petroleum. Investment in manufacturing was mainly confined to Argentina, Brazil, Cuba and Uruguay, largely in the processing of agricultural products for export.[27]

While capital imports expanded the productive capacity of the Latin American countries – and the large increase in primary exports suggests a considerable success in this respect – much of the investment was not used in the long-term interests of the region. Few countries were as successful as Venezuela, where valuable oil wells managed with great efficiency by foreign companies enabled the country to retire the whole of its public debt by 1930.[28] The concentration of investment in primary production, while it increased the efficiency of export industries and enabled the Latin American countries to increase exchange earnings, proved a mixed blessing since when prices fell world demand for the region's products proved to be highly inelastic. Apart from this more general point it is evident that a good deal of the investment was employed unwisely. Frequently capital imports were used to retire previous debts, to prevent default on existing loans or to cover domestic deficits, with little regard to the future possibilities of servicing the growing debt burden. The Bolivian government, for example, relied on U.S. loans to cover its domestic deficits while some of the proceeds were used to retire previous debts incurred in Britain and France.[29] A large part of the debt contracted by Argentina was used for unproductive purposes, in that it gave rise to little additional exchange earnings, and the success in obtaining funds abroad allowed the country to maintain persistent budgetary deficits.[30] Much of Colombia's borrowing was dissipated in public works projects, mainly communications, of an extravagant nature. Between 1924 and 1928 Colombia borrowed about $153 million, a large part of

27. United Nations, *Foreign Capital in Latin America* (1955), pp. 7–8.
28. Royal Institute of International Affairs, *The Republics of South America* (1937), p. 182.
29. S. E. Harris, *Economic Problems of Latin America* (1944), p. 264.
30. H. E. Peters, *The Foreign Debt of the Argentine Republic* (1934).

which was devoted to constructing a railway to connect two valleys separated by a range of mountains about 9,000 feet high. But, as Sir Arthur Salter recalls:

> There was no commercial justification for it, since both valleys had their own outlet to the sea. A very expensive tunnel through the top of the mountain range was begun and then abandoned; and while the Federal authorities were driving a tunnel through the mountains the local authorities were making a costly road over them. I have a vivid account from one who was in Colombia at the time of the way in which the offers of competing tenders resulted in the public authorities incurring greater and greater obligations for these extravagant ventures.[31]

While it would be misleading to imply that all investments were as misguided as this, borrowing countries did fail to utilize capital imports in a manner which permitted full servicing of their debts. Foreign short-term funds in particular were not self-liquidating in foreign exchange. Funds used to finance the holding of agricultural stocks in South America earned little foreign exchange so the borrower could not automatically amortize the debt. The same applies to short-term funds borrowed by European debtors and, as Williams points out, 'the consequence of heavy short-term borrowing was to transfer abroad effective ownership of some countries' international monetary reserves'.[32]

By the second half of the 1920s Latin America's external obligations were reaching serious proportions. The region was paying some $660 million abroad annually on its debts nearly three times its capital inflow.[33] A trade surplus balanced the external accounts for a time but when primary prices fell and capital imports dried up the servicing burden became intolerable. Drastic measures therefore had to be taken including abandonment of the gold standard, import restrictions, exchange control and ultimately default on external debts. By the end of 1935, 85 per cent of Latin American dollar bonds were in default.[34]

A similar situation developed in central and eastern Europe.

31. A. Salter, *Recovery*, 1933 edition, p. 105.
32. D. Williams, 'The 1931 Financial Crisis', *Yorkshire Bulletin of Economic and Social Research*, vol. xv (1963), p. 94.
33. United Nations, *Foreign Capital in Latin America* (1955), p. 15.
34. ibid., p. 8; Royal Institute of International Affairs, *The Republics of South America* (1937), pp. 181–3.

Apart from Germany, the largest borrower whose special position is considered separately below, most countries in this region depended on foreign capital throughout the 1920s, first for reconstruction and stabilization purposes and secondly to further economic diversification. After the war all countries in central and eastern Europe were desperately short of resources, especially capital. The immediate problems were the financing of relief and reconstruction and the stabilization of their weakened currency and financial systems. In part foreign aid was determined by political conditions since if the plight of the European countries was not alleviated and the new nations made sufficiently strong there would have been civil upheavals and defensive alliances detrimental to the security of the rest of Europe and to the new international system. Secondly, private capital for long-term development was not likely to be attracted to this area until currencies were stabilized, budgets balanced and inflation checked.

Thus in the immediate post-war years much of the capital imported into this area was designed to help relief, reconstruction and stabilization. The first aid loans, organized under the aegis of the League of Nations, were designed to provide borrowers with exchange reserves, to establish central banks and supply them with capital, and to fund short-term debts at home and abroad. For the most part imported capital in this reconstruction phase did not go directly into productive enterprise but that is no cause for criticism. Stabilization and relief loans were necessary and foreign capital played a positive role in stabilizing monetary systems and preventing total economic collapse.[35] That they were not represented by income-producing assets should not be allowed to obscure the fact that they were an essential condition of obtaining further capital which could be invested in a self-liquidating manner. On the other hand, the relief offered by foreign capital in this period was insufficient.[36]

Borrowing in the post-stabilization phase was the primary cause of the subsequent difficulties of many European countries. The need for imported capital was not in dispute yet reliance on foreign investment created more problems than it solved. Again

35. V. N. Bandera, *Foreign Capital as an Instrument of National Economic Policy: A Study Based on the Experience of East European Countries Between the World Wars* (1964), p. 130.

36. See Chapters 3, 5 and 6.

insufficient attention was given to ensuring that the increase in debts was self-liquidating. Only a small proportion of government loans were used for increasing the productive capacity of the borrowing countries. Bandera reckons that between 30 and 50 per cent of the public external loans were used directly in productive investment or as the basis for such investments. Further, he argues that private capital, motivated by profits, was not necessarily in the best interests of the debtors and probably only assisted modestly in the pursuit of national economic objectives. The flow of foreign capital was unstable and it was generally believed that to attract foreign investors sound deflationary policies were essential so as to ensure external balances adequate for the future transfers of debt services. Such policies were however self-defeating since they had an unfavourable effect on domestic capital formation.[37] This in turn hampered structural diversification and resulted in high comparative costs.

In other respects capital transfers may have aggravated the problems of the debtor countries. In so far as capital imports were employed as safeguards to plug up balance-of-payments disequilibrium they simply increased the service burden without contributing to development and rectifying fundamental imbalances. Furthermore, part of the capital receipts were used to stimulate agricultural development in an effort to boost exports, a process which merely aggravated the debt burden and led to a deterioration in the agricultural prices which provided the basis for foreign exchange earnings.

Moreover, the cost of borrowing was fairly high and inflexible. Only a small fraction of the total foreign capital absorbed by central and eastern Europe in the 1920s was directly invested in share capital, the earnings of which might decline as prosperity waned thus relieving the transfer burden.[38] Most of the capital went into fixed interest securities at a nominal interest rate of between 6 and 9 per cent, and a real rate often much higher after taking account of the low price of many issues.[39] A large proportion of the debt service burden remained fixed when

37. Bandera, *Foreign Capital as an Instrument of National Economic Policy*, pp. 66, 130–32.

38. League of Nations, *The Transition from War to Peace Economy: Report of the Delegation on Economic Depressions*, Part 1 (1943), p. 23.

39. PEP, *Economic Development in South-East Europe* (1945), p. 110.

incomes and activity declined. An additional complication was that high interest rates attracted short-term capital which, up to 1929 at least, offset autonomous declines in long-term capital inflows, since the national credit systems converted external short-term loans into long-term domestic ones. This was an obvious source of danger once the going got sticky, particularly in the latter part of 1930 and 1931, since it was then impossible to attract short-term funds with high interest rates to offset the decline in long-term borrowing when they were scuttling to safer havens. Hungary, with foreign short-term credits amounting to £18 million in 1930, was particularly affected,[40] though foreign liabilities constituted between 20 and 40 per cent of commercial bank deposits in most eastern and central European countries.[41]

Thus by the end of the 1920s the debt burdens of central and east Europe had already reached alarming proportions. By 1928 outpayments on account of capital services were 40 per cent of the net capital inflows in Hungary, 28 per cent in Poland and 70 per cent in Estonia. In many countries debt service payments constituted one-quarter or more of the value of current exports, though since servicing foreign loans called for 'strong currencies' obtainable from a limited range of exports the actual strain on the balance of payments was much heavier than these figures would suggest.[42] Given the initial strain the insolvency of these countries was simply aggravated rather than created by the depression of the 1930s. The size of the burden was much increased by the large decline in capital inflows and primary prices and the limited reserves made the burden of adjustment fall with a vengeance on the domestic economic structure.

Germany's problem was somewhat different. The magnitudes involved were much greater and her position was complicated by reparations. Furthermore, she was not dependent on primary products for exchange earnings as were her eastern neighbours. On the other hand, as did other central and east European

40. C. A. Macartney, *Hungary and Her Successors: The Treaty of Trianon and its Consequences, 1919–1937* (1937), p. 466.

41. Williams, 'The 1931 Financial Crisis', p. 94.

42. United Nations, *International Capital Movements during the Inter-war Period* (1949), p. 59; PEP, *Economic Developments in South East Europe* (1945), p. 110; Bandera, *Foreign Capital as an Instrument of National Economic Policy*, pp. 110–11.

countries though on a greater scale, she resorted to massive borrowing 'to patch up a temporary stability at the expense of the future'.[43]

That Germany should be a heavy borrower in this period is not particularly surprising. The reparations demands, the chronic imbalance on the trade account and the great scarcity of capital, especially short-term liquidity after the inflationary period, made recourse to foreign aid inevitable. In the short term it was impossible to service all these needs from her own external earnings. But the wisdom of borrowing nearly three times the reparations bill must be questioned, especially in view of the nature of the capital imports and the use to which they were put.

Large-scale borrowing began effectively with the stabilization and the floating of the Dawes Loan in 1924. Confidence in Germany was partly restored but the main attraction for investors was the high rates of interest consequent upon the scarcity of capital and the degree of risk. Lenders poured capital into Germany without a thought as to how the loans were to be serviced. Estimates of the capital inflow vary somewhat but most accounts agree that by the summer of 1930, when the peak of indebtedness was reached, Germany's external liabilities were in the region of 28 billion marks (£1,377 million), some 16 billion (£787 million) of which were in the form of short-term credits.[44] Much of the capital came from the United States, Britain and Holland.

Not much of this capital was wasted even if some did go into the building of swimming-baths, pleasure gardens, amusement halls, hotels, planetaria and the like, so much lamented by Dr Schacht in 1927.[45] Capital imports played a vital part in the

43. Royal Institute of International Affairs, *Monetary Policy and the Depression* (1933), p. 11.

44. In addition, some 6–7 billion marks were invested in German domestic securities, real property, mortgages etc., by foreigners. For the estimates see Royal Institute of International Affairs, *The Problem of International Investment* (1937), pp. 236–9; C. R. Harris, *Germany's Foreign Indebtedness* (1935), pp. 6–10; J. W. Angell, *The Recovery of Germany* (1929), p. 78; C. T. Schmidt, *German Business Cycles, 1924–1933* (1934), p. 110; H. G. Moulton and L. Pasvolsky, *War Debts and World Prosperity* (1932), p. 285; W. Fischer, *Deutsche Wirtschaftspolitik, 1918–1945* (1968), pp. 103, 109.

45. Royal Institute of International Affairs, *The Problem of International Investment* (1937), p. 235.

recovery of the German economy after the great inflation and some two-fifths of Germany's investment after 1924 came from abroad. Moreover, though some 60 per cent of long-term loans were made to government and semi-public enterprises, nearly three-quarters of total imports found their way into private industry and this facilitated re-equipment and expansion.[46] On the other hand, the borrowing process seriously increased the vulnerability of the German economy. Much foreign investment proved unproductive in that it added relatively little to the supplies of foreign exchange, though it is doubtful, even inconceivable, that it could have been employed in such a way as to create exchange earnings sufficient to service all Germany's external commitments. Part of the capital inflow was used to finance a large import surplus (6·3 billion marks), which raised the standard of living, and accumulating assets abroad (9·7 billion), but even if these two items could have been dispensed with entirely (a somewhat doubtful assumption since the first was needed for imported materials), Germany would still have had a large borrowing requirement for reparations, commercial debt and other minor items. This of course does not detract from the illogicality of lending to a country to pay former debts the servicing of which lies outside the bounds of probability.

Even more serious was the use to which short-term funds were put. A large part consisted of loans to German banks by foreign bankers (mostly American), many of which were invested in long-term projects. Since such funds were liable to sudden recall this left the German banking system vulnerable. The first indication of what lay in store came in the spring of 1929 when pressure from reparations payments on Germany's foreign exchange position caused a short financial crisis. Foreign banks withdrew their support and called in short-term loans, and the difficulties were aggravated by the decline in U.S. short-term funds as a result of the current stock market boom.[47] This crisis was soon overcome but it was merely the tip of the iceberg. Far greater disasters were to hit the German banking system in the liquidity crisis of 1931.

Throughout the latter half of the 1920s Germany was living on

46. Angell, *The Recovery of Germany*, pp. 79–80.
47. S. Flink, *The German Reichsbank and Economic Recovery* (1929), p. 253; R. Knauerhase, *An Introduction to National Socialism, 1920 to 1939* (1972), pp. 32–3.

borrowed time. Foreign debts, many of which could be recalled at short notice, were allowed to pile up to an extent which, in view of the industrial development of the country and high tariff barriers imposed by the creditors, could never be justified by her actual or potential export earnings. How Germany was supposed to meet her obligations once capital imports ceased seems never to have been considered seriously by the creditors, a lack of foresight difficult to explain. Even had there been no economic crisis or check to lending at the end of the decade it was inconceivable that Germany could have gone on absorbing such large capital imports for much longer. The alternatives were limited; any attempt to secure an improved external balance would have required severe deflation and even this would hardly have been sufficient. It is possible that the Germans shrank from more positive action to demonstrate their aversion to the obligations imposed by the Allies. That the Allies should have attempted to conceal the impossibility of the burden, at least in the short term, by pouring capital into Germany speaks volumes for their lack of economic wisdom.

The above examples constitute the most flagrant cases of over-borrowing but few debtors were immune from it. Even the Dominions and African territories, much of whose loans went through tne London market which exercised a slightly more prudent supervision over the dispensation of funds, managed to overcommit themselves. Many African states incurred large increases in their funded debts which so raised their interest burdens as to restrict the possibilities of fresh loan commitments. During the 1920s the British African territories increased their debt charges no less than eight times, a burden which increased sharply once prices fell.[48]

The British Dominions also indulged to excess. Much of the growth in post-war debt was contracted by public authorities and most of the proceeds went into public works or primary production.[49] The dependence on overseas borrowing was high, especially in the case of public authorities. In 1930, 52 per cent of Australia's public debt was held abroad, 57 per cent of New

48. W. B. Hailey, *An African Survey: A Study of Problems Arising in Africa South of the Sahara* (1938), p. 1355.
49. Royal Institute of International Affairs, *The Problem of International Investment* (1937), pp. 252–3.

Zealand's and 63 per cent of Canada's.[50] Altogether about one-fifth of Australia's total investment during the 1920s was financed by overseas borrowing, and 70 per cent of the capital imports consisted of fixed interest borrowing by public authorities, the latter accounting for about one-half of all domestic capital formation. This, together with external indebtedness incurred in the First World War, resulted in a rapid increase in the servicing burden. Interest and dividend remittances abroad as a proportion of export earnings rose from 16 per cent in 1919–20 to 28 per cent in 1928–9, and by then Australia's external debt burden per head was one of the highest in the world.[51] Because of the nature of the investment capital imports did not generate large export earnings to service the debt and pay for the increased volume of imports. Hence the balance of payments was in heavy and permanent deficit and the gap was only plugged by continuous overseas borrowing. Public foreign borrowing met two-thirds of the deficit in the balance of payments throughout the 1920s.[52] Thus as long as prices of exports remained reasonably firm and capital continued to flow into the country the accounts could be balanced. Once these props were removed the precariousness of the equilibrium was exposed and the burden of adjustment required was enormous.[53] The fall in primary product prices and the collapse in foreign lending meant that, from the latter part of 1929, Australia was engaged in a constant struggle to meet her obligations. When temporary expedients had been exhausted (e.g. allowing the reserves to fall) the burden of adjustment was

50. R. S. Gilbert, *The Australian Loan Council in Federal Fiscal Adjustments, 1890–1965* (1973), p. 112.
51. Exceeded only slightly by Canada and New Zealand. D. Copland, *Australia in the World Crisis, 1929–1933* (1934), p. 15; C. B. Schedvin, *Australia and the Great Depression* (1970), pp. 2–3, 68–75.
52. Gilbert, *The Australian Loan Council in Federal Fiscal Adjustments, 1890–1965*, p. 104.
53. In terms of either a compression of imports or expansion of exports. With the dramatic fall in export prices the upward adjustment in terms of export volume to effect external balance was very large indeed, and unobtainable given the relative inelasticity of demand for exports. Hence the major adjustment had to come from the side of imports which fell by 70 per cent in value between 1929 and 1931, and this involved severe internal deflation. See Royal Institute of International Affairs, *The Problem of International Investment* (1937), pp. 289, 292.

thrown upon the domestic economy.[54] Australia was by no means alone in this respect; primary producers the world over with heavy external debts faced similar difficulties with similar remedies. In part these problems were the price paid for extravagant and careless borrowing in the 1920s.

Responsibility of the creditors

The creditor countries must take some of the blame for the increasing vulnerability of the debtor nations during this period. Inadequate control over the volume of foreign lending and the use to which capital imports were put, together with the failure to ensure that the debts would become self-liquidating, constituted the initial lapse in responsibility. The second involved the sudden cessation of lending after the debtors had piled up obligations the servicing of which would have proved onerous even under the most favourable circumstances.

The volume of overseas lending in the 1920s was certainly too large. A smaller and more stable flow of foreign capital would have been better. Instead borrowing countries were allowed and even encouraged to live beyond their means, and the ready availability of foreign funds postponed the basic readjustments in the balances between debtors and creditors. With ample foreign funds available the economic systems of countries such as Argentina, Brazil and Australia became adjusted to a condition in which new borrowing furnished annually the rights to money abroad to pay for interest charges on old indebtedness.[55] The borrowers were not wholly to blame for this. In part overborrowing resulted from the eagerness with which creditors pressed funds on their clients with little concern for the ability to repay. Palyi quotes the example of Bolivia who pledged 80 per cent of her total tax revenues for the service of just one loan with no questions asked on how the government could manage on the remaining 20 per

54. For details see Gilbert, *The Australian Loan Council in Federal Fiscal Adjustments, 1890–1965*, pp. 117–22.
55. L. Smith, 'The Suspension of the Gold Standard in Raw Material Exporting Countries', *American Economic Review*, vol. XXIV (1934), p. 430; V. P. Timoshenko, *World Agriculture and the Depression* (1933), pp. 86–7.

cent.[56] While all foreign lending was not a product of ruthless and greedy international bankers inducing impoverished and unwilling clients to run further into debt, there is evidence that, with the lure of high profits in the background, the creditors sometimes overlooked the pecuniary welfare of the recipients.[57] The United States was particularly culpable in this respect. Competition among investment firms for business and the share-pushing activities of issue-houses intent on cashing in on the large profits to be obtained in the flotation of new issues inevitably led to ready acceptance by the potential customers. 'Enticed by the prospect of commissions much higher than those available on domestic issues and faced with the necessity for a continuous flow of new securities to keep large staffs of bond salesmen employed, American investment bankers had their agents 'sitting on the doorsteps' of prospective borrowers, as one observer put it, offering them money and many times persuading them to borrow more than they actually needed.'[58] Such practices were less prevalent in the other creditor countries but none of them restrained clients from borrowing. Even the U.K., whose long experience in this field might have made her a more obvious paragon, maintained a fairly lenient attitude to the excesses committed by her European and imperial clients.[59]

Uncontrolled lending frequently led to unwise and wasteful borrowing and it should have been obvious by the mid 1920s at least that many countries were borrowing more than they could reasonably expect to repay. Moreover, the fact that much of the lending consisted of fixed interest securities at relatively high rates of interest was bound to present difficulties once economic conditions deteriorated. Yet the creditors gave little thought to repayment or for that matter to servicing the growing burden of debt. In fact they continued 'to lend to repay' without at any time ensuring that the loans were used in such a manner as to generate sufficient foreign exchange earnings. 'Neither in lending nor in borrowing countries was it generally appreciated that debtors

56. M. Palyi, *The Twilight of Gold, 1914–1936: Myths and Realities* (1972), p. 207.

57. ibid., pp. 204–7.

58. Lary, *The United States in the World Economy*, p. 96; M. N. Rothbard, *America's Great Depression* (1963), pp. 121–2, 128–9.

59. Royal Institute of International Affairs, *The Problem of International Investment* (1937), p. 165.

could only pay the service charges on their debts by means of an export surplus of goods and services.'[60] But even had more effective control been exercised over foreign investments with a view to promoting exporting industries, it is debatable how far the debtors could have pushed their goods into the protected markets of the creditors, particularly the United States. The tariff barrier argument may be exaggerated but the basic problem still remains. Further exploitation of primary product exports would have faced increasingly inelastic demand in major consuming countries, while manufacturing exports ran up against serious cost disadvantages. Falkus, for example, doubts whether downward tariff adjustments by the major creditor, the United States, would have done much to improve the external disequilibrium of the debtors since the basically self-sufficient nature of the U.S. economy resulted in low price elasticities of demand for imports. Domestic inflation would not have had much effect either given the low marginal propensity to import, and in any case the time span for adjustment was too short.[61] In other words, debtors could not have unloaded many more exports onto the American market, suggesting fundamental structural disequilibrium in external transactions. In any case, the low import propensities of America were matched by high marginal import propensities of debtor nations undergoing internal development too rapidly.

The final mistake of the creditor nations was that, having allowed the debtor nations to run up large obligations, they suddenly turned their backs on their customers at the worst possible moment – like a man being hauled up a cliff by a rope which is slackened before he reaches the top and brings him crashing down.

The cessation of international lending

Many debtor countries, if not all, were in a precarious financial position in the latter half of the 1920s. They had borrowed freely and accumulated massive obligations which were not self-liquidating. Consequently they depended on continued capital imports to maintain external equilibrium. Though these fulfilled

60. ibid., p. 289.
61. M. E. Falkus, 'United States Economic Policy and the "Dollar Gap" of the 1920s', *Economic History Review*, vol. XXIV (1971), pp. 600–603.

this purpose in the short term they aggravated the debt burden and concealed the basic disequilibrium between creditors and debtors. This process could not continue indefinitely and any reaction by the creditors was bound to throw the burden of adjustment onto the debtors. Ultimately this was where it belonged since the failure of the debtors to live within their means was largely the cause of the problems. The notion that the creditors were at fault in not providing sufficient scope for the debtors to liquidate their commitments through increased exports is somewhat wide of the mark, since it is inconceivable that they could have managed to achieve this given the scale of their borrowing and their export potential in creditor markets. On the other hand, the abruptness with which the creditors, notably the United States, applied the brake to foreign lending and transferred the burden of adjustment to the debtors can be criticized since it was bound to have serious economic repercussions.

The critical role of foreign lending in the turning point of the business cycle now remains to be examined. This is no easy task since the data on capital movements are unsatisfactory and conflicting. But there seems little doubt that the position of the debtors as a whole deteriorated sharply between 1928 and 1929 as a result of the check in foreign lending. In 1928 the debtors of the U.K. and the U.S.A. were paying $675 million a year (in interest, dividends and amortization payments) more than they received in new loans and investments. By the following year this burden was nearly doubled.[62] Much of this increase can be

TABLE 9

NET CAPITAL MOVEMENTS OF CREDITOR COUNTRIES, 1927–31 ($ MILLION)

	France	Netherlands	Sweden	Switzerland	U.K.	U.S.A.	TOTAL
1927	−504	−95	−65	−92	−385	−829	−1,970
1928	−236	−73	−19	−94	−569	−1,250	−2,241
1929	+20	−75	−71	−86	−574	−628	−1,414
1930	+257	−66	−26	−36	−112	−380	−363
1931	+791	+259	+22	+369	+313	−330	+1,424

SOURCE: D. C. North, 'International Capital Movements in Historical Perspective', Chapter 2 of R. F. Mikesell (ed.), U.S. Private and Government Investment Abroad (1962), p. 40.

62. These figures refer only to long-term investments. Royal Institute of International Affairs, The Problem of International Investment (1937), p. 284.

attributed to the drop in overseas lending. Altogether the net outward capital movements from the main creditor countries declined by over 35 per cent between 1928 and 1929, while in 1930 the decline was even more dramatic despite a resurgence of U.S. long-term lending in the first half of the year (see Table 9). The United States and France were largely responsible for the initial setback since total British foreign lending held up fairly well until 1930. French lending was the first to decline (1927–8) though in sheer magnitude it was swamped by that of the United States in the following year. French capital exports were halved in 1928 and wiped out in 1929. Much of the movement represented the withdrawal of French short-term balances abroad (mainly from the U.K., U.S.A. and Germany) and the import of gold following the legal stabilization of the franc in June 1928. Since the French investor could not be persuaded to place his funds abroad on a long-term basis a large part of them were repatriated since, apart from increasing fears as to their safety, especially in Germany, the balances could not be attracted to any great extent by short-term rates in London, or, after the autumn of 1929, in New York. French action put strain on the major centres of credit and also on Germany – it has been suggested that it influenced the New York stock exchange collapse[63] – but for the most part it left the debtors of the periphery unscathed.

The major destabilizing influence was the check administered to American lending. This began in the summer of 1928 and was prompted by the domestic boom and the action of the Federal Reserve to restrain it by raising interest rates, both of which attracted funds towards the home market and hence discouraged foreign lending. U.S. capital issues for foreign account fell by over 50 per cent between the first and second halves of 1928 (from $841 million to $409 million); there was a slight revival in the first half of 1929 followed by a further fall in the second part of the year to $318 million, giving a total for the year of $790 million as against $1,250 million in 1928 and $1,336 million in 1927.[64] Between 1928 and 1929 new issues for the account of the six largest borrowers (Germany, Japan, Australia, Argentina, Brazil and Colombia)

63. United Nations, *International Capital Movements during the Inter-war Period* (1949), p. 36.
64. Royal Institute of International Affairs, *Monetary Policy and the Depression* (1933), p. 7. A further revival in new issues occurred in the first

fell from $570 to $52 million.[65] The drop in the total net outward flow of capital (both long and short) was even more precipitous. It was virtually halved between 1928 and 1929, and a further large fall probably occurred in 1930 (see Table 9), though there is serious discrepancy in the various estimates for that year.[66] However by this time the damage had already been done.

The curtailment of American lending and the increased flow of funds to the United States with the rise in American interest rates and stock market boom exercised a powerful deflationary impact

TABLE 10

NET CAPITAL IMPORTS OF SELECTED DEBTOR COUNTRIES, 1927–31 ($ MILLION)

	1927	1928	1929	1930	1931
Germany	+1,037	+967	+482	+129	−540
Hungary	+89	+91	+38	+22	+37
Poland	+82	+124	+68	+3	−1
Yugoslavia	+23	+27	−13	+35	+32
Bulgaria	+4	+7	+21	+1	+5
Turkey	+22	+11	+50	−6	+3
Finland	−2	+40	+12	−5	−24
Greece			+45	+34	+37
Italy	+28	+133	+97	+47	−50
Japan	+50	+80	−9	−128	−11
India *	+120	+67	+37	+92	−86
Argentina	+61	+131	−10	+287	−89
Australia †	+207	+349	+183	+194	
South Africa	−2	+40	+12	−5	−24

* Peak inflow in 1926 at $177 million.

† Fiscal year ending 30 June.

SOURCE: United Nations, *International Capital Movements during the Inter-war Period* (1949), pp. 11–12.

half of 1930. On a non-calendar basis, for example between March 1927–June 1928 and July 1928–September 1929, the decline was even greater. See H. Fleissig, 'The United States and the Non-European Periphery during the Early Years of the Great Depression', in H. van der Wee (ed.), *The Great Depression Revisited: Essays on the Economics of the Thirties* (1970), pp. 150–54.

65. Though there was a substantial rise in Canadian issues. League of Nations, *The Course and Phases of the World Economic Depression* (1931), p. 206.

66. See for example Lary, *The United States in the World Economy*, Appendix Table 3.

on the world economy. It did not affect all countries simultaneously but the impact was sufficient to undermine the fragile stability of the international economy. The second shock to the system came in the summer of 1929 with the downturn in American economic activity which effectively completed disintegration.

Data on capital imports for a selected number of countries are given in Table 10. Most countries experienced a heavy drop in their net capital inflow over the period 1928–30, and indeed the first major setback occurred between 1928 and 1929. Germany experienced a fall of 50 per cent, Hungary 58 per cent, Poland 45 per cent, Finland 70 per cent, Australia 48 per cent, India 45 per cent[67] and Italy 27 per cent, while in Yugoslavia, Japan and Argentina large capital inflows were transformed into losses of capital. The areas most severely hit initially were Latin America, eastern Europe, Germany, Australia and the Far East.

The cessation of the flow of capital affected these areas directly by leading to a tailing-off in investment and economic activity. Certainly in Germany and eastern Europe the reduced lending seems to have brought some check to activity.[68] Moreover, Fleissig argues that the decline in U.S. lending to Europe probably contributed to a decline in the rate of growth of European import demand and a curtailment of European lending to the periphery.[69] However, it was probably through the balance of payments that impact was first felt. As we have seen, most of the countries depended on capital imports to close the gap in their balance of payments. Hence when capital imports declined the only remaining way of adjusting the balance was to draw upon their limited reserves of gold or foreign exchange. Thus the collapse of foreign borrowing by the Australian governments, which had helped to fill two-thirds of the gap in the current account balance throughout the 1920s, led to a substantial liquidation of overseas reserves in 1929–30.[70] Latin America was affected severely by the sharp contraction in U.S. lending and the region suffered substantial

67. The reduction from the peak of 1926 was 79 per cent.

68. Williams, 'The 1931 Financial Crisis', p. 98.

69. Fleissig, 'The United States and the Non-European Periphery during the Early Years of the Great Depression', p. 176; European funds moved to New York and credit conditions were tightened.

70. Gilbert, *The Australian Loan Council in Federal Fiscal Adjustments, 1890–1965*, pp. 104–5; E. R. Walker, *Australia in the World Depression* (1933), p. 114.

gold losses in 1929, a large part of which came from the Argentine.[71] Germany and many east European countries faced a similar situation, while several countries on the periphery, for example in Asia and Africa, were experiencing strain in their external balances.[72] In brief, long-term lending declined, short-term loans were called in or not renewed, and the gold reserves of the debtors began to be soaked away in the backwash.[73]

The initial shock to the system might have been overcome had it not been for subsequent adverse events. Debtor countries could meet temporary difficulties by drawing on their reserves. But this process of adjustment could not cope for ever with a prolonged strain following from the collapse in primary product prices and the decline in American import demand after the downturn in economic activity in the summer of 1929. Many primary producers faced a severe deterioration in their trade balances as export values fell faster than import values, while external interest obligations, which were fixed in terms of gold, rose sharply as a proportion of export receipts.[74] Attempts to make up the deficiencies in international income by releasing stocks of commodities onto the world market only made matters worse by aggravating the fall in prices. Thus with dwindling reserves and an inability to borrow further the countries of the periphery were forced to take drastic measures to staunch the outflow of funds. The way out of the impasse was sought through devaluation, deflation, and in some cases default on debts. The initial deflation was quickly

71. Fleissig, 'The United States and the Non-European Periphery during the Early Years of the Great Depression', pp. 156–7; V. L. Phelps, *The International Economic Position of Argentina* (1938), pp. 53–4, 116.

72. Though Temin rejects the notion that the fall in American capital exports in 1929 initiated the German depression via credit restriction arising from the balance of payments deficit in that year. His argument is that the credit contraction was too small and too late to account for the turning point which can be explained primarily in terms of a decline in inventory investment. P. Temin, 'The Beginning of the Depression in Germany', *Economic History Review*, vol. XXIV (1971), pp. 242–8. But see also M. E. Falkus, 'The German Business Cycle in the 1920s', *Economic History Review*, vol. XXVIII (1975).

73. League of Nations, *The Transition from War to Peace Economy: Report of the Delegation on Economic Depressions*, Part 1 (1943), p. 23.

74. See H. Raupach, 'The Impact of the Great Depression on Eastern Europe', in H. van der Wee (ed.), *The Great Depression Revisited: Essays on the Economics of the Thirties* (1972), p. 240; Smith, 'The Suspension of the Gold Standard in Raw Material Exporting Countries', p. 447.

transmitted through the links forged by the fixed rates of the gold exchange standard, but it could never be more than a temporary expedient since to meet external obligations would have required a politically intolerable dose of deflation. Consequently the easiest solution was to abandon the gold standard. This was done by several Latin American countries and Australia and New Zealand late in 1929 and early in 1930.[75] This imposed a greater burden on the countries still on gold and hence intensified the deflationary spiral either automatically or through deliberate government action. Once started the deflationary process became cumulative and ultimately led to the complete collapse of the gold standard.[76]

The detailed events leading up to the crisis of 1931 and the final collapse are outlined fully in a subsequent volume in this series.[77] What we have been concerned with here is the immediate antecedents of the crisis and, in particular in this chapter, the role of foreign lending in the process. The drying up of international capital flows, especially from America, in 1928–9 was the initial shock to the stability of the international economic system. 'The stage was thus set for the disturbances which culminated in the international financial crisis of 1931 and the subsequent general disintegration of the international economy.'[78] Given the dependence of many debtor countries on supplies of foreign capital any break in the flow was bound to place them in a vulnerable position. This alone would have been sufficient to cause a check to economic activity of some dimension. But it occurred when primary debtors were already being weakened by sagging commodity prices, though this factor became very much more important once the downswing was under way,[79] and it was followed by a major downturn in the chief capitalist economy.[80] This convergence of unfortunate forces made a major international recession a foregone conclusion.[81]

75. G. Cassel, *The Downfall of the Gold Standard* (1936), p. 62.

76. See Chapter 7, pages 180–83.

77. C. P. Kindleberger, *The World in Depression, 1929–1939* (1973).

78. United Nations, *International Capital Movements during the Inter-war Period* (1949), pp. 66–77.

79. See Chapter 9, pages 231–6.

80. The causes of the American turning-point are dealt with in Chapter 8, pages 198–200.

81. The sequence of forces leading up to the depression are brought together in Chapter 11, pages 280–84.

11

Into Depression: Explanations of the Turning-Point of 1929

Economically if not politically the year 1929 is a historical landmark. At the beginning of that year economic activity was, with a few notable exceptions, still thriving. By the end of 1929 the U.S. stock market bubble had burst and the world was lurching into one of the most serious depressions on record. For three years or more economic conditions remained severely depressed and many countries suffered sharp declines in income and production. Not until 1933 did recovery from the slump become general and for several countries a complete cyclical revival failed to materialize even by the end of the decade.

It is not the purpose of this chapter to provide a detailed analysis of the depression itself. As the title of this volume indicates our account draws to a close with the spectacular U.S. stock market crash in autumn 1929. On the other hand, it would be unfair to leave the reader poised at one of the most exciting points in international history without drawing together the sequence of events which led up to it. After all, many of these chapters have approached the fatal year from a different angle so the various threads need to be drawn together in coherent form. Furthermore, it is instructive to examine briefly some reasons for the intensity of the downswing and also to determine how far the slump could have been avoided or alleviated. But first let us look at the verdict of some of the previous writers on this historic episode.

A variety of possibilities

There is no shortage of explanations for the downswing of 1929–32. The literature abounds with plausible suggestions and it might be presumptuous to add to the list. But they range from the particular to the general, some are partial in scope and many are conflicting so that the diligent reader may be forgiven for a sense of bewilderment at the end of his studies. However, one logical sequence of events is both comprehensive and reasonably consistent with the facts. But before we give it we look at a number of the alternative explanations which have already been put forward.

Towards the end of the crisis Hansen expressed the view that apart from its unusual severity the downturn of 1929–32 was no exception to the long-run historical sequence of cyclical activity and hence required no more explanation than a general theory of the business cycle.[1] A similar argument was expounded by Schumann in the same year.[2] This point of view is not without its attractions since the downswing, though more severe than most that occurred in the nineteenth century, came at a logical time, at a point predicted by a reading of the historical periodicity of trade cycle activity. No doubt its unusual severity could be explained partly by certain structural changes and the special circumstances of the post-war readjustments.[3] Conveniently too, it could be regarded as the grand culmination to trade cycle history, for soon after the growth cycle took its place.[4]

Unfortunately no really satisfactory general theory of the trade cycle has ever been developed. True, there has been no shortage of theoretical work in this field and the student of business cycle history has a wide range of models from which to choose. But it is doubtful whether any one particular theory has general applicability. Some economists have expressed doubts as to whether it is

1. A. H. Hansen, *Economic Stabilization in an Unbalanced World* (1932), p. 112.
2. C. G. W. Schumann, *The World Depression: South Africa and the Gold Standard* (1932), pp. 15–16.
3. Hansen, *Economic Stabilization in an Unbalanced World*, p. 112.
4. That is if we ignore the downturn in 1937–8 which was not common to all countries.

possible to develop a pure theory of the cycle. Models may throw useful light on some aspects of the cycle, but, as Wilson has pointed out, most stylized models do not adequately reflect the facts.[5] Indeed, given the wide variety of cyclical experience, even within one country, a single formal model can scarcely be expected to do justice to the facts all the time. Quite probably a true representation of the facts would require a series of models or one which was being continually adapted over time.[6]

Most early writers on business cycles plied their trade without resort to rigorous theories. Even today, after years of formal model building, it is rare to find an author who is able to integrate theory and fact successfully. Faced with reality the student of business cycle behaviour often prefers not to be constrained by the rigidities of a formal model but to rely on a more general analytical framework which provides a reasonable degree of flexibility. Hickman, for example, in his study of post-war U.S. business cycles, employs this type of framework which recognizes the need to integrate or at least utilize several types of theory.[7] This procedure may lack precision since it is sufficiently vague and general to be adaptable in any circumstances, but this may be a necessary requirement for the wide diversity of cyclical experience. Many writers, of course, employ no theory at all and are content to analyse the data and let the facts speak for themselves, while others test the validity of specific hypotheses.

Resort to formal theory in explaining the 1929–32 downturn has been very limited indeed. Possibly most writers consider it to be unique; it cannot bear resemblance to previous cycles and they are therefore content to follow Mitchell, who considered each cycle to be a unique series of events with its own special explanatory forces and its own particular effects on the economic system.[8] Though we would question this assumption the fact remains that the 1929 episode has been regarded as something of a special case for which loose and eclectic interpretations have been the order of the day.

5. T. Wilson, 'Cyclical and Autonomous Inducements to Invest', *Oxford Economic Papers*, vol. v (1953), pp. 87–8.

6. For further discussion on the role of theory in the study of the business cycle see D. H. Aldcroft and P. Fearon (eds), *British Economic Fluctuations, 1790–1939* (1972), pp. 21–5.

7. B. Hickman, *Growth and Stability of the Postwar Economy* (1960), pp. 5–6.

8. W. C. Mitchell, *Business Cycles and their Causes* (1950).

Several broad categories of interpretation may be distinguished – (1) general explanations, (2) overproduction theses with special emphasis on the role of primary commodities, (3) monetary factors, (4) the role of the United States, (5) unstable equilibrium mechanisms, (6) structural or secular problems, (7) underconsumption theories. This does not exhaust the possibilities nor for that matter are the above categories mutually exclusive. The scope for overlap is obviously wide and few writers would necessarily take a monocausal stance. Nevertheless, each thesis has its band of adherents.

One of the first and also one of the most generalized interpretations was put forward by Ohlin in a report on the world depression for the League of Nations. Though the study devoted considerable space to problems in the primary producing countries Ohlin saw the depression as an interaction between the industrial and agrarian sectors of the world economy:

> The main characteristic of the crisis, at any rate during the first two years, appears to have been that an industrial depression set in almost simultaneously with an agricultural crisis, due to quite different causes, at a time when the power of resistance and the stability of the economic situation . . . were reduced and much smaller than before the war. The industrial depression and the agricultural crisis exercised an aggravating influence upon one another. [9]

While not denying the close interrelationship between the primary and industrial sectors of the world economy, this was more a description of what was happening at the time rather than an outline of the sequential mechanism of events which led into depression.

Later writers attached greater significance to one or other of the two sectors as precursor of the depression. Some regarded overproduction in primary producing countries as the critical force initiating the downturn. According to this interpretation a depression would have occurred even without recessionary tendencies within the major industrial economies. Perhaps the most persuasive statement for this thesis was put forward in 1933 by Timoshenko who regarded the primary sector as an independent element in the depression. [10] Alpert also argued that the world depression, beginning in the primary producing countries,

9. League of Nations, *The Course and Phases of the World Economic Depression* (1931), p. 43.
10. V. P. Timoshenko, *World Agriculture and the Depression* (1933).

destroyed the unsteady balance of U.S. prosperity,[11] while Corner provided a more limited version based on sagging British exports to the periphery.[12] Some writers, while acknowledging a partial supply problem, have been less ready to accord a key role to the primary sector in the depression;[13] yet others have expressed scepticism about the thesis of overproduction and its alleged consequences.[14]

Any explanation of the depression which emphasizes its industrial origins is bound to stress the role of the United States. Any downturn in the enormous American economy would have serious repercussions on the world. Indeed, when the boom broke in the summer of 1929 the sharp decline in U.S. imports and the subsequent restrictive commercial policy spelt the end of prosperity for the rest of the world.[15] Moreover, if recessionary tendencies were developing in some countries before the American collapse these could have been partly conditioned by the prior curtailment of U.S. foreign lending to Europe and the periphery.[16] The most frequently quoted example is Germany where the contraction of foreign lending is often seen as instrumental in causing depression,[17] though this view has recently been challenged.[18] Not

11. P. Alpert, *Twentieth Century Economic History of Europe* (1951), pp. 50, 122.

12. D. C. Corner, 'Exports and the British Trade Cycle: 1929', *Manchester School*, vol. xxiv (1956).

13. H. W. Arndt, *The Economic Lessons of the Nineteen-Thirties* (1944), p. 11; M. T. Copeland, *A Raw Commodity Revolution* (1938).

14. H. Fleissig, 'The United States and the Non-European Periphery during the Early Years of the Great Depression', in H. van der Wee (ed.), *The Great Depression Revisited* (1972), p. 161; W. A. Lewis, *Economic Survey 1919–1939* (1949), pp. 46, 150–55; D. S. Landes, *The Unbound Prometheus* (1969), pp. 367–8.

15. See Arndt, *The Economic Lessons of the Nineteen-Thirties*, p. 31; Lewis, *Economic Survey 1919–1939*, p. 57; H. B. Lary, *The United States in the World Economy* (1943), pp. 171–4.

16. Fleissig, 'The United States and the Non-European Periphery during the Early Years of the Great Depression', p. 176; Lary, *The United States in the World Economy*, pp. 171–4; Lewis, *Economic Survey 1919–1939*, p. 57.

17. See, for example, Landes, *The Unbound Prometheus*, pp. 371–2; S. V. O. Clarke, *Central Bank Cooperation, 1924–31* (1967), pp. 143–50; C. T. Schmidt, *German Business Cycles, 1924–1933* (1934), pp. 47–8.

18. P. Temin, 'The Beginning of the Depression in Germany', *Economic History Review*, vol. xxiv (1971). But see M. E. Falkus, 'The German Business Cycle in the 1920s', *Economic History Review*, vol. xxviii (1975).

surprisingly therefore, several writers are convinced that developments in the United States were crucial to the downturn in world
activity as a whole. Lewis, for example, feels that 'It is hardly
necessary to look much further for the causes of the world-wide
depression. The loss of American dollars produced, through a
multiplier process, a contraction of output several times larger in
the rest of the world.'[19] Perhaps not everyone would go as far as
this but few would deny the powerful influence of the American
economy over the rest of the world.

The main bone of contention has been the causes of the U.S.
downturn itself rather than its impact on the rest of the world.
That it was internally generated is not in dispute but whether it was
caused by real or monetary forces is still a matter of some debate.
Friedman and Schwartz, Pedersen and others argue that monetary
factors were at the root of the trouble,[20] whereas Wilson, Gordon,
Hansen and Rostow prefer real forces with special emphasis on
the exhaustion of investment opportunities.[21] The latter interpretation rests primarily on the assumption that the market for
housing and consumer durables was either saturated or reaching a
state of saturation by the late 1920s. This issue has been the
subject of further scrutiny recently and the general conclusion
seems to be that while a *state* of saturation was not reached in
either the housing or automobile markets in the later 1920s, in
both cases the market was *dynamically* saturated, that is it was

19. Lewis, *Economic Survey 1919-1939*, p. 57.

20. M. Friedman and A. J. Schwartz, *A Monetary History of the United
States 1867-1960* (1963), pp. 300-308; J. Pedersen, 'Some Notes on the
Economic Policy of the United States during the Period 1919-1932', in
H. Hegeland (ed.), *Money, Growth and Methodology: Essays in Honour of
Johan Åkerman* (1961); see also L. Currie, 'The Failure of Monetary Policy
to Prevent the Depression of 1929-32', *Journal of Political Economy*, vol.
XLII (1934) and J. W. Angell, 'The General Objectives of Monetary Policy',
in A. D. Gayer (ed.), *The Lessons of Monetary Experience: Essays in Honour
of Irving Fisher* (1937), pp. 55-7.

21. T. Wilson, *Fluctuations in Income and Employment*, 3rd edition (1948),
pp. 155-6; R. A. Gordon, 'Cyclical Experience in the Interwar Period: The
Investment Boom of the 'Twenties', in National Bureau of Economic Research,
Conference on Business Cycles (1951), pp. 206-10; *Business Fluctuations*
(1952), pp. 384-8, 405-7; and 'Population Growth and the Capital Coefficient',
American Economic Review, vol. 46 (June 1956); W. W. Rostow, 'The Strategic
Role of Theory: A Commentary', *Journal of Economic History*, vol. XXXI
(1971), pp. 84-5; A. H. Hansen, *Business Cycles and National Income*
(1951).

approaching a *state* of saturation from the middle of the 1920s onwards.[22] This conclusion lends support to the Hansen–Gordon hypothesis that real forces were important in explaining the downturn, though it is clear from the debate that the issue is far from settled. As far as the initial turning-point is concerned, the latter interpretation seems the more plausible, but this is not to deny the contribution of monetary forces once the downswing was under way.

Monetary factors have been given a wider code of reference than in connection with the breaking of the American boom. Long before Friedman's writings on the United States, Angell in a study of nineteen countries had noted the close association between the money supply and national income. Variations in the quantity of money were, in his opinion, the largest single source of fluctuations in national money income and money and banking systems were inherently unstable to such a degree that they tended to intensify fluctuations in income rather than dampen them down. Angell did not specifically state how crucial monetary forces were in initiating the depression in various countries though he did maintain that much of the decline in world economic activity through to 1933 could have been avoided by stabilizing the quantity of money at the 1928–9 peaks, or better still by gradually increasing it.[23]

Two rather different monetary versions of the cyclical sequence of the 1920s and early 1930s are worth noting partly for their novelty and also partly because they run counter to the modern monetary school of thought. Melchior Palyi, in his recent controversial book dealing with the breakdown of the gold standard, challenges the Friedman and Schwartz notion that there was no

22. See L. J. Mercer and W. D. Morgan, 'Alternative Interpretations of Market Saturation: Evaluation for the Automobile Market in the Late 1920s', *Explorations in Economic History*, vol. IX (Spring 1972); 'The American Automobile Industry: Investment Demand, Capacity, and Capacity Utilization, 1921–1940', *Journal of Political Economy*, vol. LXXX (November–December 1972); 'Housing Surplus in the 1920s? Another Evaluation', *Explorations in Economic History*, vol. IX (Spring 1973); B. Bolch, R. Fels and M. McMahon, 'Housing Surplus in the 1920s?', *Explorations in Economic History*, vol. VIII (Spring 1971). See also R. F. Muth, 'The Demand for Non-Farm Housing', in A. C. Harberger (ed.), *The Demand for Durable Goods* (1960), esp. pp. 79–80, who argues that the housing stock was not excessive in the 1920s.

23. Angell, 'The General Objectives of Monetary Policy', pp. 56–7, 83–5.

inflation in the 1920s. The fact that the world-wide money and credit expansion was not reflected in the general price level has, he argues, misled the monetarists. Pressure on prices was offset by lowered costs through productivity improvements but inflationary forces were reflected in the tremendous rise in real estate values, stock market valuations and business profits. However, though monetary forces (interpreted widely to include quantitative as well as qualitative aspects) are behind this 'hidden' inflation, monetary factors of the Friedman type, e.g. high interest rates and an insufficient money supply, are not directly responsible for the downturn since credit curtailment and money contraction lag at the peak and are therefore seen as a consequence rather than a cause of underlying developments. Yet indirectly monetary factors in a broad sense are at the root of both the boom and the slump. The gold exchange standard and international capital flow permitted and fostered an enormous credit inflation both in America and elsewhere which financed rising living standards, growing inventories and overvaluation of assets. Furthermore, the expansion enlarged and duplicated the maladjustments of the decade or so before 1924 which brought excessive capacity and reduced profitability in some sectors. This was accompanied by severe speculation, a rapid increase in debt and a deterioration in credit standards which inevitably resulted in liquidity problems.[24] These developments gave rise to a world-wide fundamental disequilibrium and rigidities within the economic system which vitiated responsible decision-making by entrepreneurs and investors and impaired the functioning of the price mechanism and the efficacy of central bank policies. Palyi regards the breakdown of the strict discipline of the pre-1914 gold standard as the main cause of the problem.

While Dr Palyi's thesis is provocative it is not always well substantiated and at times conflicts with the facts. Moreover, the sequence of events is very loosely drawn; it is not clearly specified what causes the turning-point: we are merely told that a slump is indicated by the perverse results of the credit inflation.[25] The strength of Dr Palyi's case is weakened by his lack of objectivity

24. M. Palyi, *The Twilight of Gold, 1914–1936: Myths and Realities* (1972), pp. 218, 243, 304, 310–11, 337. 'It was, indeed, an illiquid overexpanded colossus of debts, rather than an excessive money supply, on which the price structure of the late 1920s rested' (ibid., p. 218).

25. ibid., p. 338.

which no doubt stems from his idealistic attachment to the discipline of the classical monetary system of the later nineteenth century.

In some respects Rothbard's analysis of the problem is similar, though his attention is focused mainly on American experience. He, like Palyi, regards the 1920s as an inflationary period; monetary inflation (quantitative more so than qualitative) imparts an upward leverage to prices but they remain stable because they are offset by lower costs from technical change and productivity improvements. However, Rothbard attributes both the boom and the depression of the business cycle directly to monetary forces for which the U.S. government and its controlled banking system were wholly responsible. The monetary inflation, on his reckoning, was virtually complete by the end of 1928 and so a depression was inevitable to adjust the economy following the distortions and malinvestment engendered by credit expansion. The correction must come and Rothbard, like Palyi, believes that the government should leave the economy free to adjust itself. But the credibility of his thesis is not enhanced by his extreme *laissez-faire* stance. Even the most ardent classicists would probably have blanched at the degree of fiscal and monetary retrenchment proposed to combat the depression.[26]

Other references to monetary factors have been less precise and frequently have been associated with the malfunctioning of the gold standard. Néré, for example, stresses the instability of the monetary system with particular reference to the large floating credits which, he maintains, could not fail to bring about a collapse.[27] Einzig regarded monetary factors, including the maldistribution of gold, as the main cause of the fall in prices, and the rise in central bank discount rates some months before the Wall Street crash as the operative weapon.[28] His references to the

26. M. B. Rothbard, *America's Great Depression* (1963), pp. 28, 56–8, 82, 147–8, 152, 164, 295. It is hard to believe that as late as the 1960s such an anti-Keynesian stance could be adopted. Rothbard's thesis is based on the Austrian theory of the trade cycle and his great mentor is Ludwig von Mises.

27. J. Néré, *La Crise de 1929* (1968), p. 59. Though later on (p. 211) he concludes that the 1929 crisis was due to a collection of circumstances which are not likely to be repeated.

28. P. Einzig, *Behind the Scenes in International Finance* (1931), pp. 67–9; see also B. M. Anderson, *Economics and the Public Welfare: Financial and Economic History of the United States, 1914–1946* (1949), pp. 198–201.

instability arising from the misuse or malfunctioning of the gold exchange standard have occasioned subsequent comment.[29] Robbins felt the gold standard had been mismanaged though he was reluctant to subscribe to a monetary theory of the depression.[30] Triffin stressed its instability and the problems arising from short-term capital movements when Britain's financial strength was seriously weakened.[31] Hicks argued that the system was trying to make do with an inadequate gold supply given the price and wage inflation between 1914 and 1920,[32] while Jacobsson suggested that the fall in agricultural prices in the latter half of the 1920s and the general deflation from 1929 were partly a reaction to the excessive gold content of currencies.[33]

While most of these interpretations explain in part the characteristics and intensity of the depression they do not add much to our knowledge of the turning-point. Even if the mismanagement of the gold standard produced a tendency towards secular or structural deflation it certainly was not the cause of the sudden downturn in 1929. It is true that the gold standard system may in time have created conditions which would have led to a downturn in economic activity, but there is no evidence that the currency problem became so much worse in 1929 as to spark off a general contraction even though some primary producers were already facing difficulties. In any case, even though recessionary tendencies were developing elsewhere the sharp break in the American boom was largely responsible for the beginning of the world-wide decline in activity. Rather the monetary links of the gold standard tended to exacerbate the downswing once it was under way.[34]

Most structural or secular theses probably have even less

29. P. Einzig, *The Tragedy of the Pound* (1932), p. 43. Einzig blamed France for her undervaluation of the franc. But his views tended to change somewhat each time he wrote.

30. L. Robbins, *The Great Depression* (1934), pp. 42–3, 97. But the genesis of the U.S. slump was attributed to overexpansion of credit in the boom (see pp. 54–5, 61).

31. R. Triffin, *Gold and the Dollar Crisis: The Future of Convertibility* (1960), p. 70, and *Our International Monetary System: Yesterday, Today and Tomorrow* (1968), pp. 29–31.

32. J. R. Hicks, *A Contribution to the Theory of the Trade Cycle* (1950), p. 163.

33. P. Jacobsson, *Some Monetary Problems: International and National* (1958), pp. 18–19.

34. See below, page 283.

bearing on the immediate problem of the turning-point itself. But they go some way to explaining why the depression was so intense or why the system was so vulnerable in the first place. Svennilson's structural transformation crisis and Hansen's secular stagnation thesis[35] reflect the view that some long-run deflationary process may have been at work. Hansen was concerned with explaining the depression by real factors, namely a dearth of investment opportunities caused by a reduced rate of population growth, the lack of new resources and inadequate technical innovation, but he also had reservations for the future on these counts.[36] To these may be added Kindleberger's proposition of structural deflation in the primary product economies as part of his rather more general instability thesis.[37] Sectoral problems of this type – both in agrarian and industrial economies – could produce an underlying deflationary trend but relative stability of sorts was maintained so long as there was an upward cyclical movement. Once the cyclical prosperity came to an end in 1929 both tendencies working in the same direction reinforced each other. Moreover, as Schumann pointed out, this also explains in part why the boom, especially in the United States, was accompanied by a gentle price decline.[38]

Most writers on this period make general reference to the unstable equilibrium of the international economy in the 1920s. In part this condition arose through the maladjustments created by the war and the half-hearted attempts to solve them. Moulton and Pasvolsky point out that the war destroyed the economic equilibrium between Europe and the United States, but that subsequent policies did not eradicate the maladjustments.[39] The economic dislocations were serious, but not irremedial. Nor was there any lack of action for, as Hodson points out, '. . . the economic history of the whole first post-war decade is a tale of

35. I. Svennilson, *Growth and Stagnation in the European Economy* (1954), p. 44; A. H. Hansen, 'Economic Progress and Declining Population Growth', *American Economic Review*, vol. XXIX (1939).

36. See G. Terborgh, *The Bogey of Economic Maturity* (1945) for a rejection of the stagnationist argument.

37. C. P. Kindleberger, *The World in Depression, 1929–1939* (1973), pp. 106, 291–6.

38. Schumann, *The World Depression*, pp. 36–7.

39. H. G. Moulton and L. Pasvolsky, *War Debts and World Prosperity* (1932), pp. 418–19.

attempts to meet or defy the disorders that the war had wrought
in the world's economic system'.[40] What was fatal was that the
policies adopted, for example in relation to war debts, reparations
and currency stabilization, were inadequate or inappropriate and
only aggravated the situation. However, the depression of 1929
cannot be attributed directly to the disequilibrium arising out of
the war. But the war did leave the international economic system
more vulnerable to shocks, and there were too many of these.
Kindleberger maintains that many of the structural dislocations
of war could have been dealt with had macroeconomic stability
been preserved. This may well have been impossible under the
grave financial distortions but it is largely irrelevant since no one
was prepared to shoulder the burden. Britain and France alone
were unable, and the United States was unwilling, to take responsibility for stabilizing the system. This abdication of responsibility
on the part of the great powers helps to explain the depth and
intensity of the crisis.[41]

Theories of under-consumption have never attracted widespread
support in explaining cyclical turning-points partly because the
more volatile swings in investment, the other major component of
national income, have usually been regarded as of greater significance. Yet in so far as investment magnitudes are determined by
changes in levels of consumption or income, fluctuations in
consumption, though much less dramatic than those in investment, may be crucial at the turning points of the cycle. For
example, the breaking of the boom in Britain in 1920 was preceded
by a decline in domestic consumption, while the initial revival
from the slump of 1929–32 was almost certainly assisted by the
high floor to consumption throughout the crisis and the early
upturn in this component of national income.

In a sense of course, under-consumption or a deficiency of
demand in Keynesian terms prevailed throughout the 1920s,
which gave rise to an equilibrium, albeit unstable, below the full
employment level. To a large extent this was a structural problem
which reflected changes in tastes, technologies, population movements and the distribution of income changes both within and
between countries. Within this context it was still possible for a

40. H. V. Hodson, *Slump and Recovery, 1929–1937: A Survey of World
Economic Affairs* (1938), p. 50.
41. Kindleberger, *The World in Depression, 1929–1939*, pp. 293–5.

cyclical upswing to take place, the termination of which would depend on short-run shifts in the demand function rather than on secular or sectoral demand deficiencies.

As far as American experience is concerned there is certainly some evidence that consumption patterns moved unfavourably in the later stages of the boom and therefore contributed to the turning-point. The skewed distribution of income gains – with a large share going to profits – meant that real wages rose very slowly, and this, together with the mortgaging of future incomes by excessive instalment buying, inevitably checked the rate at which consumption expanded.[42] Between 1928 and 1929 the rate of growth of consumption fell sharply and this was bound to affect investment expectations adversely given the drying-up of investment opportunities at that time in building and consumer durable trades. Wilson regards this combination of circumstances as critical to the breaking of the boom.[43] Rostow is more emphatic about the role of consumption. He argues that the momentum of the leading sectors (consumer durables and building) depended on a continued expansion of consumers' income since their products were subject to a high-income elasticity of demand. Once a hiatus occurred an exogenous rise in consumers' income was required to set them in motion again.[44]

It is doubtful whether many other countries experienced similar developments of the same magnitude as America. And in any case, if one believes that the breaking of the U.S. boom was critical in triggering off a world-wide slump the matter is very much an academic one. In a wider context one could extend the argument in as much as the sudden curtailment of U.S. foreign lending in 1928–9 caused a check to consumption in say central Europe and Latin America.

A synthesis

We have by no means exhausted the possible explanations of the downturn of 1929 but it is clear that nearly every author who has written about the subject has put forward his own particular version. The version we shall present below incorporates several

42. See P. Einzig, *The World Economic Crisis 1929–1931* (1931), pp. 41–2.
43. Wilson, *Fluctuations in Income and Employment*, p. 156.
44. Rostow, 'The Strategic Role of Theory', pp. 84–5.

elements of earlier theories but also attempts to assemble the course of events in some logical and coherent sequence.

We should state at the onset that the First World War and its aftermath was not the prime causal factor in the crisis that began in 1929. Certainly the repercussions of the war created maladjustments and instability within the world economy which made it more vulnerable to shocks, but the turning-point of the cycle cannot be attributed directly to the war itself. Indeed, though the war imparted a severe shock to the economic mechanism it did not, because of its timing, upset the cyclical pattern. It distorted the economic system in several ways and also aggravated the amplitude of subsequent cyclical movements but it did little, if anything, to destroy the time sequence or periodicity of cyclical activity. After the war economic systems for the most part reverted to their previous cyclical course and in all probability a downturn could have been anticipated towards the end of the 1920s even in the absence of a European war.

The origins of the world-wide slump of 1929–32 must be located in the United States. This is not to say that there were not cyclical weaknesses elsewhere; indeed it is probable that several countries would have experienced a moderate recession in the early 1930s even had conditions not deteriorated in the U.S.A. But events in the United States, together with its power over the world economic system, determined to a large extent the timing, the severity and the extent of the depression. The United States administered two severe shocks to the world economic system when it was vulnerable and least able to withstand them. The initial shock came with the curtailment in foreign lending in 1928–9 which was aggravated by a downturn in U.K. long-term lending in 1929–30. The brunt of this contraction was borne by the countries already heavily in debt, many of which were already facing some difficulties because of falling commodity prices. This gave rise to pressure on their external accounts and the attempts to counter this by domestic retrenchment reduced their import requirements from the industrialized countries. Britain, as we have seen, suffered early in this respect.

However, this initial shock might well have been overcome (for example by the resumption of some foreign lending in the first half of 1930) had it not been quickly followed by an even more disastrous blow. In the summer of 1929 the U.S. boom petered out.

This domestic collapse can be attributed mainly to real forces rather than monetary ones. The temporary exhaustion of investment opportunities and a severe restraint on consumer expenditure growth in 1929, together with a deterioration in business confidence, were mainly responsible for the turning of the cycle. Monetary factors probably played a relatively minor part in determining the peak though once the downswing was under way it was certainly aggravated and prolonged by the policy of severe monetary contraction adopted by the Federal Reserve System. The rapidity of the American slide into depression was assisted by the complete collapse of business confidence after the crash of the stock market in October 1929.

The American downturn was accompanied by a further reduction in foreign lending and a sharp contraction in import demand. This could hardly fail to have a severe impact on the rest of the world given America's preponderant influence in the world economy. Attrition in debtor and primary producing countries was completed as commodity prices fell dramatically. Industrialized countries in Europe felt the impact directly from America and indirectly via the periphery. By early 1930 all but a few countries were engulfed in depression.

Though the role of the United States is crucial in any interpretation of the world-wide depression it should be stressed that the sequence of events in that country came at a weak time for the international economy. For one thing cyclical forces were reaching their apogee in a number of other countries, for example the U.K. and Germany, in the late 1920s, and in some cases independently of the U.S.A. Secondly, the cyclical developments of the period must be set against the background of an unstable international economy, partly as a legacy from the war. Thus the cyclical downturn came at a time when many countries were still struggling with post-war distortions to their economies which left them inherently unstable. Structural or sectoral deflationary tendencies were common and these were reflected in excess capacity problems, both in primary producing and industrialized countries, and in external account imbalances, arising from reparations and war debts, the distortions produced by the ill-conceived currency stabilization process and tariff policies, among other things. The position was aggravated by the transformation of economic power relationships by the war and the lack of strong and enlightened economic leadership which would have helped to stabilize the system. These disequilibrating forces were not crucial to the initial downturn. But they were sufficient to ensure that the system exploded once the initial shocks had been imparted, thereby producing a depression of unusual severity.

That the depression was so intense and widespread is not altogether surprising. Given the severity of the American depression and its repercussions on foreign lending and U.S. import demand the multiplier effects were bound to be large. Moreover, the cyclical downturn occurred against a backdrop of structural deflation and international disequilibrium and this was bound to intensify the process. Misguided government policies also aggravated the deflationary spiral. Monetary and fiscal retrenchment, tariffs and other restrictive measures made things worse. The spread of depression was encouraged by the fairly close economic relationships between nations; in particular, the complex and precarious monetary relationships and the fixed exchange rates forged by the gold standard system facilitated the transmission of recession from one country to another.

Enlightened government policies rapidly applied could have alleviated the crisis. But it is difficult to believe that a depression could have been avoided altogether. Lag effects would have required the appropriate action to have been taken a few months before the peak; and governments would have needed the foresight, skill and aptitude to do so, which clearly at that time they had not. In fact it is doubtful even today whether they are any better at forecasting turning-points of the cycle. But expertise apart, it is doubtful whether such action would have been forthcoming. The burden of adjustment lay with the United States initially and would have entailed two courses of action: first, reversing the contraction in foreign lending and secondly, taking measures to refuel the boom. Neither would have been very logical in the conditions of 1928–9. By that time it was apparent that debtor countries had borrowed far too much and that their capacity to repay was being strained. To have kept up the rate of lending or even stepped it up would only have postponed the date at which adjustment had to be made. The mistake in the 1920s was that creditor nations had been too generous with their funds: debtors had been allowed to overborrow and had made little attempt to adjust their economies and develop within their means.

That the crunch came in 1928–9 as a result of the U.S. boom was unfortunate, but it was bound to come in the end since creditors were hardly likely to lend indefinitely to insolvent borrowers at the previous high rate. The difficulties of debtor countries could have been alleviated by scrapping reparations and a more liberal commercial policy on the part of the United States but such adjustments would have by no means solved the problem.

In 1929 the last thing the authorities were likely to do was to revitalize the boom. After all, with memories of the boom of 1919–20 and the subsequent European inflations still close at hand, the authorities were more concerned with bringing it under control, and especially with curbing excessive stock market speculation. Moreover, for much of 1929 most Americans were convinced that the country had entered perpetual prosperity and there seemed little indication of the dire consequences which were soon to follow. In the circumstances it was unlikely that any government would have acted differently. Only after the stock market crash in October did America realize that the halcyon days were over, and by then it was too late. Economic activity and business confidence deteriorated so rapidly, both in America and elsewhere, that it is unlikely that any policy action could have saved the situation in the short term. This is not an apology for inaction on the part of governments. Clearly had they made a concerted effort to combat the depression late in 1929 and early in 1930 the duration and severity of the downswing and the accompanying financial crisis could have been lessened. Indeed, cooperation on the part of the major economic powers could even have saved the gold standard. What we would stress however is that some degree of recession was inevitable in 1929-30; that it developed into a global crisis of such intensity can be attributed not only to the convergence of a combination of unfavourable circumstances, but also to the fact that governments resorted to policies which made things worse rather than better.

12

Trends in the World Economy

The final chapter provides a contrast, and perhaps a welcome one, to the rest of the book. Up to now we have traced and analysed in detail some problems and issues of the post-war decade. It is time now to take an overview of the 1920s by examining the trends in economic activity through the decade as a whole, and, where possible, putting these in historical perspective. This is clearly a somewhat hazardous task given the dubious statistical data for certain countries. Moreover, in some cases, the trade figures in particular, there are conflicting estimates. However, it is important to attempt the exercise to provide a more meaningful understanding of the 1920s within the context of long-term historical development. The reader is warned that the figures on which this survey is based can only be regarded as broad measures of magnitude.

Income trends and distribution

Indicators of national income combined with those of population still provide the most convenient overall method of measuring economic change or progress, though they certainly are not ideal in every respect. Fortunately comparison has been eased by the laborious and painstaking work of Zimmerman who has collected and analysed virtually all the known country income estimates available for the period 1860 to 1960. The tally is incomplete since there are still several countries and regions for which long-term income estimates do not exist; there is very little on Africa or the Near East, while the farther one goes back in time the fewer countries are represented. Nevertheless, coverage is sufficient to give a fairly representative sample from which to compile world income trends together with a breakdown for major regions and countries. Many figures are still very tentative, especially those for the lesser developed areas; the estimates for south-east Europe, for example, are based on data covering three-fourths of the population, while the sample in Latin America and China is considerably worse, and for these areas the estimates are only rough approximations. Those for the developed countries in North America, north-west Europe, etc. are more accurate though the figures are continually being revised and improved, and it is doubtful even here whether some of the data would stand close scrutiny. Nevertheless, considerable effort has been devoted to income analysis since the Second World War and the income series are probably more reliable than some of the indicators of activity which are currently in use. Zimmerman expresses considerable confidence in the results: 'Because we have been engaged in collecting the material for quite some time and have had rather extensive correspondence with insiders in various parts of the world, we do not think that it will be possible, for the time being, to improve our basic material fundamentally.'[1] In fact it has been necessary to correct several of his estimates (mainly as a result of recording errors), while a comparison with other estimates published in the same year throws up some interesting contrasts.[2]

Some basic data have been assembled in convenient form in Table 12 for the years 1913 and 1929 and for longer periods for purposes of comparison. The most striking fact is the marked deceleration of income growth throughout the world between 1913 and 1929. Growth was by no means negligible but both income and income per head (in real terms) slowed down appreciably compared with the long period of expansion before 1914, while the performance shows up badly against twentieth-century

1. L. J. Zimmerman, 'The Distribution of World Income, 1860–1960', in E. de Vries (ed.), *Essays on Unbalanced Growth* (1962), p. 35.
2. Namely those by J. Tinbergen, *Shaping the World Economy* (1962), p. 9.

experience as a whole (1913–59). Of the regions listed only Japan recorded an acceleration in income per capita. Japan's performance was quite exceptional and for the most part reflected the rapid boost to her development during the war when advantage was taken of the indisposition of the belligerent nations. One or two other countries, notably New Zealand, Denmark, France and probably Peru and Malaya, managed to improve on their pre-war performance, but for the most part the trend was towards lower rates of growth.

It is evident therefore that the war checked the full growth potential of most countries, and that what was lost during the hostilities was not made good during the first post-war decade.[3]

For purposes of comparison the percentage increases in real per capita income for the main regions of the world over the period 1913 and 1929 are as follows:

	Tinbergen	Zimmerman
North America	35·6	18·0
Oceania	18·9	0·0
North-west Europe	16·3	10·9
Soviet Union	9·9	12·5
South-east Europe	−9·1	5·0
Latin America	15·3	12·5
Japan	78·8	55·6
Far East	14·0	14·0
South-east Asia	4·6	3·1
China	0·0	4·3

The most serious discrepancies are in the figures for North America, Oceania, Japan and south-east Europe. Differences in coverage probably explain the discrepancy in the last case but not for the other three regions. For North America both estimates are incorrect since the rise in real per capita income in the United States for this period was of the order of one-quarter, very similar to the Canadian increase. For the United States see J. W. Kendrick, *Productivity Trends in the United States* (1961), pp. 298–9. Tinbergen's estimates for Japan are too high and the figures given by Zimmerman follow those in K. Ohkawa, *The Growth Rate of the Japanese Economy since 1878* (1957), pp. 248–9. After correction of the population figure for 1913 the Zimmerman estimates for Oceania yield a nil rate of growth for the period. This rather surprising result seems correct since, according to Butlin's estimates, Australia, the largest component, suffered a decline in real income per head. See N. G. Butlin, *Australian Domestic Product, Investment and Foreign Borrowing, 1861–1938/39* (1962), pp. 7, 33, and the comments below.

3. Taking the 1920s alone the record of growth for many countries was

TABLE 11
ANNUAL COMPOUND GROWTH RATES OF NATIONAL INCOME,
INCOME PER CAPITA AND POPULATION FOR SELECTED REGIONS,
1860–1959 (PER CENT)

	1860–1913			*1913–29*			*1913–59*		
	In- come	*Popu- lation*	*In- come per capita*	*In- come*	*Popu- lation*	*In- come per capita*	*In- come*	*Popu- lation*	*In- come per capita*
North America	3·8	2·1	1·7	2·8	1·6	1·2	2·9	1·5	1·4
Oceania	4·0	3·1	0·9	1·7	1·7	0·0	2·4	1·3	1·1
North–west Europe	2·1	0·8	1·3	0·9	0·2	0·7	1·6	0·3	1·3
Soviet Union	2·2	1·2	1·0	1·1	0·5	0·6	4·4	0·9	3·5
South-east Europe	1·9	0·8	1·1	1·6	1·3	0·3	2·3	0·9	1·4
Latin America	2·3	1·4	0·9	2·8	1·9	0·9	3·6	2·0	1·6
Japan	2·4	0·9	1·5	4·0	1·2	2·8	3·8	1·3	2·5
Far East	2·8	1·6	1·2	2·4	1·6	0·8	2·1	1·5	0·6
South-east Asia	1·1	0·5	0·6	0·9	0·6	0·3	1·3	1·2	0·1
China	0·4	0·3	0·1	0·5	0·3	0·2	1·4	0·6	0·8
TOTAL	2·2	0·7	1·5	1·7	0·7	1·0	2·6	1·0	1·6

SOURCE: Calculated from data in L. J. Zimmerman, 'The Distribution of World Income, 1860–1960', in E. de Vries (ed.), *Essays on Unbalanced Growth* (1962), pp. 54–5.

Even in North America growth slowed down which is perhaps contrary to what one might expect given the fact that this area, like Japan, stood to benefit from the war. Growth was above average (and there was not much to choose between Canada and the United States in this respect), yet income expansion w·ns some way below that of the latter half of the nineteenth century. The estimates given in Table 11 probably understate growth in North America but even allowing for this the performance still falls short of the pre-war record. This suggests that America did not do quite so well out of the war as one often imagines, and also possibly

comparable and often better than pre-war, but this tends to provide a rather unfair basis of comparison since production levels were low in many countries immediately after the war.

belies the arguments often put forward that the American economy was overextended in the 1920s and hence a reaction was inevitable. It is possible to have a little of both sides of the coin. American development was somewhat lopsided in the 1920s. Manufacturing and exports (in both the U.S.A. and Canada) boomed in these years with emphasis on the newer sectors of activity, while residential construction was also buoyant for part of the period; in contrast, certain service sectors stagnated and agriculture was in some difficulties, both of which tended to dampen the growth potential.

But the most surprising result must surely be the stagnation of income per capita growth in Oceania, and the more so since population growth declined considerably compared with pre-war. Moreover, it was Australia which was responsible for the poor result since total income in New Zealand doubled between 1913 and 1929, and even though population expanded rapidly the per capita income increase was still a hefty 57 per cent. This was one of the largest increases recorded in this period and it placed New Zealand in third place (behind America and Canada) in levels of income per head. On the other hand, Australia's income per head remained below the pre-war level for most of the 1920s and by the end of the decade it was some 10 per cent down on that of 1913–14. This is indeed curious given the substantial growth in manufacturing activity during the period and so far the lapse has not been satisfactorily explained.[4] One suspects the statistics themselves though even an upward revision of the income estimates would hardly throw up a substantial growth in income.[5] There are however several possible explanations. Australia attained a very high level of income per capita at an early stage in her development; by the 1890s the first major phase of extensive expansion was petering out and the country entered a fairly long period of retardation. Though manufacturing activity tended to increase in importance structural shifts towards high-productivity sectors were limited, and there was little offset in terms of a decline in the rural sector. After 1913 growth in most sectors was lower while productivity over a wide sector of the economy appears to have taken a sharp dive downwards. Apart from these long-term

4. For manufacturing see C. Forster, *Industrial Development in Australia, 1920–1930* (1964).

5. H. F. Lydall, 'N. G. Butlin's Anatomy of Australian Economic Growth', *Business Archives and History*, vol. III (1963).

factors there were more immediate forces at work. The war produced a severe check to income growth in Australia, while some sectors were far less buoyant in the 1920s than before. Exports stagnated, the rural sector lost its former dynamism, mining continued to decline, while, apart from manufacturing, the sectors which tended to advance, public and government services and finance, had a relatively low level of productivity.[6] This probably does less than justice to the position but it is the best that can be offered in the present state of research.

The relative impoverishment of Europe is also very apparent. Despite some efforts to recover lost ground, in both the east and the west, during the latter half of the decade income per capita growth was appreciably less than before the war. In south-east Europe part of the problem was the rapid upsurge in population, one of the few regions, apart from Latin America, to experience a marked acceleration in this field. Some countries in this region, for example Romania, Yugoslavia and Greece, scored massive increases in population but in part these reflected the acquisition of new territories, migrants or refugees in the post-war settlements. However, though the natural rate of population increase in this region as a whole no doubt dampened income per capita growth the experience of certain countries does not suggest a very close correlation. In Greece, for example, the population more than doubled, a large part of the increase being derived from refugee migrants, yet per capita income rose by one-quarter, a sharp contrast with the decade or two before the war when both income and population were virtually stagnant. On the other hand, Bulgaria, which had a quite modest population increase, managed to record a 10 per cent fall in per capita income over the period 1913–29. Elsewhere the pattern was mixed though the absence of figures for certain countries precludes comment in detail, and one is doubtful about the reliability of what data are available given the huge reorganization of territorial boundaries. Poland came off very badly with an income per capita drop of 26 per cent, which seems large but is certainly in the right direction given the difficulties in the way of recovery.[7] Poland too was afflicted by a large

6. C. Forster (ed.), *Australian Economic Development in the Twentieth Century* (1970), especially Chapters 2, 5, 6; Butlin, *Australian Domestic Product, Investment and Foreign Borrowing, 1861–1938/39*, pp. 12–13, 460–61.

expansion of population, again largely derived from the peace settlements. Austria and Hungary, especially the former, did reasonably well, while Czechoslovakia must surely have recorded the best performance though unfortunately there are no estimates for this country. The slow down in the Soviet Union reflects the battering which the economy received in the post-war cata-strophes and in view of this the overall performance must be considered quite creditable.

Population growth was no problem in north-west Europe since it almost ground to a halt after the war. The halving of the growth rate clearly reflects the war-time setback. However, there were rather sharp differences in experience among the countries within this region. The overall deceleration can be attributed almost entirely to two countries, the U.K. and Germany, which accounted for about one-half the combined income of this area. The U.K. registered below-average growth while Germany's per capita income was still slightly below pre-war by the end of the decade. France and Belgium, partly through a rapid burst of expansion later in the 1920s, coupled in France with a very low rate of population growth, showed very respectable performances, better than in the immediate pre-war decades. But it was the neutrals, Denmark, Norway, Sweden, Switzerland and the Netherlands, which set the pace with increases in per capita income of around a third or more. Norway, Denmark and the Netherlands had very large increases in total income, two-thirds or more, but their population growth was also very much higher than the average.

The Latin American region provides several interesting con-trasts. On the surface the continent as a whole appeared peaceful and prosperous through the 1920s. The output of primary commodities and industrial production rose steadily and national income in absolute terms showed a notable acceleration over the pre-war period. But population growth also rose sharply, cutting the per capita increase down to the same level as before 1914. Yet population changes are not the crux of the problem in all cases since experience was far from uniform. Brazil and Peru both recorded similar rates of population change but income per head

7. Manufacturing indices for Poland support the trend in income. Indices of gross domestic product for many European countries are contained in A. Maddison, *Economic Policy and Performance in Europe, 1913–1970* (1973), Appendix B.

moved quite differently: in Peru it nearly doubled whereas in Brazil it was virtually stagnant. Moreover, prior to 1914 (1900–1913), Brazil had managed a substantial rise in per capita income with a population increase greater than was attained later. And again Colombia and the Argentine had larger rises in population than Brazil yet they both managed to score gains in income per head. These contrasts clearly reflect the different structures of individual economies. Though industrialization was advancing throughout the region most of Latin America was still heavily dependent upon primary products as a source of income, and in particular on the export of these commodities. Their economic progress was determined very much by world markets for primary products. There was a considerable expansion in demand for many of them during the 1920s but not all countries were equally fortunate. Brazil, for example, suffered from periodic crises of overproduction in coffee and lost its privileged position in the rubber trade after the First World War. Brazil's problems in coffee were partly aggravated by expansion elsewhere (partly because high prices were secured for coffee for a time through the coffee valorization policy), especially in Colombia which gained an increasing share of the world market in the 1920s.[8] Brazil did enjoy considerable expansion outside agriculture but this barely kept pace with population growth with the result that real income per head more or less stagnated over the period 1913 to 1929.[9] Chile also went through a difficult patch when the trade in nitrates closed in on her as a consequence of the development of synthetic substitutes. Fortunately the rapid exploitation of her copper resources and steady industrial development enabled her to counteract this blow.[10] One might also mention here the difficulties encountered by Cuba, Java and Jamaica in sugar as a result of oversupply problems together with the recovery of European beet production, which checked their income growth.

8. W. P. McGreevey, *An Economic History of Columbia, 1845–1930* (1971), pp. 11, 202–5.

9. G.N.P. rose by 4·1 per cent between 1920 and 1929. N. H. Neff, 'Long-term Brazilian Economic Development', *Journal of Economic History*, vol. xxix (1969), pp. 486–7; C. Furtado, *Economic Development of Latin America* (1970), pp. 82–3, and *The Economic Growth of Brazil* (1963), pp. 201–2.

10. P. T. Ellsworth, *Chile: An Economy in Transition* (1945), p. 4; M. Mamalakis and C. W. Reynolds, *Essays on the Chilean Economy* (1965), pp. 221–30.

The real benefits of progress in Latin America occurred in those countries fortunate enough to specialize in raw materials where oversupply problems were far less prevalent. This was particularly true of the newer products such as petroleum and tin where the enormous demand from the car-owning countries brought significant benefits to the fortunate, particularly Venezuela, Mexico, Peru, Colombia, Ecuador and Bolivia. The biggest oil discoveries were in Venezuela, and from negligible beginnings in 1918 the country was producing more than 10 per cent of the world's supply by 1930 nearly all of which was exported. The income from oil enabled Venezuela to finance a growing import bill and raise the standard of living and she was the only Latin American republic not encumbered with public debts. Most of the other states had important oil interests but none became so dependent on it as Venezuela. Colombia's prosperity was based on a rapid expansion in foreign trade which more than doubled, and included exports of coffee, cocoa, sugar as well as oil. This country also possessed important mining and textile activities. Peru also had a reasonably diversified export structure, including copper, cotton, sugar, other agricultural products and oil.[11] The Argentine, on the other hand, which depended very much on the export of agricultural products, had a much lower rate of increase in per capita income despite fairly vigorous industrial growth in the 1920s, though a rapid increase in population was a drag.[12] But in nearly every Latin American republic, prosperous or otherwise, the basis of development was very insecure; it depended heavily on one or two commodities and on foreign sources of supply for capital and equipment. Once the market for primary products contracted and foreign aid dried up almost every country found itself in severe difficulties.

China and Asia continued to stagnate with very little relief from the vicious circle of poverty. True there were developments on the industrial front in both India and China but modernization was very limited and the advanced areas were isolated from the rest of the economy. The traditional sector of agriculture and handicrafts continued to dominate these economies and growth

11. J. H. Parry, 'Latin America', Chapter 19 of C. L. Mowat (ed.), *The Shifting Balance of World Forces, 1898–1945* (1968, vol. xii of the *New Cambridge Modern History*), p. 598.

12. C. Furtado, *Economic Development of Latin America* (1970), p. 8.

elsewhere was barely sufficient to counteract population increase so that there was very little gain in income per head.[13] Thus despite rapid industrial growth in the modern industrial sector during the 1920s industrial production only accounted for a very small proportion of the Chinese national product by the early 1930s (about 10 per cent in total or 3 per cent without handicrafts), while the traditional sector still bulked large.[14] Moreover, much of the modern development was concentrated around one or two areas or enclaves, notably Shanghai and Manchuria, which depended heavily for their progress upon imported capital from Britain and Japan. But the total foreign investment was small in relation to the capital needs of the economy; and even if it had all been used for productive purposes it could not have effected a significant transformation of the economy.[15] The Far East did

TABLE 12

DISTRIBUTION OF WORLD INCOME AND POPULATION BY REGIONS, 1860, 1913 AND 1929 (PER CENT)

	1860		1913		1929	
	Income	Population	Income	Population	Income	Population
North America	14·8	0·1	32·9	6·3	38·3	7·4
Oceania	0·5	3·1	1·4	0·4	1·3	0·4
North-west Europe	29·3	11·1	27·6	11·5	24·0	10·7
Soviet Union	7·2	6·7	7·3	8·7	6·6	8·4
South-east Europe	9·8	7·9	8·5	8·2	8·4	8·9
Latin America	3·8	3·4	4·0	5·0	4·7	6·0
Japan	1·4	2·9	1·5	3·3	2·1	3·5
Far East	1·4	2·4	1·9	3·8	2·0	4·4
South-east Asia	11·8	22·3	6·9	20·3	6·0	19·9
China	20·0	40·1	8·0	32·5	6·6	30·4
TOTAL	100·0	100·0	100·0	100·0	100·0	100·0

SOURCE: L. J. Zimmerman, 'The Distribution of World Income, 1860–1960', in E. de Vries (ed.), *Essays on Unbalanced Growth* (1962), pp. 54–5.

13. A. K. Bagchi, *Private Investment in India, 1900–1939* (1972), pp. 84–8; V. B. Singh, *Economic History of India, 1857–1956* (1965), pp. 656–60, 700–702.

14. J. K. Chang, *Industrial Development of Pre-Communist China* (1969), pp. 87–8, 97, 109.

15. For China see C. Hou, *Foreign Investment and Economic Development in China, 1840–1937* (1965), pp. 13–22; C. F. Remer, *Foreign Investments in China* (1933), pp. 73–7, 98–100; Y. K. Cheng, *Foreign Trade and Industrial Development of China* (1956); F. H. H. King, *A Concise Economic History of*

somewhat better thanks partly to the short-lived rubber boom in Malaya. Finally, Indonesia and the Philippines achieved substantial gains in total income but most of these were offset by large accretions to their populations.

The distribution of income among the ten major regions changed quite significantly for such a short period, a reflection both of the impact of war and the shifting population structure. The main gains were made by North America, Latin America and Japan (see Table 12). Much of the Japanese increase was due to the marked acceleration in income per capita growth whereas in Latin America population growth produced the rise in world income share. Both factors served to raise the North American share. On the other hand, north-west Europe and the Soviet Union, as might be expected, declined in relative importance, while significant losses were also recorded by China and south-east Asia. However, in terms of the inequality of income distribution in relation to population the overall effect was very limited. The distribution of income among nations remained very unequal in 1929 and even more so compared with 1860. In 1929, 18·5 per cent of the world's population (that is, North America, Oceania and north-west Europe) accounted for nearly two-thirds of world income, while just over one-third of the global population (the addition of south-east Europe and the Soviet Union to the first three regions) accounted for nearly four-fifths of world income. Nearly two-thirds of the world's population had little more than one-fifth of the world income. These proportions were almost identical in 1913 so the period saw a temporary halt to the steady increase in inequality which had been evident from 1860 through to the present. In 1860 income distribution was considerably less skewed since one-third of the world's population accounted for only two-thirds of total income. The top ten nations in terms of income per head actually increased their combined share of world income from 52·0 to 56·3 per cent between 1913 and 1929.[16]

Modern China, 1840–1961 (1961); J. W. Davidson and C. Forster, 'China, Japan and the Pacific, 1900–1931', Chapter 12 of C. L. Mowat (ed.), *The Shifting Balance of World Forces, 1898–1945* (1968, vol. XII of the *New Cambridge Modern History*), pp. 361–4.

16. These ten nations (the U.S.A., Canada, Australia, New Zealand, the U.K., Belgium, France, Switzerland, Denmark and Sweden) contained 13·1 and 13·9 per cent of the world's population in 1913 and 1929 respectively.

The contrasts in inequality seem even more startling when one compares what the average person in the rich countries had to spend compared with that of the typical inhabitant of the impoverished nations. In 1929 the average American had over 5 times more to spend than the average world income recipient, while the people of Oceania and north-west Europe had treble and double the world per capita income. In all other regions income per head fell below the world average. Expressed even more sharply, the American had 24 times more income to spend than his Chinese counterpart and nearly 18 times more than the inhabitant of south-east Asia,[17] while the European had 10 and 7·6 times more respectively. These comparisons take no account of differences in price levels between countries, but even when allowance is made for these the discrepancies remain very substantial.

Trends in production

Both output and trade in primary products expanded rapidly in the 1920s. Between 1913 and 1929 world production of raw materials and foodstuffs rose by nearly one-third,[18] and the trade in primary products probably expanded by a similar amount.[19] There was, however, a marked contrast between the two groups. The demand for foodstuffs weakened considerably, partly as dietary habits changed and population growth in the main consuming regions slowed down, and some prices sagged noticeably in the later 1920s. Overall therefore the output of food products rose by only 18 per cent with a notable lag in cereals production, though in some cases, especially coffee, cocoa, sugar, tea, vegetable oils and tobacco, there was a marked rise in production despite falling prices.[20] By contrast the demand for most raw materials was very buoyant throughout the period and overall

17. China and south-east Asia, the poorest regions on the earth, contained no less than one-half the world's population, but accounted for slightly less than 13 per cent of global income. But their share of manufacturing activity was even lower. See below, page 300.

18. Based on League of Nations data. League of Nations, *Production and Prices 1925–1932* (1933); cf. A. Maizels, *Industrial Growth and World Trade* (1963), pp. 79–80.

19. P. L. Yates, *Forty Years of Foreign Trade* (1959), p. 39.

20. Royal Institute of International Affairs, *World Agriculture: An International Survey* (1932), pp. 9–11. See also Chapter 9.

production expanded by around 60 per cent, a rate of increase slightly higher than that for world manufacturing production. A substantial part of this increase occurred in the last five or six years of the period when economic activity was booming in a good part of the world. Variations in growth between different commodities reflected the changes in the structure of output in the industrial countries. Thus coal gave way to oil and textile raw materials to artificial silk. Some of the largest rises in production occurred in fertilizers, metallic ores, fuels (petroleum), non-metallic minerals, wood-pulp and rubber, while agricultural-based textile materials, hemp, jute, cotton and wool, either stagnated or grew very modestly.

TABLE 13
REGIONAL INDICES OF OUTPUT OF FOODSTUFFS AND RAW MATERIALS, 1928 (1913 = 100)

	Foodstuffs	Raw materials	All products
Eastern and Central Europe (excluding U.S.S.R.)	106	124	111
Eastern and Central Europe (including U.S.S.R.)	109	118	112
Rest of Europe	107	126	116
Europe (excluding U.S.S.R.)	106	125	114
Europe (including U.S.S.R.)	109	122	113
North America	127	147	137
South America	139	181	155
Africa	134	180	153
Asia (excluding Asiatic Russia)	112	194	136
Oceania	146	126	136
WORLD	117	148	129

SOURCE: A. Loveday, *Britain and World Trade* (1931), p. 49.

A regional breakdown of production (Table 13) shows again Europe's serious lag behind the rest of the world. Production of all primary commodities in Europe expanded by barely one-half the world average, although in the later 1920s European primary production advanced more rapidly than most of the rest of the world and eastern Europe was gaining ground over the west.[21] Food production in Europe by the late 1920s only registered a modest increase over pre-war and it was in Oceania (meat, dairy products, cereals), Africa (vegetable oils) and South America

21. See Chapter 8, page 189.

(meat, wheat, sugar, coffee, etc.) that the really substantial gains were made. A similar pattern is evident in raw material production. Though Europe did not lag so far behind her performance was still mediocre compared with the massive increases in production recorded in South America, Africa and Asia which benefited considerably from the surge in demand for newer products such as oil. Not surprisingly these regions, together with North America, registered the largest gains in trade in primary commodities, though again Europe was recovering lost ground in the later 1920s when trade was expanding more rapidly than the output of primary commodities. Loveday summed up the whole period as one of retrogression and recovery for important areas of the world capped here and there by real advance.[22]

TABLE 14
PERCENTAGE INCREASE IN MANUFACTURING PRODUCTION FOR
SELECTED AREAS, 1913-29

	Percentage increase 1913–29
Europe (18 countries) *	27·8
U.S.A.	81·8
U.S.S.R.	81·4
Rest of world (i.e. excluding the three areas above)	81·6
WORLD	53·3

* Includes U.K., Germany, France, Italy, Belgium, Netherlands, Switzerland, Sweden, Denmark, Norway, Finland, Austria, Czechoslovakia, Hungary, Poland, Romania, Greece, Spain.

SOURCES: League of Nations, *Industrialisation and Foreign Trade* (1945), p. 134, and I. Svennilson, *Growth and Stagnation in the European Economy* (1954), pp. 304–5.

Though growth of manufacturing production slowed down over the period as a whole, the 1920s saw a significant advance and by the end of the decade world output was some 50 per cent or more above the 1913 level (see Table 14). Trade in manufactured products however slowed down appreciably and did not match the growth in manufactured output.[23] Unfortunately a regional breakdown comparable to the one used earlier is not available for manufacturing production but a less elaborate one compiled from data given by the League of Nations and Svennilson provides

22. A. Loveday, *Britain and World Trade* (1931), p. 51.
23. This aspect is covered in the next section.

approximate orders of magnitude for several broad areas. This shows clearly Europe's loss to the rest of the world; European production expanded at just about one-half the world rate and only one-third that outside Europe. The spectacular advance in the Soviet Union may occasion surprise given its turbulent and disastrous history in the early 1920s. The questionable nature of the statistics apart, however, most of the advance was achieved in the last couple of years of the decade under the impetus of the First Five Year Plan. Most of the European shortfall can be ascribed to the slow growth experienced in Germany, the U.K. and eastern Europe where some countries, for example Poland, failed even to attain their pre-war level of output. Czechoslovakia, on the other hand, was a major exception with an increase in manufacturing output well above the world average. Most of the neutrals, especially the Netherlands, Sweden and Denmark, together with one or two other countries in the European grouping, notably Italy, Finland and Greece,[24] achieved impressive rates of expansion.[25] Outside Europe the most impressive advances occurred in Japan, South Africa, the United States, Canada and New Zealand, while a number of underdeveloped countries in Asia and Latin America scored worthwhile gains, though often much of the advance was recorded during the war and early post-war years after which manufacturing activity tended to stagnate, as in India and Brazil, or grew from a very low base, as in Chile.

Figures for the distributional shares in manufacturing for the major nations are given in Table 15. These throw up some rather interesting results. Between 1913 and the late 1920s the major losses occurred in four European countries, Germany, the U.K., France and Belgium; their combined share fell from 37·5 to 29·5 per cent. This loss was matched almost exactly by a gain from 42 to 50·4 per cent in four other countries, the U.S.A., Canada, Japan and Italy. These eight countries, with only 22 per cent of the world's population, dominated manufacturing activity of the world throughout the period, for in both 1913 and 1926–9

24. Greece was the odd one out with a spectacular 259 per cent increase though from a fairly low base.

25. While Spain as usual did nothing good and nothing bad. Perhaps its persistent mediocrity is one reason why the country gets neglected by the texts.

TABLE 15
PERCENTAGE DISTRIBUTION OF WORLD MANUFACTURING
PRODUCTION, 1913–29

	1913 *	1926–9
U.S.A.	35·8	42·2
Germany	14·3	11·6
U.K.	14·1	9·4
France	7·0	6·6
Italy	2·7	3·3
Canada	2·3	2·4
Belgium	2·1	1·9
Japan	1·2	2·5
Soviet Union	4·4	4·3
Sweden	1·0	1·0
India	1·1	1·2
Rest of World	14·0	13·6
TOTAL	100·0	100·0

* The percentages for 1913 represent the distribution according to the frontiers established after the First World War.

SOURCE: League of Nations, *Industrialisation and Foreign Trade* (1945), p. 13.

they accounted for almost 80 per cent of global production.[26] This was an even more unequal distribution than in the case of national income since the same eight countries accounted for 61·1 per cent of world income in 1913 and 63·4 per cent in 1929.

That nearly four-fifths of the world's population had only some 20 per cent of all manufacturing production is disturbing in itself. What is even more so is the fact that distribution at the lower end of the scale was very skewed. China and India, with roughly half the world's population, probably had less than 2 per cent of all manufacturing production. An even larger area, Africa, Asia (excluding Russia), Latin America, south-east Europe and Oceania, had 69 per cent of the world's population but only 10 per cent of manufacturing industry, while Japan accounted for one-quarter of all manufacturing in these areas and most of the increase between 1913 and 1929. Furthermore, because the eight industrial nations listed above retained their monopoly intact over this period, though there were shifts in relative importance among them, any gains made by individual underdeveloped countries were at the

26. Though this represented an improvement on 1870 when the same countries accounted for over 85 per cent of all manufacturing.

expense of other countries within this large, non-industrialized group. The bulk of the world's population could do no more than keep pace with industrialization, and many countries failed to do even this.

The bare figures tell us next to nothing about the nature of the industrialization process in different regions, though since this has already been discussed we need give only a brief review here.

The characteristics of industrialization varied a great deal from region to region. For the underdeveloped areas of Latin America, eastern Europe and Asia it meant basically the expansion of textile activity, the processing of certain primary products, and various semi-handicraft and similar unsophisticated activities characteristic of low-income countries. Much of the development was inefficient compared with the standards of the western industrial nations and therefore had to be protected by tariffs. In the sparsely populated high-income countries of Oceania and Canada it was a matter of shifting away from the staple primaries which had served as a strong basis of expansion in the past towards manufacturing activities based on advanced technology. Thus in Canada, for example, the emphasis shifted away from wheat and railways towards newsprint, metals, electric power and developments related to the spread of the motor car. Rapid growth in these and the service industries gave a significant boost to investment and determined to a significant degree the nature of development after 1929.[27] A similar though less rapid shift was going on in Australia at the same time. The most advanced stage was of course reached in the United States where the boom of the 1920s was based on the products of a high-income society, motor cars, other consumer durables, residential building and industries involving highly complex technologies such as chemicals. By contrast, a future giant of the industrial world,[28] the Soviet Union, was struggling to reform her agriculture and at the same time

27. A. E. Safarian, *The Canadian Economy in the Great Depression* (1959), pp. 22–3.

28. And a not very distant future at that. While most countries were floundering under the impact of the slump of the early 1930s the Soviet Union forged ahead rapidly under successive Five Year Plans. Almost unbelievably she became, overnight so to speak, the second largest manufacturing nation in the world after the U.S.A. by the end of the 1930s, when she accounted for 18·5 per cent of world production, that is almost as much as the U.K. and Germany combined.

industrialize. Here the First Five Year Plan, launched at the end of the decade, placed heavy emphasis on the expansion of capital goods production.

Old Europe, or western Europe to be more precise, was at an awkward stage. Many new developments based on modern technologies along American lines marched side by side with a host of declining staple industries. It had a severe problem of structural transformation and the delay in making adjustments impeded the growth process. Britain suffered most acutely in this respect, and while progress in the newer trades was by no means meagre it could not cope with the mass of resources flung redundant from the great staple industries of coal, cotton, shipbuilding, etc., to which Britain had probably been overcommitted in the past. Britain was by no means alone in this problem though some countries adapted more quickly to changing conditions. Germany's dramatic revival after the 1923–4 stabilization crisis was in no small measure due to the massive overhauling of her industrial structure and processes in the name of rationalization.[29] Sweden's industrial metamorphosis was even more impressive and it is no coincidence that throughout the whole inter-war period this country achieved one of the fastest rates of growth in the western hemisphere.[30]

Incomes and production may have risen more slowly in the 1920s than formerly but the fact that they did expand is, as Landes points out, 'testimony to the power of continued technological change to stimulate investment and raise productivity in the most adverse circumstances'.[31] The period was not noted for spectacular new inventions, rather there was a widespread application of known techniques or production processes in a large area of the economy. Technical change was evident in both old and

29. See R. Brady, *The Rationalization Movement in German Industry: A Study in the Evolution of Economic Planning* (1933), p. xix. Brady also suggests (p. xii) that rationalization *as carried out* must bear a considerable share of the responsibility for the 1929–32 debacle; but it is not very clear what exactly he means by this.

30. For an excellent account of structural transformation in Sweden between the wars see E. Dahmén, *Entrepreneurial Activity and the Development of Swedish Industry, 1919–1939* (1970; translated by A. Leijonhufvud).

31. D. S. Landes, *The Unbound Prometheus: Technological Change and Industrial Development in Western Europe from 1750 to the Present* (1969), p. 419.

new industries though rates of development were very uneven both by industry and by country. In the older sectors such as coal, cotton, and iron and steel one can list a range of improvements – new machines, mechanized methods of production, fuel economies, etc. – which were being introduced by various countries. Many new product innovations were initiated or stimulated by wartime demands, while the pressure of war requirements often gave a considerable boost to developing more efficient methods of production, in engineering and machine tools for example.[32]

But in this period the centre of gravity shifted towards the newer products. Most of the basic inventions had been perfected before the war and in the 1920s they were exploited intensively. They included the massive application of electricity and the internal combustion engine, the introduction of a wide range of household appliances, new chemical products, rayon and aircraft production. Often the whole format of production was revolutionized by continuous assembly line production, particularly in the car industry, but the manufacture of a whole range of products both old and new was being transformed by more efficient and streamlined production. The changes occurred most rapidly in the United States though Europe too was beginning to 'enjoy new technical marvels, like mass-produced cars, aircraft, radios and the cinema, together with an undreamt-of expansion or improvement of older consumption goods and services, including housing, medical services, holidays, and mass-produced clothing, confectionary and preserved foods'.[33] Indeed, the benefits of modern consumer technology were even penetrating outside the confines of the western world, into Asia, Africa and Latin America.[34]

Thus despite the dislocations and crises of the inter-war years the rate of technical change was probably as great, if not greater, than in the later nineteenth century. It is difficult to prove this

32. See Landes, *The Unbound Prometheus*, Chapter 6 for a very extensive survey of developments in Western Europe, and also I. Svennilson, *Growth and Stagnation in the European Economy* (1954).

33. S. Pollard and C. Holmes (eds), *Documents of European Economic History, Vol. 3: The End of the Old Europe 1914–1939* (1973), p. XIII.

34. 'This revolution, which has affected to a greater or less extent all classes of society in all parts of the world, is one of the outstanding phenomena in the social history of the decade preceding the present depression.' League of Nations, *The Course and Phases of the World Economic Depression* (1931), pp. 23–4.

point statistically since data on output per unit of input are obtainable for only a few countries. The figures for output per man-hour estimated by Maddison can only act as a proxy since they take no account of changes in capital inputs, and in any case they reflect shifts of employment from low- to high-productivity sectors as well as the ejection of redundant labour from

TABLE 16
RATES OF GROWTH OF OUTPUT PER MAN-HOUR, 1870–1929

	1870–1913	1913–1929
Belgium	2·1	2·0
Denmark	2·5	1·7
France	1·8	2·8
Germany	2·1 *	0·8
Italy	1·3	2·3
Netherlands	1·1 †	2·6
Norway	1·8 *	3·0
Sweden	2·7	0·9
Switzerland	1·6	3·2
U.K.	1·5	2·1
Canada	2·1	1·3
U.S.A.	2·3 *	2·8
* 1871–1913		
† 1900–1913		

SOURCE: A. Maddison, *Economic Growth in the West* (1964), p. 232.

declining industries. Nevertheless, whatever the deficiencies of these statistics for our purpose they do show that between 1913 and 1929 the majority of western countries were able to improve on their pre-war productivity (see Table 16).[35] In some countries the improvements reflect shifts of labour out of low-productivity sectors or the discharge of manpower from industries with excess labour resources. These factors probably account for much of the rise in productivity in the U.K. and Italy for instance. Even so, if all the productivity gains over and above the rates recorded for the period 1870–1914 could be attributed to non-technical factors it would still mean that technical progress was no less a contributor to productivity growth than previously.

35. For the 1920s alone productivity growth was, as a rule, considerably above the long-term average. Cf. the data given by C. D. Paige *et al.*, 'Economic Growth: The Last Hundred Years', *National Institute Economic Review*, vol. XVI (July 1961), p. 36.

Patterns of international trade

International trade never regained its former momentum in the inter-war years. The worst period was in the 1930s, but even in the 1920s the recovery of trade to pre-war levels was sluggish and it was not until the boom later in the decade that it regained its former sparkle. Estimates of the extent of the recovery vary considerably. Both Maddison and Woytinsky suggest a fairly high

TABLE 17
RATES OF GROWTH OF WORLD EXPORTS, 1880-1929

	1880–1913	*1913–29*
Belgium	3·6	0·4
France	2·6	2·4
Germany	4·3 *	0·1
Italy	3·1 *	2·4
Netherlands	4·6 *	2·3
Sweden	3·4 *	2·3
Switzerland	3·6 *	0·05
U.K.	2·6	−0·8
Western Europe	3·0	0·7
Canada	4·6	4·5
U.S.A.	3·2	3·0
Third countries	4·0	3·5
WORLD	3·4	2·2

* Germany, 1881–1913; Italy, 1872–1913; Netherlands, 1885–1913; Sweden, 1872–1913; Switzerland, 1900–1913.
SOURCE: A. Maddison, 'Growth and Fluctuation in the World Economy, 1870–1960', *Banca Nazionale del Lavoro Quarterly Review*, vol. xv, June 1962, pp. 185–6.

rate of increase in the volume of world trade between 1913 and 1929, 41·5 and 35·1 per cent respectively,[36] but other authorities incline towards lower estimates.[37] However, what is not open to dispute is that world trade grew less rapidly between 1913 and 1929 than it had in the later nineteenth and early twentieth centuries. The figures in Table 17 show that in virtually all areas

36. A. Maddison, 'Growth and Fluctuation in the World Economy, 1870–1960', *Banca Nazionale del Lavoro Quarterly Review*, vol. xv (June 1962), p. 186; W. S. and E. S. Woytinsky, *World Commerce and Governments* (1955), p. 39.
37. See Maizels, *Industrial Growth and World Trade*, p. 80 and Yates, *Forty Years of Foreign Trade*, pp. 31, 39, 62.

the rate of growth was slacker than before 1913, though the U.S.A. and Canada came very close to their previous records. The worst performance was undoubtedly western Europe, where the rate of growth was barely one-quarter that of the period 1880–1913. Some countries, notably Germany, Switzerland and the U.K., did very badly; France was the one exception to an otherwise depressing record.

Retardation in trade was more marked than in production. Before 1913 both trade and production generally had marched in step but thereafter this was no longer true. Even with the burst of expansion in trade in the late 1920s it is very unlikely that the foreign trade proportion recovered to its 1913 level.[38] It is quite probable that world trade in primary products kept pace with the output of such commodities – though the statistical material available is unreliable[39] – but there can be no doubt that trade in manufactures failed to keep pace with production. Between 1913 and 1929 world manufacturing production expanded by 2·7 per cent per annum whereas the corresponding figure for world trade was only 1·6 per cent per annum.[40] Before 1913 both had grown at approximately 3·3 per cent per annum.

Many countries therefore suffered a decline in the proportion of foreign trade to national income, though in a few cases, for example Canada, the reverse was true. The most noticeable declines occurred in European countries which is not surprising given the check administered by the war, and the more widespread impediments to trade after the war, for example, nationalistic policies, tariffs, etc., though these became a greater influence in the 1930s. However, the decline in the trade–income ratio has been seen as a particular characteristic inherent in the long-term development of advanced economies. Deutsch and Eckstein have argued that the main trading nations of the non-communist world experienced a rise in the trade–income ratio in the early stages of industrialization which reached a peak between 1870 and 1919. Under the impact of war and depression the ratios decline sharply but even after 1945 they do not return to the former peaks. This,

38. A. G. Kenwood and A. L. Lougheed, *The Growth of the International Economy 1820–1960* (1971), p. 223. The authors' suggestion that it more or less regained the pre-war level is incorrect.

39. Maizels, *Industrial Growth and World Trade*, p. 80, suggests that it did.

40. A. K. Cairncross, *Factors in Economic Development* (1962), p. 235.

they feel, suggests that reasons other than the upset imparted by shocks cause the ratio to fall as an economy matures.[41] In particular, as economies become more advanced the domestic and service sectors gain in importance. Sectors such as housing, education, welfare and service industries, which contribute little to foreign trade, take up more of a nation's resources. Secondly, the advanced technology of industrial nations involves economies in imported raw materials or replaces imported materials by substitutes from local sources, for example, synthetic rubber, nitrates and fibres.[42] Modern technology also increases the importance of the refining and finishing stages in the processing of raw materials. Other forces working in a similar direction are the spread of industrialization elsewhere and the declining proportion of income spent on food.

While these assertions certainly have some validity it is difficult to find hard evidence that they were instrumental in forcing down

TABLE 18
WORLD EXPORTS AND IMPORTS BY REGIONS, 1876–1937
(PERCENTAGES OF ALL COUNTRIES)

	1876–80		1913		1928		1937	
	Ex-ports	Im-ports	Ex-ports	Im-ports	Ex-ports	Im-ports	Ex-ports	Im-ports
North America	11·7	7·4	14·8	11·5	19·8	15·2	17·1	13·9
U.K. and Ireland	16·3	22·5	13·1	15·2	11·5	15·8	10·6	17·8
North-west Europe*	31·9	31·9	33·4	36·5	25·1	27·9	25·8	27·8
Rest of Europe†	16·0	11·9	12·4	13·4	11·4	12·5	10·6	10·2
Oceania			2·5	2·4	2·9	2·6	3·5	2·8
Latin America‡	24·1	26·3	8·3	7·0	9·8	7·6	10·2	7·2
Africa			3·7	3·6	4·0	4·6	5·3	6·2
Asia			11·8	10·4	15·5	13·8	16·9	14·1

* All countries west and north of a line drawn down the eastern frontiers of Finland, Germany and Austria.
† Including U.S.S.R.
‡ Including all colonial territories in the western hemisphere.
SOURCE: P. L. Yates, *Forty Years of Foreign Trade* (1959), Tables 6, 7, pp. 32–3.

41. K. W. Deutsch and A. Eckstein, 'National Industrialisation and the Declining Share of the International Economic Sector, 1890–1959', *World Politics*, vol. XIII (1961), pp. 292–6.
42. ibid., p. 296.

the trade–income ratio. Moreover, there are economic forces operating in the reverse direction, notably rising real incomes of industrial countries which encourage trade expansion. In any case, it is too much of a coincidence that the peak in the trade–income ratio occurred in the period up to the First World War after which it declined. Given the impact of two wars, a severe economic depression and all that these entailed in barriers to foreign trade, it is not surprising that the trade–income ratio took time to recover. Indeed, since the 1950s world trade in manufactures has risen more rapidly than production[43] and many countries should have now regained their former trade–income ratios.

There were significant shifts in the proportional distribution of trade among various regions of the world between 1913 and the late 1920s. Broadly speaking, North America and the underdeveloped world gained at the expense of Europe including the U.K. (see Table 18). The significant increase in Asia's share of world trade is partly accounted for by the rapid advances made by Japan, while the sharp fall in north-west Europe was mainly due to the losses incurred by Germany and Belgium.[44] Eastern Europe, it should be noted, maintained its position remarkably well given that it includes the Soviet Union whose share of world trade shrank from about 4 per cent in 1913 to 1·5 per cent at the end of the 1920s. However, these major shifts cannot be attributed simply to the disruptive effects of the war since some trends were already evident before 1913. North America and to a lesser extent the main underdeveloped or non-industrial regions (Latin America, Asia, Africa and Oceania) had been gaining ground, while the U.K. and eastern Europe had been declining. Nevertheless, industrial countries continued to account for the bulk of world exports throughout the period.[45]

This dominance was particularly marked in manufactured exports. Though the shares of the U.K. and north-west Europe declined significantly between 1913 and 1929 the combined loss was almost made good by the increased North American share.

43. In fact after 1948–50 the world trade volume in manufactures was rising more rapidly than the production of manufactures. See Maizels, *Industrial Growth and World Trade*, p. 80.

44. It should be noted that in the later 1920s Europe as a whole recovered some lost ground.

45. About two-thirds. Yates, *Forty Years of Foreign Trade*, pp. 56–7.

TABLE 19

WORLD EXPORTS AND IMPORTS OF MANUFACTURES BY REGIONS,
1876–1937 (PERCENTAGES OF ALL COUNTRIES)

	1876–80		1913		1928		1937	
	Ex-ports	Im-ports	Ex-ports	Im-ports	Ex-ports	Im-ports	Ex-ports	Im-ports
North America	4·4	7·7	10·6	12·1	19·2	12·8	19·7	10·6
U.K. and Ireland	37·8	9·1	25·3	8·2	21·8	9·1	19·5	8·8
North-west Europe	47·1	18·1	47·9	24·4	40·9	17·5	41·8	17·5
Rest of Europe	9·2	13·3	8·3	15·4	4·6	15·7	5·8	13·3
Oceania			0·1	5·0	0·2	5·1	0·4	5·7
Latin America	1·5	51·8	0·7	11·9	0·6	13·5	0·5	12·9
Africa			0·4	6·1	0·4	8·3	0·5	12·3
Asia			6·7	16·9	12·3	18·0	11·8	18·9

SOURCE: P. L. Yates, *Forty Years of Foreign Trade* (1959), Tables 21, 23, pp. 49–50.

These three regions accounted for almost 82 per cent of all manufactured exports as against 83·8 per cent in 1913 and 89·3 per cent in the late 1870s. The scope for gain elsewhere was very limited; the only area which showed a significant advance was Asia (largely under the influence of Japan), while all other underdeveloped regions remained static or lost ground, eastern Europe particularly. On the other hand, most of the underdeveloped areas increased their shares of imported manufactures at a time when the relative importance of Europe was declining (see Table 19).

Fortunately the underdeveloped areas had somewhat greater success in exporting primary products. All the non-industrial regions increased their shares of world trade, the most significant advances being those for Latin America and Asia. North America also increased its share. The only areas to suffer losses were northwest Europe and the U.K., in part a reflection of the diminishing importance of coal and farm product exports. As regards relative import shares the major changes occurred in North America and Asia with a significant increase in their dependence on imported raw materials (Table 20).

Thus despite notable shifts in the composition of world trade the industrial countries still dominated the international markets at the end of the decade. They monopolized the trade in manufactures – if anything manufactured exports as a proportion of

TABLE 20
WORLD EXPORTS AND IMPORTS OF PRIMARY PRODUCTS BY
REGIONS, 1876–1937 (PERCENTAGES OF ALL COUNTRIES)

	1876–80		1913		1928		1937	
	Ex-ports	Im-ports	Ex-ports	Im-ports	Ex-ports	Im-ports	Ex-ports	Im-ports
North America	16·1	7·2	17·3	11·3	20·0	16·7	15·5	15·8
U.K. and Ireland	3·1	29·7	6·2	19·0	4·8	19·9	4·8	22·9
North-west Europe	22·6	39·3	25·2	43·1	14·5	34·2	15·6	33·7
Rest of Europe	20·2	11·2	14·7	12·3	16·0	10·5	13·7	8·5
Oceania			3·7	0·9	4·6	1·1	5·5	1·1
Latin America	38·0	12·6	12·6	4·3	15·8	4·1	16·4	3·9
Africa			5·6	2·2	6·4	2·3	8·3	2·8
Asia			14·7	6·9	17·9	11·2	20·2	11·3

SOURCE: P. L. Yates, *Forty Years of Foreign Trade* (1959), Tables 19, 25, pp. 47, 51.

their total exports increased in this period – while the greater part of their exports were traded with one another. Except for Japan and one or two other cases, most of the export gains made by the underdeveloped regions were in primary products. These commodities formed the overwhelming proportion of their exports (over 90 per cent in the case of Latin America, Africa and parts of Asia, and also of Oceania) and for the most part they were directed to the industrial countries, though an increasing proportion was traded within this group.[46]

There were also several shifts in the structure of trade by commodity. Trade in foodstuffs and agricultural-based raw materials declined in importance while the shares of other raw materials and manufactures rose. But probably of greater importance was the shifting composition within groups since not all the commodities in a particular category shared the same experience. In foodstuffs the main area of stagnation was cereals partly as dietary standards shifted and western European production recovered. On the other hand, there was a big expansion in sugar, fruit and vegetables, especially tropical fruits, dairy produce, oilseeds and fats and in certain classes of meat and beverages, coffee and cocoa. In some cases shifts in the sources of supply affected established producers. For example, the rapid rise of meat

46. See Yates, *Forty Years of Foreign Trade*, pp. 56–8.

and dairy interests in New Zealand and Australia threatened existing producers in Europe (for example Denmark) and in Latin America (Argentine and Uruguay), though the full force of these developments did not materialize until the following decade. The emergence of Africa as a source of cocoa, coffee and vegetable oils posed similar problems for Latin American exporters.

The least buoyant sector was agricultural raw materials. Here the main problem was the depressed conditions in textile fibres (cotton, raw silk, hemp and flax) and hides and skins, the trade of which was affected adversely by spreading industrialization and substitutes. The trade in raw cotton was one of the most seriously affected. Consumption of raw cotton began to fall in the mid 1920s with the decline in American demand,[47] while the spread of the manufacturing process in countries with their own supply of the raw product, India, Brazil and Egypt, together with the rise of competition from man-made fibres (rayon), checked the expansion of trade in raw cotton. Similarly raw silk exports of Japan and China were affected by competition from rayon, while the trade in hides and skins, which fell by some 10 per cent between 1913 and 1929, declined as a result of changes in fashion and the development of rubber substitutes. By contrast, the demand for natural rubber rose rapidly in the 1920s, despite synthetic-based compounds, while the centre of production shifted from the Americas to south-east Asia, with Malaya becoming the chief source of supply for North America.[48] Exports of tobacco leaf also received a significant boost from rising cigarette consumption in the western world.

Virtually all mineral exports rose rapidly during the 1920s. The only major exception was coal where stagnant world consumption following the development of new sources of energy, together with the contraction in the European coal export trade (mainly the British), checked this once-flourishing intercourse. By contrast the trade in copper, lead, zinc, tin, aluminium and iron ores rose by 60 per cent or more, and in some cases more than doubled. This was a product of rising demand from industrial countries for use in motor-car production, housing and the engineering trades together with a growing deficiency in mineral production in these

47. V. P. Timoshenko, *World Agriculture and the Depression* (1933), p. 22.
48. Lim, Chong-Yah, *Economic Development of Modern Malaya* (1967), pp. 128–9.

countries, notably the United States which became a net importer of copper, lead and zinc. But the most spectacular development was the trade in oil, which from negligible beginnings before the war became a major industry in its own right by the end of the 1920s. In 1930 crude oil output was more than double that of 1920 (1411 million barrels as against 688 million) and over four times that of 1910 (327 million barrels). The industry benefited from the combined demands for motor fuel, aviation spirit and the substitution of oil for traditional fuels in shipping and industrial activities. Europe became the largest importer while the United States and several Latin American countries provided the main sources of supply.

Finally, the main changes in the manufactured category were a shift away from textiles and a rise in the importance of many engineering products. The expanding groups in world trade were motor vehicles and aircraft, industrial equipment, electrical goods and iron and steel, while drink and tobacco, railways and ships, textiles, clothing and miscellaneous manufactures were the declining sectors.[39] This partly reflected a shift away from consumption goods in international trade, as import substitution occurred in such products as textiles and clothing in the more underdeveloped countries, while the latter increasingly depended on imports of capital equipment based on sophisticated technology supplied by the industrial west.

One would expect from these trends that countries which shifted resources away from declining towards expanding sectors would benefit most in international trade. This was not always the case. True America's large gain in the share of world trade in manufactures can be explained primarily by her concentration of resources in the expanding lines of production, thereby gaining the lion's share of the increased trade in this category. On the other hand, Canada and Japan benefited relatively little from a more favourable structural composition of their trade. Canada's main growth in trade share came from the stable group of manufactures, while Japan did best in the declining sector. This suggests that the ability to compete was more crucial to a country's export

49. H. Tyszynski, 'World Trade in Manufactured Commodities, 1899–1950', *Manchester School*, vol. XIX (1951), p. 240. Stable groups included chemicals, agricultural equipment, non-ferrous metals, books and films and miscellaneous metal products.

performance than structural shifts in the composition of trade.[50] Even Britain, which had a higher proportion of resources tied up in the declining sector (especially textiles) than any other major industrial country, found her loss in trade share was due more to her poor competitive position in expanding sectors and to import substitution than to the structural format of her productive process.[51]

50. ibid., p. 298.
51. See Maizels, *Industrial Growth and World Trade*, p. 231; cf. R. E. Baldwin, 'The Commodity Composition of Trade: Selected Industrial Countries, 1900–1954', *Review of Economics and Statistics*, vol. XL (1958), pp. 57–60.

Bibliography

AITKEN, H. G. J. (ed.), *The State and Economic Growth*, Social Science Research Council, New York, 1959.

ALBRECHT-CARRIÉ, R., *Italy at the Paris Peace Conference*, Columbia University Press, New York, 1938.

ALBRECHT-CARRIÉ, R., *France, Europe and the Two World Wars*, Minard, Paris, 1960.

ALDCROFT, D. H., 'Economic Progress in Britain in the 1920s', *Scottish Journal of Political Economy*, vol. XIII, 1966.

ALDCROFT, D. H., 'Economic Growth in Britain in the Inter-War Years: A Reassessment', *Economic History Review*, vol. XX, 1967.

ALDCROFT, D. H., and RICHARDSON, H. W., *The British Economy, 1870–1939*, Macmillan, London, 1969.

ALDCROFT, D. H., 'The Development of the Managed Economy before 1939', *Journal of Contemporary History*, vol. IV, 1969.

ALDCROFT, D. H., 'The Impact of British Monetary Policy, 1919–1939', *Revue Internationale d'Histoire de la Banque*, vol. III, 1970.

ALDCROFT, D. H., *The Inter-War Economy: Britain, 1919–1939*, Batsford, London, 1970.

ALDCROFT, D. H., and FEARON, P. (eds), *British Economic Fluctuations, 1790–1939*, Macmillan, London, 1972.

ALDCROFT, D. H., 'British Monetary Policy and Economic

Activity in the 1920s', *Revue Internationale d'Histoire de la Banque*, vol. v, 1972.

ALIBER, R. Z., 'Speculation in the Foreign Exchanges: The European Experience, 1919–1926', *Yale Economic Essays*, vol. II, Spring 1962.

ALLEN, G. C., 'The Industrialization of the Far-East' in Habakkuk, H. J., and Postan, M. (eds), *Cambridge Economic History of Europe*, vol. VI, Part II, Cambridge University Press, Cambridge, 1965.

ALMOND, N., and LUTZ, R. H. (eds), *The Treaty of St Germain: A Documentary History of its Territorial and Political Clauses*, Stanford University Press, Stanford, 1935.

ALPERT, P., *Twentieth Century Economic History of Europe*, Schuman, New York, 1951.

ALPERT, P., 'The Impact of World War I on the European Economy', in Scoville, W. C., and Clayburn La Force, J., *The Economic Development of Western Europe from 1914 to the Present*, D. C. Heath, Lexington, Mass., 1969.

ANDERSON, B. M., *Economics and the Public Welfare: Financial and Economic History of the United States, 1914–1946*, Van Nostrand, New York, 1949.

ANDERSON, B. M., Jnr, *Effects of the War on Money, Credit and Banking in France and the United States*, Oxford University Press, New York, Carnegie Series, 1919.

ANGELL, J. W., *The Recovery of Germany*, Yale University Press, New Haven, 1929; revised edition 1932.

ANSTEY, V., *The Economic Development of India*, 4th edition, Longmans, London, 1952.

APOSTOL, P. N., BERNATZKY, M. W., and MICHELSON, A. M., *Russian Public Finance During the War*, Yale University Press, New Haven, 1928.

ARNDT, H. W., *The Economic Lessons of the Nineteen-Thirties*, Oxford University Press, London, 1944; reprinted Cass, London, 1963.

ATKIN, J., 'Official Regulation of British Overseas Investment, 1914–1931', *Economic History Review*, vol. XXIII, 1970.

AUBERT, L., *The Reconstruction of Europe*, Yale University Press, New Haven, 1925.

AWAD, F. H., 'Diversification and Export Trade', *Yorkshire Bulletin of Economic and Social Research*, vol. X, 1958.

BACON, L. B., and SCHLOEMER, F. C., *World Trade in Agricultural Products*, Institute of Agriculture, Rome, 1940.

BAER, W., *Industrialization and Economic Development in Brazil*, Irwin, Homewood, Ill., 1965.

BAGCHI, A. K., *Private Investment in India 1900–1939*, Cambridge University Press, Cambridge, 1972.

BALDWIN, R. E., 'The Commodity Composition of Trade: Selected Industrial Countries, 1900–1954', *Revue of Economics and Statistics*, vol. XL, 1958.

BALOGH, T., 'The Import of Gold into France', *Economic Journal*, vol. XL, 1930.

BANDERA, V. N., *Foreign Capital as an Instrument of National Economic Policy: A Study Based on the Experience of East European Countries between the World Wars*, Nijhoff, The Hague, 1964.

BARUCH, B. M., *The Making of the Reparation and Economic Sections of the Treaty*, Harper, New York, 1920.

BAUDHUIN, F., *Histoire économique de la Belgique, 1914–1939*, 2 vols, 2nd edition, Emily Bruylant, Brussels, 1946.

BAUER, P. T., 'Some Aspects of the Malayan Rubber Slump 1929–1933', *Economica*, vol. XI, 1944.

BAUER, P. T., *The Rubber Industry: A Study in Competition and Monopoly*, Longmans, Green, London, 1948.

BELL, A. C., *A History of the Blockade of Germany, Austria–Hungary, Bulgaria, and Turkey 1914–1918*, H.M.S.O., London, 1937.

BENHAM, F. C., *The Prosperity of Australia*, P. S. King, London, 1928.

BENNETT, E. W., *Germany and the Diplomacy of the Financial Crisis, 1931*, Harvard University Press, Cambridge, Mass., 1962.

BEREND, I. T. and RANKI, G., *Economic Development in East Central Europe in the 19th and 20th Centuries*, Columbia University Press, New York, 1974.

BEREND, I. T., and RANKI, G., *Hungary: A Century of Economic Development*, David & Charles, Newton Abbot, 1974.

BERGMAN, C., *The History of Reparations*, E. Benn, London, 1927.

BERRIDGE, W. A., 'The World's Gold Supply Again Considered', *Review of Economic Statistics*, vol. XVI, 1934.

BERTRAM, G. W., 'Economic Growth in Canadian Industry,

1870–1915: The Staple Model and the Take-Off Hypothesis', *Canadian Journal of Economics and Political Science,* vol. XXIX, 1963.

BETTELHEIM, C., *Bilan de l'économie française, 1919–1946*, Presses Universitaires de France, Paris, 1947.

BEYEN, J. W., *Money in Maelstrom*, Macmillan, London, 1951.

BLAINEY, G., *Gold and Paper: A History of the National Bank of Australasia Ltd*, Melbourne, 1958.

BLOOMFIELD, A. I., *Monetary Policy under the International Gold Standard, 1880–1914*, Federal Reserve Bank, New York, 1959.

BLYN, G., *Agricultural Trends in India, 1891–1947: Output, Availability and Productivity*, University of Pennsylvania Press, Philadelphia, 1966.

BOGART, E. L., *Direct and Indirect Costs of the Great World War*, Oxford University Press, New York, Carnegie Series, 1919.

BOLCH, B., FELS, R., and MCMAHON, M., 'Housing Surplus in the 1920s', *Explorations in Economic History*, vol. VIII, Spring 1971.

BOLCH, B., and PILGRIM, J. D., 'A Reappraisal of Some Factors Associated with Fluctuations in the United States in the Inter-war Period', *Southern Economic Journal*, vol. XXXIX, January 1973.

BOSWELL, J. L., 'Some Neglected Aspects of the World War Debt Payments', *American Economic Review*, vol. XXI, 1931.

BOWLEY, A. L., *Prices and Wages in the United Kingdom 1914–1920*, Oxford University Press, Oxford, 1921.

BOWLEY, A. L., *Some Economic Consequences of the Great War*, Thornton Butterworth, London, 1930.

BRADY, R. A., *The Rationalization Movement in German Industry; A Study in the Evolution of Economic Planning*, University of California Press, Berkeley, 1933.

BRESCIANI-TURRONI, C., *The Economics of Inflation: A Study of Currency Depreciation in Post-War Germany*, Allen & Unwin, London, 1937.

BRIGGS, A., 'The World Economy: Interdependence and Planning', Chapter 3 of Mowat, C. L. (ed.), *The Shifting Balance of World Forces, 1898–1945*, vol. XII of the *New Cambridge Modern History*, Cambridge University Press, Cambridge, 1968.

BRONFENBRENNER, M. (ed.), *Is the Business Cycle Obsolete?* Wiley, New York, 1969.

BROWN, W. A., Jnr, 'German Reparations and the International

Flow of Capital: Discussion', *American Economic Review, Papers and Proceedings*, vol. xx, 1930.

BROWN, W. A., Jnr, *The International Gold Standard Reinterpreted, 1914–1934*, 2 vols, National Bureau of Economic Research, New York, 1940.

BROWN, W. A., Jnr, 'Gold as a Monetary Standard 1914–1949', *Journal of Economic History*, vol. IX, Supplement, 1949.

BRUCK, W. F., *Social and Economic History of Germany from William II to Hitler 1888–1938*, University Press Board, Cardiff, 1938.

BRY, G., *Wages in Germany, 1871–1945*, Princeton University Press, Princeton, 1960.

BUCHANAN, N. S., and LUTZ, F. A., *Rebuilding the World Economy*, Twentieth Century Fund, New York, 1947.

BUCK, PEARL S., *How it Happens: Talk about the German People, 1914–1933, with Erna von Pustau*, John Day, New York, 1947.

BUTLIN, N. G., *Australian Domestic Product, Investment and Foreign Borrowing, 1861–1938/9*, Cambridge University Press, Cambridge, 1962.

BUXTON, N. K., 'Economic Progress in Britain in the 1920s: A Reappraisal', *Scottish Journal of Political Economy*, vol. XIV, June 1967.

CAGAN, P., 'The Monetary Dynamics of Hyperinflation', in M. Friedman (ed.), *Studies in the Quantity Theory of Money*, University of Chicago Press, Chicago, 1956.

CAHILL, J. R., *Report on Economic and Industrial Conditions in France in 1928*, H.M.S.O., London, 1928.

CAHILL, J. R., *Report on Economic Conditions in France*, H.M.S.O., London, 1934.

CAIRNCROSS, A. K., and FAALAND, J., 'Long-Term Trends in Europe's Trade', *Economic Journal*, vol. LXII, 1952.

CAIRNCROSS, A. K., 'World Trade in Manufactures since 1900', *Economia Internazionale*, vol. VIII, 1955.

CAIRNCROSS, A. K., *Factors in Economic Development*, Allen & Unwin, London, 1962.

Carnegie Endowment for International Peace and the International Chamber of Commerce (Joint Committee), *International Economic Reconstruction*, Paris, 1936.

CASSEL, G., *The World's Monetary Problems*, Constable, London, 1921.

CASSEL, G., *Post-war Monetary Stabilisation*, Columbia University Press, New York, 1928.

CASSEL, G., *The Crisis in the World's Monetary System*, Clarendon Press, Oxford, 1932.

CASSEL, G., *The Downfall of the Gold Standard*, Oxford University Press, London, 1936.

CAVES, R. E., and HOLTON, R. H., *The Canadian Economy: Prospect and Retrospect*, Harvard University Press, Cambridge, Mass., 1959.

CHAMBERLAIN, W. C., *Economic Development of Iceland through World War II*, Columbia University Press, New York, 1947.

CHANDLER, L. V., *Benjamin Strong, Central Banker*, Brookings Institution, Washington D.C., 1958.

CHANG, J. K., 'Industrial Development of Mainland China, 1912–1949', *Journal of Economic History*, vol. XXVII, 1967.

CHANG, J. K., *Industrial Development in Pre-Communist China: a Quantitative Analysis*, Edinburgh University Press, Edinburgh, 1969.

CHARLESWORTH, E. K., 'The Contribution of Rationalization to Industrial Development in Sweden 1918–1939', *Economy and History*, vol. XII, 1969.

CHENG, S. H., *The Rice Industry of Burma 1852–1940*, University of Malaya Press, Kuala Lumpur, 1968.

CHENG, Y. K., *Foreign Trade and Industrial Development of China*, University Press of Washington, Washington D.C., 1956.

CLARK, C., *The Conditions of Economic Progress*, Macmillan, London, 1957.

CLARK, H., *Swedish Unemployment Policy, 1914–1940*, American Council on Public Affairs, Washington D.C., 1941.

CLARK, J. M., *The Costs of the World War to the American People*, Yale University Press, New Haven, Carnegie Series, 1931.

CLARKE, S. V. O., *Central Bank Cooperation, 1924–31*, Federal Reserve Bank, New York, 1967.

CLAY, H., *Lord Norman*, Macmillan, London, 1957.

CLOUGH, S. B., *France: A History of National Economics, 1789–1939*, Charles Scribner's Sons, New York, 1939.

CLOUGH, S. B., *The Economic History of Modern Italy*, Columbia University Press, New York, 1964.

CLOUGH, S. B., *The Economic Development of Western Civilization*, revised edition, McGraw-Hill, New York, 1968.

CLOUGH, S. B., MOODIE, T., and MOODIE, C. (eds), *Economic History of Europe: Twentieth Century*, Macmillan, London, 1969.

COHEN, J. H., 'The 1927 Revaluation of the Lira: A Study in Political Economy', *Economic History Review*, vol. XXV, 1972.

COLLINET, P., and STAHL, P., *Le Ravitaillement de la France Occupée*, Presses Universitaires de France, Paris, 1928.

Commission of Enquiry into National Policy in International Economic Relations, *International Economic Relations*, University of Minnesota Press, Minneapolis, 1934.

COMSTOCK, A., 'Reparation Payments in Perspective', *American Economic Review*, vol. XX, 1930.

CONDLIFFE, J. B., *The Reconstruction of World Trade*, Allen & Unwin, London, 1941.

CONDLIFFE, J. B., *The Commerce of Nations*, Allen & Unwin, London, 1951.

CONZE, W., and RAUPACH, H., *Die Staats- und Wirtschaftskrise des deutschen Reichs, 1929–33*, Klett, Stuttgart, 1967.

COPELAND, M. A., *Trends in Government Financing*, Princeton University Press, Princeton, 1961.

COPELAND, M. T., *A Raw Commodity Revolution*, Business Research Studies, no. 19, Harvard University Graduate School of Business Administration, Cambridge, Mass., 1938.

COPLAND, D. B., 'The National Income and Economic Prosperity', in T. Sellin and D. Young (eds), *An Economic Survey of Australia*, for *Annals of the American Academy of Political and Social Science*, vol. CLVIII, 1931.

COPLAND, D. B., *Australia in the World Crisis 1929–1933*, Cambridge University Press, Cambridge, 1934.

CORNER, D. C., 'Exports and the British Trade Cycle: 1929', *Manchester School*, vol. XXIV, 1956.

COURT, W. H. B., 'The Years 1914–1918 in British Economic and Social History', in Court, W. H. B., *Scarcity and Choice in History*, Edward Arnold, London, 1970.

COURTENAY, P. P., *A Geography of Trade and Development in Malaya*, G. Bell, London, 1972.

CROSS, C., *Adolf Hitler*, Hodder & Stoughton, London, 1973.

CROWTHER, J. G., *Discoveries and Inventions of the 20th Century*, 5th edition, Routledge & Kegan Paul, London, 1966.

CURRIE, L., 'The Failure of Monetary Policy to Prevent the Depression of 1929–32', *Journal of Political Economy*, vol. XLII, 1934.

CURRIE, L., *The Supply and Control of Money in the United States*, Harvard University Press, Cambridge, Mass., 1934.

CZADA, P., 'Ursachen und Folgen der grossen Inflation', in Winkel, H. (ed.), *Finanz- und Wirtschaftspolitische Fragen der Zwischenkriegzeit*, Duncker & Humblot, Berlin, 1973.

DAHMÉN, E., *Entrepreneurial Activity and the Development of Swedish Industry, 1919–1939*, translated by A. Leijonhufvud, Irwin, Homewood, Ill., 1970.

DALTON, H., *et alia, Unbalanced Budgets*, G. Routledge, London, 1934.

DANA, A. G., *'Prosperity' Problems*, University Press, New Haven, 1931.

DANAILLOW, G. T., *Les effets de la guerre en Bulgarie*, Presses Universitaires de France, Paris, 1932.

DANIELS, R. V., *Red October, The Bolshevik Revolution of 1917*, Charles Scribner's Sons, New York, 1967.

DARBY, H. C., and FULLARD, H. (eds), *New Cambridge Modern History:* vol. 14, *Atlas*, Cambridge University Press, Cambridge, 1970.

DAVIDSON, D., *The Rationalization of the Gold Standard*, Almquist & Wicksells, Stockholm, 1933.

DAVIS, J. S., 'World Currency Expansion during the War and in 1919', *Review of Economic Statistics*, vol. II, 1920.

DAVIS, J. S., 'Recent Economic and Financial Progress in France', *Review of Economic Statistics*, vol. III, 1921.

DAVIS, J. S., 'Recent Economic and Financial Progress in Germany', *Review of Economic Statistics*, vol. III, 1921.

DAVIS, J. S., 'Recent Developments in World Finance', *Review of Economic Statistics*, vol. IV, 1922.

DAVIS, J. S., 'Economic and Financial Progress in Europe', *Review of Economic Statistics*, vol. V, 1923.

DAVIS, J. S., 'Economic and Financial Progress in Europe, 1923–24', *Review of Economic Statistics*, vol. VI, 1924.

DAVIS, J. S., 'Economic and Financial Progress in Europe, 1924–25', *Review of Economic Statistics*, vol. VII, 1925.

DAVIS, J. S., *The World Between the Wars, 1919–39: An Economist's View*, Johns Hopkins University Press, Baltimore, 1969.

DAWSON, P., *Germany's Industrial Revival*, Williams & Norgate, London, 1926.

DAY, J. P., *An Introduction to World Economic History since the Great War*, Macmillan, London, 1939.

DEAK, F., *Hungary at the Paris Peace Conference: The Diplomatic History of the Treaty of Trianon*, Columbia University Press, New York, 1942.

DEAN, W., *The Industrialisation of the Western Pacific*, Institute of Pacific Relations, Quebec, 1942.

DEAN, W., *The Industrialisation of Sao Paulo, 1800–1945*, University of Texas Press, Austin, 1969.

DELLE DONNE, O., *European Tariff Policies Since the World War*, Adelphi, New York, 1928.

Department of Overseas Trade, *Economic Conditions in Chile*, H.M.S.O., London, 1932.

Department of Overseas Trade, *Economic Conditions in Venezuela*, H.M.S.O., London, 1932.

DEUTSCH, K. W., and ECKSTEIN, A., 'National Industrialisation and the Declining Share of the International Economic Sector, 1890–1959', *World Politics*, vol. XIII, 1961.

DIAZ ALEJANDRO, C. F., *Essays on the Economic History of the Argentine Republic*, Yale University Press, New Haven, 1970.

DOBB, M., *Soviet Economic Development since 1917*, revised edition, International Publishers, New York, 1968.

DONALD, R., *The Tragedy of Trianon*, Thornton Butterworth, London, 1928.

DORFMAN, J., *The Economic Mind in American Civilisation 1919–1933*, Viking, New York, 1959.

DOUGLAS GIBSON, J. (ed.), *Canada's Economy in a Changing World*, Macmillan, Toronto, 1948.

DOWD, D. F., 'Economic Stagnation in Europe in the Interwar Period', *Journal of Economic History*, vol. XV, 1955.

DOWIE, J. A., 'Growth in the Inter-War Period: Some More Arithmetic', *Economic History Review*, vol. XXI, 1968.

DOWIE, J. A., '1919–20 is in Need of Attention', *Economic History Review*, vol. XXVIII, August 1975.

DRABBLE, J. H., *Rubber in Malaya, 1876–1922: The Genesis of an Industry*, Oxford University Press, Kuala Lumpur, 1973.

DRUMMOND, I. M., *British Economic Policy and the Empire, 1919–1939*, Allen & Unwin, London, 1972.

DULLES, E. L., *The French Franc 1914–1928: The Facts and Their Interpretation*, Macmillan, New York, 1929.

DULLES, E. L., *The Dollar, the Franc and Inflation*, Macmillan, New York, 1933.

DUNNING, J. H., 'Capital Movements in the 20th Century', *Lloyds Bank Review*, no. LXXII, April 1964.

DUNNING, J. H., *Studies in International Investment*, Allen & Unwin, London, 1970.

DU PLESSIS, J. C., *Economic Fluctuations in South Africa, 1910–1949*, Bureau for Economic Research, University of Stellenbosch, Stellenbosch, 1950.

EASTERBROOK, W. T., and AITKEN, H. G. J., *Canadian Economic History*, Macmillan, Toronto, 1956.

EASTMAN, H. C., 'French and Canadian Exchange Rate Policy', *Journal of Economic History*, vol. XV, 1955.

EBERSOLE, J. F., 'Deflationary Indemnity Hopes and War Debts', *Harvard Business Review*, vol. X, 1931.

ECKSTEIN, A., 'National Income and Capital Formation in Hungary, 1900–50', in S. Kuznets (ed.), *Income and Wealth*, Series 5, Bowes & Bowes, London, 1955.

EDIE, L. D., *Gold Production and Prices before and after the World War*, Indiana University, Bloomington, Ind., 1928.

EDIE, L. D., *Capital, the Money Market and Gold*, University of Chicago Press, Chicago, 1929.

EINZIG, P., *Behind the Scenes of International Finance*, Macmillan, London, 1931.

EINZIG, P., *The Fight for Financial Supremacy*, Macmillan, London, 1931.

EINZIG, P., *The World Economic Crisis 1929–1931*, Macmillan, London, 1931.

EINZIG, P., *International Gold Movements*, Macmillan, London, 1932.

EINZIG, P., *The Tragedy of the Pound*, Kegan Paul, Trench Trubner, London, 1932.

EINZIG, P., *The Comedy of the Pound*, Kegan Paul, London, 1933.

EINZIG, P., *The Economic Foundations of Fascism*, Macmillan, London, 1933.

EINZIG, P., *France's Crisis*, Macmillan, London, 1934.

EINZIG, P., *World Finance Since 1914*, Kegan Paul, Trench Trubner, London, 1935.

ELLIS, E. R., *A Nation in Torment: The Great American Depression, 1929–1939*, Coward McCann, New York, 1970.

ELLIS, H. S., *German Monetary Theory 1905–33*, Harvard University Press, Cambridge, Mass., 1934.

ELLSWORTH, P. T., *Chile: An Economy in Transition*, Macmillan, New York, 1945.

ELLSWORTH, P. T., *The International Economy*, 3rd edition, Macmillan, New York, 1964.

FALKUS, M. E., 'United States Economic Policy and the "Dollar Gap" of the 1920s', *Economic History Review*, vol. xxiv, 1971.

FALKUS, M. E., 'The German Business Cycle in the 1920s', *Economic History Review*, vol. xxviii, 1975.

FEAVEARYEAR, A. E., *The Pound Sterling*, revised edition by E. V. Morgan, Clarendon Press, Oxford, 1963.

FEIS, H., 'The Industrial Situation in Great Britain from the Armistice to the Beginning of 1921', *American Economic Review*, vol. xi, 1921.

FEIS, H., *The Changing Pattern of International Economic Affairs*, Harper Bros., New York, 1941.

FELDMAN, G. D., 'Economic and Social Problems of German Demobilisation, 1918–19', *Journal of Modern History*, vol. xlvii, 1975.

FELIX, D., *Walter Rathenau and the Weimar Republic: The Politics of Reparations*, Johns Hopkins University Press, Baltimore, 1971.

FERENCZI, I., and WILLCOX, W. F. (eds), *International Migrations*, 2 vols, National Bureau of Economic Research, New York, 1929–31.

FETTER, F. W., *Monetary Inflation in Chile*, Princeton University Press, Princeton, 1931.

FEUERWERKER, A., *The Chinese Economy 1912–1949*, Michigan Papers in Chinese Studies, University of Michigan Press, Ann Arbor, 1968.

FISCHER, W., *Deutsche Wirtschaftspolitik 1918–1945*, C. W. Leske, Opladen, 1968.

FISHER, I., *The Stock Market Crash and After*, Macmillan, New York, 1930.

FISK, H. E., *The Inter-Ally Debts. An Analysis of War and Post-War Public Finance, 1914–1923*, Bankers Trust Company, New York and Paris, 1924.

FLEMING, D. F., *The United States and World Organization 1920–1933*, Ams Press, New York, 1966.

FLINK, S., *The German Reichsbank and Economic Recovery*, Columbia University Press, New York, 1929.

FLUX, A. W., 'Our Food Supply before and after the War', *Journal of the Royal Statistical Society*, vol. XCIII, 1930.

FONTAINE, A., *L'industrie francaise pendant la Guerre*, Presses Universitaires de France, Paris, 1924.

FORD, A. G., 'The Truth about Gold', *Lloyds Bank Review*, no. LXXVII, July 1965.

FORSTER, C., 'Australian Manufacturing and the War of 1914–1918', *Economic Record*, vol. XXIX, 1953.

FORSTER, C., *Industrial Development in Australia 1920–1930*, Australian National University Press, Canberra, 1964.

FORSTER, C. (ed.), *Australian Economic Development in the Twentieth Century*, Allen & Unwin, 1970

FRANKEL, S. H., 'The Situation in South Africa, 1929–1932', *Economic Journal*, vol. XLIII, 1933.

FRANKEL, S. H., 'South African Monetary Policy', *The South African Journal of Economics*, vol. I, 1933.

FRANKEL, S. H., *Capital Investment in Africa: Its Course and Effects*, Oxford University Press, London, 1938.

FRANKEL, S. H., 'An Analysis of the Growth of the National Income of the Union of South Africa in the Period of Prosperity before the War', *South African Journal of Economics*, vol. XII, 1944.

FRIEDMAN, M., and SCHWARTZ, A. J., *A Monetary History of the United States, 1867–1960*, Princeton University Press, Princeton, 1963.

FURNIVALL, J. S., *Netherlands India: A Study of Plural Economy*, Cambridge University Press, Cambridge, 1939; 1967 reprint.

FURTADO, C., *The Economic Growth of Brazil*, University of California Press, Berkeley, 1963.

FURTADO, C., *Economic Development of Latin America*, Cambridge University Press, Cambridge, 1970.

GADGIL, D. R., *The Industrial Evolution of India in Recent Times, 1860–1939*, 5th edition, Oxford University Press, Bombay, 1971.

GALBRAITH, J. K., *The Great Crash, 1929*, Hamish Hamilton, London, 1955; Penguin, 1961.

GANDOLFI, A. E., 'Stability of the Demand for Money during the

Great Contraction', *Journal of Political Economy*, vol. LXXXII, 1974.

GAYER, A. D., 'The Nature and Functioning of the Post-War Gold Standard', in MacIver, R. M. (ed.), *Economic Reconstruction: Report of the Columbia University Commission*, Columbia University Press, New York, 1934.

GAYER, A. D., 'Non-Monetary Factors Affecting the Functioning of the Post-War Gold Standard', in MacIver, R. M. (ed.), *Economic Reconstruction: Report of the Columbia University Commission*, Columbia University Press, New York, 1934.

GAYER, A. D. (ed.), *The Lessons of Monetary Experience: Essays in Honour of Irving Fisher*, Farrer & Rinehart, New York, 1937.

GAYER, A. D., *Monetary Policy and Economic Stabilization: A Study of the Gold Standard*, 2nd edition, A. & C. Black, London, 1937.

GIDE, C., *Effects of the War upon French Economic Life*, Oxford University Press, Oxford, Carnegie Series, 1923.

GIDE, C., and OUALID, W., *Le bilan de la guerre pour la France*, Presses Universitaires de France, Paris, 1931.

GILBERT, C., *American Financing of World War I*, Greenwood, Westport, Conn., 1970.

GILBERT, M., *Currency Depreciation*, University of Pennsylvania Press, Philadelphia, 1939.

GILBERT, M., *First World War Atlas*, Weidenfeld & Nicolson, London, 1970.

GILBERT, R. S., *The Australian Loan Council in Federal Fiscal Adjustments, 1890–1965*, Australian National University Press, Canberra, 1973.

GLADE, W., *The Latin American Economies: A Study of their Institutional Evolution*, American Book Company, New York, 1969.

GLYNN, S., 'Government Policy and Agricultural Development: Western Australia 1900–1930', *Australian Economic History Review*, vol. VII, 1967.

GLYNN, S., and LOUGHEED, A. L., 'A Comment on United States Economic Policy and the "Dollar Gap" of the 1920s', *Economic History Review*, vol. XXVI, 1973.

GOETSCHIN, P., *L'Évolution du marché monétaire de Londres, 1931–1952*, Ambilly–Annemasse, Geneva, 1963.

GORDON, M. S., *Barriers to World Trade: A Study of Recent Commercial Policy*, Macmillan, New York, 1941.

GORDON, R. A., 'Cyclical Experience in the Interwar Period: The Investment Boom of the Twenties', in National Bureau of Economic Research, *Conference on Business Cycles*, N.B.E.R., New York, 1951.

GORDON, R. A., 'Investment Opportunities in the United States before and after World War II', in E. Lundberg (ed.), *The Business Cycle in the Post-War World*, Macmillan, London, 1957.

GORDON, R. A., *Business Fluctuations*, 2nd edition, Harper, New York, 1961.

GORECKI, R., *Poland and Her Economic Development*, Allen & Unwin, London, 1935.

GOTTLIEB, L. R., 'Indebtedness of Principal Belligerents', *Quarterly Journal of Economics*, vol. XXXIII, 1918–19.

GRAHAM, F. D., 'Germany's Capacity to Pay and the Reparation Plan', *American Economic Review*, vol. XV, 1925.

GRAHAM, F. D., *Exchange, Prices and Production in Hyperinflation Germany, 1920–23*, Publication of the International Finance Section of the Department of Economics and Social Institutions in Princeton University, vol. I, Princeton, 1930.

GRAHAM, F. D., and WHITTLESEY, C. E., *Golden Avalanche*, Princeton University Press, Princeton, 1939.

GRAMM, W. P., 'The Real-Balance Effect in the Great Depression', *Journal of Economic History*, vol. XXXII, 1972.

GRANT, A. T. K., *A Study of the Capital Market in Britain from 1919–1936*, Macmillan, London 1934; reprinted Cass, London, 1967.

GRAUBARD, S. R., 'Military Demobilization in Great Britain Following the First World War', *Journal of Modern History*, vol. XIX, 1947.

GREBLER, L., and WINKLER, W., *The Cost of the War to Germany and Austria–Hungary*, Yale University Press, New Haven, 1940.

GREER, G., *The Ruhr–Lorraine Industrial Problem*, Brookings Institution, Washington D.C., 1925.

GREGORY, T. E., *The First Year of the Gold Standard*, E. Benn, London, 1926.

GREGORY, T. E., *The Gold Standard and its Future*, 3rd edition, Methuen, London, 1934.

GROTKOPP, W., *Die grosse Krise, Lehren aus der Überwindung der Wirtschaftskrise, 1929–1932*, Econ–Verlag, Düsseldorf, 1954.

GRUBER, J., *Czechoslovakia: A Survey of Economic and Social Conditions*, Macmillan, New York, 1924.

GUTTMAN, W., and MECHAN, P., *The Great Inflation*, Saxon House, New York, 1975.

HABERLER, G., *International Trade and Economic Development*, National Bank of Egypt, Cairo, 1959.

HAHN, A., 'Stabilisation of Business in Germany', *Harvard Business Review*, vol. VII, 1929.

HAHN, L. A., *Fünfzig Jahre zwischen Inflation und Deflation*, J. C. B. Mohr, Tübingen, 1963.

HAIG, R. M., *The Public Finances of Post-war France*, Columbia University Press, New York, 1929.

HAIGHT, F. A., *A History of French Commercial Policies*, Macmillan, New York, 1941.

HAILEY, W. B., *An African Survey: A Study of Problems Arising in Africa South of the Sahara*, Oxford University Press, Oxford, 1938.

HALASZ, A., *New Central Europe – In Economical Maps*, R. Gergely, Budapest, 1928.

HANCOCK, W. K., *Survey of British Commonwealth Affairs: Vol. 2. Problems of Economic Policy 1918–1939*, Oxford University Press, London, 1940.

HANCOCK, W. K., *Four Studies of War and Peace in this Century*, Cambridge University Press, Cambridge, 1961.

HANSEN, A. H., *Economic Stabilisation in an Unbalanced World*, Harcourt, Brace, New York, 1932.

HANSEN, A. H., *Full Recovery or Stagnation?*, A. & C. Black, London, 1938.

HANSEN, A. H., 'Economic Progress and Declining Population Growth', *American Economic Review*, vol. XXIX, 1939.

HANSEN, A. H., *America's Role in the World Economy*, Allen & Unwin, London, 1945.

HANSEN, A. H., *Business Cycles and National Income*, Norton, New York, 1951.

HARDACH, G., *The First World War, 1914–1918*, Allen Lane, London; University of California Press, Stanford, 1977.

HARDY, C. O., *Is There Enough Gold?* Brookings Institution, Washington D.C., 1936.

HARMAJA, L., *Effects of the War on Economic and Social Life in Finland*, Yale University Press, New Haven, 1933.

HARRIS, C. R. S., *Germany's Foreign Indebtedness*, Oxford University Press, Oxford, 1935.

HARRIS, S. E., *Monetary Problems of the British Empire*, Macmillan, New York, 1931.

HARRIS, S. E., *Twenty Years of Federal Reserve Policy*, 2 vols, Harvard University Press, Cambridge, Mass., 1933.

HARRIS, S. E. (ed.), *Economic Problems of Latin America*, McGraw-Hill, New York, 1944.

HARRISON, A., *The Framework of Economic Activity*, Macmillan, London, 1968.

HARROD, R. F., *The Life of John Maynard Keynes*, Macmillan, London, 1951.

HART, A. G., and KENEN, P. B., *Money, Debt and Economic Activity*, 3rd edition, Prentice-Hall, Englewood Cliffs, N.J., 1961.

HAWKE, G. R., 'New Zealand and the Return to Gold in 1925', *Australian Economic History Review*, vol. XI, 1971.

HAWKE, G. R., 'The Government and the Depression of the 1930s in New Zealand: An Essay towards a Revision', *Australian Economic History Review*, vol. XIII, 1973.

HAWTREY, R. G., *Monetary Reconstruction*, 2nd edition, Longmans, London, 1926.

HAWTREY, R. G., *The Gold Standard in Theory and Practice*, 5th edition, Longmans, Green, London, 1947.

HECKSCHER, E. F., *et alia*, *Sweden, Norway, Denmark and Iceland in the World War*, Oxford University Press, New York, Carnegie Series, 1930.

HEILPERIN, M. A., *La Problème monétaire d'après-guerre et sa solution en Pologne, en Autriche et en Tchécoslovaquie*, Recueil Sirey, Paris, 1931.

HENDERSON, H. D., *The Inter-war Years and Other Papers*, Clarendon Press, Oxford, 1955.

HENNING, F. W., 'Die Liquidität der Banken in der Weimarer Republik', in Winkel, H. (ed.), *Finanz- und Wirtschaftspolitische Fragen der Zwischenkriegszeit*, Duncker & Humblot, Berlin, 1973.

HERTZ, F., *The Economic Problem of the Danubian States: A Study in Economic Nationalism*, Gollancz, London, 1947.

HESSE, F., *Die deutsche Wirtschaftslage von 1914–1923: Krieg, Geldblähe und Wechsellagen*, Fischer, Jena, 1938.

HIBBARD, B., *Effects of the Great War upon Agriculture in the United States and Great Britain*, Oxford University Press, New York, Carnegie Series, 1919.

HILL, M., *The Economic and Financial Organization of the League of Nations: A Survey of Twenty-Five Years Experience*, Carnegie Endowment for International Peace, Washington D.C., 1946.

HILL, R. L., 'The Role of Rigidities in the Failure of the Gold Standard', *Weltwirtschaftsliches Archiv*, vol. LXXVII, 1956.

HIRSCHMAN, A. O., 'The Commodity Structure of World Trade', *Quarterly Journal of Economics*, vol. LVII, 1943.

HODSON, H. V., *Slump and Recovery 1929–37*, Oxford University Press, Oxford, 1938.

HOLLAND, W. L., *Commodity Control in the Pacific Area: A Symposium on Recent Experience*, Allen & Unwin, London, 1935.

HOOKER, A. A., *The International Grain Trade*, Putnam, London, 1938.

HORSEFIELD, J. K., 'Currency Devaluation and Public Finance, 1929–37', *Economica*, vol. VI, 1939.

HOU, C., *Foreign Investment and Economic Development in China 1840–1937*, Harvard University Press, Cambridge, Mass., 1965.

HOWSON, S., ' "A Dear Money Man?": Keynes on Monetary Policy, 1920', *Economic Journal*, vol. LXXXIII, 1973.

HOWSON, S., 'The Origins of Dear Money, 1919–20', *Economic History Review*, vol. XXVII, 1974.

HUBBARD, G. E., *Eastern Industrialization and Its Effects on the West*, Oxford University Press, Oxford, 1938.

HUME, L. J., 'The Gold Standard and Deflation: Issues and Attitudes in the Nineteen-Twenties', *Economica*, vol. XXX, 1963.

HURST, W., 'Holland, Switzerland, and Belgium and the English Gold Crisis of 1931', *Journal of Political Economy*, vol. XL, 1932.

HUTCHISON, T. W., *A Review of Economic Doctrines, 1870–1929*, Clarendon Press, Oxford, 1933.

INNIS, H. A., *Essays in Canadian Economic History*, Toronto University Press, Toronto, 1956.

International Conference of Economic Services, *International*

Abstract of Economic Statistics 1919–1930, International Conference of Economic Services, London, 1934.

International Institute of Agriculture, *International Yearbook of Agricultural Statistics*, International Institute of Agriculture, Rome.

International Institute of Agriculture, *The Agricultural Situation in 1930–31*, International Institute of Agriculture, Rome, 1932.

International Institute of Agriculture, *The Course of the Agricultural Depression in 1931–32*, International Institute of Agriculture, Rome, 1933.

ISSAWI, C., *Egypt in Revolution: An Economic Analysis*, Oxford University Press, London, 1963.

IVERSON, C., *Aspects of the Theory of International Capital Movements*, Oxford University Press, London, 1935.

JACK, D. T., *The Economics of the Gold Standard*, P. S. King, London, 1925.

JACK, D. T., *The Restoration of European Currencies*, P. S. King, London, 1927.

JACOBSSON, P., *Some Monetary Problems: International and National*, Oxford University Press, London, 1958.

JASNY, N., *Soviet Economists of the Twenties: Names to be Remembered*, Cambridge University Press, Cambridge, 1972.

JÈZE, G., 'The Economic and Financial Position of France in 1920', *Quarterly Journal of Economics*, vol. xxxv, February 1921.

JOHNSON, P. B., *Land Fit for Heroes; The Planning of British Reconstruction, 1916–1919*, University of Chicago Press, Chicago, 1968.

JORDAN, W. M., *Great Britain, France and the German Problem, 1918–1939: A Study of Anglo-French Relations in the Making and Maintenance of the Versailles Settlement*, Oxford University Press, Oxford, 1943; reprinted Cass, London, 1971.

JOSLIN, D., *A Century of Banking in Latin America*, Oxford University Press, London, 1963.

KAHN, A. E., *Great Britain in the World Economy*, Columbia University Press, New York, 1946.

KALDOR, N., 'The Economic Situation of Austria', *Harvard Business Review*, vol. xi, 1932–3.

KANE, N. S., 'Bankers and Diplomats: The Diplomacy of the Dollar in Mexico, 1921–1924', *Business History Review*, vol. xlvii, 1973.

KAPP, K. W., *The League of Nations and Raw Materials, 1919–1939*, Geneva Studies, vol. XII, no. 3, Geneva Research Centre, Geneva, 1941.

KEMMERER, D. L., 'The Changing Pattern of American Economic Development', *Journal of Economic History*, vol. XVI, 1956.

KEMMERER, E. W., *High Prices and Deflation*, Princeton University Press, Princeton, 1922.

KEMMERER, E. W., *Gold and the Gold Standard*, McGraw-Hill, New York, 1944.

KEMP, T., 'The French Economy Under the Franc Poincaré', *Economic History Review*, vol. XXIV, 1971.

KEMP, T., *The French Economy, 1919–39: The History of a Decline*, Longmans, London, 1972.

KENDRICK, J. W., *Productivity Trends in the United States*, Princeton University Press, Princeton, 1961.

KENWOOD, A. G., and LOUGHEED, A. L., *The Growth of the International Economy, 1820–1960*, Allen & Unwin, London, 1971.

KERCHOVA DE DENTERGHEM, C., *L'industrie belge pendant l'occupation allemande, 1914–1918*, Presses Universitaires de France, Paris, 1927.

KEYNES, J. M., *The Economic Consequences of the Peace*, Macmillan, London, 1919.

KEYNES, J. M., *A Revision of the Treaty*, Macmillan, London, 1922.

KEYNES, J. M. 'The German Transfer Problem', *Economic Journal*, vol. XXXIX, 1929.

KINDLEBERGER, C. P., *International Short-term Capital Movements*, Columbia University Press, New York, 1937.

KINDLEBERGER, C. P., *The Terms of Trade: A European Case Study*, Chapman & Hall, London, 1956.

KINDLEBERGER, C. P., 'Foreign Trade and Growth: Lessons from the British Experience since 1913', *Lloyds Bank Review*, no. LXV, 1962.

KINDLEBERGER, C. P., *Economic Growth in France and Britain, 1851–1950*, Cambridge University Press, Cambridge, 1964.

KINDLEBERGER, C. P., *The World in Depression, 1929–1939*, Allen Lane, London; University of California Press, Stanford, 1973.

KING, F. H. H., *A Concise Economic History of Modern China (1840–1961)*, Pall Mall Press, London, 1969.

KIRK, D., *Europe's Population in the Inter-war Years*, League of Nations, 1946.

KIRK, J. H., *Agriculture and the Trade Cycle (1926–1931)*, P. S. King, London, 1933.

KJELLSTROM, E. J. H., *Managed Money: The Experience of Sweden*, Columbia University Press, New York, 1934.

KNAUERHASE, R., *An Introduction to National Socialism 1920–1939*, C. E. Merrill, Columbus, Ohio, 1972.

KNORR, K. E., *Tin Under Control*, Food Research Institute, Stanford University, Stanford, 1945.

KNORR, K. E., *World Rubber and Its Regulation*, Stanford University Press, Stanford, 1945.

KNOWLES, L. C. A., *Economic Development of the British Overseas Empire*, 3 vols, G. Routledge, London, 1924.

KNOX, F. A., 'Canadian War Finance and the Balance of Payments, 1914–1918', *Canadian Journal of Economics and Political Science*, vol. VI, 1940.

KOBAYASHI, U., *The Basic Industries and Social History of Japan, 1914–1918*, Yale University Press, New Haven, 1930.

KOCK, F., *Crises, Depression and Recovery in Sweden, 1929–1937*, C. E. Fritze, Stockholm, 1938.

KOHN, S., and MEYENDORFF, A. F., *The Cost of the War to Russia*, Yale University Press, New Haven, 1932.

KOOY, M. (ed.), *Studies in Economics and Economic History: Essays in Honour of Professor H. M. Robertson*, Macmillan, London, 1972.

KRIZ, M. A., 'Postwar International Lending', *Essays in International Finance*, No. 8, International Finance Section, Department of Economics and Social Institutions, Princeton University, Princeton, Spring 1947.

KUCZYNSKI, R., *American Loans to Germany*, Institute of Economics, New York, 1927.

KULISCHER, E. M., *Europe on the Move: War and Population Changes, 1917–1947*, Columbia University Press, New York, 1948.

KUZNETS, S., MOORE, W. E., and SPENGLER, J. J. (eds), *Economic Growth: Brazil, India, Japan*, Duke University Press, Durham, N.C., 1955.

LANDES, D. S., *The Unbound Prometheus: Technological Change and Industrial Development in Western Europe from 1750 to the Present*, Cambridge University Press, Cambridge, 1969.

LANK, R., *Der Wirtschaftskrieg und die Neutralen 1914–1918*, Junker & Dünnhaupt, Berlin, 1940.

LARY, H. B., *The United States in the World Economy*, Government Printing Office, Washington D.C., 1943; H.M.S.O., London, 1944.

LAURSEN, K., and PEDERSEN, J., *The German Inflation, 1918–1923*, North-Holland Publishing Company, Amsterdam, 1964.

LAYTON, W., and RIST, C., *The Economic Situation of Austria*, League of Nations, Geneva, 1925.

League of Nations, *Currencies After the War: A Survey of Conditions in Various Countries*, League of Nations, Geneva, 1920.

League of Nations, International Financial Conference, Brussels, 1920: vol. I, *Report of the Conference;* vol. 2, *Statements on the Financial Situation of the Countries Represented at the Conference*, 1920–21.

League of Nations, *The General Transport Situation in 1921*, League of Nations, Geneva, 1922.

League of Nations, *Report on Certain Aspects of the Raw Materials Problems*, 2 vols, League of Nations, Geneva, 1922.

League of Nations, *Report of the Financial Committee of the League of Nations on the Economic and Financial Situation of Estonia*, League of Nations, Geneva, 1925.

League of Nations, *The Financial Reconstruction of Austria*, League of Nations, Geneva, 1926.

League of Nations, *The Financial Reconstruction of Hungary*, League of Nations, Geneva, 1926.

League of Nations, *International Economic Conference: Final Report of the Trade Barriers Committee of the International Chamber of Commerce*, League of Nations, Geneva, 1927.

League of Nations, International Economic Conference, Geneva, May 1927: *Report and Proceedings of the World Economic Conference*, 2 vols, League of Nations, Geneva, 1927.

League of Nations, *Tariff Level Indices*, League of Nations, Geneva, 1927.

League of Nations, *The Problem of the Coal Industry: Interim Report on its International Aspects*, League of Nations, Geneva, 1929.

League of Nations, *The World Sugar Situation*, League of Nations, Geneva, 1929.

League of Nations, *Interim Report of the Gold Delegation of the Financial Committee*, League of Nations, Geneva, 1930.

League of Nations, *Legislation on Gold*, League of Nations, Geneva, 1930.

League of Nations, *Principles and Methods of Financial Reconstruction Work Undertaken under the Auspices of the League of Nations*, League of Nations, Geneva, 1930.

League of Nations, *Ten Years of World Cooperation*, League of Nations, Geneva, 1930.

League of Nations, *The Agricultural Crisis*, 2 vols, League of Nations, Geneva, 1931.

League of Nations, *The Course and Phases of the World Economic Depression*, League of Nations, Geneva, 1931.

League of Nations, *Second Interim Report of the Gold Delegation of the Financial Committee*, League of Nations, Geneva, 1931.

League of Nations, *Conference for the Economic Restoration of Central and Eastern Europe*, League of Nations, Stresa, 1932.

League of Nations, *Final Report of the Gold Delegation of the Financial Committee*, League of Nations, Geneva, 1932.

League of Nations, *Report on Economic Conditions in Russia with Special Reference to the Famine of 1921–22 and the State of Agriculture*, League of Nations, Geneva, 1932.

League of Nations, *World Economic Survey, 1931–32*, League of Nations, Geneva, 1932.

League of Nations, *Report of the Committee for the Study of the Problem of Raw Materials*, League of Nations, Geneva, 1937.

League of Nations, *International Trade in Certain Raw Materials and Foodstuffs, 1937*, League of Nations, Geneva, 1938.

League of Nations, *Raw Materials and Foodstuffs: Production by Countries 1935–38*, League of Nations, Geneva, 1939.

League of Nations, *Europe's Trade*, League of Nations, Geneva, 1941.

League of Nations, *Commercial Policy in the Inter-War Period,* League of Nations, Geneva, 1942.

League of Nations, *Economic Fluctuations in the United States and the United Kingdom 1918–1922*, League of Nations, Geneva, 1942.

League of Nations, *The Network of World Trade*, League of Nations, Geneva, 1942.

League of Nations, *Agricultural Production in Continental Europe during the 1914–18 War and the Reconstruction Period*, League of Nations, Geneva, 1943.

League of Nations, *Europe's Overseas Needs 1919–1920 and How They Were Met*, League of Nations, Geneva, 1943.

League of Nations, *Quantitative Trade Controls: Their Causes and Nature*, League of Nations, Geneva, 1943.

League of Nations, *Relief Deliveries and Relief Loans 1919–1923*, League of Nations, Geneva, 1943.

League of Nations, *The Transition from War to Peace Economy: Report of the Delegation on Economic Depressions, Part I*, League of Nations, Geneva, 1943.

League of Nations, *International Currency Experience: Lessons of the Inter-War Period*, League of Nations, Geneva, 1944.

League of Nations, *Economic Stability in the Post-War World: Report of the Delegation on Economic Depressions, Part II*, League of Nations, Geneva, 1945.

League of Nations, *Industrialisation and Foreign Trade*, League of Nations, Geneva, 1945.

League of Nations, *League of Nations' Reconstruction Schemes in the Inter-War Period*, League of Nations, Geneva, 1945.

League of Nations, *Transport Problems which Arose from the War of 1914–18 and the Work of Restoration Undertaken in This Field by the League of Nations*, League of Nations, Geneva, 1945.

League of Nations, *The Course and Control of Inflation: A Review of Monetary Experience in Europe after World War I*, League of Nations, 1946.

League of Nations, *Raw Materials Problems and Policies*, League of Nations, 1946.

League of Nations, Statistical Memoranda:

League of Nations, *Balances of Payments, 1933–1938;* from 1924 to 1926 published as vol. I of *Memorandum on Balance of Payments and Foreign Trade Balances;* from 1927 to 1928 as vol. I of *Memorandum on International Trade and Balances of Payments;* from 1929 to 1930 as vol. II of *Memorandum on International Trade and Balances of Payments;* in 1931 as vol. II of *Memorandum on Trade and Balances of Payments.*

League of Nations, *International Trade Statistics, 1933–1938;* from 1924 to 1926 published as vol. II of *Memorandum on Balance of Payments and Foreign Trade Balances;* from 1927 to 1928 as vol. II of *Memorandum on International Trade and Balances of Payments;* from 1929 to 1930 as vol. III of *Memorandum on International Trade and Balances of Payments;* in 1931 as vol. III of *Memorandum on Trade and Balances of Payments.*

League of Nations, *Money and Banking:* vol. I *Monetary Review.* vol. II *Commercial and Central Banks since 1931;* in continuation of *Memorandum on Commercial Banks, 1913–1929 and 1925–1933,* 1931 and 1934, and *Commercial Banks, 1929–1934,* 1935 and *Memoranda on Currencies and Central Banks,* 1922–6.

League of Nations, *Public Finance, 1928–1935,* 1936; similar studies published intermittently in the 1920s under the title of *Memorandum on Public Finance.*

League of Nations, *Review of World Trade, 1933–1938;* from 1924 to 1926 published as vol. I of *Memorandum on Balance of Payments and Foreign Trade Balances;* for 1931 to 1932 as vol. I of *Memorandum on Trade and Balances of Payments.*

League of Nations, *Statistical Yearbook,* 1927 onwards.

League of Nations, *World Production and Prices, 1933–1939;* from 1926 to 1932 published as *Memorandum on Production and Trade;* and in 1932 as *Review of World Production 1925–1931.*

LEE, C. H., 'The Effects of the Depression on Primary Producing Countries', *Journal of Contemporary History,* vol. IV, 1969.

LEE, M. W., *Macroeconomics, Fluctuations, Growth, and Stability,* 5th edition, Irwin, Homewood, Ill., 1971.

LEFF, N. H., 'Long-Term Brazilian Economic Development', *Journal of Economic History,* vol. XXIX, 1969.

LEHFELDT, R. A., *Restoration of the World's Currencies,* P. S. King, London, 1923.

LEITH-ROSS, F., *Money Talks: Fifty Years of International Finance,* Hutchinson, London, 1968.

LEKACHMAN, R., *The Age of Keynes,* Allen Lane, London, 1967; Penguin, Harmondsworth, 1969.

LESTER, R. A. (ed.), *Monetary Experiments,* 1939; reprinted David & Charles, Newton Abbot, 1970.

LETICHE, J. M., 'Differential Rates of Productivity Growth and International Imbalance', *Quarterly Journal of Economics,* vol. LXIX, 1955.

LEVIN, J., *The Export Economies*, Harvard University Press, Cambridge, Mass., 1960.

LEVY, H., *Industrial Germany*, Cambridge University Press, Cambridge, 1935.

LEVY, H., *The New Industrial System*, G. Routledge, London, 1936.

LEWIS, CLEONA, *America's Stake in International Investments*, Brookings Institution, Washington D.C., 1938.

LEWIS, W. A., *Economic Survey, 1919–1939*, Allen & Unwin, London, 1949.

LEWIS, W. A., 'World Production, Prices and Trade, 1870–1960', *Manchester School*, vol. XX, 1952.

LEWIS, W. A., *Aspects of Tropical Trade 1883–1965*, Almquist & Wicksell, Stockholm, 1969.

LIEPMANN, H., *Tariff Levels and the Economic Unity of Europe*, Allen & Unwin, London, 1938.

LIM, C. Y., *Economic Development of Modern Malaya*, Oxford University Press, Kuala Lumpur, 1967.

LINDER, S. B., *An Essay on Trade and Transformation*, Wiley, New York, 1961.

LINDERT, P. H., *Key Currencies and Gold 1900–1913*, Princeton University Press, Princeton, 1969.

LINEHAM, B. T., 'New Zealand's Gross Domestic Product, 1918–1938', *New Zealand Economic Papers*, vol. II, 1968.

LLOYD, E. M. H., *Stabilisation*, Allen & Unwin, London, 1923.

LLOYD GEORGE, D., *The Truth about Reparations and War-Debts*, Heinemann, London, 1932.

LLOYD PRICHARD, M. F., *An Economic History of New Zealand to 1939*, Collins, Auckland, 1970.

LOCKWOOD, W. W., 'The Scale of Economic Growth in Japan, 1868–1938', in Kuznets, S., Moore, W. E. and Spengler, J. (eds), *Economic Growth: Brazil, India, Japan*, Duke University Press, Durham, N. C., 1955.

LOCKWOOD, W. W., *The Economic Development of Japan: Growth and Structural Change*, Princeton University Press, Princeton, 1968.

LORCH, A., *Trends in European Social Legislation Between the Two World Wars*, Editions de la Maison Française, New York, 1943.

LOUIS, L. J., and TURNER, I. (eds), *The Depression of the 1930s*, Cassell, Australia, 1968.

LOVEDAY, A., *Britain and World Trade*, Longmans, Green, London, 1931.

LUKE, R. E., *Von der Stabilisierung zur Krise*, Polygraphischer Verlag, Zurich, 1958.

LUNDBERG, E. (ed.), *The Business Cycle in the Post-War World*, Macmillan, London, 1955.

LUNDBERG, E., *Business Cycles and Economic Policy*, Allen & Unwin, London, 1957.

LUNDBERG, E., *Instability and Economic Growth*, Yale University Press, New Haven, 1968.

LUTZ, H. L., 'Inter-Allied Debts, Reparations and National Policy', *Journal of Political Economy*, vol. XXXVIII, 1930.

MACARTNEY, C. A., *National States and National Minorities*, Oxford University Press, Oxford, 1934.

MACARTNEY, C. A., *Hungary and Her Successors: The Treaty of Trianon and its Consequences 1919–1937*, Oxford University Press, London, 1937.

MacCLINTOCK, S., 'French Finances and Economic Resources', *Journal of Political Economy*, vol. XXX, 1922.

MacDOUGALL, D., *Studies in Political Economy*, vol. I, *The Inter-war Years and the 1940s*, Crane-Russak, New York, 1975.

McGREEVEY, W. P., *Statistical Series on the Columbian Economy*, Mimeo. pub. No. 388067, Dept of Geography, University of California.

McGREEVEY, W. P., *An Economic History of Columbia 1845–1930*, Cambridge University Press, London, 1971.

McGUIRE, C. E., *Italy's International Economic Position*, Allen & Unwin, London, 1927.

MCIVER, R. M., *et alia*, *Economic Reconstruction: Report of the Columbia University Commission*, 1934; reprinted Columbia University Press, New York, 1964.

Macmillan Committee, *Report of the Committee on Finance and Industry*, Cmd. 3897, H.M.S.O., London, 1931.

MACROSTY, H. W., 'Inflation and Deflation in the United States and the United Kingdom, 1919–23', *Journal of the Royal Statistical Society*, vol. XC, 1927.

MADDISON, A., 'Economic Growth in Western Europe, 1870–1957', *Banca Nazionale del Lavoro Quarterly Review*, vol. XII, 1959.

MADDISON, A., 'Growth and Fluctuation in the World Economy,

1870–1960', *Banca Nazionale del Lavoro Quarterly Review*, vol. xv, 1962.

MADDISON, A., *Economic Growth in the West*, Allen & Unwin, London, 1964.

MADDISON, A., *Economic Growth in Japan and the U.S.S.R.*, Allen & Unwin, London, 1969.

MADDISON, A., *Class Structure and Economic Growth: India and Pakistan since the Moghuls*, Allen & Unwin, London, 1971.

MADDISON, A., *Economic Policy and Performance in Europe, 1913–1970*, Collins/Fontana, 1973.

MADGEARU, V., *Rumania's New Economic Policy*, P. S. King, London, 1930.

MAIZELS, A., *Industrial Growth and World Trade*, Cambridge University Press, Cambridge, 1963.

MALACH, V. W., 'Internal Determinants of the Canadian Upswing, 1921–9', *Canadian Journal of Economics and Political Science*, vol. xvi, 1950.

MALACH, V. W., *International Cycles and Canada's Balance of Payments 1921–33*, University of Toronto Press, Toronto, 1954.

MALENBAUM, W., *The World Wheat Economy 1885–1939*, Harvard University Press, Cambridge, Mass., 1953.

MAMALAKIS, M., and REYNOLDS, C. W., *Essays on the Chilean Economy*, Irwin, Homewood, Ill., 1965.

MANTOUX, E., *The Carthaginian Peace or the Economic Consequences of Mr Keynes*, Oxford University Press, London, 1946.

MARCUS, E., 'The Cyclical Adjustment Pattern of an "Open Economy": Canada, 1927–1939', *Economic Journal*, vol. LXII, 1952.

MARCUS, E., *Canada and the International Business Cycle 1927–1939*, Bookman Associates, New York, 1954.

MARKOVITCH, T. J., 'L'industrie française de 1789 à 1964 – Conclusions générales', in *Histoire quantitative de l'économie française*, Institut de Science Économique Appliquée, Paris, 1966.

MARSTON, F. S., *The Peace Conference of 1919: Organization and Procedure*, Oxford University Press, London, 1944.

MARTIN, G., 'The Industrial Reconstruction of France since the War', *Harvard Business Review*, vol. V, 1927.

MARTIN, K., and THACKERAY, F. G., 'The Terms of Trade of Selected Countries, 1870–1938', *Bulletin of the Oxford University Institute of Statistics*, vol. X, 1948.

MARWICK, A., *The Deluge*, Bodley Head, London, 1965.

MARWICK, A., *Britain in the Century of Total War: War, Peace and Social Change, 1900–1967*, Penguin, Harmondsworth, 1968.

MARWICK, A., 'The Impact of the First World War on British Society', *Journal of Contemporary History*, vol. III, 1968.

MATOLESY, M., and VARGA, S., *The National Income of Hungary, 1924/25–1936/37*, P. S. King, London, 1938.

MEAKIN, W., *The New Industrial Revolution*, Gollancz, London, 1928.

MELVILLE, L. G., 'Gold Standard or Goods Standard' (The Joseph Fisher Lecture in Commerce, 26 September 1934), Hassell Press, Adelaide.

MENDERSHAUSEN, H., *The Economics of War*, Prentice–Hall, New York, 1941.

MENDERSHAUSEN, H., Two Postwar Recoveries of the German Economy, North Holland Publishing Company, Amsterdam, 1955.

MERCER, L. J., and MORGAN, W. D., 'Alternative Interpretations of Market Saturation: Evaluation for the Automobile Market in the late Twenties', *Explorations in Economic History*, vol. IX, 1972.

MERCER, L. J., and MORGAN, W. D., 'The American Automobile Industry; Investment Demand, Capacity and Capacity Utilisation in the 1920s', *Journal of Political Economy*, vol. LXXX, 1972.

MEREDITH, D., 'The British Government and Colonial Economic Policy, 1919–39', *Economic History Review*, vol. XXVIII, 1975.

MEYER, F. V., and LEWIS, W. A., 'The Effects of an Overseas Slump on the British Economy', *Manchester School*, vol. XVII, 1949.

MEYER, R. H., *Bankers' Diplomacy: Monetary Stabilisation in the Twenties*, Columbia University Press, New York, 1970.

MIKESELL, R. F. (ed.), *U.S. Private and Government Investment Abroad*, University of Oregon Books, Eugene, 1962.

Midland Bank Review, 'The German Inflation of 1923', *Midland Bank Review*, November 1975.

MILLER, H. E., 'The Franc in War and Reconstruction', *Quarterly Journal of Economics*, vol. XLIV, 1930.

MILWARD, A. S., *The Economic Effects of the World Wars on Britain*, Macmillan, London, 1970.

MINGS, T. R., *An Inter-Country Comparison of the Factors Determining Cyclical Behaviour in Sweden, Canada, Austria and Belgium, 1929–1937*, University Microfilms, Ann Arbor, Michigan, 1968.

MINTZ, I., *Deterioration in the Quality of Foreign Bonds Issued in the United States 1920–1930*, National Bureau of Economic Research, New York, 1951.

MINTZ, I., *Trade Balances during Business Cycles: U.S. and Britain since 1880*, National Bureau of Economic Research, New York, 1959.

MITCHELL, B. R., and DEANE, PHYLLIS, *Abstract of British Historical Statistics*, Cambridge University Press, Cambridge, 1962.

MITCHELL, B. R., *European Historical Statistics, 1750–1970*, Macmillan, London, 1975.

MITCHELL, K. L., *Industrialisation of the Western Pacific*, Institute of Pacific Relations, New York, 1942.

MITRANY, D., *The Land and the Peasant in Rumania. The War and Agrarian Reform (1917–1921)*, Oxford University Press, London, 1930.

MITRANY, D., *The Effect of the War in Southeastern Europe*, Yale University Press, New Haven, 1936.

MLYNARSKI, F., *Gold and Central Banks*, Macmillan, New York, 1929.

MLYNARSKI, F., *The Functioning of the Gold Standard*, League of Nations, Geneva, 1931.

MOGGRIDGE, D. E., *The Return to Gold, 1925: The Formulation of Economic Policy and its Critics*, Cambridge University Press, Cambridge, 1969.

MOGGRIDGE, D. E., 'British Controls on Long Term Capital Movements, 1924–1931', Chapter 4 of McCloskey, D. N. (ed.), *Essays on a Mature Economy: Britain after 1840*, Methuen, London, 1971.

MOGGRIDGE, D. E., *British Monetary Policy 1924–1931: The Norman Conquest of $4.86*, Cambridge University Press, Cambridge, 1972.

MONTGOMERY, G. A., *The Rise of Modern Industry in Sweden*, P. S. King, London, 1930.

MONTGOMERY, G. A., *How Sweden Overcame the Depression 1930–33*, Benniers, Stockholm, 1938.

MOON, P. T., 'The Young Plan in Operation', *Proceedings of the Academy of Political Science*, vol. XIV, 1931.

MOORE, W. E., *Economic Demography of Eastern and Southern Europe*, League of Nations, Geneva, 1945.

MORGAN, E. V., *Studies in British Financial Policy, 1914–25*, Macmillan, London, 1952.

MORGAN, O. S. (ed.), *Agricultural Systems of Middle Europe*, Macmillan, London, 1933.

MORGAN, T., 'The Long-Run Terms of Trade between Agriculture and Manufacturing', *Economic Development and Cultural Change*, vol. VIII, 1959.

MORGENSTERN, O., *International Financial Transactions and Business Cycles*, Princeton University Press, Princeton, 1959.

MORLEY, J. W. (ed.), *Dilemmas of Growth in Prewar Japan*, Princeton University Press, Princeton, 1971.

MOSELEY, G., *China: Empire to People's Republic*, Batsford, London, 1968.

MOULTON, H. G., 'Economic Conditions in Europe', *American Economic Review*, vol. XIII, 1923.

MOULTON, H. G., and MCGUIRE, C. E., *Germany's Capacity to Pay*, McGraw-Hill, New York, 1923.

MOULTON, H. G., *The Reparation Plan*, McGraw-Hill, New York, 1924.

MOULTON, H. G., and LEWIS, C., *The French Debt Problem*, Macmillan, New York, 1925.

MOULTON, H. G., 'Economic Problems Involved in the Payment of International Debts', *American Economic Review, Papers and Proceedings*, vol. XVI, 1926.

MOULTON, H. G., and PASVOLSKY, L., *World War Debt Settlements*, Brookings Institution, Washington D.C., 1926.

MOULTON, H. G., *Japan: An Economic and Financial Appraisal*, Brookings Institution, Washington D.C., 1931.

MOULTON, H. G., and PASVOLSKY, L., *War Debts and World Prosperity*, Brookings Institution, Washington D.C., 1932.

MOWAT, C. L., *Britain Between the Wars. 1918–1940*, Methuen, London, 1955.

MOWAT, C. L. (ed.), *The Shifting Balance of World Forces, 1898–1945*, New edition of vol. XII of *New Cambridge Modern History*, Cambridge University Press, Cambridge, 1968.

MUNOZ, O. E., 'An Essay on the Process of Industrialization in Chile since 1914', *Yale Economic Essays*, vol. VIII, 1968.

MYERS, MARGARET G., *Paris as a Financial Centre*, P. S. King, London, 1936.

MYERS, MARGARET G., 'The League Loans', *Political Science Quarterly*, vol. LX, 1945.

NAPIER, E. S., *The German Credit Problem*, London General Press, London, 1931.

NEFF, N. H., 'Long-Term Brazilian Economic Development', *Journal of Economic History*, vol. XXIX, 1969.

NEISSER, H., *Some International Aspects of the Business Cycle*, University of Pennsylvania Press, Philadelphia, 1936.

NEISSER, H., and MODIGLIANI, F., *National Incomes and International Trade: A Quantitative Analysis*, University of Illinois Press, Urbana, 1953.

NÉRÉ, J., *La Crise de 1929*, Colin, Paris, 1968.

NEUMARK, S. D., 'The World Agricultural Crisis: A Review of Recent Economic Literature', *South African Journal of Economics*, vol. II, 1934.

NEVIN, E., *The Mechanism of Cheap Money; A Study of British Monetary Policy, 1931–1939*, University of Wales Press, Cardiff, 1955.

NEYTZELL DE WILDE, A. and MOLL, J. TH., *The Netherlands Indies during the Depression: A Brief Economic Survey*, J. M. Meulenhoff, Amsterdam, 1936.

NICHOLSON, J. S., *Inflation*, P. S. King, London, 1919.

NOLDE, B. E., *Russia in the Economic War*, Yale University Press, New Haven, 1928.

NORTH, D. C., 'International Capital Movements in Historical Perspective', in Mikesell, R. F. (ed.), *U.S. Private and Government Investment Abroad*, University of Oregon Books, Eugene, 1962.

NOTESTEIN, F. W., *et alia*, *The Future Population of Europe and the Soviet Union*, League of Nations, Geneva, 1944.

NOVE, A., *An Economic History of the U.S.S.R.*, Allen Lane, London, 1969.

NOYES, A. D., *The War Period of American Finance, 1918–1925*, Putnam, New York, 1926.

O'BRIEN, P., *The Revolution in Egypt's Economic System*, Oxford University Press, London, 1966.

OGBURN, W. F., and JAFFÉ, W., *The Economic Development of Postwar France: A Survey of Production*, Columbia University Press, New York, 1929.

OHKAWA, K., *The Growth Rate of the Japanese Economy since 1878*, Kinokuniya Bookstore, Tokyo, 1957.

OHLIN, B., 'The Reparation Problem: A Discussion', *Economic Journal*, vol. XXXIX, 1929.

OLSON, M., *The Economics of the Wartime Shortage. A History of British Food Supply in the Napoleonic War and in World Wars I and II*, Duke University Press, Durham, N. C., 1963.

OLSSON, C. A., 'Swedish Agriculture During the Interwar Years', *Economy and History*, vol. XI, 1968.

Organisation for Economic Cooperation and Development, *Basic Statistics of Industrial Production, 1913–1960*, OECD, Paris, 1962.

Organisation for European Economic Cooperation, *Industrial Statistics, 1900–1959*, OEEC, Paris, 1960.

PAIGE, C. D., *et alia*, 'Economic Growth: The Last Hundred Years', *National Institute Economic Review*, vol. XVI, July 1961.

PALYI, M., *Managed Money at the Crossroads*, University of Notre Dame Press, Notre Dame, 1958.

PALYI, M., *The Twilight of Gold 1914–1936: Myths and Realities*, Henry Regnery, Chicago, 1972.

PANANDIKAR, S. G., *Some Aspects of the Economic Consequences of the War for India*, Bombay, 1921.

PARETTI, V., and BLOCH, G. G., 'Industrial Production in Western Europe and the United States, 1901–1955', *Banca Nazionale del Lavoro Quarterly Review*, vol. IX, 1956.

PARKER, R. A. C., *Europe 1919–45*, Weidenfeld & Nicolson, London, 1969.

PASVOLSKY, L., and MOULTON, H. G., *Russian Debts and Russian Reconstruction*, McGraw-Hill, New York, 1924.

PASVOLSKY, L., *Economic Nationalism of the Danubian States*, Allen & Unwin, London, 1928.

PASVOLSKY, L., *Bulgaria's Economic Position*, Brookings Institution, Washington D.C., 1930.

PASVOLSKY, L., *Current Monetary Issues*, Brookings Institution, Washington D.C., 1933.

PATEL, S. J., 'Rates of Industrial Growth in the last century 1860–1958', *Economic Development and Cultural Change*, vol. IX, Part 2, 1961.

PATEL, S. J., *Essays on Economic Transition*, Asia Publishing House, Bombay, 1965.

PATTERSON, R. T., *The Great Boom and Panic, 1921–1929*, Henry Regnery, Chicago, 1965.

PEACOCK, A. T., and WISEMAN, J., *The Growth of Public Expenditure in the United Kingdom*, Oxford University Press, London, 1961.

PEDDIE, J. T., *The Flaw in the Economic System: The Case against the Gold Standard*, J. Murray, London, 1928.

PEDERSEN, J., *Economic Conditions in Denmark after 1922*, Copenhagen, 1931.

PEDERSEN, J., 'A Chapter of the History of Monetary Theory and Policy', in G. Bombach (ed.), *Stabile Preise in Wachsender Wirtschaft: Das Inflationsproblem*, J. C. B. Mohr (Paul Siebeck), Tübingen, 1960.

PEDERSEN, J., 'Some Notes on the Economic Policy of the United States during the Period 1919–32', in Hegeland, H. (ed.), *Money, Growth and Methodology: Essays in Honour of Johan Åkerman*, C.W.K. Gleerup, Lund, 1961.

PEEL, A. G. V., *The Financial Crisis of France*, Macmillan, London, 1925.

PEEL, A. G. V., *The Economic Impact of America*, Macmillan, London, 1928.

PEEL, A. G. V., *The Economic Policy of France*, Macmillan, London, 1937.

PERROT, M., *La Monnaie et l'opinion en France et en Angleterre (de 1924 à 1936)*, Colin, Paris, 1955.

PESELJ, B., *The Industrialisation of Peasant Europe*, Mid-European Studies Centre, New York, 1953.

PETERS, H. E., *The Foreign Debt of the Argentine Republic*, Johns Hopkins Press, Baltimore, 1934.

PHELPS, V. L., *The International Economic Position of Argentina*, University of Pennsylvania Press, Philadelphia, 1938.

PHELPS BROWN, E. H., and BROWNE, M. H., *A Century of Pay*, Macmillan, London, 1968.

PHILPOTT, B. D., and STEWART, J. D., 'Capital, Income and Output in New Zealand Agriculture, 1922–1956', *Economic Record*, vol. xxxIV, 1958.

PIGOU, A. C., *Aspects of British Economic History 1918–1925*, Macmillan, London, 1947.

PILGRIM, J. D., 'The Upper Turning Point of 1920', Ph.D. thesis, Vanderbilt University, Nashville, Tenn., 1969.

PILGRIM, J. D., 'The Upper Turning Point of 1920: A Reappraisal', *Explorations in Economic History*, vol. XI, 1974.

PIM, A., *The Financial and Economic History of the African Tropical Territories*, Clarendon Press, Oxford, 1940.

PINOT, P., *Le Contrôle du ravitaillement de la population civile*, Presses Universitaires de France, Paris, 1925.

POLAK, J. J., 'European Exchange Depreciation in the Early Twenties', *Econometrica*, vol. II, 1943.

POLANYI, K., *The Great Transformation*, Farrar & Rinehart, New York, 1944.

Political and Economic Planning, *Report on International Trade*, PEP, London, 1937.

Political and Economic Planning, *Economic Development in S. E. Europe*, PEP, London, 1945.

Political and Economic Planning, *Britain and World Trade*, PEP, London, 1947.

POLLARD, S., *The Development of the British Economy, 1914–1950*, Edward Arnold, London, 1962.

POLLARD, S., and HOLMES, C., *Documents of European Economic History*, vol. III: *The End of the Old Europe, 1914–1939*, Edward Arnold, London, 1973.

POLONSKY, A., *The Little Dictators*, Routledge & Kegan Paul, London, 1975.

PRESTON, H. H., 'Europe's Return to Gold', *Harvard Business Review*, vol. IX, 1931.

PRINGLE, W. H. (ed.), *Economic Problems in Europe Today*, A. & C. Black, London, 1927.

PUXLEY, H. L., *A Critique of the Gold Standard*, Allen & Unwin, London, 1933.

RAPPARD, W. E., *Post-War Efforts for Freer Trade*, Geneva Studies, vol. IX, Geneva Research Centre, Geneva, 1938.

REES, G., *The Great Slump: Capitalism in Crisis, 1929–33*, Weidenfeld & Nicolson, London, 1970.

REINHOLD, P., *The Economic, Financial and Political State of Germany since the War*, Yale University Press, New Haven, 1928.

REMER, C. F., *Foreign Investments in China*, Macmillan, New York, 1933.

RENOUVIN, P., *Les Crises du XXᵉ siècle: I. De 1914 à 1929* (*Histoire des relations internationales*, vol. VII), Hachette, Paris, 1957.

RICHARDSON, H. W., 'The New Industries between the Wars', *Oxford Economic Papers*, vol. XIII, 1961.

RICHARDSON, H. W., *Economic Recovery in Britain, 1932–9*, Weidenfeld & Nicolson, London, 1967.

RICHARDSON, H. W., 'The Economic Significance of the Depression in Britain', *Journal of Contemporary History*, vol. IV, 1969.

RINGER, F. K. (ed.), *The German Inflation of 1923*, Oxford University Press, New York, 1969.

RIST, C., and SCHWOB, P., 'Vingt-cinq ans d'évolution dans la balance des paiements française', *Revue d'Économie Politique*, vol. LIII, 1939.

ROBBINS, L., *The Great Depression*, Macmillan, London, 1934.

ROBINSON, E. A. G., 'The Changing Structure of the British Economy', *Economic Journal*, vol. LXIV, 1954.

ROBINSON, N., 'German Foreign Trade and Industry after the First World War', *Quarterly Journal of Economics*, vol. LVIII, 1944.

ROEPKE, W., *Crises and Cycles*, Hodge, London, 1936.

ROESLER, K., *Die Finanzpolitik des Deutschen Reiches im Ersten Weltkrieg*, Duncker & Humblot, Berlin, 1967.

ROGERS, J. H., *The Process of Inflation in France 1914–1927*, Columbia University Press, New York, 1929.

ROLL, E., *Spotlight on Germany: A Survey of her Economic and Political Problems*, Faber & Faber, London, 1933.

ROOSE, K. D., 'The Production Ceiling and the Turning Point of 1920', *American Economic Review*, vol. XLVIII, 1958.

ROPKE, W., *International Economic Disintegration*, William Lodge, London, 1942.

ROSENBERG, W., 'Capital Imports and Growth – the Case of New Zealand – Foreign Investment in New Zealand, 1840–1958', *Economic Journal*, vol. LXXI, 1961.

ROSENSTEIN-RODAN, P. N., 'Problems of Industrialization of Eastern and South-Eastern Europe', *Economic Journal*, vol. LIII, 1943.

ROSOVSKY, H., *Capital Formation in Japan 1868–1940*, Free Press, Glencoe, 1961.

ROSTOW, W. W., 'The Strategic Role of Theory: A Commentary', *Journal of Economic History*, vol. XXXI, 1971.

ROTHBARD, M. N., *America's Great Depression*, Van Nostrand, Princeton, 1963.

ROTHSCHILD, J., *East Central Europe between the Two World Wars*, American University Publishers Group, Washington D.C., 1975.

ROTHSCHILD, K. W., *Austria's Economic Development between the Two Wars*, Frederick Muller, London, 1947.

ROWE, J. W. F., *Markets and Men: A Study of Artificial Control Schemes in Some Primary Industries*, Cambridge University Press, Cambridge, 1936.

ROWE, J. W. F., *The World's Coffee*, H.M.S.O., London, 1963.

ROWE, J. W. F., *Primary Commodities in International Trade*, Cambridge University Press, Cambridge, 1965.

ROWE, L. S., *Early Effects of the War upon the Finance, Commerce and Industry of Peru*, Oxford University Press, New York, Carnegie Series, 1920.

Royal Institute of International Affairs, *The International Gold Problem: Collected Papers*, Oxford University Press, London, 1932.

Royal Institute of International Affairs, *World Agriculture: An International Survey*, Oxford University Press, London, 1932.

Royal Institute of International Affairs, *Monetary Policy and the Depression*, Oxford University Press, London, 1933.

Royal Institute of International Affairs, *The Future of Monetary Policy*, Oxford University Press, London, 1935.

Royal Institute of International Affairs, *Unemployment: An International Problem*, Oxford University Press, London, 1935.

Royal Institute of International Affairs, *The Balkan States: I. Economic. A Review of the Economic and Financial Development of Albania, Bulgaria, Greece, Roumania and Yugoslavia since 1919*, Oxford Uiniversty Press, London, 1936.

Royal Institute of International Affairs, *The Problem of International Investment 1937*, Oxford University Press, Oxford, 1937; reprinted Frank Cass, London, 1965.

Royal Institute of International Affairs, *The Republics of South America*, Oxford University Press, London, 1937.

Royal Institute of International Affairs, *The Baltic States*, Oxford University Press, London, 1938.

Royal Institute of International Affairs, *South-Eastern Europe: A Political and Economic Survey*, Oxford University Press, London, 1939.

Royal Institute of International Affairs, *South-Eastern Europe: A Brief Survey*, Oxford University Press, London, 1940.

Royal Institute of International Affairs, *The Scandinavian States and Finland: A Political and Economic Survey*, Oxford University Press, London, 1951.

SAFARIAN, A. E., *The Canadian Economy in the Great Depression*, University of Toronto Press, Toronto, 1959.

SALTER, A., *Recovery: The Second Effort*, Bell, London, 1932.

SALTER, A., *et alia*, *The World Economic Crisis*, Kennikat Press, New York, 1932.

SAMUEL, H. B., *The French Default: An Analysis of the Problems Involved in the Debt Repudiation of the French Republic*, E. Wilson, London, 1930.

SARTI, R., 'The Battle of the Lira 1925–27', *Past and Present*, vol. XLVII, 1970.

SARTI, R., *Fascism and the Industrial Leadership in Italy, 1919–1940*, University of California Press, Berkeley, 1971.

SAUVY, A., 'L'inflation en France jusqu'à la Dévaluation de 1928', in *Mélanges d'histoire économique et sociale en hommage au Professeur Antony Babel*, vol. II, Geneva, 1963.

SAUVY, A., *Histoire économique de la France entre les deux guerres, 1918–1931*, Fayard, Paris, 1965.

SAYERS, R. S., *Central Banking after Bagehot*, Oxford University Press, London, 1957.

SAYERS, R. S., 'The Return to Gold, 1925', Chapter 12 of Pressnell, L. S. (ed.), *Studies in the Industrial Revolution*, Athlone Press, London, 1960.

SCAMMELL, W. M., *International Monetary Policy*, Macmillan, London, 1957.

SCAMMELL, W. M., *International Monetary Policy*, 2nd edition, Macmillan, London, 1961.

SCAMMELL, W. M., 'The Working of the Gold Standard', *Yorkshire Bulletin of Economic and Social Research*, vol. XVII, 1965.

SCHACHT, H. H. G., *The Stabilization of the Mark*, Allen & Unwin, London, 1927.

n.

SCHACHT, H. H. G., *The End of Reparations*, Cape, London, 1931.

SCHEDVIN, C. B., *Australia and the Great Depression: A Study of the Economic Development and Policy in the 1920s and 1930s*, University of Sydney Press, Sydney, 1970.

SCHEDVIN, C. B., 'Monetary Stability and the Demand for Money in Australia between the Wars', *Australian Economic History Review*, vol. XI, 1971.

SCHMID, G. C., 'The Politics of Currency Stabilisation: The French Franc, 1926', *Journal of European Economic History*, vol. III, 1974.

SCHMIDT, C. T., *German Business Cycles 1924–1933*, National Bureau of Economic Research, New York, 1934.

SCHMITZ, J., *Inflation und Stabilisierung in Frankreich, 1914–1928*, K. Schroeder, Bonn, 1930.

SCHUMANN, C. G. W., *The World Depression: South Africa and the Gold Standard*, Juta, Cape Town, 1932.

SCHUMANN, C. G. W., 'Business Cycles in South Africa 1910–1933', *South African Journal of Economics*, vol. II, 1934.

SCHUMANN, C. G. W., *Structural Changes and Business Cycles in South Africa 1806–1936*, P. S. King, London, 1938.

SCHUMPETER, J. A., *Business Cycles*, vol. II, McGraw-Hill, New York, 1939.

SCHWARTZ, ANNA J., 'Secular Price Change in Historical Perspective', *Journal of Money, Credit and Banking*, vol. V, 1973.

SCHWOB, P., 'French Monetary Policy and its Critics', *Economica*, vol. II, August 1935.

SCOTT, J. B. (ed.), *The Paris Peace Conference: History and Documents*, 6 vols, Columbia University Press, New York, 1934–42.

SCOVILLE, W. C., and LA FORCE, J. C. (eds), *The Economic Development of Western Europe from 1914 to the Present*, D. C. Heath, Lexington, Mass., 1969.

SEIDEL, R. N., 'American Reformers Abroad: The Kemmerer Missions in South America, 1923–1931', *Journal of Economic History*, vol. XXXII, 1972.

SELLIN, T., and YOUNG, D. (eds), 'An Economic Survey of Australia', *Annals of the American Academy of Political and Social Science*, vol. CLVIII, 1931.

SERING, M., *Germany Under the Dawes Plan*, P. S. King, London, 1929.

SETON-WATSON, H., *Eastern Europe between the Wars, 1918–1941*, Cambridge University Press, Cambridge, 1945.

SHANN, E. O. G., and COPLAND, D. B., *The Crisis in Australian Finance*, Angus & Robertson, Sydney, 1931.

SHEPHERD, H. L., *The Monetary Experience of Belgium 1914–1936*, Princeton University Press, Princeton, 1936.

SHORTT, A., and ROWE, L. S., *Early Economic Effects of the European War upon Canada and Chile*, Oxford University Press, New York, Carnegie Series, 1918.

SIMUTIS, A., *The Economic Reconstruction of Lithuania after 1918*, Columbia University Press, New York, 1942.

SINGH, V. B., *Economic History of India 1857–1956*, Allied Publishers Private, Bombay, 1965.

SMITH, J. G., 'Economic Nationalism and International Trade', *Economic Journal*, vol. XLV, 1935.

SMITH, L., 'Suspension of the Gold Standard in Raw Material Exporting Countries', *American Economic Review*, vol. XXIV, 1934.

SOBEL, R., *The Great Bull Market: Wall Street in the 1920s*, W. W. Norton, New York, 1968.

SOBEL, R., *Panic on Wall Street: A History of America's Financial Disasters*, Macmillan, New York, 1968.

SOULE, G., *Prosperity Decade*, Holt, Rinehart & Winston, New York, 1947.

SPAHR, W. E., *The Case for the Gold Standard*, Economists' National Committee on Monetary Policy, New York, 1940.

SPULBER, N., 'The Role of the State in Economic Growth in Eastern Europe since 1860', in Aitken, H. G. J. (ed.), *The State and Economic Growth*, Social Science Research Council, New York, 1959.

SPULBER, N., *The State and Economic Development in Eastern Europe*, Random House, New York, 1966.

STALEY, E., *War and the Private Investor*, Doubleday, Doran, New York, 1935.

STALEY, E., *Raw Materials in Peace and War*, Council on Foreign Relations, New York, 1937.

STALEY, E., *World Economy in Transition*, Council on Foreign Relations, New York, 1939.

STALEY, E., *World Economic Development: Effects on Advanced Industrial Countries*, 2nd edition, International Labour Office, Montreal, 1945.

STAMP, J., *The Financial Aftermath of War*, Benn, London, 1932.

STAMP, J., *Taxation During the War*, Oxford University Press, London, 1932.

STEARNS, P. N., *European Society in Upheaval*, Macmillan, New York, 1967.

STEIN, S. J., *The Brazilian Cotton Manufacture: Textile Enterprise in an Underdeveloped Area, 1850–1950*, Harvard University Press, Cambridge, Mass., 1957.

STERN, S., *Fourteen Years of European Investments 1914–1928*, Bankers Publishing Company, New York, 1929.

STEWART, M., *Keynes and After*, Penguin, Harmondsworth, 1967.

STOLPER, G., *et alia, The German Economy, 1870 to the Present*, 2nd edition, Weidenfeld & Nicolson, London, 1967.

STOLPER, W. F., 'Purchasing Power Parity and the Pound Sterling, 1919–1925', *Kyklos*, vol. II, 1948.

STRANGE, S., *Sterling and British Policy: A Political Study of an International Currency in Decline*, Oxford University Press, London, 1971.

STUCKEN, R., *Deutsche Geld- und Kreditpolitik, 1914 bis 1963*, Mohr, Tübingen, 1964.

SVENNILSON, I., *Growth and Stagnation in the European Economy*, United Nations, Geneva, 1954.

TAMAGNA, F., *Central Banking in Latin America*, Centro de Estudios Monetarios/Latinoamericanos, Mexico, 1965.

TANNENBAUM, E. R., *The Fascist Experience: Italian Society and Culture, 1922–1945*, Basic Books, New York, 1972.

TASCA, H. J., *World Trading Systems*, League of Nations, Paris, 1939.

TAWNEY, R. H., 'The Abolition of Economic Controls, 1918–21', *Economic History Review*, vol. XIII, 1943.

TAYLOR, H. C., and TAYLOR, A. D., *World Trade in Agricultural Products*, Macmillan, New York, 1943.

TAYLOR, J., *The Economic Development of Poland 1919–1950*, Cornell University Press, Ithaca, 1952.

TEICHERT, P. C. M., *Economic Policy, Revolution and Industrialization in Latin America*, Bureau of Business Research, University of Mississippi, 1959.

TEICHOVA, A., *An Economic Background to Munich: International Business and Czechoslovakia, 1918–1938*, Cambridge University Press, Cambridge, 1974.

TEMIN, P., 'The Beginning of the Depression in Germany', *Economic History Review*, vol. XXIV, 1971.

TEMPERLEY, H. W. V. (ed.), *A History of the Peace Conference of Paris*, 6 vols, Oxford University Press, London, 1920–24.

TERBORGH, G., *The Bogey of Economic Maturity*, Machinery and Allied Products Institute, Chicago, 1945.

THOMAS, B., *Monetary Policy and Crises: A Study of Swedish Experience*, Routledge, London, 1936.

THOMSON, D., *Europe Since Napoleon*, Penguin, Harmondsworth, 1966.

THORNER, D., and THORNER, C., *Land and Labour in India*, Asia Publishing House, London, 1962.

TILTMAN, H. H., *Slump? A Study of Stricken Europe Today*, Jarrolds, London, 1932.

TIMOSHENKO, V. P., *World Agriculture and the Depression*, University of Michigan Business Studies, vol. V, Ann Arbor, Michigan, 1933.

TINBERGEN, J., *Shaping the World Economy*, Twentieth Century Fund, New York, 1962.

TRACY, M., *Agriculture in Western Europe: Crisis and Adaptation Since 1880*, Cape, London, 1964.

TRIANTIS, S., *Cyclical Changes in Trade Balances of Countries Exporting Primary Products 1927–33*, University of Toronto Press, Toronto, 1967.

TRIFFIN, R., *Gold and the Dollar Crisis: The Future of Convertibility*, Yale University Press, New Haven, 1960.

TRIFFIN, R., *The Evolution of the International Monetary System: Historical Reappraisal and Future Perspectives*, Princeton Studies in International Finance, No. 12, Princeton University Press, Princeton, 1964.

TRIFFIN, R., *Our International Monetary System: Yesterday, Today and Tomorrow*, Random House, New York, 1968.

TRIVANOVITCH, V., *Rationalization of German Industry*, National Industrial Conference Board, New York, 1931.

TRUCHY, H., *Les finances de guerre de la France*, Presses Universitaires de France, Paris, 1926.

TSIANG, S. C., 'Fluctuating Exchange Rates in Countries with Relatively Stable Economies: Some European Experiences After War I', International Monetary Fund *Staff Papers*, vol. VII, 1959–60.

TUGWELL, R. G., 'The Agricultural Policy of France', *Political Science Quarterly*, vol. XLV, 1930.

TYSZYNSKI, H., 'World Trade in Manufactured Commodities, 1899–1950', *Manchester School*, vol. XIX, 1951.

United Nations, *International Cartels*, United Nations, New York, 1947.

United Nations, *Public Debt, 1914–1946*, United Nations, New York, 1948.

United Nations, *International Capital Movements during the Inter-war Period*, United Nations, New York, 1949.

United Nations, *Foreign Capital in Latin America*, United Nations, New York, 1955.

United Nations (ECLA), *The Process of Industrial Development in Latin America*, United Nations, New York, 1966.

United States Bureau of the Census, *Historical Statistics of the United States: Colonial Times to 1957*, Government Printing Office, Washington D.C., 1960.

URQUHART, M. C., and BUCKLEY, K. A. H. (eds), *Historical Statistics of Canada*, Cambridge University Press, Cambridge, 1965.

UTLEY, F., *Lancashire and the Far East*, Allen & Unwin, London, 1931.

VAN DER FLIER, M. J., *War Finances in the Netherlands up to 1918*, Oxford University Press, Oxford, 1923.

VAN DER WEE, H. (ed.), *The Great Depression Revisited: Essays on the Economics of the Thirties*, Martinus Nijhoff, The Hague, 1972.

VAN WALRÉ DE BORDES, J., *The Austrian Crown*, P. S. King, London, 1924.

VON HAYEK, F. A., *Monetary Nationalism and International Stability*, Longmans, Green, London, 1937.

VINER, J., 'Who Paid for the War?', *Journal of Political Economy*, vol. XXVIII, 1920.

VINSKI, I., 'National Product and Fixed Assets in the Territory of Yugoslavia, 1900–1959', *Income and Wealth*, vol. IX, 1961.

WALKER, E. R., *Australia in the World Depression*, P. S. King, London, 1933.

WALKER, G., 'The Payment of Reparations', *Economica*, vol. XI, 1931.

WALLACE, B. B., and EDMINSTER, L. R., *International Control of*

Raw Materials, Brookings Institution, Washington D.C., 1930.

WALTER, J. T., *Foreign Exchange Equilibrium*, University of Pittsburgh Press, Pittsburgh, 1951.

WALTERS, A. A., *Money in Boom and Slump*, Institute of Economic Affairs, London, 1969.

WARBURTON, C., 'The Volume of Money and the Price Level Between the World Wars', *Journal of Political Economy*, vol. LIII, 1945.

WARE, R. G., 'The Balance of Payments in the Inter-war Period: Further Details', *Bank of England Quarterly Bulletin*, vol. XIV, March 1974.

WARREN, G. F., and PEARSON, F. A., *Prices*, Chapman & Hall, London, 1933.

WARRINER, D., *Combines and Rationalisation in Germany, 1924–1928*, P. S. King, London, 1931.

WARRINER, D., *Economics of Peasant Farming*, Oxford University Press, London, 1939.

WASSERMAN, M. J., 'Inflation and Enterprise in France, 1919–1926', *Journal of Political Economy*, vol. XLII, 1934.

WASSERMAN, M. J., 'The Compression of French Wholesale Prices During Inflation, 1919–1926', *American Economic Review*, vol. XXVI, 1936.

WELK, W. G., *Fascist Economic Policy*, Harvard University Press, Cambridge, Mass., 1938.

WELLISZ, L., *Foreign Capital in Poland*, Allen & Unwin, London, 1938.

WHEELER-BENNETT, J., and LATIMER, H., *Information on the Reparations Settlement*, Allen & Unwin, London, 1930.

WHEELER-BENNETT, J., *The Wreck of Reparations: Being the Political Background of the Lausanne Agreement 1932*, Allen & Unwin, London, 1933.

WHITE, D. A., *Business Cycles in Canada*, Staff Study No. 17, Economic Council of Canada, Ottawa, 1967.

WHITTLESEY, C. R., and WILSON, J. S. G. (eds), *Essays in Money and Banking in Honour of R. S. Sayers*, Clarendon Press, Oxford, 1968.

WICKER, E. R., *Federal Reserve Monetary Policy, 1917–1933*, Random House, New York, 1966.

WICKIZER, V. D., and BENNETT, M. K., *The Rice Economy of Monsoon Asia*, Stanford University Press, California, 1941.

WICKIZER, V. D., *The World Coffee Economy with Special Reference to Control Schemes*, Food Research Institute, Stanford University, Stanford, 1943.

WICKIZER, V. D., *Tea Under International Regulation*, Food Research Institute, Stanford University, Stanford, 1944.

WIGGS, K. I., *Unemployment in Germany since the War*, P. S. King, London, 1933.

WILLIAMS, D., 'Montagu Norman and Banking Policy in the 1920s', *Yorkshire Bulletin of Economic and Social Research*, vol. XI, 1959.

WILLIAMS, D., 'London and the 1931 Financial Crisis', *Economic History Review*, vol. XV, 1962–3.

WILLIAMS, D., 'The 1931 Financial Crisis', *Yorkshire Bulletin of Economic and Social Research*, vol. XV, 1963.

WILLIAMS, D., 'The Evolution of the Sterling System', in Whittlesey, C. R., and Wilson, J. S. G. (eds), *Essays in Money and Banking in Honour of R. S. Sayers*, Oxford University Press, London, 1968.

WILLIAMS, J. H., 'Latin American Foreign Exchange and International Balances during the War', *Quarterly Journal of Economics*, vol. XXXIII, 1918–19.

WILLIAMS, J. H., 'The Future of Our Foreign Trade: A Study of Our International Balance in 1919', *Review of Economic Statistics*, vol. II, Supplement, 1920.

WILLIAMS, J. H., 'Reparations and the Flow of Capital', *American Economic Review, Papers and Proceedings*, vol. XX, 1930.

WILSON, T., *Fluctuations in Income and Employment with Special Reference to Recent American Experience and Post-War Prospects*, 3rd edition, Pitman, London, 1948.

WINCH, D., *Economics and Policy: An Historical Study*, Hodder & Stoughton, London, 1970.

WINKEL, H. (ed.), *Finanz- und Wirtschaftspolitische Fragen der Zwischenkriegzeit*, Duncker & Humblot, Berlin, 1973.

WINKLER, M., *Investments of United States Capital in Latin America*, World Peace Foundation, Boston, Mass., 1929.

WIRTH, J. D., *The Politics of Brazilian Development 1930–54*, Stanford University Press, Stanford, 1970.

WOLFE, M., *The French Franc between the Wars 1919–1939*, Columbia University Press, New York, 1957.

WOLFF, J., 'Fiscalité et development en France entre 1919 et

1939', in R. Schnerb (ed.), *Deux siècles de fiscalité française, XIXᵉ – XXᵉ siècle: histoire, économie, politique*, Mouton, Paris, 1973.

WOOD, G. L., 'War Debts of the British Dominions', *Economic Record*, vol. VII, 1931.

WOOD, G. L., 'Reparations and War Debts', *Economic Record*, vol. VIII, Supplement, 1932.

WOYTINSKY, W. S., and WOYTINSKY, E. S., *World Population and Production: Trends and Outlook*, Twentieth Century Fund, New York, 1953.

WOYTINSKY, W. S., and WOYTINSKY, E. S., *World Commerce and Governments*, Twentieth Century Fund, New York, 1955.

WRIGHT, G., *France in Modern Times: 1760 to the Present*, Murray, London, 1962.

WRIGHT, P. Q. (ed.), *Unemployment as a World Problem*, University of Chicago Press, Chicago, 1931.

WRIGHT, P. Q. (ed.), *Gold and Monetary Stabilization*, University of Chicago Press, Chicago, 1932.

WYNNE, W. H., 'The French Franc, June 1928–February 1937', *Journal of Political Economy*, vol. XLV, 1937.

WYTHE, G., 'Brazil: Trends in Industrial Development', in Kuznets, S., Moore, W. E. and Spengler, J. (eds), *Economic Growth: Brazil, India, Japan*, Duke University Press, Durham, N. C., 1955.

YAMASAKI, K., and OGAWA, G., *The Effect of the World War upon the Commerce and Industry of Japan*, Yale University Press, New Haven, 1929.

YATES, P. L., *Food Production in Western Europe*, Longmans, London, 1940.

YATES, P. L., *Commodity Control: A Study of Primary Products*, Cape, London, 1943.

YATES, P. L., and WARRINER, D., *Food and Farming in Postwar Europe*, Oxford University Press, London, 1943.

YATES, P. L., *Forty Years of Foreign Trade*, Allen & Unwin, London, 1959.

YEAGER, L. B., *International Monetary Relations: Theory, History and Policy*, Harper & Row, New York, 1966.

YOUNGSON, A. J., *Britain's Economic Growth, 1920–1966*, Allen & Unwin, London, 1967.

ZALESKI, E., *Planning for Economic Growth in the Soviet Union*,

1918–1932, University of North Carolina Press, Chapel Hill, N.J., 1971.

ZAUBERMAN, A., *Russia and Eastern Europe, 1920–1970*, Collins/ Fontana, 1974.

Index of Subjects

Index of Names